THE BREACH

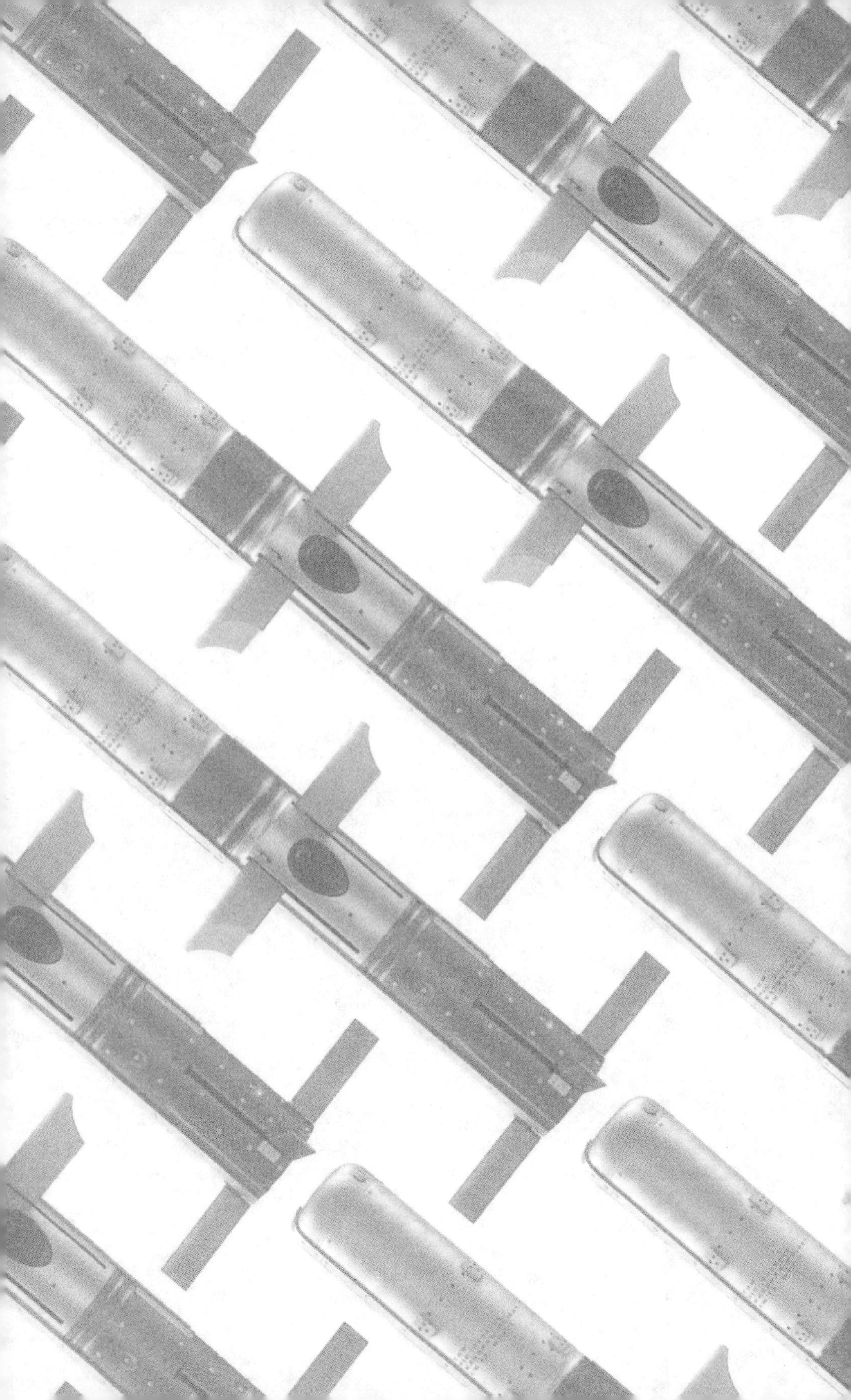

THE BREACH

IRAN-CONTRA AND THE ASSAULT ON AMERICAN DEMOCRACY

Alan McPherson

THE UNIVERSITY OF NORTH CAROLINA PRESS

Chapel Hill

Designed by Jamison Cockerham
Set in Scala, Officina Sans, and Trade Gothic
by codeMantra

Cover art: dpa picture alliance / Alamy Stock Photo

Manufactured in the United States of America

LIBRARY OF CONGRESS CATALOGING-IN-PUBLICATION DATA
Names: McPherson, Alan L., author.
Title: The breach : Iran-Contra and the assault on
American democracy / Alan McPherson.
Description: Chapel Hill : The University of North Carolina Press,
[2025] | Includes bibliographical references and index.
Identifiers: LCCN 2024045150 | ISBN 9781469686332
(cloth ; alk. paper) | ISBN 9781469686349 (pbk. ; alk. paper) |
ISBN 9781469683614 (epub) | ISBN 9781469687889 (pdf)
Subjects: LCSH: Iran-Contra Affair, 1985–1990. | Political corruption—United
States—History—20th century. | Democracy—United States—History. |
Executive power—United States—History—20th century. |
Constitutional law—United States. | Impunity—United States—
History—20th century. | United States—Politics and government—
20th century. | BISAC: HISTORY / United States / 20th Century |
POLITICAL SCIENCE / International Relations / Diplomacy
Classification: LCC E876 .M433 2025 | DDC 973.927—dc23/eng/20241009
LC record available at https://lccn.loc.gov/2024045150

TO MY STUDENTS AT TEMPLE UNIVERSITY:

YOU ARE THE FUTURE OF DEMOCRACY

CONTENTS

PART THREE **SCRUTINY**

ILLUSTRATIONS

ACKNOWLEDGMENTS

I conceived of this book in 2019, with a nudge from Meredith Hindley, as I considered the antecedents to the first impeachment of Donald Trump. Then the COVID-19 pandemic hit, shutting all physical archives.

Fortuitously, members of Congress, investigators, and scholars had long pushed for the declassification of Iran-Contra documents since the scandal, and so I found that most sources for this book were published or online. Most voluminous among these were the transcripts of the Iran-Contra joint committee hearings of 1987, accompanied by hundreds of documents, and the report that followed. Also crucial were the thousands of Iran-Contra documents that the National Security Archive made available online in its unparalleled digital collections, as well as memoirs by administration officials and investigators and several hundred newspaper and magazine articles. I could not have plowed through these sources without Temple University student research assistants. The bibliographical, transcription, and cataloging work of Emily Collopy, Zeinah Latefa, Igor Piovezan, Iuri Piovezan, Josh Stern, and Raina Welch made this project see the light of day much sooner than otherwise. Kathryn Perrone did a brilliant job thinking through the basic tenets of democracy for me. And David Devine put in the most hours. At Charles Library, Rebecca Lloyd was a consummate professional when I hit walls looking for rare books and documents.

Starting in 2021, I did visit a few archives to complete the research, and I thank the staffs of the Hoover Institution at Stanford University, the National Archives at College Park, and the Manuscript Division of the Library of

Congress in Washington, DC. At UNC Press, Debbie Gershenowitz ushered the project to completion with the help of Alexis Dumain, Dino Battista, and two anonymous readers. As usual, Heather Dubnick produced a thorough index.

Alan McPherson
Philadelphia, May 2024

ABBREVIATIONS

AECA	Arms Export Control Act
CIA	Central Intelligence Agency
CIPA	Classified Information Procedures Act
DCI	Director of Central Intelligence
FBI	Federal Bureau of Investigation
FDN	Fuerza Democrática Nicaragüense
HAWK	Homing-All-the-Way-Killer
HPSCI	House Permanent Select Committee on Intelligence
IOB	Intelligence Oversight Board
NEPL	National Endowment for the Preservation of Liberty
NHAO	Nicaraguan Humanitarian Assistance Office
NSC	National Security Council
NSDD	National Security Decision Directive
NSPG	National Security Planning Group
OIC	Office of Independent Counsel
PROFS	Professional Office System
RIG	Restricted Interagency Group
S/LPD	State Department Group on Latin American Public Diplomacy
SSCI	Senate Select Committee on Intelligence
TOW	Tube-launched, Optically tracked, Wire-guided missile

THE BREACH

INTRODUCTION

DEMOCRACY IN SIX STANDARDS

When it broke, no one knew what to call the scandal. "Iranscam," "Iranscab," or "Iranaffair" to denote its seediness? "Irangate" to evoke the Watergate affair of the previous decade? For those partial to puns, "Iranamok"? The link between Iran and the Contras in Nicaragua produced "Iragua." Other ideas included "Contraversions," "Ronnybrook," and "North by Mideast."[1] Eventually came "Iran-Contra," the moniker that stuck.

The convoluted quest for a term reflected the struggle to grasp the crisis as its facts came to light in late 1986. The Ronald Reagan administration, having pledged never to bargain with terrorists, had sold weapons to Iran, a state sponsor of terrorism, in the hopes of freeing American hostages. Meanwhile, it had slighted the will of Congress by secretly coordinating the private funding of—and giving military advice to—the counterrevolutionary or "Contra" rebels fighting the socialist government of Nicaragua. To top it off, the National Security Council (NSC), through arms dealers, had diverted profits from sales to Iran to fund the Contras. Thus "Iran-Contra."

Confusion reigned. Were these schemes illegal, and if so, which parts broke which laws? How high did the scandal go? What did President Reagan know and do? Would the US government be able to investigate itself? Would any investigation turn into a political witch hunt? Were these premeditated crimes and a moral breakdown? Just errors of judgment? An underappreciated bending of rules by brave mavericks? The conservative editors of the *Wall Street Journal* perceived "a gleefully destructive reaction wholly out of proportion to any errors that have been alleged."[2]

Many read the scandal as a threat to American democracy. Liberal journalists, legal scholars, judges, and especially the Democrats in Congress identified several tenets of democratic rule that the Reagan administration had disregarded. The most obvious and important was the separation of powers, which should lead the executive to acknowledge the coequal status of the legislative branch, including in the funding if not the formulation of foreign policy. After investigating, Congress raised "serious questions about the adherence of the Administration to the Constitutional processes of Government," including the privatization of foreign policy, the breaking of laws, lies to Congress and the American people, and quid pro quos with foreign nations.[3] Years later, a special prosecutor uncovered a broader cover-up that telegraphed the Reagan and George H. W. Bush administrations' disregard for the truth and its obstruction of justice to dodge guilty verdicts. "What set Iran-Contra apart from previous political scandals," concluded the prosecutor Lawrence Walsh, "was the fact that a cover-up engineered in the White House of one president and completed by his successor prevented the rule of law from being applied to the perpetrators of criminal activity of constitutional dimension."[4]

Republican Party efforts to evade justice worked. While the president's polling tanked in 1987, the party paid no political price in 1988, seeing Vice President Bush succeed a still-popular Reagan into the Oval Office. Claims of executive privilege resulted in a trickle of light sentences. On his way out of the White House, Bush pardoned everyone still in legal jeopardy, signaling impunity for crimes against American democracy.

.....

The Iran-Contra scandal is an object lesson in how the supposed guardians of democracy—elected officials—can themselves threaten its norms. Donald Trump and the Republican Party's onslaught against those norms led to their backsliding in several areas. In the 2020s, a general erosion of democratic beliefs beset the United States, accompanied by a rise of authoritarianism among Republican voters.[5] In late 2021, only 42 percent of Republicans had confidence in elections overall.[6] Two years later, 48 percent of them believed America needed "a leader who is willing to break some rules," and one-third advocated political violence.[7]

Democracy is a fragile thing, its norms needing constant reinforcement. "Manners"—another word for norms—"are of more importance than laws," wrote conservative philosopher Edmund Burke in 1795. "In great measure the laws depend upon them."[8] The informal nature of norms means that they can prove easy to threaten and those threats can be tricky to perceive and impossible to prosecute in courts. For all their vulnerability, norms matter no less. "Like a pickup basketball game without a referee, democracies work best when unwritten rules of the game, known and respected by all players, ensure a minimum of civility and cooperation," write scholars Steven Levitsky and Daniel Ziblatt. "Norms serve as the soft guardrails of democracy, preventing political competition from spiraling into a chaotic, no-holds-barred conflict."[9]

To be sure, several crucial democratic norms not at stake during Iran-Contra have come under duress since the 1990s—for instance, the protection of voting rights, respect for election results, and the acceptance of legitimate opposition. Still, Iran-Contra threatened basic standards in a healthy democracy. In this book, I identify six, which are, more or less, in declining order of importance:

1. The **separation of powers**, violated by discarding Congress's role in foreign affairs.
2. The **rule of law**, desecrated by breaking several statutes.
3. The independence of the judicial branch, infringed by **obstructing justice**.
4. The importance of **truth**, despoiled by lying and attacking the press.
5. The consent of the governed, sullied by **privatizing foreign policy** and removing it from public scrutiny.
6. The active participation of citizens in government, interrupted by reaching **quid pro quo agreements** with foreign governments and thus reducing the role of American citizens.

There is no universally agreed-upon set of norms for democracy, but scholars and institutions have advanced several lists, most of which contain some of these basic standards and many others besides. Among nine elements of democracy enumerated by the United Nations, for instance, are the separation of powers, the rule of law, and an independent judicial branch.[10]

Larry Diamond, a scholar of democracy, has emphasized the participation of citizens in society and the equal application of law to all.[11] Transparency and accountability in government, an element essential to many scholars, depends on trust, which in turn leans on truth.[12]

These six norms overlap. The separation of powers includes the independence of the judiciary from the other two branches. The rule of law relies on the courts functioning independently. Privatizing foreign policy and quid pro quos tend to flourish in secret, or, in other words, when transparency and truth suffer. These overlaps are strengths of democracy in that each reinforces others—when properly defended.[13]

There is no need to be a purist about democracy. Some backsliding will always occur, and norms need reinforcement precisely because citizens tend to defy them. Yet one of the costliest errors a regressing democracy can make is to ignore its own erosion. Author Fareed Zakaria has been foremost in warning against the threat to world order by "illiberal democracies" or countries that present forms of democracy yet fail to reinforce its norms.[14] The United States is becoming an illiberal democracy, and the Iran-Contra scandal widened the breach between citizens' standards for democracy and its reality.

.....

Historians have contributed to blurring the lessons of Iran-Contra. At the time of the scandal, its antidemocratic nature could have been hazy to many, containing as it did opaque minutiae about congressional prohibitions, faraway hostages, a war between Middle Eastern states, a guerrilla conflict consuming Central America, and shady intermediaries shifting funds between Swiss bank accounts.

Although most of the public may have tired of the scandal after its first year, a minority paid attention and understood the stakes for democratic norms. As early as 1986, two scholars asked whether the American people were witnessing the "de-democratising" of US foreign policy.[15] Scandal expert Louis Fisher called Iran-Contra "a stunning collapse of democratic government."[16] After Bush's late-1992 pardons, Theodore Draper, who wrote the most comprehensive early book on the scandal, warned, "If ever the constitutional democracy of the United States is overthrown, we now have a better idea of how this is likely to be done."[17]

Yet most legal scholars at the time, and historians since, have narrowed our understanding of the norms at risk by focusing on only one of them: the separation-of-powers clash between the executive and Congress. They have called Iran-Contra a "constitutional confrontation," "constitutional crisis," or "constitutional perversion" between only two branches of government, a tug-of-war over foreign policy and little more.[18] In 1987, three scholars reached an early and typical conclusion condemning the Reagan team: "they turned the power of the presidency against Congress and the American people in the course of turning it against foreign enemies."[19] In 1990, Edwin Timbers called Iran-Contra "one of the most important constitutional confrontations between Congress and the White House in United States history." The "specific issues of this conflict" that Timbers enumerated all related to the separation of powers.[20]

Other historians have focused not on the democratic consequences of the scandal but on its foreign policy sides—its origins and failures, its fit within the Cold War, its illustration of Reagan's style, and more.[21] Harold Hongju Koh, an oft-cited early scholar of the scandal, called it "a nearly successful assault upon the constitutional structures and norms that underlie our postwar *national security system*."[22] Malcolm Byrne, working with a much broader array of documents and interviews a generation later, wrote the most updated book yet focused on Reagan's role in foreign policy rather than on democracy more broadly.[23] Others have focused on discrete norms, such as the rule of law,[24] truth,[25] privatization,[26] or obstruction of justice,[27] but never all holistically.[28] Finally, few scholars have linked the scandal to future episodes of democratic decline.[29]

Republicans, meanwhile, unwilling to cop to their antidemocratic leanings, fell in line behind the myth of the honest slipup. In his memoirs, Caspar Weinberger called Iran-Contra "the one serious mistake the Administration made during the several years I worked as Secretary of Defense."[30] A Republican report from Congress dismissed the affair as "mistakes" by "Reagan and his staff."[31]

By 1992, as the scandal dissolved, journalist Richard Cohen feared "that the American public will continue to see Iran-Contra as the policy equivalent of quantum physics—hopelessly complicated and of interest only to specialists."[32] In 2023, Steve Martin's character in the streaming series *Only Murders in the Building* explained to a bored millennial that Iran-Contra was "worse than Watergate, just not as interesting."[33] Yet, when boiled down to its impact on democracy, the scandal becomes intelligible to anyone who can count to six.

.....

Each of the half-dozen norms under assault during Iran-Contra had a history of both mattering to democracy and of being maligned in US government long before the Reagan administration.

SEPARATION OF POWERS

The separation of powers may be the most fundamental principle in American democracy. "It has in fact come to define the very character of the American political system," wrote historian Gordon Wood.[34] Yet in the making of foreign policy as elsewhere, it has not been without controversy.

The division of government into branches, each held by different people and with identifiable functions, is "essential for the establishment and maintenance of political liberty," wrote M. J. C. Vile.[35] The doctrine of separation of powers combines with checks and balances to ensure some dependence of each branch on the others—and a measure of control over them.

In *The Spirit of Laws*, published in 1748, Montesquieu defined the three powers wielded in most democracies today and premised their separation on the survival of liberty. "When the legislative and executive powers are united in the same person, or in the same body of magistrates, there can be no liberty," he wrote. "Again, there is no liberty, if the judiciary power be not separated from the legislative and executive."[36]

Before Montesquieu, others had separated powers into only two branches, beginning with Aristotle and practiced in the Greek states. The distinction between powers weakened in republican Rome, and then broke down during the Middle Ages, when kings, counts, and others arrogated all administrative functions.[37] In 1689, John Locke redivided powers into three, but his third was the "federative," which he defined as "the power of war and peace, leagues and alliances" and located within the executive. Locke notably tied separation of powers to the rule of law, envisioning that, if those who made laws also enforced them, "they may exempt themselves from obedience to the laws they make." He also called the legislative the "one supreme power . . . to which all the rest are and must be subordinate."[38]

The Founding Fathers had read their Locke and Montesquieu, wary as they were of the "factions" in any democracy. In *Federalist No. 47*, James Madison warned, "The accumulation of all powers, legislative, executive, and judiciary, in the same hands, whether of one, a few, or many, and whether hereditary, self-appointed, or elective, may justly be pronounced the very definition of tyranny."[39] The Virginian called the separation of powers "a first principle of free government."[40] His generation enshrined Montesquieu's ideas in state constitutions. In 1779 Williamsburg, Virginia, conventioneers proclaimed that "the legislative, executive and judiciary departments shall be separate and distinct."[41] Maryland, North Carolina, and Georgia made similar statements, codifying their colonial experience of encroaching on the powers of royal governors.

The separation would be clearest in the US Constitution, as would checks and balances. In it, "each department should have a will of its own," Madison added in *Federalist No. 51*, "and consequently should be so constituted that the members of each should have as little agency as possible in the appointment of the members of the others."[42] Thus, justices of the Supreme Court would be nominated by the executive, the Senate would advise and consent, and, once appointed, justices could be removed by neither.

Article I of the Constitution grants several foreign policy powers to Congress, including the right to declare war and to approve budgets, including items pertaining to foreign relations. Article II states, "The executive Power shall be vested in a President of the United States." From those potentially contradictory passages comes a weighty debate about the "unitary executive," the theory that only the president wields executive powers. Some scholars have argued that precisely because Congress's foreign policy powers are enumerated and the executive's powers are not, nonenumerated powers—some say all—reside with the executive.[43] Supreme Court Justice Antonin Scalia, in a famous dissenting opinion in *Morrison v. Olson*, declared that Article II gives the president not "some of the executive power, but all of the executive power."[44]

Too often, proponents of executive power have made exaggerated theoretical claims. To the arguments that the president is unique in representing the national interest, that his or her staff may have superior expertise, and that the White House may enjoy better institutions with which to implement policy, Larry George noted, the notion of "national interest" has been chimerical, and institutions and expertise may fail disastrously especially when couched in the assumption of superiority and secrecy.[45] Besides, wrote Stephen Elkin, congressional involvement in foreign affairs may be helpful, for instance in helping the president avoid miscalculation in putting troops in harm's way.[46]

.....

In practice, the separation of powers in the United States has been a drawn-out tug-of-war between the executive and the legislative, one increasingly inching—sometimes leaping—toward the former.

It remains unclear whether the framers of the Constitution meant to restrain the executive or legislative branch more regarding foreign affairs. Records of the Constitutional Convention suggest "a lingering fear of the

President becoming too strong an executive," wrote William Shendow. Some thought Congress should have the bulk of the power in foreign affairs, while most anti-Federalists interpreted the Constitution as at least intending a shared power.[47] Louis Fisher has asserted that the framers "very consciously" rejected Locke's vision of exclusive presidential control over foreign policy and war.[48]

Some of the framers and the executive branch itself soon asserted its authority. Alexander Hamilton argued in *Federalist No. 70* for "energy in the Executive" as "good government. It is essential to the protection of the community against foreign attacks."[49] Madison imagined the Constitution as a tool to restrain *legislative* power because "the tendency of republican governments is to an aggrandizement of the legislative," and "the weakness of the executive," therefore, "may require . . . that it should be fortified."[50]

Fortified it was. President George Washington responded to foreign communiqués and issued a proclamation of neutrality unilaterally. In 1794, after the Senate approved the Jay Treaty, Jeffersonians in the House who opposed it demanded Washington's instructions to John Jay and other measures. Washington judged giving the House his papers "a dangerous precedent" and kept them sealed on the grounds of secrecy.[51]

Using the pseudonym "Pacificus," Hamilton put forth a theory to warm the hearts of conservatives for centuries. The Constitution, he wrote, granted all authority on foreign policy to the executive except as expressly provided in Article I. John Marshall, when still a member of Congress in 1799, declared, "The President is the sole organ of the nation in its external relations, and its sole representative with nations."[52] The "sole organ" phrasing returned in the 1936 case *U.S. v. Curtiss-Wright Export Co.*, in which Justice George Sutherland reasoned that the ability to defend the United States existed before the Constitution did and that therefore those rights resided in the executive, "the sole organ of the federal government in the field of international relations—a power which does not require as a basis for its exercise an act of Congress."[53] Sutherland specified that such power "must be exercised in subordination to applicable provisions of the Constitution."[54] William Weaver and Robert Pallitto pushed back against Sutherland's logic, writing that the idea that the power to defend the state "is pre-constitutional and acquired naturally without authorization of constitution or state, is hardly self-evident," especially when all political power derived from the Constitution.[55]

In the mid-twentieth century, Edward Corwin saw the separation of powers as "an invitation to struggle for the privilege of directing American foreign policy," with the president enjoying a "clear advantage."[56] President after president played that advantage. Franklin Roosevelt penned the destroyer deal in 1940 in open defiance of the Congress, and Harry Truman ordered troops to Korea in violation of constitutional and statutory constraints.[57]

In the Dwight Eisenhower era, the term "executive privilege" came into use to describe the right of the president to keep documents from investigators. Richard Nixon was the first chief executive to invoke it to shield himself from an impeachment inquiry.[58] He was hardly the first, however, to bypass Congress in making foreign policy. Before him, Lyndon Johnson had committed half a million troops to Vietnam without declaring war. Nixon bombed Cambodia without even telling Congress.[59]

The Watergate scandal, which featured not only Nixon's claims of executive privilege but also a slew of dirty tricks and cover-ups from the White House, prompted a rare era of congressional assertion over foreign affairs. There was some precedent. Beginning in 1791, the House looked into the executive's handling of a war against Native Americans.[60] During the Cold War, Congress proposed but rejected formally overseeing the Central Intelligence Agency (CIA) in 1956 and again in 1966.[61]

Only in the wake of Nixon's ignominy did Congress for the first time place the CIA and other intelligence bodies under its authorization and appropriation procedures. The 1973 War Powers Resolution forced the executive to consult and report to Congress within sixty days of sending troops abroad—yet it failed to include covert wars and short-term military strikes.[62] The Hughes-Ryan Amendment of 1974 required that the president report on CIA covert actions in a "timely fashion" to the "appropriate committees of the Congress" and that the president "find" that the proposed actions were "important to the national security of the United States." Soon after, both chambers established special committees to investigate intelligence activities.[63] In 1976, the Senate established its Select Committee on Intelligence (SSCI, pronounced "sissy"), and the following year, the House formed its own Permanent Select Committee on Intelligence (HPSCI, pronounced "hipsy").[64]

In 1980, the Intelligence Oversight Act inserted the concepts of prior notice and, if not, "timely fashion," into the National Security Act of 1947. The president *had* to inform Congress before any intelligence or military activity. If this proved impossible, then the executive had to do so immediately after. "The presumption of this bill," said Senator Robert Byrd (D-WV), "is that prior notice must be given to the Congress, period."[65]

After Nixon dismissed a Watergate special prosecutor, in 1978, Congress also limited the executive's power over investigations of itself. The Ethics in Government Act provided for a court-appointed independent counsel to investigate senior members of the executive.[66] The conflict harked back to the president's long-standing claim to "removal power"—the idea, and the reality up to the 1970s, that the chief executive could fire anyone within his branch for incompetence or disagreement over policy. In the 1830s, the Senate had censured Andrew Jackson for removing his treasury secretary. A generation later, the House impeached Andrew Johnson for removing his secretary of war. Franklin Roosevelt failed to abolish independent agencies. According to scholars Steven Calabresi and Christopher Yoo, "all of our nation's presidents have believed in the theory of the unitary executive."[67]

In the 1970s, the judiciary joined the tug-of-war on the legislature's side, in this instance against the president's right to hoard tapes of White House conversations. In *United States v. Nixon,* the Supreme Court acknowledged—maybe invented—an executive right to withhold some information from Congress to allow the president to confer with advisors in confidence. This right of confidentiality, however, could not "prevail over the fundamental demands of due process of law in the fair administration of criminal justice." The Court ordered the tapes to be produced, and Nixon resigned.[68]

Starting in the 1970s, presidents both Democratic and Republican, but especially Republican, pushed back against congressionally imposed limitations on their foreign policy power.[69] Harold Koh found that each element of the Iran-Contra scheme "repeated historical events that had first occurred during the Nixon Era," including selling arms, funding secret wars, operationalizing the NSC staff, and organizing secret operations.[70] In 1975, National Security Advisor Henry Kissinger secretly funded anticommunist guerrillas in Angola.[71] The Gerald Ford and Jimmy Carter administrations issued executive orders to increase their control over intelligence activities. They hated having to report covert operations to eight different committees (fifty years later, the number was down to two).

The Reagan administration, especially, embraced the unitary executive theory in a "very open and public" way, wrote Calabresi and Yoo.[72] Reagan's attorney general, Edwin Meese III, "who would promote the concept of the 'unitary executive,'" according to historian Malcolm Byrne, suggested that independent counsels and agencies were unconstitutional.[73] The Republican attitude in the 1980s, especially embraced by William Casey, Reagan's director of the CIA, was that Congress could not be trusted, especially with information. "You can't have 535 members of the House and Senate administer foreign policy," Reagan wrote in his memoir, in his seemingly commonsense but misleading way. The members of Congress who legally needed to be in the loop numbered a mere eight.[74]

The president himself fired a dozen inspectors general without informing Congress, pocket vetoed an act to protect whistleblowers, and opposed the Ethics in Government Act.[75] He bemoaned the "rash of congressional initiatives to limit the president's authority" in the 1970s. Acknowledging that "Congress is a partner with the president in foreign affairs," he nevertheless argued that "there are some situations in which only the president can and does know all the facts [and] he should be permitted to *lead* the nation and make decisions based upon what he knows and the trust placed in him by the voters—although I never felt these views should justify overriding or ignoring validly enacted laws."[76] Reagan's "leadership" during Iran-Contra would betray his penchant for making those decisions without even consulting Congress. Also, what were *invalidly* enacted laws?

RULE OF LAW

"There appears to be widespread agreement, traversing all fault lines, on one point, and one point alone: that the 'rule of law' is good for everyone."

So wrote scholar Brian Tamanaha in *On the Rule of Law*. He noted that not only democracies but also dictatorships have endorsed the norm to ensure freedom, order, or economic development. "No other single political ideal has ever achieved global endorsement."[77] Aristotle first preached in writing that all citizens should be subject to laws and treated equally by them: "It is more proper that law should govern than any one of the citizens." Those who wield the power of the laws, even autocrats, "should be appointed to be only guardians, and the servants of the laws."[78] Plato and others preferred the terms "isonomy" or "isonomia," meaning "equality of laws to all manners of persons." Rule of law became not a synonym but a sine qua non of democracy. "Where there is no law, there is no freedom," declared Locke.[79] The causal link between rule of law and democracy is that the former "enables individual autonomy," wrote José María Maravall and Adam Przeworski. "Rule of law makes it possible for people to predict the consequences of their actions and, hence, to plan their lives." Machiavelli explained that political leaders also perceive their self-interest in the rule of law, which allows them to gauge the behavior of other powerful groups.[80]

From A. V. Dicey to F. A. Hayek, modern scholars have laid out the secondary "conceptions" (as Dicey called them) that regulated the tenet that "no man is above the law." First among these was that only the law can decide the punishment for an offense. Second, all are subject to the *same* "ordinary law" in "ordinary tribunals." Third was that courts—and not just constitutions—interpret the law to determine the rights of individuals.[81] Yet, as Aristotle explained, "well drawn laws should themselves define all the points they possibly can, and leave as few as possible to the decision of the judges."[82] Modern scholars have also warned that the rule of law can exist in principle yet the law itself can generate inequalities and harm democracy—not to mention that those who write or enforce the law may not consider that it applies to them. Laws should rule not only people but also governments. Rules should be open, clear, stable, and general. Courts, the arbiters of laws, should be accessible and free of bias and have the right to review laws made by parliaments or congresses. All these norms enhance human dignity.[83]

.....

The reality of the rule of law has been shaky throughout the West in the past century or so, and the United States has been no exception.

In Ancient Greece, equality before law did not mean equality between different groups but instead within them. As Tamanaha explained, "The law recognized categories of individuals (for example, women, children, slaves, and non-citizens) with different legal implications. Rather, equality meant that the law would be applied to all in accordance with its terms without regard to whom, whether aristocrat or lowly artisan, stood before it." Athens strove for neither equality nor popular democracy. After the slow demise of the concept during Roman times, for half a millennium, the rule of law disappeared from Europe. Only slowly did the principle of having kings and other nobles subject to the law reemerge in Germany and England, but the competing doctrine of the "divine right of kings" removed the law as a restraint. To Thomas Hobbes, the rule of law was illogical: a sovereign made the law and therefore could not be bound by it.[84]

Still, by the eighteenth century, the words of Locke, Montesquieu, and *The Federalist Papers* firmly established the democratic basis for the rule of law. Montesquieu argued that the law protected individual liberty because it secured society from tyranny. A government restrained by law would be one in which "power should be a check to power."[85] The nineteenth century added the principle of judicial review. Dicey and Hayek, while hailing the rule of law in principle, criticized it on the conservative basis that large governments were becoming burdensome to liberty and thus threatening to the rule of law.

The US government seemed to confirm such suspicions as its ballooning executive branch skirted the edge of the law or openly broke it. Before World War II, Roosevelt violated neutrality laws, having his attorney general justify the transfer of fifty warships to Britain in return for naval bases as legal when it almost certainly was not. Yet he paid no price, either politically or militarily.[86] Throughout the Cold War, the CIA spied on American citizens, experimented with drugs on American subjects, and helped assassinate foreign leaders, all of which was illegal.[87]

After a string of illegalities during Watergate, journalist David Frost asked a retired Nixon if "the president can decide that it's in the best interests of the nation or something, and do something illegal?"

"Well," responded Nixon infamously, "when the president does it that means that it is *not* illegal."

At the time, Ronald Reagan was asked what he thought of Nixon's negation of the rule of law. He could "understand" it, he said. "When the commander in chief of a nation finds it necessary to order employees of the government or agencies from the government to do things that would technically break the law, he has to be able to *declare* it legal for them to do that."[88]

TRUTH

"Lying lips are an abomination to the Lord" (Proverbs 12), written around 350 BCE, tells us.

So are they an affront to democracy. Telling the truth is essential for establishing popular trust in leaders, imbuing them with the authority to lead, and for voters to feel that they are participating in the representative governance that flows from popular sovereignty.

In a democracy, citizens need to be fully informed. In defending the Freedom of Information Act in 1963, Senator Edward Long (D-MO) said, "free people are, of necessity, informed; uninformed people can never be free."[89] The governed need to consent, and to consent, they need accurate information.[90] Secrecy is an obstacle to the free flow of information and to the accountability of leaders to the public.

Eliding the truth, of course, can be a winning tool in politics. Machiavelli counseled a leader to try to be honest but also to lie when telling the truth might "put him at a disadvantage."[91] In *The Prince,* the Florentine advised anyone who wanted to be a great leader "to be a great pretender and dissembler . . . he who deceives will always find someone who allows himself to be deceived."[92]

The more common rationale for lying in a democracy is the need for secrecy, which comes up in justifications of "reason of state," the concept that the state may have interests above those of the citizenry. One Iran-Contra schemer, Michael Ledeen, advanced what appears to be common sense about secrecy: "We need candor, but we do not need large meetings or a large number of participants, or full public debate at every stage of the policy process, or even of every aspect of policy." Presidents need to be assured of the confidentiality of their conversations with advisors and foreign leaders precisely to achieve honesty. Using private individuals as back channels in diplomacy, therefore, is good for democracy: "Secrecy actually encourages the free flow of information and candid expression, while exposure limits the flow of knowledge and forces top officials to speak guardedly, if at all."[93]

The Dutch philosopher Hugo Grotius argued that deception, if intended to confuse enemies, can also be in the collective interest. Such was the raison d'état that reigned from the Middle Ages to Napoleon and Bismarck.[94] Leaders could get "dirty hands" if their motives proved pure.[95] An offshoot of this realism is consequentialism or utilitarianism, which holds that the immorality of one's actions is justified if the results prove beneficial.[96]

Especially in a democracy, this rationale for lying in politics can be both exaggerated and, well, deceptive. Concealment and manipulation endanger the principles of "accountability, participation, consent, and representation" that are fundamental to democracy.[97] Access to information allows free and open discussion, from which alternatives may emerge and which perpetuate an active citizenry.

Lies to foreign leaders—morally acceptable for many—might easily morph into lies to the public, the media, legislators, and the internal bureaucracy of the executive. The slippery slope can take many paths: Lies can target internal political opponents rather than external enemies, or they can advance private political gain rather than national interests or the reason of state. In times of diplomatic or military urgency, lying is even more alluring but also more damaging. Many argue that the unhurried openness of democratic processes cannot satisfy the need for speed and efficiency of national security. Leaders thus engage in "perception management," one of the many euphemisms for lying.[98] And although covert operations may be legitimate, wrote James Pfiffner, covert policies—"when the government says it is pursuing policy X, but it is in fact pursuing policy Y"—are not.[99] Successful secrecy can lead to what Hannah Arendt called "organized lying," which corrodes "the chief stabilizing factor in the ever-changing affairs of men."[100]

Lying is corrosive to democracy. Politicians who lie habitually become desensitized to the truth and are no longer representative of the will of their constituents because voters no longer know the will of their representatives.

When the public uncovers lies, more lies may emerge to cover those lies.[101] If lying becomes so pervasive to the point where truth is no longer distinguished from falsity, the entire democratic system can come crashing down. Citizens trust no one in politics, politicians disbelieve one another, and no deal gets done that requires keeping one's word. "If we cannot persuade one another to agree with reference to some shared system of meaning," wrote journalist Quinta Jurecic, "the only thing left is to compel agreement through force."[102]

.....

One of the contradictions out of which the United States emerged was its lie about telling the truth. Mason Locke "Parson" Weems's 1806 biography of George Washington taught citizens of a budding, uncertain democracy that their first president, as a boy, had admitted to chopping down a cherry tree. The United States presented to the world what Martin Jay has called "its steadfast rejection of Machiavellian duplicity."[103] Its Constitution was written and explicit; its language, intelligible; its leaders, accountable.

But the cherry tree tale had no basis in fact.[104] Weems told it to attach to Washington and his young nation a set of virtues: not only honesty but also repentance, contrition, and remorse.[105] The intent may have been admirable, but the deception reflected the little trust that American leaders put in their constituents.

Scholar David Merwin has argued that the US political system compels chief executives to lie, with its antiauthority political culture, separation of powers, "formidable array of pressure groups," "virulent, uninhibited media," "notoriously undisciplined bureaucracy," and disloyal cabinet members. He has found democratic forms "not really workable when it comes to national security."[106] If a president has tried and failed to persuade, the argument goes, he should lie. After all, Edmund Burke claimed, political leaders should use their best judgment rather than offer subservience to their constituents. This argument overlooks the counter that a policy that fails to persuade might be a poor one.

Because of America's growing military and intelligence involvement in the world, presidents kept more and more secrets. Scholars judged many of them as justifiable—when Franklin Delano Roosevelt (FDR) lied about the USS *Greer* incident to pull the country into World War II; when Nixon, in his 1960 presidential campaign, kept mum about Eisenhower's support for anti–Fidel Castro Cuban forces; or when Kennedy hid the withdrawal of US missiles from Turkey to resolve the missile crisis with the Soviets.[107] But presidents told other lies to prevent embarrassment, such as when Eisenhower fibbed about the U-2 flights over the Soviet Union.

Perhaps the most consequential foreign policy lie of the Cold War era proved to be the Gulf of Tonkin incident used to secure Johnson's resolution averring that North Vietnamese ships had attacked US counterparts in international waters. "Hell, those dumb, stupid sailors were just shooting at flying fish!" the president admitted. By lying, the White House started a war that took millions of lives and broke the US foreign policy consensus.[108] Projected failure in Vietnam, in turn, convinced Nixon to conceal his bombing of neighboring Cambodia. "My administration was only two months old," the president wrote as justification, "and I wanted to provoke as little public outcry as possible at the outset."[109] The *Pentagon Papers* revealed that every administration since Truman's had lied about Vietnam.[110]

In the 1960s, as political lies increased, so did the credibility gap. Before Tonkin, in 1964, 76 percent of the US public trusted the government to "do what is right most of the time."[111] By 1971, 69 percent felt that Nixon and his team were not telling them enough about Vietnam.[112] The era saw the proliferation of "sunshine laws," of which the Freedom of Information Act was but one.[113] Another poll asking when Americans "trust the government to do what is right" found that, in 1964, 77 percent answered either "always" or "most of the time." By 2022, that number was down to 20 percent.[114]

"I will never lie to you," pledged Jimmy Carter during his 1976 presidential campaign, demonstrating that the public's longing for honesty had become a political asset.[115] Gerald Ford said much the same in the Republican primary.[116]

Yet the late 1970s and early 1980s witnessed an acrid debate over leaks of information. The executive accused members of Congress of being sieves for state secrets. House member Henry Hyde (R-IL) recalled that "every new covert action disclosed to Congress in 1975 was leaked." A report by the Senate Intelligence Committee found that the White House was actually responsible for 66 percent of these leaks, but Hyde argued that, given the lower rate of security clearance in Congress, "a cleared person in Congress is 60 times more likely than his counterparts elsewhere to engage in unauthorized disclosures." A 1987 survey of 900 people in the capital found that 28 percent admitted leaking information to the media. Capitol Hill staffers did so 31 percent of the time, slightly higher than average. To Hyde, these numbers confirmed "the widespread existence of a permissive culture regarding unauthorized disclosures to the media." He believed that the public would reject its own "right to know."[117]

Believing Congress to be untrustworthy, many who testified before it lied, and largely with impunity. Between about 1947 and 2007, only six people were convicted of perjury before Congress or related charges. Given that 2,000 to 4,000 persons testify to Congress per year, the abysmal ratio of successful prosecutions—1 in about 30,000 witnesses—must have emboldened fabricators.[118]

Also accelerating in the 1970s were political leaders' attacks on the media—especially on outlets that exposed their lies. Condemning the press has existed since at least the days of Jefferson. Abraham Lincoln had troops shut down newspapers.[119] Woodrow Wilson censored journalists. LBJ was especially paranoid about his coverage. The Nixon administration made denigrating the news-gathering profession a common strategy. As a losing gubernatorial candidate in 1962, he scolded the press for "giv[ing] him the shaft."[120] Once president, his disgraced vice president, Spiro Agnew, was an early proponent of not countering media claims with facts or arguments but instead "attacking the institution of the free press itself," wrote journalists Rachel Maddow and Michael Yarvitz. Agnew suggested censorship of the press. He assailed journalists for being unelected. His attacks spiked anti-Semitic denunciations of local television stations for putting "Jew-Commies on the air."[121] Such attacks bore fruit among the public. In Watergate days, more than 70 percent of the public trusted the news. A generation later, only half did.[122]

The election of Reagan gave a boost to deception and secrecy. The former actor was probably the most prolific fabricator among presidents up to then, his genial style concealing it better than Nixon could. He made up quotes, told tall tales—often about his own life—cited outrageously erroneous statistics, and repeated inaccuracies even after being corrected.[123] As president, the Republican reversed Carter's pledge of openness in favor of withholding more materials from the public. Funding for intelligence skyrocketed, and covert action and Federal Bureau of Investigation (FBI) domestic spying both returned with a vengeance. In 1982, Reagan signed a law prohibiting the press from publishing some information even when it was already available in the public domain.

INDEPENDENCE OF COURTS

The independence of the judicial system is an offshoot of the separation of powers, the courts exercising, in most democracies, the third basic function of government. For justice to be open and impartial, members of the judiciary branch must be protected from punitive or coercive acts by the legislative and executive. In *Federalist No. 78*, Hamilton argued that courts must be independent also to check the power of the other branches.[124]

The US Constitution protects judicial independence in two passages. Article III first states that judges "shall hold their Office during good Behavior." This may sound restrictive, but it protects judges from being removed by either branch for any reason other than a serious breach of ethics, thus ensuring lifetime appointments and the independence that comes with them. Article III also ensures that judges' salaries "shall not be diminished," abating the bribery of impoverished judges.[125]

Independence does not, by itself, ensure justice. Within the system, any counsel, accuser, or defendant can obstruct the processes of the court, including when the legislative or, more often, the executive is involved. Probably the most common obstruction of justice from inside government is the refusal to produce evidence, either by withholding it from the courts or, less commonly, by overwhelming prosecutors with mountains of worthless documents. The executive, especially, may withhold evidence legally by claiming national security exemptions.[126] Intent matters in the courts, too. For an obstruction of justice accusation to stick, Title 18 of the US Code requires proof of knowing that an investigation is pending and intending to corrupt it.[127]

.....

In their history, US courts have witnessed obstruction of justice by the other branches, mostly in two areas: the granting of pardons and the withholding of evidence.

In the first area, Article II of the Constitution grants the president the power to pardon anyone accused of any federal crime "except in Cases of Impeachment." The president also has the powers of commutation of sentence, remission of fine or restitution, and reprieve. Pardons can come at any point, including before any charges are filed. The power of the pardon is tremendous and open to abuse. The Founding Fathers "seriously considered whether to grant the new President such an important power," wrote scholars Anthony Eksterowicz and Robert Roberts. Anti-Federalists suspected collusion between the president and senators.[128] To be sure, a pardon is not legally obstruction of justice. But it can harm democracy if its intent is to circumvent or nullify the independence of the courts.

In the second area, the growth of the national security apparatus—the personnel involved, the paperwork churned out—led to clashes over the state's right to keep secrets from the courts. In 1953, the secretary of the Air

Force refused to deliver secret documents to a judge when the family members of civilians who died in a plane crash while testing secret electronic equipment sued the US government. The case made its way to the Supreme Court, which found in favor of the government but declared that the privilege of state secrets must not be "lightly invoked." The case set a challenging task for judges—to rule on whether such claims for documents were appropriate "without forcing a disclosure of the very thing the privilege is designed to protect."[129] In the Cold War, the bureaucracy did its share of obstruction of justice, often in the form of destroying documents that could be politically embarrassing. The CIA did so with its "MKUltra" program of behavior modification experiments. The Joint Chiefs of Staff "disappeared" its own records of meetings from 1947 to 1974. The CIA-led coup in Iran in 1953 also led to what Kate Doyle has called "large-scale destruction of files."[130]

Rarely, however, have top US leaders been charged with obstruction of justice. Maddow and Yarvitz accuse George H. W. Bush, when he was chair of the Republican National Committee, of having delivered a message to a senator that amounted to obstruction of justice. Most infamously, Nixon stood accused of it in the case against Vice President Agnew, and "obstruction of justice" was the first article of impeachment against Nixon during Watergate.[131]

PRIVATIZATION

The use of private actors in diplomacy and war can be appropriate for democracies. It can provide expertise that governments lack, and no training or long-term employment are involved. There is no inherent reason why weapons manufacturers, bankers, or mercenaries cannot participate in the execution of foreign policy, just as governments contract private actors to manage computer systems, run cafeterias, and collect garbage.

Dangers do exist, however, the first being profiteering. Stuart Brandes defines war profiteering as "a gain in economic well-being obtained as a result of military conflict. The gain is usually monetary, but it may also come in the form of appreciated stock prices or payment in kind, such as the acquisition of government facilities."[132] Profiteering may occur whenever private actors make excessive profits off their collaboration with a government. Although there is no clear definition of "excessive" (20 percent? 200 percent?), keeping contracting transparent and competitive can shine needed light on profiteers. A related danger to privatization is that mercenaries and weapons manufacturers depend on wars for their way of life. They engage in war not out of ideology, patriotism, or self-protection, but for private gain. Therefore, they might *want* wars to happen or to continue.

More perilous for democracy, it follows, is when private actors make foreign policy. When those neither elected by voters nor under the clear command of elected officials start formulating policy, the governed no longer have a mechanism for consenting. Privatized policymaking, like profiteering, almost always occurs in the shadows.

In a democracy, wrote Samuel Huntington, the state monopolizes the military profession and therefore so does the citizenry. According to P. W. Singer, "Society has a direct, continuing, and general interest in the employment of this skill for the enhancement of its own military security."[133] Once the public monopoly over the military profession breaks down, democracy is under threat. Tellingly, private military actors thrive where governance is weak. Privatization, Laura A. Dickinson has asserted, erodes democratic accountability.[134]

.....

As in other democratic traditions, Americans established the relationship between government and private foreign policymakers in defiance of an undemocratic past. According to the Bible, the Pharaoh chased the Israelites out of Egypt with an armed force that included hired non-Egyptians. Ancient Greek and Roman armies also included mercenaries. In medieval Europe, warriors with special skills, such as the crossbow, rented themselves out to kings and princes. A contract system regulated these commercial relationships, and the words "commission," "companies," and "freelance" trace their origin to mercenary culture. Mercenaries prolonged war and suffering by taking prisoners for ransom and by pillaging towns that refused to pay for protection. War for profit became so common, wrote Singer, that "'patriotism' was a meaningless concept to the average soldier of the period."[135]

The founding of America coincided with the nation-state in Europe solidifying its monopoly on the use of force and with armies, for the first time, becoming loyal to nations rather than to rulers. Patriot leaders excoriated the so-called Hessians during their revolution against the British. In 1775, Washington bemoaned that "this whole Continent at a vast expence of Blood & Treasure is endeavoring to establish its Liberties, [yet] there are Men among us so basely sordid as to Counteract all our Exertions for the Sake of a little Gain."[136]

Americans first prohibited mercenariness in the US Neutrality Act of 1794.[137] They aimed not to eradicate war profits but rather to bring them under the reasonable control of the state—what Stuart Brandes calls "a special category of semilegitimate wealth"—not illegal but "not entirely ethical, either." The opprobrium came from the accusation that individuals made money—often fortunes—from a conflict that killed fellow citizens and injured or bankrupted countless others.

As the US war machine grew in the twentieth century, so did the ways private entities could profit from it. "Large corporate salaries, commodity speculation, excessive construction costs for military posts, black market trading, evasion of price controls, and gains from postwar reconversion sparked new controversies," wrote Brandes. To counter this and other schemes, the government bought its own weapons plants, restricted profits, audited military contractors, and renegotiated contracts.[138]

Still, by the 1970 and 1980s, it seemed there were US mercenaries in every global conflict, calling themselves "freedom fighters," leafing through *Soldier of Fortune* and similar magazines, attending US-based mercenary schools and training camps, and usually supporting right-wing causes from Angola to the Congo, from El Salvador to Rhodesia.[139] These "paramilitary assets" often fought low-intensity wars not *for* the US government but *instead* of it. When conflicts were too politically sensitive for US troops, mercenaries were there to "shake off the Vietnam syndrome," as Klaas Voß has argued.[140]

At times, private actors manipulated US diplomacy to substitute their priorities for those of the American people. In the early 1900s, entrepreneurs Philippe Bunau-Varilla and William Nelson Cromwell changed the US target site for an interoceanic canal from Nicaragua to Panama because they owned a concession in the latter. World War I produced the fear that weapons manufacturers had prompted Woodrow Wilson into the conflict.[141] In the interwar years, the United Fruit Company "virtually guided foreign policy in Central America," wrote Michael A. Cohen and Maria Figueroa Küpçü.[142] By 1961, Eisenhower warned of a "military-industrial complex" in which "pressure groups" gained undue influence on policy. "The aggressive demands of various groups and special interests, callous or selfish, or even well-intentioned," he argued, "contradicted the American tradition that no part of our country should prosper except as the whole of America prospered."[143]

During the Cold War, privatized military firms (PMFs) entered the arena of war and diplomacy. Many were the creations of former soldiers or spies who profited from former expertise in government.[144] Some companies showed significant independence and control over aspects of war or diplomacy, thus marrying profiteering and policymaking. One of these, California Analysis Center Inc., commonly known as CACI, started operating in Northern Virginia's Dulles Corridor in 1972.[145] Several more would follow.

Reagan entered the Oval Office preaching the privatization of many public purviews. He thought the private sector could do a better job in most instances, and he saw little conflict of interest in the proposition. "Reagan consistently dismissed the accusations [of private abuse] as unfair, gratuitous, or simply unimportant," wrote Jane Mayer and Doyle McManus. "He openly disdained the post-Watergate 'ethics in government' laws, which required officials to keep their private businesses at arm's length from the public business." More than 100 members of his administration would resign or be forced out, accused of using their office for private gain. "In a decade whose cultural heroes included Donald Trump, Lee Iacocca, and T. Boone Pickens, Jr.," added Mayer and McManus, "Reagan's blurring of the distinctions between wealth and commonwealth caused him no political damage."[146]

Many titans of industry built upon Reagan's political philosophy to interfere directly in foreign affairs. Armand Hammer dangled trade in front of the Soviets in exchange for the release of a Jewish dissident. Ross Perot offered a $2 million ransom for hostages held in Lebanon. And former Green Beret "Bo" Gritz led at least two private missions to find missing American prisoners of war.[147]

QUID PRO QUOS

Exchanging favors with foreign nations entails an inherent peril to democracy. On one hand, common sense—and the translation of the Latin phrase *quid pro quo* as "something for something"—dictates that to receive, one must give something of similar value. These positive incentives might include "symbolic gratifications, policy concessions, and economic favors," according to Miroslav Nincic.[148] Intelligence agencies, for example, might offer information or analysis to a foreign nation.[149] Unless it coerces foreign governments, Washington should expect to cede a *quid* to obtain a *quo*. As Larry George wrote, a common argument in favor of quid pro quos is that foreign leaders will not cooperate otherwise—often insisting that exchanges also be secret.

On the other hand, actual exchanges are more layered, rarely explicit, seldom equitable, and brimming with risk. Just as US policymakers might reap the better part of a bargain with their foreign counterparts, so too might the foreign nation. More common is the damage that the secrecy of a quid pro quo inflicts on democracy by keeping the American people—even all its representatives—out of the decision-making loop. According to George, the argument for quid pro quos "purports that Americans' rights to democratic accountability should be subordinated to foreign leaders' political need to deceive their own people."[150] A related danger is that foreign leaders might *not* keep a confidence, or threaten not to, thus gaining leverage on the US government and the American people. Sharing of intelligence leads to what Chris Clough sees as "a reduction of sovereignty." Moreover, either of the "sharing" governments might be deceiving the other with false information or unkept promises. Either way, truth and trust can easily be casualties of quid pro quos.[151] A quid pro quo, as Deborah Levy wrote, brings up "an old American fear: that foreign interests, by employing influential Americans, may be able to exploit the U.S. system of checks and balances to gain unfair advantage."[152]

In short, quid pro quos may be legitimate and useful in diplomacy, but they must be sincerely reached with the national interest in mind and with the knowledge of relevant actors within the contracting governments.

One relevant actor is Congress, and here quid pro quos intersect not only with truth but also with the separation of powers. The Constitution does not forbid the president from trading favors with a third-party government, for instance, to contribute funding toward a US foreign policy that might benefit that third party, as occurred in Iran-Contra. The Constitution, however, does forbid the executive from misspending those funds. Congress may be on thin ice when prohibiting quid pro quos because it could encroach on the prerogative of the executive in making foreign policy. However, wrote Alex Whiting, quid pro quos "threaten to render Congress's power over the purse meaningless . . . by allowing the executive to use appropriated funds indirectly for purposes explicitly denied funding by Congress."[153]

.....

US history is replete not only with quid pro quos that have been in the US interest but also with deals that, because of their flawed design, secrecy, or poor intentions, foreign governments and private actors—without the US national interest at heart—exploited.

During the Cold War, Washington commonly asked allies for assistance to a regional problem. The Saudis, for instance, aided Afghan refugees. The United States asked Japan and Western Europe to help Eastern European countries.[154]

But "wherever there was a quid, there was a quo," warned Secretary of State George Shultz.[155] All assistance provided by third countries came with strings attached. Often, allies responded positively without asking for an explicit return favor but knowing that they had either earned a future favor with the United States or else repaid a past debt.

.....

The rest of this book examines Iran-Contra in hopes of marrying a lively narrative of this "worse than Watergate, just not as interesting" scandal with a meditation on the sprawling, long-term damage it inflicted on US democracy. The five chapters of part I, "Scheme," cover the plot—funding the Contras, trading arms for hostages, and diverting the money, from 1983 to late 1986. They focus more on the six behaviors of the plotters that most endangered democracy and less on the foreign policy causes and consequences of Iran-Contra. The three chapters of part II, "Scandal," cover the most public phase of the scandal, from its inklings in the press in 1985 to its reckoning before Congress in 1987. During those two years, disrespect for the separation of powers, privatization, and attacks on the truth and the press stood out as the major themes. The four chapters in part III, "Scrutiny," shift the focus to the investigation by the Office of Independent Counsel starting in 1987, the trials that followed, and the pardons by President Bush in late 1992. This six-year, most drawn-out phase of the scandal, rarely covered by historians, revealed some of the fiercest menaces to democracy—the disrespect for the rule of law, continued mendacity, and a cover-up and eventual pardon that constituted grave, widespread obstruction of justice.

The "long" Iran-Contra saga of 1983–1992 was a pivotal moment when the Reagan administration engaged in these six democracy-eroding behaviors and took a major step in the assault on democracy that the American people have since witnessed. Although the NSC most bluntly assailed those already deteriorating norms, the same intent pervaded the actions and words of Reagan's CIA, Defense Department, and State Department; the Republican members of Congress; and conservative judges and media figures. All demonstrated a disdain for democracy while often posing as its defenders. This contradiction also marked their stated foreign policy goals, which included encouraging democracy in both Iran and Nicaragua. The schemers of Iran-Contra may have been sincere in their so-called democracy promotion. Naming their secret funding of the Contras "Project Democracy" was not likely a bit of dark humor but instead a promise to themselves and their subjects. Men like Oliver North, Robert McFarlane, John Poindexter, and many others seemed at times truly patriotic. Some were war heroes. But the damage they inflicted on democracy while claiming to defend it must be part of the historical record.

PART ONE

SCHEME

1

THE COUNTER-CONGRESS CONTRAS

One of the great ironies of Iran-Contra is that the Reagan administration disregarded the doctrine of the separation of powers, the rule of law, and truth—harming its own democracy—to bring to Central America what it claimed to be democracy. As National Security Advisor John Poindexter testified to Congress, the president "was very secure in his belief that [funding the Contras] was the only way that we could bring about a democratic change to the government in Nicaragua."

It was Reagan's zealous anticommunism and his conviction that the Contras, short for *contrarevolucionarios*, would restore democracy to Nicaragua that led him, as Poindexter described it, "to take unilateral action." Poindexter's definition of unilateralism: "The President exercising his constitutional authority without necessarily getting the agreement from Congress."[1] As Congress banned Contra aid, the executive branch froze out its legislative partner, lied, and broke the law.

.....

Reagan and his staff sidestepped Congress because of their frustration at seeing legislators agree with the basic ends of US foreign policy in Central America while denying Reagan the means to achieve those ends. President Jimmy Carter, in the Oval Office when the leftist Sandinistas took over the small Central American nation of Nicaragua in July 1979, used a variety of responses to moderate the revolution. He first showed goodwill with emergency food and economic assistance packages.[2] But the Democrat also helped Nicaraguan politicians, trade unionists, journalists, business people, and religious leaders who opposed the Sandinistas.[3]

Reagan's advisors, in contrast, saw only coercion as the proper remedy. They suspended the final $15 million payment on a $75 million Carter promise of aid.[4] When Reagan did present a treaty to the Sandinistas in 1983, he backed it with the existing military threat of the armed paramilitary Contras, and no one in the White House seriously thought Managua would sign. Throughout much of the 1980s, US peace overtures toward Central America often proved a façade.[5] In February 1984, Reagan openly called for the Sandinistas' "removal" unless they joined to "form a truly democratic government" with the Contras.

Did he mean overthrowing the Sandinistas? asked reporters. "Not if the present government would turn around and say 'uncle' to the rebels," the president responded. Reagan wanted neither moderation nor negotiation—just surrender.[6]

This rigidity emerged from the broader Reagan doctrine, which held that all anti-capitalist or anti-Western revolutions, whether in Nicaragua, Angola, or Afghanistan, were manifestations of a worldwide offensive by the Soviets. "Let's not delude ourselves," Reagan had said during his 1980 campaign. "The Soviet Union underlies all the unrest that is going on. If they weren't engaged in this game of dominoes, there wouldn't be any hot spots in the world."[7] Secretary of State Alexander Haig, in his first press conference, blamed the Soviet Union for "the training, funding and equipping" of terrorists throughout the world.[8] In Central America, he later explained, "what we are watching is a four-phased operation of which phase one has already been completed—the seizure of Nicaragua. Next is El Salvador, to be followed by Honduras and Guatemala . . . a hit list, if you will, for the ultimate take-over of Central America."[9] Reagan saw a Sandinista Nicaragua as endangering trade and transportation to the United States, impoverishing the region, and sending untold millions to the US border.[10] "What is going on is a general revolution aimed at all of Central Am[erica] & yes, Mexico," he wrote in his diary.[11]

Compounding Reaganite zeal was a Manichean worldview that painted Nicaragua as part of a global struggle "between right and wrong and good and evil," wrote historian Arthur Schlesinger Jr. If members of Congress disagreed with the ends of the good, it followed, they were evil. White House communications director Patrick Buchanan traced the line in the sand: "With the vote on contra aid, the Democratic party will reveal whether it stands with Ronald Reagan and the resistance—or [Sandinista leader] Daniel Ortega and the Communists."[12] In contrast, said Reagan, the Contras were the "moral equal of our Founding Fathers."[13]

Such a reading of Nicaragua was ahistorical and based on little evidence on the ground. Moral exemplars the Contras were not. Edgar Chamorro, a disenchanted former leader of the Contras, called them the most "undemocratic force" in Central America. Many of its commanders were former guardsmen of Anastasio Somoza, the US-supported dictator whom the Sandinistas had overthrown. Greed rather than democracy motivated many. They committed murder, torture, and rape and had no program for social or economic reform. "If the contras ever took power," Chamorro predicted, "they would simply replace the communists with their law-and-order regime and no one would be any better off."[14] One lobbyist for the Contras saw some decent elements in the coalition, but he judged the "thugs" of the Fuerza Democrática Nicaragüense (FDN) to be anything but democratic: "The clique that runs the FDN would put a couple of families in power, it would not create anything like a democratic system."[15]

Painted into their own corner, Reagan's foreign policy advisors disdained those in Congress who held up Contra aid as well as those in the American public who indicated insufficient concern. Polls in the 1980s consistently showed not only that US citizens knew little about conflicts in Central America but also that those who did disagreed with Reagan. About 60 to 70 percent of those polled opposed aid.[16] The president confided to his diary that he found it "astonishing how few people even know where El Salvador & Nicaragua are."[17] One Republican pollster called the issue of Nicaragua "pure poison."[18]

Frustrated, Reagan resorted to exaggerating, dissembling, and increasing the violence. In 1982, at an NSC meeting on Central America, he asked, "How can we solve this problem with Congress and public opinion being what they are? . . . Can covert actions be traced back to us?"[19] In 1983, when he ordered the invasion of the tiny island of Grenada to roll back a radical

Marxist takeover, he explained why he barred the US press from the island: "You can't let your people know [what the government is doing] without letting the wrong people know—those who are in opposition to what you're doing." *Time* magazine denounced the Reagan notion that "truth should be a controlled substance."[20]

Among the embellishments about Nicaragua that the executive branch told were that its Sandinista leaders wanted to overthrow their Central American neighbors and that Washington's counterpolicy consisted only of stemming the flow of arms from Nicaragua to neighboring insurgents. State and Defense officials often stated that they did not believe the first lie.[21] Poindexter himself let it slip to Congress that the end of the Contra funding was to bring "about a change to this [Sandinista] Government."[22]

.....

While Reagan set the tone and priorities for the Contras, the CIA and its director of central intelligence (DCI), William Casey, constituted the driving forces in shaping them as a political and military power in Nicaragua and then keeping them funded regardless of the will of Congress.

As soon as Reagan took office in January 1981, he ramped up assistance to the Contras. Israeli and Argentine officials had already launched the counterrevolutionaries with some help from Carter, but Argentina withdrew after Reagan supported the United Kingdom against the South American nation in the Falklands/Malvinas War of 1982.[23] On November 17, 1982, the president signed National Security Decision Directive 17, which created a 500-man force under US influence.[24]

From 1981 to 1984, Congress did appropriate significant resources to the Contras, including $24 million in the fall of 1983.

No funding was ever enough for Bill Casey, who proved more contemptuous of Congress than any other DCI in US history. Casey had the physique of a dissembler extraordinaire (see fig. 1). "A large, shambling old man, flabby-faced and buck-toothed," as one journalist described him, he mumbled everything he said, calling the Central American nation "Nica-wog-wa." Or was it "Nic-a-wha-wha." Or "Nica-wa-wa"? No one could tell.[25] "Not zestful" is how reporter Bob Woodward described Casey. Nancy Reagan thought he was "grotesque," wrote Rick Perlstein: "a sartorial unmade bed, . . . with table manners like a hobo."[26] Casey also suffered from gingivitis, and some of his teeth were loose. None of this helped his diction; it did wonders for his deceptiveness.[27]

FIGURE 1
Director of Central Intelligence William Casey tended to mumble, which helped obscure facts from Congress. (Shepard Sherbell/Corbis Historical/Getty)

Yet Casey proved attentive and cunning. From a poor Catholic family in Queens, he was a determined product of public schools who first studied social work, only to conclude that the profession was for women and to leave it for law school. During the Great Depression, the young lawyer pioneered the idea of "sheltering" the wealthy from taxes and authored books on the subject. During World War II in Europe, he served as a spymaster in the Office of Strategic Services, the precursor to his beloved CIA. He rose to chair of the Securities and Exchange Commission (SEC) in 1973–74. He had become rich through his own investments and helping others hide their fortunes from the Treasury. His overriding political philosophy was a privatized view of government in which any service that could be taken over by corporations, from garbage collection to firefighting, should be. Needless to say, he was a devout Republican. He headed the Import-Export bank for President Gerald Ford, and candidate Reagan tapped him to chair his presidential campaign.[28] In this role, Casey's staff got hold of the briefing books used by Carter to prepare for debates, and Casey boasted of this "intelligence operation." He may also have sabotaged Carter's plans to have US hostages in Iran freed before the election.[29]

Casey was investigated twice for his lying. A federal judge ruled that he knowingly misled investors in an agribusiness firm he helped found. The SEC also investigated him, for perjury. He had gotten thirty-four boxes of documents and thirteen "politically sensitive" memos and letters shipped to the Justice Department despite a congressional subpoena. Casey denied the shipment was his idea. "Casey's entire statement here is deceptive," one prosecutor concluded. Prosecutors declined to charge him, citing not his likely innocence but their low chance of success.[30]

At the CIA, Casey valued secrecy and hated leaks. He complained to Secretary of State George Shultz that "agencies take too long to recognize unauthorized disclosures, to report them, and to begin investigations."[31] He was particularly angry when he talked to a congressional committee about a secret finding only to learn that "the press knew the outcome within one-half hour after the hearing was closed."[32]

Partly to prevent leaks, Casey kept other parts of the executive branch in the dark. Shultz accused him of distorting data and of lying to and misleading the State Department.[33] In Central America, the DCI valued armed resistance over Shultz's multilateral negotiating. "More than once," recalled Reagan in his memoir, "Shultz threatened to resign because of Casey."[34]

In summer 1981, Casey appointed Duane "Dewey" Clarridge as his liaison to the Contras. Clarridge was a longtime clandestine service officer and former CIA station chief. As a boy from a loyal Republican family, Clarridge recounted, "political gatherings at our home were not all that unusual." He forever spoke in "the clipped Yankee tones of Nashua, New Hampshire."[35] Once in Washington, Clarridge's opinions were as loud as his sartorial affectations, which included a monocle, pastel silk safari suits, flamboyant suspenders, a cowboy hat, and a cigar.[36]

Clarridge and Casey developed what the former called "a strong working relationship," bypassing channels so that Clarridge could report directly to the director.[37] Upon his appointment to Central America, he knew he was no expert: "I got out my atlas to see what countries we were talking about."[38] But Clarridge was aggressive and smart. Casey saw in him "a doer, a take-charge guy." What about his zero experience in Latin America? His nonexistent Spanish? Casey waved them off: "He can handle it." Clarridge's plan for Latin America was "simple," as he said: "(1) Take the war to Nicaragua and (2) Start Killing Cubans."

Robert Gates of the CIA agreed that Clarridge was "talented. One of our best operations officers. Just make sure you have a good lawyer at his elbow—Dewey's not easy to control."[39]

.....

In the face of Casey and Clarridge's bold moves to overthrow the Nicaraguan government, Congress passed increasingly restrictive bans on Contra aid.

Congressional suspicions formed early in the Reagan presidency. Michael Barnes, a young Maryland Democrat representative, grew apprehensive of the CIA in Nicaragua. In the winter of 1981–1982, he had breakfast at the plush Hay-Adams hotel with Tom Enders, in charge of Latin American affairs at the State Department.

Making sure no one could hear them, Barnes leaned in: "I have a report that the CIA is hiring mercenaries to blow up bridges in Nicaragua."

Enders did not quash the rumor. "You'll need to go to the Intelligence Committee" is all he said.

Enders meant the chair of the HPSCI, Edward Boland of Massachusetts. Boland explained to Barnes that the CIA planned to use Argentina to train Contras to interdict arms from Nicaragua to El Salvador.

Barnes thought the plan reckless: *The CIA will never be able to control the Argentines.* He asked Enders to lunch this time and said as much. Enders reassured Barnes that there would be no assassinations, no human rights violations. If the Sandinistas found out about CIA involvement, Barnes warned, they would shut down all remaining democratic opposition in Nicaragua—the press, the labor movement, the political parties—on the pretext that the CIA was infiltrating them.

"Trust me," were Enders's final words.

The CIA increased the size of the Contras from 500 to thousands, divided into a northern front based along the border with Honduras and a southern front in Costa Rica. Their training, weaponry, and boldness swelled. One Sandinista leader publicly concluded, "There are too many things happening at once to be a coincidence. All these elements lead to one conclusion. The CIA is the only force with the power to do these things at once." Just as Barnes had predicted.

The more the CIA got involved, the more the Sandinistas invited Cubans to guide them, Soviets to provide equipment, and opposition Nicaraguans to shut their mouths.

And, in response, the more members of Congress called for the DCI to brief them. Whenever Casey begrudgingly did so, he proved impatient. Congressman Dave McCurdy (D-OK) once asked him how much the Sandinistas were spending on schools, roads, and hospitals.

"I don't know," snapped Casey.

Was this because Casey himself didn't know, or the CIA didn't?

"What's your point, Mr. Congressman?" Casey blurted.

When he appeared before a Senate committee with Shultz, Casey again exhibited a thin skin. Republican senators urged him to admit that the US goal was to overthrow the Sandinistas.

"Why don't we say what we believe?" one senator asked.

"Sounds okay to me," chimed in Barry Goldwater (R-AZ).

"We ought to overthrow 'em," agreed Jake Garn (R-UT).

Casey refused. He privately called the senators "these fuckers." He agreed with the overthrow policy but thought the idea of overtness was "bullshit."[40] He believed Democrats opposed his Contra policy for political reasons. Bipartisanship? "A waste of time."[41]

By 1983, Duane Clarridge grew dissatisfied with the meager progress of the Contras. They now numbered maybe 15,000 against the 75,000-strong Sandinista military and police yet seemed unable to secure any territory in Nicaragua. Clarridge planned to attack Sandinista coastal fuel depots not with Contras but with full-time agency men called "unilateral controlled Latino assets" or UCLAs. On January 6, 1984, Reagan approved the plan. Some complained that this smacked of an act of war. "That's what the President wants," replied Clarridge.[42]

Clarridge also came up with the idea of dropping mines in Nicaragua's harbors. It would scare off suppliers of the Sandinistas' oil and skyrocket shipping insurance rates at Lloyd's of London. As Oliver North explained the plot to his superior, "once a ship has been sunk no insurers will cover ships calling in Nicaraguan harbors.[43]

The mining of Nicaraguan waters set off a decisive confrontation with Congress. On the SSCI, when Joe Biden (D-DE) found out about the direct involvement of the CIA in the mining, he handed a classified memo to his colleague William Cohen (R-ME). Cohen walked over to Goldwater. "Barry, what the fuck is this? Is this true? Why haven't I been told?"[44]

On March 8, 1984, Casey had, in fact, briefed the SSCI on the mining but had buried the ten-second reference to it, delivered in the passive voice and camouflaged by the director's mumbling, in a two-hour-eighteen-minute presentation. He even failed to mention that it was the CIA, not the Contras, who had dropped the mines. SSCI staff members had to replay the tape several times to unearth the admission. Only three weeks later did the HPSCI also question Casey and catch the allusion to the mining.[45]

Goldwater, who had been advocating for more Contra funding, felt betrayed. "You get hold of Bill Casey," he told his staff director Rob Simmons, "and find out what the fuck's going on." Once he found out the full extent of the damage—yes, some ships turned back and exports piled up on the docks, but merchant seamen or fishermen were wounded, a British ship was damaged, a hit on a Soviet vessel could have started World War III, and Nicaragua sued the United States at the World Court—Goldwater told Simmons, "I feel like a boob. I misled my colleagues. . . . You tell Casey that he's on his own. I've pulled his nuts out of the fire often enough." Senator David Durenberger (R-MN) assessed that, "on a 0 to 10 scale, Casey rates a 2 on the trust factor."[46] A joke went around the House committee: If your coat was on fire, Casey would not tell you unless you asked, "Is my coat on fire?"[47]

Some Republicans believed that Casey's lone sentence on mining had been notification enough. "You're all assholes!" Garn of Utah screamed at his colleagues, "you're all assholes—the whole Congress is full of assholes, all five hundred thirty-five members are assholes!"

"Smile when you call me an asshole," the chair of the committee, Senator Daniel Patrick Moynihan (D-NY), responded calmly.[48]

On April 9, 1984, Goldwater was in no mood to smile. "Dear Bill," he wrote Casey. "I've been trying to figure out how I can most easily tell you my feelings about the discovery of the President having approved mining some of the harbors of Central America. It gets down to one, little, simple phrase: I am pissed off!"

Bemoaning the White House's disregard of both transparency and the rule of law, he added, "Bill, how can we back his foreign policy when we don't know what the hell he is doing? . . . This is an act violating international law."[49]

Moynihan, equally outraged, briefly resigned in protest from the SSCI, explaining that Casey's briefing had been neither "full," "current," nor "prior" as required by the Intelligence Oversight Act of 1980 and calling his deception a "challenge to American constitutional government."[50] The New Yorker spoke for most of his colleagues: "Casey was running a disinformation operation against our committee."[51] Simmons of the SSCI recalled that "the committee kept digging because Casey kept telling them to go fuck themselves."[52] When the Iran-Contra scandal broke two years later, Moynihan would reflect that "in the history of the American Republic I do not believe there has even been so massive a hemorrhaging of trust and integrity. The very processes of American Government were put in harm's way by a conspiracy of faithless or witless men: sometimes both."[53]

Moynihan also chafed under Clarridge's disrespectful appearances before his committee, once leaning in to his microphone to scold, "Mr. Clarridge, you are *snapping* your suspenders. You are engaging in chitchat with people behind you. Need I remind you, this is an official body?"

Clair George, chief of the Latin American Division, also had a "mind-set . . . the same as Casey's—suspicious, minimal notification," recalled Simmons. "That's fine at a station overseas, but it doesn't work in a democratic forum." According to Bob Gates, Casey's deputy, the attitude of Clair, Casey, and Clarridge "toward the Hill was screw 'em. . . . Don't tell Congress anything unless you're driven to the wall."[54]

Moynihan and Goldwater did just that, forcing Casey to sign what became known as the "Casey Accords": an agreement to report every "planned intelligence activity" to the SSCI even if "part of an ongoing covert action operation within the scope of an existing Presidential Finding."[55] Casey apologized to Moynihan and then to the SSCI. "He mouthed the words," one Congressman observed. "But true contrition was not in his vocabulary."

Casey confirmed: "I sure as hell didn't want to do it. I gagged on it."[56]

Further dividing the CIA from Congress, the press in late 1984 revealed that a CIA guerrilla-warfare training manual advised the Contras on the "selective use of violence" to "neutralize carefully selected and planned targets such as court judges, police and state security officials, etc." In short, *Psychological Operations in Guerrilla Warfare*, which Clarridge had commissioned but not read because it was in Spanish, taught assassination—in addition to kidnapping, blackmailing, terror, and overthrowing the Sandinistas. Representative Boland denounced the publication as "the doctrine of Lenin, not Jefferson."[57]

In damage-control mode, Casey replaced the brash Clarridge with Alan Fiers Jr. (pronounced "fires"), who became chief of the Central American Task Force. But relations between the intelligence community at Langley and the intelligence committees on Capitol Hill proved nearly beyond repair. A resolution by Senator Edward Kennedy (D-MA) condemning the mining of the ports passed 84 to 12.

Still, the Contra army grew. By the mid-1980s, it numbered 20,000, forty times larger than originally sold to Congress. Clarridge declared it "the largest guerrilla force ever seen in Latin America."[58]

Then came the Boland Amendments. Starting in late 1982 until late 1986, there would be from three to six of them, depending on whom one asked. As their opponents complained, they could be confusing and, as White House chief of staff Donald Regan testified, "a constantly micromanaging affair."[59] But the second—known as Boland II and signed by Reagan on October 12, 1984—stated unequivocally its prohibition of Contra aid: "During fiscal year

1985, no funds available to the Central Intelligence Agency, the Department of Defense, or any other agency or entity of the United States involved in intelligence activities may be obligated or expended for the purpose or which would have the effect of supporting, directly or indirectly, military or paramilitary operations in Nicaragua by any nation, group, organization, movement, or individual."[60] When word of the House vote on Boland II reached Casey at Langley, Gates was there. "He gnashed his teeth," Gates said. "Casey literally gnashed his teeth. You could hear it."[61]

Lest anyone doubt his intent, Boland added, "Let me make very clear that this prohibition applies to all funds available for fiscal year 1985 regardless of any accounting procedure at any agency. It clearly prohibits any expenditure, including those from accounts for salaries and all support costs. The prohibition is so strictly written that it also prohibits transfers of equipment acquired at no cost. To repeat, the compromise provision clearly ends U.S. support for the war in Nicaragua."[62]

"This secret war should end—today," said Boland. His Republican colleague Henry Hyde, a strong supporter of the Contras, agreed that Boland forbade "any assistance to the freedom fighters in Nicaragua. . . . No food, no medicine, no ammunition, not even moral support."[63]

Another Republican House member, Bob Livingston of Louisiana, had not quite gotten it: "Are there no exceptions to this prohibition?"

"There are no exceptions to the prohibition," Boland reiterated.

Dick Cheney (R-WY), then also in the House, called Boland II a "killer amendment," intended to compel the Contras "to lay down their arms."[64] It thus proved a hard sell when others dismissed all the Boland Amendments as "each more opaque than the last."[65]

Some executive branch members did get the message. Under Stanley Sporkin, the Office of General Counsel at the CIA grasped that not even "staff salaries" could be used "in any activities which would have the effect of supporting paramilitary operations in Nicaragua by anyone." The Boland language also meant that the CIA had to know the "effect" of any aid. Medical supplies to the Contras, for instance, "arguably has the 'effect' of 'indirectly' supporting their paramilitary activities."[66] "We are going to be under very close scrutiny on this question," predicted the agency's lawyers, "and we must take every precaution to ensure that we are not in violation of congressional prohibition either in fact or in spirit."[67]

Contradicting Sporkin, other executive branch lawyers came up with legal justifications to circumvent Boland. Most were exercises in splitting hairs. One, for instance, differentiated between the purpose of the CIA and

Defense in providing funds to the Contras—outwardly, to interdict gunrunning to El Salvador—versus the purpose of the Contras themselves, which was regime change. The first could not be barred, said the president's Intelligence Oversight Board (IOB), but the second could.[68] Some legal scholars argued that Congress could certainly "withhold" funds from the executive but not "condition" them, which would restrict the president's prerogative over how to disburse foreign policy moneys.[69]

Armed with such justifications, Casey informed Boland that he would indeed be helping the Contras but that none of the aid would be offensive. The CIA, for instance, was "contemplating providing defensive intelligence," he wrote in December 1984. That intelligence would leave out "the specific details requisite for the planning/launching of offensive operations" and be aimed only to "prevent loss of life."[70]

No dice, Boland told Casey. "Your stated intention to provide 'defensive intelligence' . . . is troubling . . . particularly if such information will enable [the Contras] to avoid tactical contact with the enemy and thus be in a better position to continue military operations of its own." Boland knew—as Casey surely also did—that all aid, whether defensive or humanitarian, was fungible and thus allowed the Contras to fight another day.[71]

"Those guys at Langley must have thought we were walking around with 'Kick me' signs on our backs," muttered one SSCI staffer.[72]

.....

With Congress unwilling to let the CIA directly fund the Contras, Casey identified Marine Lieutenant Colonel Oliver North as the instrument of his will over at the NSC. Their offices were around the corner from each other in the old Executive Office Building.[73] Clair George testified that Casey "loved North very much, he liked action people."[74]

North's life had led him to be able and willing to fund a covert counterrevolutionary force against the will of Congress. Everyone who met him in the 1980s described him as strong-willed, results-focused, arrogant, stupefyingly hard working, and contemptuous of any individual or group failing to share his righteousness or sense of urgency.

Physically, he impressed many as an all-American male specimen. "A man with an intense, magnetic personality and riveting blue eyes, he looked as though he had stepped out of a Marine Corps recruiting poster," wrote two men who worked with him.[75]

North was born in 1943 "in the midst of the war that America won for the world," he wrote in his autobiography. Among those who triumphed figured his father, who served in Patton's army. Raised by this "staunch Republican" and a "devout Catholic" mother in a "Norman Rockwell painting" small town in New York State, young Oliver, known then by his middle name Larry, fished, hunted, and learned to shoot a .22 rifle before he could drive. After a strict and patriotic upbringing, he joined the Marines and proudly attended the Naval Academy because "anyone who is blessed to live in this great country ought to give something back to it."[76]

At Annapolis, he majored in international relations and warned his roommate about the coming Cold War peril in Central America. "Johnny, that's where communism is going to be in the late seventies or eighties."[77]

One Contra leader described North as "a living metaphor for the Empire."[78] North copped to sharing the military's arrogance as "a well-deserved pride. That swaggering, macho attitude, the confidence that comes with being part of an elite group like the Marines, that lack of patience with our civilian counterparts—these qualities were earned on battlefields all over the world." North sought his own battlefield. After graduation, he gave up his leave time to make it to Vietnam before the war ended. There, North displayed bravery and loyalty to his men. In nine months of combat, he was wounded twice.[79] He earned a Bronze Star with Combat "V," a Silver Star, two Purple Hearts, and a Navy Commendation Medal. As an officer, he also dished out the fastidiousness of his father, who, if North had come home from school with a grade of 95 percent, would ask him why he didn't earn 100.[80] In Southeast Asia, one Marine joked, "if you took a piss, Lieutenant North would critique you on how you held your dick."[81]

North deemed his leadership of a platoon as "an exercise in frustration. You'd take a hill and move on, and three days later you'd have to come back and fight again over the same piece of ground because there weren't enough troops to occupy it." He added: "We were angry at the politicians back in Washington who set the rules, who made us risk our lives while putting up with enormous obstacles."[82]

When Reagan became president, North got the invitation to join the NSC on a temporary assignment that would end up lasting six years. There, he focused on issues as diverse as counterterrorism, disaster response, and Central America. He was promoted to lieutenant colonel and earned a reputation as a workhorse.

"North is truly an extreme example of workaholism," observed Robert "Bud" McFarlane, the national security advisor and North's superior. "Because it wasn't fourteen hours a day, it was almost sixteen, on average, except Sundays. Sundays he might knock off with about eight hours. Every day of every year." In the 1970s, North's near-total absence from family life nearly drove him and his wife Betsy to divorce and North to depression and suicide. By the 1980s, it appeared she had accepted his extreme schedule.[83] At the Executive Office Building, wrote a colleague of North, "there were many occasions when he did not sleep at all. He found that it was possible to take a late-night flight to Miami, meet with *contra* leaders and/or supporters in the early hours of the morning, and catch the first flight to Washington, in order to be at his desk by the time most people were arriving at work after a night's sleep."[84]

The evening North's daughter Dornin turned five, she called her father three times at the office. "Daddy, when are you coming home?"

"Don't worry, honey. Daddy's coming home as soon as he can," he said each time. "I've just got to finish this work."

By the time he got home—well after nine o'clock—Dornin was fast asleep.[85]

Once entrenched at the NSC, North believed in the exclusive power of the executive to make foreign policy.[86] He interpreted broadly the 1936 *Curtiss-Wright* decision as giving the president unlimited powers in foreign policy.[87] His memoir even assessed that Reagan "wasn't forceful enough when it came to fighting for the constitutional prerogatives of the Executive Branch."[88] Like Casey, North blamed leaks overwhelmingly on Congress, once citing two instances of counterterrorism operations when legislators or their aides had disclosed sensitive information. It turned out that White House officials were to blame for one leak—and North himself for the other.[89]

.....

Casey and North were keen to interpret Boland II as not covering North's NSC at all. If it did not, the NSC could serve as a lifeboat for the Contras until Congress funded them anew.

Trouble was, common sense indicated that an organization that analyzed, disseminated, and directed intelligence was, in the language of Boland II, "involved in intelligence activities." Some Republicans allowed this plain logic.[90] Also, Executive Order 12333 stated that the "NSC shall act as the highest Executive Branch entity that provides review of, guidance for and direction to the conduct of all national foreign intelligence, counterintelligence, and special activities, and attendant policies and programs."[91]

Lee Hamilton (D-IN), chair of the HPSCI, recalled Congress's intent. "We drafted the Boland Amendment broadly for precisely the reason that we wanted to cover the National Security Council. And we briefed in the

Committee and the intent of the Committee was to cover the National Security Council because it was involved in intelligence activities."[92] Another member of Congress wrote: "It would be stretching the integrity of the law to suggest that this prohibition was not intended to cover the NSC."[93] There was also the matter that both North and Poindexter were at the NSC on loan from the Pentagon, and therefore were uniformed members of the Department of Defense and very much subject to Boland.[94] Had the NSC not been covered by Boland, Pentagon salaries were.[95]

National Security Advisor McFarlane understood that the Boland Amendment applied to his outfit, and he told his staff so.[96] Bud McFarlane was a die-hard Republican military man. The son of a congressman from Texas, he graduated from the Naval Academy and spent twenty years in the Marines before joining the Nixon administration as a White House fellow and later military assistant to Henry Kissinger. Under Reagan, he became the deputy to his predecessor, William Clark. As national security advisor, he all but conceived of the Strategic Defense Initiative or "Star Wars" missile defense system.[97]

Under McFarlane, NSC staffers understood that "the legislative intent of the [Boland] Amendment is to end funding in support of paramilitary operations in Nicaragua."[98] North himself wrote in a memo, along with another NSC official, that "notwithstanding our own interpretation" of Boland, "it is very clear from the colloquy during the [congressional] debate . . . that the legislative intent was to deny *any* direct or indirect support for military/paramilitary operations in Nicaragua."[99]

Yet many willfully interpreted the amendment as excluding them from its prohibition. They assumed that the Boland Amendments did not apply to the president—even though he could count as an "entity" involved in intelligence—and inferred that the NSC was a personal agency of the president's and therefore also not covered. A more popular argument was that the authorization act to which Boland II was attached listed intelligence agencies that were affected, and the list included neither the president nor the NSC. Besides, they thought, no criminal penalties were attached to Boland II, so what was the harm in violating it? (It *was* a crime to spend funds in ways not appropriated by Congress.)[100] And shouldn't anybody, including the NSC staff, have the First Amendment right to *talk* to the Contras?[101]

As the IOB also argued, the NSC was "not considered part of the intelligence community by law or executive order" and did "not function as a member of the intelligence community" because it coordinated rather than implemented policy. Maybe North was officially from Defense, it added, but even then, Boland II did not prohibit his activities.[102] Lawyer Bretton Sciaroni, who researched and wrote the IOB memo, conducted only a cursory interview with North in preparation. Sciaroni asked for none of North's files, piled on the desk between the two men. He left believing the lie that "the NSC had not raised funds or given military support or helped give military support to the Contras."[103] It was true that, as Sciaroni wrote McFarlane, "If the intent [of Boland] was to include the NSC [in its prohibited agencies], that could have been easily done."[104] But legislators probably never conceived of the NSC, an advisory body, running operations. Sciaroni's memo tackled neither why coordinating intelligence did not "involve" the NSC in intelligence activities nor the fact that funding the Contras was very much an operation.

This casuistry was all North and others at the NSC needed to keep ignoring Congress. North feared "unhelpful speculation" among the lawyers.[105] In later testimony, he admitted withholding facts from the IOB and relying only on its favorable opinions.[106] His relief was palpable when the IOB memo landed on his desk because it "reinforced" his opinion that Boland II did not cover the NSC.

"Was there any consideration of the fact that you didn't want to go outside for an opinion because you might get an answer you didn't like?" he was asked.

"I don't think that crossed my mind."

"That was never discussed amongst your staff?"

"No, not that I initiated or participated in."[107]

North stated that he discussed legalities with "John Norton Moore of the American Bar Association on a number of occasions," but Moore said he never talked to North.[108]

In the rest of the White House, many wondered how the Contras hung together despite Boland II, but they looked the other way. Chief of Staff Don Regan admitted he asked no one at the NSC about the void left by the CIA's abandonment and was not aware that the men differed on whether Boland II covered their agency. "I never looked into the legalities of the Boland Amendment. . . . I left that up to the NSC." He did ask—twice—that Reagan's lawyers look at the matter. The NSC's answer: "That is not necessary, we have our own legal opinion."[109]

.....

North also was lucky to get a new superior a few months after the IOB memo. In December 1985, Admiral John Poindexter replaced McFarlane as national security advisor.

FIGURE 2
When Admiral John Poindexter served as national security adviser, "secretiveness applied to all issues," said one NSC official. (Cynthia Johnson/The Chronicle Collection/Getty)

Poindexter had spent a career coming to substantially the same beliefs as North, but with a different demeanor. "He was never a little boy," his mother said. "He was born an old man" (see fig. 2).[110] Also from a small town, Poindexter, too, had risen in the military, but his medals were for paperwork, not combat. In high school, he was valedictorian and school president.[111] At Annapolis, he graduated first in his class of more than 900—compared with 468th in a class of 835 for North.[112] In the Navy, one of Poindexter's evaluators called him "the most outstanding officer I have met in the naval service."[113] He earned a doctorate in nuclear physics and commanded a destroyer squadron. Colleagues described him as efficient and photographic-memory brilliant.

Reclusive, too. Poindexter often ate all three meals in his office. "The Admiral," said his secretary, "was not a very social bird."[114]

"More than any man I've ever known," recalled North, "the admiral kept his feelings to himself. He actually made McFarlane seem colorful."[115]

With Poindexter, "secretiveness applied to all issues," said one NSC official. "He changed the NSC routine from constant meetings to one-on-one negotiations where only he saw all the cards."[116]

Poindexter's schedule mirrored North's. He worked from 7 a.m. to 9 p.m., went home for dinner, and worked there until midnight, six days a week. On the seventh day, he might go to church, and then do paperwork.[117] With none of North's flash, Poindexter nevertheless shared his subordinate's distrust of those outside the executive branch. According to North, his superior "seem[ed] to have no friends in Congress, and certainly none in the media."[118]

Like Casey and North, Poindexter resented Congress for its oversight of foreign policy funding and intelligence. He considered leaks to be "bad faith" on the part of congressional opponents of Contra aid. The press, he added, "did not present a clear and complete picture to the American public about many of the issues that we were faced with."[119]

Continuing Contra aid despite the prohibition was an open secret between the CIA and NSC. Alan Fiers, who showed more integrity than his predecessor Duane Clarridge, once reported to Clair George that North might be working with the Contras. He was summoned to Casey's office with George and North.

There, Casey leaned back in his chair: "Ollie, Alan says you're operating in Central America. Are you operating in Central America?" He turned to Fiers: "Alan, tell Ollie what you told—what you said."

Taken aback, Fiers gave a "softened" version of his concerns.

"Now Ollie, I don't want you operating in Central America," Casey said. "You understand that?"

"Yes, sir. I understand it," North said.

"Alan," George told Fiers after the meeting, "you've got to understand what happened in there. What we saw was for our consumption. Sometime in the dark of night Bill Casey has told the President: 'I'll take care of Central America, Mr. President; don't worry about it.' And what you saw was essentially for our consumption."

"Wow," Fiers told George. "If that's true and if it blows it will be worse than Watergate."[120]

.....

To prevent secrets from "blowing," the NSC staff evaded oversight efforts by Congress under Boland.

In August 1985, Congressman Barnes, now chair of the House Subcommittee on Western Hemisphere Affairs, wrote to McFarlane about press allegations of a certain Marine lieutenant colonel "providing 'tactical influence' on rebel military operations, facilitating contacts for prospective financial donors, and otherwise organising and coordinating rebel efforts."[121] North later admitted to Congress to advising the Contras "that they could not or should not attack certain types of targets because it would indeed have the effect of alienating the population."[122]

North did much more. He traveled to Contra camps several times, discussing strategy and needs. Contras gave him wish lists of weapons, and he edited them. One Contra leader testified to Congress that North "commented, let's say, on military things." Asked if North shared intelligence, the Contra answered, "We did discuss positions of Sandinista troops, and he did tell me about the Sandinistas massing up [*sic*] at some point and about the Sandinista troops threatening." Yet he insisted that "we never planned nor carried out any operation" based on conversations with North.[123]

An aide warned Barnes that asking the White House for documents was tricky, "both because of executive privilege and because we don't know what we are looking for, and they were probably smart enough not to leave much of a paper trail anyway."[124] Yet Barnes sought breadcrumbs linking the NSC to the Contras.

In response to Barnes's request for documents, McFarlane's staff schemed to keep Congress (and State) in the dark. *We need to proceed carefully*, North urged them.[125] One aide suggested an old bureaucratic trick—"to be terribly forthcoming and bury Mr. Barnes in logs of dates and/or names re meetings and telecons." In the end, the NSC went with the opposite tactic. To the suggestion by Barnes that North may have been having discussions with the Contras after the October 1984 Boland prohibition, one aide counseled, "we should search the files only on that basis," and Poindexter, McFarlane's deputy at the time, approved.[126] After a "narrowly focused" search of only North's computer files, they found a grand total of nine items.[127]

McFarlane first responded to Barnes not that Boland did not apply to the NSC but that "we have scrupulously abided by the spirit and the letter of the law." North urged the Contras only "to forge a representative political front."[128] When Barnes insisted on seeing documents, McFarlane plainly refused, calling his files "the appropriate purview of the Executive branch." He hinted that Barnes had leaked his first response.[129]

Unable to shake off Barnes, McFarlane had him visit his office, where, rather than present him with just a few documents, he piled hundreds of them, a foot thick, on his desk.

"There they are," he told Barnes. "You're welcome to read them. But I'm afraid I can't let them leave my office."

Barnes shook his head. "I'll have my staff go through them."

"I'm afraid we can't do that," said McFarlane coldly. "Some of these documents include highly sensitive, highly classified information."

"We have procedures for dealing with highly classified information," Barnes reassured him.

"I'm sorry. We can't do it."

"I can't accept this," Barnes insisted. "You'll hear from us," he added, and walked out. Upon his return to Capitol Hill, he told aides, "I've just met a man who's afraid he's going to go to jail."[130]

McFarlane kept refusing to share documents until the issue faded. He thwarted Lee Hamilton of the HPSCI in a similar fashion.

McFarlane eventually sent Barnes six of the nine documents his staff had curated.[131] According to North, his boss had him first remove all traces of McFarlane's knowledge of North's illegal activities: "He was cleaning up the historical record."[132] Or, as he told Fiers "in a very ominous way, . . . Bud McFarlane just perjured himself."[133] One administration official brazenly said that Barnes "was informed as fully as we thought necessary."[134]

North later admitted that he was deeply involved in moving military supplies, and "I didn't want to show Congress a single word on this whole thing." One of the lines he and McFarlane used in their response to Barnes—"The right of the executive to maintain confidentiality of information important to the conduct of our foreign policies must be sustained"—came right from a law book about executive privilege.

"I take it you intended to mislead the Congress?" asked Republican counsel George Van Cleve of North, at later hearings.

"I did," replied North.[135]

When Poindexter took over as national security advisor, he closed the matter by declaring that his predecessor had answered enough questions. He provided no further documents.[136]

.....

With Congress effectively sidelined, North created what he and colleagues called "the Enterprise" or "Project Democracy." With Fiers, the CIA Central American Task Force chief, and Elliott Abrams, the assistant secretary of state first for human rights and humanitarian affairs and, after mid-1985, for inter-American affairs, North operated within a Restricted Interagency Group (RIG)—which itself grew out of a larger RIG—that ran funding and propaganda operations out of the NSC. In 1987, Abrams evaded responsibility for those operations, saying, "Most of us were careful not to ask North lots of questions."[137] But one deputy chief of mission in mid-1980s Costa Rica saw all three RIG members as "central, the 'Anillo' (the ring) we called them. Of course others were involved too. . . . But for us it was these three."[138]

One RIG project was the State Department Group on Latin American Public Diplomacy (S/LPD), otherwise known as the Office of Public Diplomacy. As early as 1982, this gang of eight staffers originally headed by Walter

Raymond targeted the districts of anti-Contra lawmakers to pressure them to vote for aid. Maryland's Barnes, who prodded McFarlane for documents, was one mark. "We all . . . wanted to nail Barnes's ass," admitted one official.[139] Concealing government sponsorship, the S/LPD's nearly $1 million yearly budget funded private entities, such as International Business Communications, to ghost-write and place TV and newspaper ads that attacked the Sandinistas, for instance in the *Wall Street Journal.* Taxpayers also unwittingly paid for Contra leaders to visit Washington and lobby Congress. In its first year, S/LPD booked more than 1,500 speaking engagements, published three booklets, and sent materials to 1,600 college libraries, 520 political science faculties, 122 editorial writers, and 107 religious groups. Otto Reich, the later head of S/LPD, met with editors and journalists to press for more favorable coverage. His goal was not to correct errors but to complain of "bias." Reich and his staff also made up "crises," such as an alleged plan for Soviet MiG fighter planes to be delivered to Nicaragua.[140]

He often succeeded. "Without blowing our own horn," Reich later testified, "it got to the point where the President of the United States, the Secretary of State, the National Security Advisor, Cabinet officials and lots of other people relied on our information and used it verbatim. I mean, it was that good."

In 1984, Oliver North personally oversaw an S/LPD "sting" operation. In it, smuggler Barry Seal—played by Tom Cruise in the movie *American Made*—flew his usual shipment of cocaine into Nicaragua. There, he secretly photographed a Sandinista official carrying a sack of it to a second plane. The photo allowed Reagan to claim that the Sandinistas were running drugs, but the Drug Enforcement Agency acknowledged no evidence of such activity by any other Nicaragua official.[141]

In 1987, the US comptroller general found that S/LPD "engaged in prohibited, covert propaganda activities." Soon after, the office shut down.[142] By law, government funds cannot be "designed to influence a Member of Congress" or for covert propaganda.[143]

Those who planned this internal propaganda adopted as a "major theme" that Contra "freedom fighters are fighting democracy's battle."[144] Yet to Robert Parry and Peter Kornbluh, S/LPD operated "against the three key institutions of American democracy: Congress, the press, and an informed electorate."[145]

.....

Another scheme for getting around Boland sprouted from Congress's appropriation in August 1985 of $27 million for the newly created Nicaraguan

Humanitarian Assistance Office (NHAO). Congress put the NHAO under the jurisdiction of the State Department, and Abrams at State lamented its founding "over our dead body. We all, the Secretary on down, felt that that was crazy." He argued: "What did the State Department know about buying boots and shipping them down to Central America? There were two agencies of government that do it, that know how to do it, that know how to account for it that are all set, CIA and the Defense Department."[146]

The NHAO's very name helped to blur the distinction between lethal and nonlethal aid. Journalist Ann Wroe traced the overlap: "Presumably radios were non-lethal; on the other hand, how were signals given to attack targets? A truck carrying wounded soldiers was obviously humanitarian, but what if there were bullets on board?" Could the NHAO pay for wristwatches for the Contras? asked its director of Abrams. "Well, you know, unless you have a very large wristwatch and hit somebody with it," was Abrams's positive answer.[147] At Ilopango air base in El Salvador, lethal and nonlethal cargo lay side by side. "We didn't differentiate between one and the other," one operative admitted. "I was just handling both like the same thing."[148]

The slope got slippery, and quickly. In December 1985, the NHAO's mission changed to allow exchanges of intelligence between the CIA and the Contras.[149] Alan Fiers of the CIA recalled that North could now infiltrate the NHAO or "piggyback the activities of his Enterprise onto the fledgling humanitarian program." Air crews were "NHAO by night, private benefactors by day"—meaning that they placed military goods donated by private donors on US government planes.[150]

The Government Accountability Office audited the NHAO a few months after its establishment, concerned that it could not account for $7 million of its expenses. How could one verify that the Contras were using the humanitarian aid the NHAO sent and not bartering it for weapons? One could not, the NHAO responded. But "the resistance forces cannot survive without basics—food, clothing, medicines—which NHAO provides; they have no incentive to divert or exchange these supplies, and even if they tried, that would become immediately apparent in the highly parochial environment in which they operate."[151] The Government Accountability Office still investigated. It found "$80,000 based on false receipts," adding that "some funds were used to purchase ammunition and grenades."[152]

.....

As for President Reagan, everything he said and did regarding the Contras telegraphed his support to those who wanted them funded, Congress be damned. In his diary, the president often complained of congressional opposition from "far out liberals & left wingers," yet he knew that most Americans also opposed aid.[153] Reagan lobbied Congress, and when he lost votes, the disappointment stung. Advisors kept him briefed on the Contras often, if not in detail, and he was pleased that they survived as a force under Boland II. He testified that "whatever we did in trying to maintain the existence of the contras" had to be done within the law, a point he "always" stressed to aides.[154] But he told those same aides that Boland did not apply to the NSC and that the US government had to keep the Contras alive "body and soul," as McFarlane told Congress.[155] The contradiction, perhaps the most careless in Reagan's career, placed subordinates in an impossible situation.

2

WAR, INC.

Besides the disregard for the separation of powers—not to mention for the law and for truth—another major antidemocratic facet of President Reagan's Contra operation was its privatization. Oliver North, Bill Casey, Elliott Abrams, and many others solicited money from both third countries and private US citizens to fund a war that they knew the people's representatives had forbidden. Reagan knowingly participated as a fundraiser.

As privatization tends to do, the Contra variety led not only to profiteering but also to lawbreaking—including bribery and drug smuggling—and a chipping away at the truth. A form of corruption was the making of quid pro quo arrangements with foreign governments, who used secrecy as a fulcrum to make demands of US foreign policymakers.

.....

In October 1983, one month after Congress imposed the first limits on Contra spending, privatizing that spending also began.[1] North and his crew at the National Security Council coordinated most of the funds that came in, but they relied on non-government individuals who solicited donations directly.

The lieutenant colonel called these people, and donors to them, "private patriotic Americans."[2]

A major propagandist and private fundraiser for the Contras was retired general John Singlaub, the head of the World Anti-Communist League.[3] Singlaub was a legend for his daring. During World War II, he had volunteered for the Office of Strategic Services. In 1944, he led a three-man parachute team into the Massif Central to head a French resistance unit behind Nazi lines. Later that year he trained Chinese guerrillas against the Japanese on the border between China and Indochina. He even parachuted into a war camp off the coast of China to free some 400 prisoners. After the war, he served in Manchuria, Korea, Germany, and Vietnam and taught at Forts Benning and Leavenworth. He organized CIA missions behind enemy lines during the Korean War.[4] In Southeast Asia, he directed the CIA-linked Special Operations Group, conducting raids without consulting Congress.[5] His then-case officer, none other than William Casey, once offered him cyanide pills to commit suicide if caught by the enemy. "No sir, I don't intend to be captured," responded Singlaub.[6] Oliver North served under him in Vietnam.[7]

Singlaub's years as a hero of war preceded those as a critic of peace. In the Carter administration, Singlaub found himself chief of staff of United Nations forces in the Korean Peninsula until he publicly criticized the president's plans to withdraw US troops. Carter removed Singlaub from his command. When he again went public to denounce his commander in chief, this time over canceling the neutron bomb, Carter fired him. The president briefly rehired him, only to see Singlaub retire and become a vocal detractor of the Democrat's foreign policies, from negotiating away the Panama Canal to being soft on Soviet nuclear plans. Among his enemies Singlaub counted "our own State Department and the pressure from New York bankers," the latter usually a veiled anti-Semitic reference. The Republicans welcomed him. He helped craft the defense language of their 1980 platform.[8]

In Central America, Singlaub threw himself into counterguerrilla training in El Salvador and then fundraising for the Contras—about $250,000 each in 1985 and 1986. He claimed that he "devoted my life to trying to advance the cause of freedom" and "did not make any money" off his cause, and there was indeed no evidence of Singlaub profiteering. In a classic example of the dangers to policymaking that privatization can pose, however, he once flirted with impersonating the US government. He reached an agreement with Contra leader Edén Pastora about Pastora reentering Nicaragua from Costa Rica. Singlaub claimed that Abrams of the State Department "posed no objections to my doing this, although he pointed out the hazards involved."

Singlaub also knew that North would object to further collaborating with the infamously unreliable Comandante Cero and was aware that "I had no authority to represent the United States." Yet Singlaub made promises about what "the United States" would do, telegraphing to the Nicaraguan that he represented Washington.[9] Secretary of State Shultz warned: "Pastora might attempt to use the Singlaub agreement to pressure or embarrass the USG[overnment.]"[10] The State Department eventually sent Singlaub clear signals to cease and desist.[11]

The private individual who most directly reported to North, meanwhile, was Robert Owen, whom North's biographer described as "his liaison and man Friday with the Contras." A generation younger than Singlaub, Owen devoted himself to anticommunism after his older brother died at the hands of the Vietcong. After majoring in political science at Stanford, he went to work for arch-conservative Senator Dan Quayle (R-IN). Owen left politics for a public relations firm that considered working for the Contras. In 1983, during a meeting about the threat from the Sandinistas, he met North. The two brainstormed about how to win in Nicaragua, for instance by establishing a front company to ship goods to the Contras. North loved the young man's enthusiasm. He had the Contras hire him, initially at $2,500 a month.[12] Owen was not a government employee, yet he and North developed a close working relationship. In correspondence, Owen was "TC" for "The Courier"—appropriate as he shuttled from Washington to Central America—while North called himself "The Hammer," "Steelhammer," or "BG" for "Blood and Guts." When Congress appropriated the $27 million in "humanitarian" aid, North extracted $4,850 per month for "the full time services of Mr. Owen."[13]

.....

On the afternoon of June 25, 1984, Reagan gathered his National Security Planning Group (NSPG) in the Situation Room, a windowless, wood-paneled meeting space in the basement of the White House. The subject was Central America. Casey of the CIA was there, along with Shultz, Secretary of Defense Caspar Weinberger, Counselor to the President Ed Meese III, National Security Advisor Bud McFarlane, Vice President George H. W. Bush, and various aides. These men were about to make a momentous decision despite knowing they might be denigrating the rule of law and the sanctity of truth, not to mention indebting the United States to foreign nations.

The CIA, began Casey, was authorized "to cooperate and seek support from third countries" for the Contra effort. He ticked off Latin American countries that would receive it. "If we notify the oversight committees" of Congress, he added, "we can provide direct assistance to help the FDN [a Contra organization] get the money they need from third countries."

Shultz's antennae went up. He warned that James Baker, a lawyer, current secretary of the Treasury, and recent White House chief of staff opposed to funding the Contras, "said that if we go out and try to get money from third countries, it is an impeachable offense."

Not if we notify committees such as the SSCI and the HPSCI, Casey countered.

But Shultz was categorical: "Jim Baker's argument is that the US Government may raise and spend funds only through an appropriation of the Congress."

Weinberger took Casey's side, arguing that the US government would not be spending its own money, only that of other countries or sources.

Can we do that? the skeptical Shultz asked. *We should get the attorney general's opinion.*

Meese—who would soon be attorney general—suggested that he could produce any legal opinion that his president wanted. "It's important to tell the Department of Justice that we want them to find the proper and legal basis which will permit the United States to assist in obtaining third party resources for the anti-Sandinistas." He failed to add *or not.* "You have to give lawyers guidance when asking them a question," he did add, to make himself understood.

Casey got it. "We need the legal opinion which makes clear that the US has the authority to facilitate third country funding for the anti-Sandinistas." He left no door open for an opinion that would bar such aid.

Bush, who spoke little, agreed with "third parties" helping but warned that foreign nations could then trap the United States into quid pro quos. "The only problem that might come up is if the United States were to promise to give these third parties something in return so that some people could interpret this as some kind of exchange."

Groupthink was congealing too fast, sensed McFarlane. "I propose that there be no authority for anyone to seek third party support for the anti-Sandinistas until we have the information we need. . . and I certainly hope none of this discussion will be made public in any way." McFarlane thus said aloud what they all thought: that privatization, legal or not, would run against the will of Congress and prove unpopular with the American people.

"If such a story gets out," joked Reagan, "we'll all be hanging by our thumbs in front of the White House until we find out who did it."[14]

The next day, Stanley Sporkin, the CIA's top lawyer, confirmed that Casey was looking for a legal way of getting money to the Contras, possibly through third countries. That might happen, said Sporkin, but only absent "any monetary promises or inducements from the United States Government."[15] In other words, no quids from Washington in return for foreign funds.

In August, Sporkin repeated the proviso and added that Boland II "is not limited by its language to *appropriated* funds. The broadness of the wording of this section appears to prohibit the use of funds made 'available' to the Agency by other nations, groups or individuals."[16]

As for Shultz, he claimed he never got a legal opinion from the attorney general. "The subject seemed to die down."[17] Yet at CIA, Casey did get Attorney General William French Smith to give him oral assurances that there was "no legal concern" so long as contributing governments "could not look to the United States to repay that commitment in the future."[18]

.....

What McFarlane did not share with the rest of the NSPG was that Saudi Arabia had already started contributing to the Contras. Until Boland II in December 1984, soliciting such aid was legal. In his memoir, Reagan described donor countries as sharing "our concern about the threat to democracy in Latin America. . . . Several countries responded and extended help."[19] Six months before Boland II, McFarlane, who had the original idea of asking third countries, told Saudi Prince Bandar bin Sultan that the Reagan administration was likely to lose Congress's support of the Contras. Two or three days later, Bandar promised $1 million per month. When McFarlane told the president, Reagan "made clear to me that no one should [know about it] and let's keep it that way."[20]

In February 1985, after Boland II, Reagan met privately with Saudi King Fahd, who agreed to double his monthly contribution to $2 million.[21]

Because he had not expressly asked the Saudis for a contribution, McFarlane rationalized it as a gift. He testified that he told North not to solicit money from foreign countries or private sources. North denied receiving such instructions.[22]

McFarlane hated passing the hat around to third countries: "I believe strongly that we could not and should not expect to sustain the [pro-Contra] policy with this kind of support." But he felt pressure from other Republicans. In March 1985, he met with four members of the HPSCI—Robert Stump (R-AZ), Robert Livingston (R-LA), Henry Hyde (R-IL), and Robert McCollum (R-FL). All approved of third-country funding and quid pro quos, even though both ran against the spirit of Boland II.[23]

Congress's lawyer, Arthur Liman, later asked McFarlane, "Were you uncomfortable that you might be creating some implicit quid for a quo?"

"Yes," answered McFarlane. "You always have to consider what is it that you may invite by way of reciprocal gesture or concession, what obligation do you incur for having had some contribution of this kind. Yes." He clarified that there was no "quid for the quo," for instance with the Saudis, but "we were vulnerable to the possibility that one day a quid pro quo would be asked or urged."

McFarlane believed that even post–Boland II donations were not illegal because the US government had not solicited them. Senator William Cohen judged this a "sort of a metaphysical exercise in the definition of 'solicitation.' "[24]

.....

Senior officials eventually made solicitations of some two dozen governments.[25] Between June 1984 and early 1986, the White House, including the president, secretly raised $34 million from other countries for the Contras. Almost all of it came from the Saudis.

In 1983, Israel provided hundreds of tons of weapons to the Department of Defense, which transferred them to the CIA, in an operation codenamed Tipped Kettle. The following year, the sequel came out: Tipped Kettle II. The CIA told Congress that these weapons would be used for "various purposes," a 1989 document revealed, but "in fact many of them were provided to the Nicaraguan Resistance as appropriated funds ran out." As a quid, "the U.S. Government would be as flexible as possible in its approach to Israeli military and economic needs."[26]

Outside the US government, in late 1984, John Singlaub solicited donations from Taiwan and South Korea, in each country's embassy in Washington. According to Singlaub, officials from both countries "expressed sincere interest in being helpful if this could be done in a way that did not attract attention" from Congress. North agreed that Singlaub should follow up those meetings with visits in the two countries' capital and report back to North. Singlaub was not to state overtly that he represented the US government but instead that his request supported the president's policy. As Singlaub put it, he signaled that he was not an "unguided missile."

"In fact," one sly member of Congress asked Singlaub, "there wasn't any great reason for these countries to make this contribution unless they thought it was with the approval of the U.S. Government, was there?"

"No," allowed Singlaub.

Abrams at State agreed to give a "signal" from the US government, yet soon after instructed Singlaub not to make the request—after Singlaub had already made an appointment.

This is embarrassing, Singlaub told Abrams when he returned.

Abrams replied that "the solicitation was going to be made at the highest level." Singlaub assumed that meant someone from the White House and above Shultz. Probably the president himself.[27]

In summer 1985, North asked Gaston Sigur, who worked on Asian affairs at the NSC, to approach Taiwan for a donation, assuring Sigur that North was following McFarlane's orders and that the solicitation was legal.

Asked whether he considered "what those countries could expect in the future as a quid pro quo for having supported this initiative of ours," Sigur responded, "I saw no quid pro quo there at all."[28] Yet, in exchange for Taiwan's offer of $1 million, North promised the unlikely quid that the Contras, once in power, would recognize the Taiwanese regime. Again he made the promise for an additional million.[29] To Taiwan's nemesis, the People's Republic of China, meanwhile, North also promised Contra recognition.[30] Had the Contras triumphed, they would have faced a wrenching dilemma in the Taiwan Strait.

Poindexter once foresaw the typical risks of quid pro quos:

- Public exposure would exacerbate the current partisan atmosphere.
- The foreign contributors would ultimately expect
  that their largesse would result in some kind of
  USG[overnment] concession in their favor.[31]

As Shultz explained, in "countries with which we had a big military or economic assistance relationship," the ask could be "misinterpreted." "We would, in a sense, be giving them a major marker and [a quid pro quo] could wind up compromising us."[32]

Abrams, on whom fell the job of soliciting third countries, interpreted Shultz's instructions as "two rules": "no country which was a right-wing dictatorship, such that the political link to the Contras would be negative, and no country which was getting a lot of aid or help from us, because then you would be accused of putting the arm on them even if it weren't true." This eliminated from contention "countries like Taiwan and South Korea because of the political relationship with them."[33] It is not clear if Abrams knew that both were approached.

The State Department contacted Hassanal Bolkiah, the Sultan of Brunei, a tiny, oil-rich nation on the island of Borneo. In August 1986, Abrams made a hush-hush trip to London under the name "Mr. Kenilworth." As he strolled in Hyde Park with General Ibnu, an aide to the sultan, they exchanged pleasantries.

Then Ibnu bluntly asked, "How much money?"

"Ten million dollars." Abrams justified the donation on the grounds of US national security.

"What do we get out of this? What's in it for us?" asked Ibnu.

"The gratitude of the secretary [of state] and of the President for getting us out of this jam."

"But what *concrete* do we get out of this?" Ibnu pressed.

"You don't get anything concrete out of it."

Miraculously, it worked—sort of. The richest man in the world at the time, the Sultan did pledge $10 million, but North's secretary, Fawn Hall, got two digits transposed on the receiving account number. What would have been a fortune for the Contras lingered in the wrong account until the scandal broke. The $10 million eventually returned to Brunei, none of it reaching the rebels.[34]

.....

Among the most contentious legal questions of the Iran-Contra affair was whether US government employees could encourage not just foreign government but also private US donors to the Contras. The Neutrality Act of 1794 made it illegal for any US citizen to wage war against a country at peace with the United States.

McFarlane stressed to NSC staffers "not to solicit, encourage, coerce or otherwise broker financial contributions to the contras."[35] He followed US government regulations, which forbade soliciting contributions on US government property or for use by the US government.

Yet Reagan himself skirted the edge of the law on this issue. In his memoirs, he recalled telling White House staff, "There has to be a way to help these private citizens who otherwise wouldn't know how to get help to the Contras . . . ; somebody ought to be able to tell them what channel to use." As with keeping the Contras alive "body and soul," he coupled his policy direction with a contradictory directive to stay "within the law."[36]

On March 27, 1984, Casey broached the subject with McFarlane, foreseeing that Congress would cut off funding. "After examining legalities, you might consider appropriate private U.S. citizens to establish a foundation."[37] The DCI kept pressing private funding during the summer of 1984.[38] By the fall, so did North.[39] In September, North requested of McFarlane "that you approve my approaching a private donor for the provision of a replacement *civilian* helicopter." McFarlane said no. "I don't think this is legal," he wrote by hand on the memo.[40]

"What have you been doing on occasions when somebody asks, can they contribute to the contras for military or other purposes?" McFarlane once asked North.

I can't be party to any transfers of monies, responded North. *If they wished to be helpful, they should go on their own, contact the Contra leaderships. I've not been involved in brokering that.*[41]

.....

In reality, North was a crucial "party" in private donations. In early 1985, Carl "Spitz" Channell, a short West Virginian conservative fundraiser with a thin blonde mustache, became the nodal point of private financing for the Contras. Having formed, in late 1984, the National Endowment for the Preservation of Liberty (NEPL), officially a tax-exempt, nonprofit educational foundation, Channell met North shortly after working on a Nicaraguan Refugee Fund dinner at which Reagan delivered the keynote. The dinner raised $200,000, but "consultants" took half of it, and only about $3,000 trickled down to the Contras. The pattern for profiteering off private fundraising was set. To Channell, North's codename became "Green"—the color of money.[42]

The NEPL became the major conduit for large private donations meant for the Contras, under the coordination of North—and of President Reagan. One senator later called this tactic "the one-two punch": First, potential donors met with North to hear of the Contras' specific needs, followed by North's caveat that he could not legally ask for money. Second, he pointed donors to Channell and left the room so that Channell could collect donations. Blurring lines further, North wrote fundraising appeals on NSC stationary.[43]

A direct appeal from the NEPL explained the process to donors: "You are cordially invited to a private meeting concerning Nicaragua which will be held here in Washington. A very high level national security official will be briefing the group of 10 who've been invited. . . . The President needs your personal support to win in Nicaragua."[44] The official was North.

North qualified his nonsolicitation of beer baron Joseph Coors in the following conversation with congressional counsel:

"You asked Joseph Coors for $65,000—"

"Wrong," interrupted North.

" —to buy a Maule airplane, didn't you?"

"Not so. He offered the money, and I told him where to send it, and an airplane was bought with it."

"I did tell people I could not and would not solicit," specified North, "and I do not recall ever being in the presence of Mr. Channell at any time when he asked someone for money. . . . Nor do I ever recall Mr. Channell offering someone a visit to the Oval Office or the President of the United States of America for a price." Yet North took credit for the donations. "If someone wants to say, 'It was a speech by Ollie North that made me want to give money to help the Nicaraguan Resistance,' I appreciate that." He once called Contra fundraising "my private U.S. operation" and admitted, "One of the purposes of my talking to people was indeed to encourage that they do whatever they felt moved to do to support the cause of a democratic outcome in Nicaragua." North also believed that Reagan was fully aware of this campaign. "Why should he tell me to stop? We weren't breaking any laws."[45]

The entangled role of government officials in the process raised red flags. Channell and North met Ellen Garwood, the daughter of a Texas cotton magnate, for dinner at the Hay-Adams. They presented her with a $1.5 million menu of weapons she could choose from. She recalled that options included "bullets, cartridge belts, possibly surface-to-air missiles, and there were quantities opposite each category, and after that there was a sum of money that was needed."

In this instance, North got up and left, and Channell asked for a contribution. "This is the list of things needed, and can you do something about it? Can you help provide for this and some of the other needs Colonel North had described?"[46] She purchased a $65,000 helicopter that was christened the "Lady Ellen."[47] Garwood had "no doubt," as she said in a deposition, that "this was the executive department of the government that was asking for this help," and it was North's participation that convinced her. White House officials just "were never that blunt in requesting funds. . . . The President himself had said so publicly many times that he wanted private people to give humanitarian aid to the Nicaraguans. . . . It isn't very vague."[48] She never explained how bullets could be humanitarian aid.

Oil and gas businessman William O'Boyle recalled a similar one-two sales pitch. NEPL representatives invited him to Washington, met him at the airport in a limousine, and took him to the Hay-Adams, where he met Channell. They walked over to the Executive Office Building to join a group of ten to twelve prospective donors, including North. What followed was an alarmist presentation about Nicaraguan air bases for Russian planes, enlarged Nicaraguan harbors, "the refugee problem" caused by communism,

Russians "managing the diplomacy of the Nicaraguans before the United Nations," and Nicaraguan officials "involved in smuggling dope." Much of it was untrue or exaggerated. The group returned to the Hay-Adams sans North, where a reception awaited them.

"I am a wealthy person; I have financial resources; is there any way that I can help?" asked O'Boyle of Channell's representatives.

"Well, yes," they responded helpfully. "It is possible that we might be able to do something. For example, a blowpipe missile costs $20,000."

Channell held out the promise of a fifteen-minute "off-the-record" meeting with Reagan for $300,000 or more. And, of course, the record of O'Boyle's stay at the Hay-Adams would be scrubbed.

A few weeks later, O'Boyle hand delivered to Channell a check for $130,000 to purchase two Maule aircraft. North "acknowledged" the contribution. O'Boyle's eventual total gift was $160,000. O'Boyle considered his donation to be for humanitarian purposes because such small planes could be shot down easily and "can be used just for carrying materials from one base to another."

O'Boyle's $160,000 was not enough for a meeting with Reagan. But Garwood, whose gifts to NEPL totaled $2,518,135, did meet the president. So did elderly widow Barbara Newington, who gave $2,866,025.[49] In all, the NEPL raised $10.4 million for the Contra cause.[50]

White House lawyers hesitated when Reagan took on this role of being "a very important prop in this whole operation," in the words of one congressman.[51] North explained to Poindexter, "The President obviously knows why he had been meeting with several select people to thank them for their 'support for Democracy' in Cent[ral] Am[erica]."[52]

North's claim that donations were all legal was bunk. The Neutrality Act forbade any private military aid. It was also illegal for tax-exempt organizations to raise funds for lethal aid. Channell told donors that their gifts were tax deductible because the NEPL was a tax-exempt 501(c)(3) organization. This was a lie: Gifts to foreign organizations such as the Contras were not deductible. When donors expressed misgivings, Channell told them that "the money couldn't be traced."[53] If the gifts had been legal and deductible, US taxpayers would have "effectively subsidized a portion of contributions intended for lethal aid to the Contras," as congressional investigators put it.[54]

After a private donation, North continued to be involved by sending letters of thanks. "The hope [for?] freedom and democracy in Nicaragua was kept alive with the help of the National Endowment for the Preservation of

Liberty and fine Americans such as you," he wrote one donor. "You can be proud that you have made a crucial contribution in helping our President in this vital endeavor."[55] Implicating the president was not casual; it was why donors donated.

.....

To be sure, Channell described himself as fighting an ideological war. "I don't care if they have to mortgage their homes or sell their children," he allegedly said of donors. "What we are doing is more important."[56]

But the war proved vital to his wallet, too. Of the $10.4 million the NEPL received, $6.3 million was intended for the Contras, but only about $3.3 million reached them—a mere 10 percent of what third countries gave, and much of *that* ended up in the pockets of arms smugglers. Channell and his colleagues kept the rest for expenses and salaries, including lobbying, political action committees, and TV ads for Republicans running against anti-Contra Democrats, such as Michael Barnes, and for other Republicans who were not.[57] In other words, the Contra war became a way to advance other conservative causes, serve Republican campaigns, and pad bank accounts in Switzerland and the Cayman Islands. Channell himself bought a $300,000 condo next to Rock Creek Park—worth well over $1 million in the 2020s. He was driven around in a stretch limo. He used his tax-exempt organization to pay his personal credit card bills, housecleaning, and federal income taxes. In two years, his salary alone totaled $345,000 while a fellow fundraiser, Daniel Conrad, pocketed more than $270,000—"extraordinary earnings for nonprofit fundraisers," commented Congress in its report.[58]

When the widow Garwood gave $10,000 for Oliver North's legal defense after the scandal broke, Channell skimmed 35 percent off the top without telling her. She got her money back but was disappointed.

"You mean that he was mixing a little patriotism with a little profiteering?" asked a member of Congress.

"Well, I suppose you could put it that way," answered Garwood. "But the patriotism came first," she still believed.[59]

The Democratic Congressional Campaign Committee charged that Channell's groups violated laws by abusing their tax-exempt status. Channell and his partner Richard Miller would eventually plead guilty to one criminal charge of conspiring to defraud the US government. They named North as coconspirator.[60]

Miller, who funneled donations to the NEPL through his own firm, International Business Communications, charged a 10 percent commission, which netted him and his business partner, Francis Gomez, more than $1.7 million.[61] Reagan's personal assistant, David Fischer, also pocketed $50,000 from Channell and Miller for every donor-president visit he arranged.[62]

.....

Privatization led to claims on policy, typical when philanthropists are involved. In August 1985, Garwood wrote to Reagan, first informing him of her current donations. "But now I've reached the end of my rope in enthusiasm to give for freedom's defense," she proclaimed, "because of the undermining by the State Department under Secretary Shultz of your strong stand against the expansion of totalitarian communism." She had problems with the comparatively moderate diplomat's policies in Angola, Afghanistan, and Mozambique. She demanded that Jeane Kirkpatrick, at the time ambassador to the United Nations, replace Shultz, threatening to otherwise turn off her aid spigot.[63]

.....

Everyone involved in privatization kept Congress and the press in the dark. "Too much is becoming known by too many people," North wrote to Contra leader Adolfo Calero (see fig. 3). "We need to make sure that this new financing does *not* become known. The Congress must believe that there continues to be an urgent need for funding."[64]

In September 1985, McFarlane met with Senators David Durenberger (R-MN) and Patrick Leahy (D-VT) of the SSCI. He assured them that "no NSC staff member either personally assisted the Resistance or solicited outside assistance on their behalf. At no time did anyone act as a go between or focal point for such aid." The senators clarified that helping with private aid would constitute assistance as barred by Boland II. The White House agreed, McFarland assured them.[65]

In October 1985, McFarlane testified to Congress: "There is no official or unofficial relationship with any member of the NSC staff regarding fundraising for the Nicaraguan democratic opposition."[66] Yet that very month, one senator later noted, "the President himself was aware of the existence of the plan to coordinate private donations within the administration."[67]

"I wanted to withhold information on the NSC operational activities in support of the Contras from most everybody," Poindexter later admitted. He and North shared messages through an early IBM email system called PROFS (for Professional Office System) that they both thought private. "Be Cautious," Poindexter titled one PROFS message to North. "I am afraid you

FIGURE 3 Reagan in Robert McFarlane's office with Contra leader Adolfo Calero and Oliver North standing in the back. "We need to make sure that this new financing does *not* become known," North wrote Calero. "The Congress must believe that there continues to be an urgent need for funding." (Courtesy Ronald Reagan Presidential Library)

are letting your operational role become too public. From now on I don't want you to talk to anybody else, including Casey, except me about any of your operational roles. In fact you need to quietly generate a cover story that I have insisted that you stop."[68]

As ordered, North met with members of the HPSCI in the Situation Room in August 1986. He lied to them, stating that "he did not in any way, nor at any time violate the spirit, principles or legal requirements of the Boland Amendment." He denied raising money for the Contras or giving them military advice. He lied that his relationship with Rob Owen was "casual" and that he had not been in touch with John Singlaub at all in 1985 or 1986.

After the scandal broke, North revisited that episode in front of Congress:

"I will tell you right now, counsel, and all the Members here gathered, that I misled the Congress. I misled—"

"At that meeting?"

"At that meeting."

"Face to face?"

"Face to face."

"You made false statements to them about your activities in support of the Contras?"

"I did. . . . [Poindexter] did not specifically go down and say, 'Ollie, lie to the Committee.' I told him what I had said afterwards, and he sent me a note saying, 'Well done.' "

Poindexter confirmed: "I did think that he would withhold information and be evasive, frankly, in answering questions. My objective all along was to withhold from the Congress exactly what the NSC staff was doing in carrying out the President's policy. . . . There was no doubt about that in my mind."[69]

Reagan certainly knew about the secret private network financing the Contras. A few of his comments suggested, as late as May 1987, that he thought donations were merely funding pro-Contra ads on US television. But Poindexter, again, confirmed that "[Reagan] knew the NSC staff was running support for the Contras."

Did Reagan know North coordinated with Contras on military issues?

"Yes."[70]

.....

With the stated goal of getting more funding to the Contras, the NSC further privatized the war by associating with private arms merchants, who got involved out of a mixture of patriotism and greed. Private involvement again resulted in profiteering and the handover of foreign policy reins to nongovernment actors.

According to North, it was Casey who suggested setting up "private entities" to "comply" with (Casey's doublespeak for "violate") Boland II.[71] North described Casey's wish as "an existing, as he put it, off-the-shelf, self-sustaining, stand-alone entity that could perform certain activities on behalf of the United States."[72] Although North led the private operation, Casey and the CIA never retreated completely.

The most prominent of the arms merchants was retired Air Force major general Richard Secord. Secord had served twenty-eight years in the force, cutting his teeth in covert operations in Vietnam and Laos. He had commanded the Air Force Mission to Iran before the 1979 overthrow of the Shah and risen to deputy assistant secretary of defense in charge of the Middle East, Africa, and South Asia. In 1982, while still legal, he had shipped Israeli arms to the Contras through a CIA depot in Texas.[73] In 1983, his suspected ties to former CIA officer Edwin Wilson, who had been sentenced to life in prison for selling arms to Libya, sent Secord into retirement. Wilson accused him of steering a sale of weapons to Egypt to benefit a company in which he had invested—a clear conflict of interest.[74] The Justice Department decided not to bring up charges, but Secord was denied a security clearance.[75] He called the Wilson charges "absolutely false."[76] Still, as Clair George later told Congress as the agency's deputy director, "the good General Secord's reputation inside the CIA was not of the highest." In addition to his association with Wilson, "General Secord worked the edges of those guys out there in the world who were buying and selling in the arms business."[77]

North had met Secord while selling weapons to Saudi Arabia, and in the summer of 1984, he asked him to become "actively engaged" in the Contra struggle.[78] *I'm no expert on Central America*, replied Secord.

"That doesn't matter," North said. "You're an expert in special ops. You've been all over the world, know how to size people up. And—according to Bill Casey—you know how to keep your mouth shut."[79] Secord also had a Swiss shell company, Lake Resources, which was a destination for private donations.

Albert Hakim, who would be very active in the Iran portion of Iran-Contra, offered Secord half of an operation called Stanford Technology Trading Group International (STTGI) if Secord ran it while Hakim financed it. "I hired a secretary and authorized myself a salary of $60,000 (raised to $72,000 the next year)," wrote Secord in his memoir—"about what I had been making as an active-duty major general at the time I retired."

Soon, STTGI's only activity was "the Enterprise," as Secord called the private funding network. In joining the Contra cause, Secord recalled his "main motivation" was "the nagging sense that things were getting screwed up again in our covert operations, and there weren't a lot of guys around who could fix them."[80]

But there was also plenty of money to be made. To the Contras, Secord sold about $11 million of arms and other equipment in total, charging a markup of 20–30 percent on average, with sometimes another 20 percent to his partner, Hakim. In 1985 and 1986, Secord made more than $3 million in "direct personal benefits."[81] Contra leader Calero testified that Secord said nothing about a markup, leading the Contra to understand that he was obtaining his arms at cost. "I believe I was told that he was not making a profit." Learning that Secord lopped off a hefty percentage came as "a revelation."[82] In his autobiography and elsewhere, Secord denied profiteering from the Contras. "Like Caesar's wife, I would have to avoid even the *appearance* of profiteering for my chance of returning to government service to be realized." Yet he did admit to making a 20 percent profit. He claimed that Calero never complained of the markup.[83]

To be fair, Secord at this point was a businessman and, North, with some exaggeration, wrote that "everybody understood that he would be making a profit."[84] North compared Secord's price list with that of others: "Some [prices] were higher, some were lower."[85] Singlaub, however, surprised the Contras with prices that were much lower than Secord's: $135 for an AK-47 rifle instead of $260; $165,000 for an SA-7 missile instead of $180,000. "We were getting twice as many weapons for the same amount of money," testified a Contra. But Casey wanted more control over the weapons, so orders tended to go through Secord instead of Singlaub.[86]

North admitted that "Secord and I should have agreed then and there on a set fee for his work. We never discussed exactly what fair and just compensation would entail—an omission that eventually led to major problems for both of us."[87]

Secord arguably shared with North two beliefs typical of mercenaries: first, that they know better than an elected government what foreign policies should be, and second, that using the resources of a government for private purposes was legitimate. Secord's exchange with Louis Stokes (D-OH) demonstrated these two tenets:

"Doesn't it look to you like we have two governments?" asked Stokes. "There is one Government run by the United States which Mr. Reagan heads where you cannot utilize appropriated funds for the purposes we have already enunciated, and this other government run by you, and you can utilize these funds for whatever purposes you deem necessary, though they be contrary to the use for which appropriated funds can be put?"

"I didn't see it that way," answered Secord. "The President has certain rights in the foreign policy area. I never saw myself as being a foreign policy operative. I believe that the funds that we had were private funds and could be sent to the Contra project, which project we believed deeply in, and we did that."

"You see nothing wrong with those operations?"

"I did not see anything wrong with it then."

"Did Colonel North's salary come from appropriated funds?"

"I am sure it did."

"How about the airplane pilots who flew Mr. North around the world to the various meetings he had with you and others?"

"To the extent they were government pilots, of course they were paid the same way."

"Then how do you square this fact with the fact that you say no appropriated funds were used in any manner in conjunction with your operation?"[88]

. . . . .

Some Contra leaders also profited handsomely from private aid. As journalists Jane Mayer and Doyle McManus reported, "Saudi Arabia's millions had gone straight into the hands of Calero, a former manager of Coca-Cola of Nicaragua who had schemed his way to the top of the rebel leadership. Calero ran the rebels' cash fund from his hip pocket, handling millions of dollars with little accountability."[89] In fact, Calero kept $1 million of one delivery of $3.3 million to the Contras.[90]

Owen once threw up his arms in a memo to North about the Contras: "These people don't know they are even in a war—they think they're running a business."[91] Of the Contras around Calero he opined, "they are not first rate people: in fact they are liars and greed and power motivated. They are not the people to rebuild a new Nicaragua." Contra buyers of privately funded goods pocketed the difference between the black market exchange rate and the legal rate and they provided false receipts, Owen explained. "THE WAR HAS BECOME A BUSINESS TO THEM."[92]

. . . . .

With the help of Owen, Secord, and Singlaub, North operated the Enterprise, or, as he preferred to call it, Project Democracy.[93] They purchased five planes, a ship, and warehouses; hired pilots; bought weapons from Europe and elsewhere; and flew hundreds of thousands of pounds of arms, food, uniforms, and other materiel to the northern and southern fronts of the Contra war.[94]

To assist the southern front, perhaps the largest single US-government supported "private" initiative came when the CIA and US Embassy oversaw the construction of a secret airstrip in Costa Rica—that country's quid in return for CIA support for a secret project.[95] Private benefactors put up the funds, but a CIA proprietary company called Udall Resources purchased the 100 acres needed and cleared a 3,000-foot strip starting in late 1985.[96] "The Boland amendments never caused me a moment of concern," recalled a top embassy official who worked on the project.[97] US Ambassador to Costa Rica Lewis Tambs, whose salary funded his time overseeing the airstrip, also felt that it was legitimate because the manual labor on the airfield was privately funded. As he testified to Congress, US government employees "were not out there driving a bulldozer."[98]

Except that the CIA was getting increasingly reinvolved. At the southern front airfield, the station chief oversaw construction. Now allowed to provide coded communications equipment, the spy agency stretched its mission to include radios, satellite data, aerial photographs, weather reports, flight vectors, secret intelligence, and training—anything that was not direct aid to specific combat operations. One CIA officer who read a memo on this aid scribbled on it, "This is not kosher! We should not [be] using our coms [communications equipment] to help this."[99] Yet the aid continued.

All the while, North gave Robert Dutton, a retired Air Force colonel and on-the-ground manager of airdrops, intelligence on the weather, locations of troops, and whether to fly inside Nicaragua, all aiding in the delivery of military materiel. North told Dutton "that we were working for the President of the United States."

"Bob, you're never [going to] get a medal for this," said North, "but someday the President will shake your hand and thank you for it." Dutton never met Reagan.

Dutton instead asked about the legality of these sales, and Secord gave him talking points from the NSC. "Do you regard it as the normal, prudent thing to do when you go to work somewhere, to ask whether what you have been asked to do is legal?" an incredulous member of Congress later asked of Dutton.

"I thought it was somewhat of an unusual situation, sir," he replied.[100]

Almost everyone involved had doubts about Project Democracy, but they largely failed to ask questions about the separation of powers, the rule of law, the assault on truth, or the perils of privatization. The ends justified the means. As one senior US military officer opined of the US employees of the project, "Sure they bent the rules. It was for a good cause."[101]

The CIA's Joseph Fernandez later admitted "that it was an airfield to be used eventually for the contras, yes, that is true, but in and of itself, it wasn't necessarily an illegal or an intelligence activity, by my interpretation." In late 1985, Fernandez was on a hotel veranda with Alan Fiers of the CIA, telling him about the airstrip.

Fiers snapped back, "Jesus, Joe, watch what you do. Stay legal. Stay within the bounds."

"I know what I'm doing," said Fernandez.

The lines were so blurred that North grew cavalier in his disregard of Boland and other laws. At one meeting at the State Department, North pulled out pictures of the secret airstrip in Costa Rica and showed them to "a whole bunch of people," said Fiers. "'Look at this!' he was saying. 'Isn't this great?'"

"My God, this is dumb," thought Fiers.[102]

.....

While the Reagan administration sometimes avoided promising quid pro quos to donors to the Contras, they made explicit and routine promises to Nicaragua's neighbors in return for their cooperation.

Guatemala's president, for instance, requested of Shultz that, in return for his government's support, the United States "triple military assistance . . . [and] double economic assistance to Guatemala."[103] The Central American government also asked for US support in its negotiations with the International Monetary Fund and an increase in its sugar quota. North called these demands "a *quid pro quo* system."[104] He identified equipment of the "highest priority for the Guatemalan Army" to "compensate the Guatemalans for the extraordinary assistance they are providing to the Nicaraguan freedom fighters," North told McFarlane.[105] As a favor to the United States, Guatemala also falsified end-user certificates: Its military lied that it would use $8 million of munitions that it instead passed on to the Contras.[106]

In February 1985, Reagan sent a formal letter to President Roberto Suazo of Honduras offering increased aid for continuing to harbor Contra bases. "Incentives" to Honduras included CIA covert support, faster military assistance from Defense, and more economic aid. In helping craft the letter, McFarlane explained, "We should dispatch our envoy to carefully explain the linkage between our additional support and the critical issue of Honduran performance in backing the cause of liberty in Central America."[107]

That envoy was Vice President Bush, who proffered the quid pro quo in person upon visiting Honduras. Reagan himself had a meeting with Suazo, before which a briefing memo suggested, "Without making the linkage too explicit, it would be useful to remind Suazo that in return for our help—in the form of security assurances as well as aid—we do expect cooperation in pursuit of our mutual objectives."[108]

Meanwhile, Panama's strongman, Manuel Noriega, had already donated $100,000 to the Contras in Costa Rica. He proposed to assassinate Sandinista leaders in return for a clean-up of his image and permission to buy US weapons. Although North and Poindexter did not seriously entertain the killings, they did consider "assistance with sabotage." In September 1986 in London, North spoke with Noriega about attacking an oil refinery, an airport, and a harbor in Nicaragua. Plans collapsed when the Iran-Contra scandal broke the following month.[109]

As for El Salvador, Reagan promised to support trade legislation that favored Nicaragua's neighbor, from which supplies flew to the Contras.

Throughout, North said, he never explicitly asked Central American leaders "that if they did this, then we would do that. Never did I do that." He recalled that these leaders helped out of their shared anticommunism.[110] Yet US correspondence and Central American demands made it plain that each side thought in terms of tit for tat.

. . . . .

One day North announced to several colleagues, "Once this all comes out, I'm going to jail."[111] They likely took it as a joke, just as he meant it. North was many things—an ideologue, a manipulator, a liar. But he never asked for bribes nor took a percentage of the many sales he brokered or had associates broker. His government salary paid for a modest middle-class home in the suburbs of Northern Virginia. He was clean.

Mostly. Three exceptions indicate that the network of private channels and self-interest that he cobbled together ensnared him in the petty corruption typical of privatization efforts.

In the first, Albert Hakim, Secord's partner in STTGI, began setting up a Swiss investment account, in the name of "B. Button," to provide for North's wife Betsy and their children in the event of his death.

The origin of this initiative may have lain in North once asking Secord, "Suppose both of you guys [Secord and Hakim] go down on the same airplane, flitting back and forth to Europe or wherever you are going; what happens then?"

"Don't worry about it," said Secord, "arrangements will be made so that these operations can continue."

Another theory went that Hakim was concerned that North might cave to his wife's complaints about his toiling long hours for middling pay and take another job, which would cut off Hakim from Iran-Contra contracts. The "button" account was to "quiet" Betsy North.[112] The name of the account came from a lawyer's joke to Hakim: "What do you want me to do, rub belly buttons with this lady?"[113]

Hakim suggested that Betsy meet with Hakim's lawyer in Philadelphia, and she did have a preliminary appointment with him.[114] Hakim then set aside $200,000 as a death benefit, allegedly without telling Oliver North. "I had become emotionally very attached to Ollie," he explained. "Ollie, you are part of the family," Hakim said. "For as long as one of us is alive, you need not worry about your family." But Hakim's lawyer could not find a legal route to get the Norths the funds, which clearly would appear a kickback if made public. One congressional investigator suggested to Hakim an interpretation somewhere in the middle: "It just seems to me the logical conclusion that what you were trying to do with Ollie North was to influence him, you were trying to have him beholden to you." Whatever the case, the Norths decided not to proceed, and the contract remained unsigned.[115]

The second exception was North's careless and perhaps criminal use of traveler's checks. As part of Project Democracy, the lieutenant colonel kept an operational account of $150,000 to $175,000 for various expenses. His superiors knew about it. Sometimes he handed out so much cash that the account went "down to zero," as he said. He would then pay for expenses, such as snow tires, with his own salary and reimburse himself by cashing traveler's checks. "I never took a penny that didn't belong to me," North swore.[116] However, Iran-Contra prosecutors concluded that "North had used some $4,000 for personal expenses."[117] Some $90,000 worth of checks came from the Contras' Adolfo Calero, who recycled private donations. North told some of his associates to record their expenses as he did his, but he said that he destroyed his ledger on the advice of DCI Casey.

The most serious of the three exceptions was the possible bribery and admitted forgery that ended with the North family benefiting from a security fence around their home. In late April 1986, recalled North, the FBI informed him of death threats from extremist Palestinian guerrilla leader Abu Nidal, then known, in North's words, as the "foremost assassin in the world." Nidal's threat was likely retaliation for North's role in a counterterrorist raid on Libya. The FBI declined to protect North and his family, and Poindexter never followed up on North's request for security. As a result, the Norths moved for five days to Camp Lejeune, North Carolina. The worried husband and father called security companies for estimates for a system, but the process looked to take too long. He told Secord of his problems and cursed his government for putting him in this situation.

"Don't worry about that," replied Secord. "I have a good friend who is an expert. This guy has a company that does these things." By early May, Glenn Robinette, a former CIA employee who had worked for Secord, showed up at North's house and gave him an estimate of $8,000–$8,500 for a security fence. He could do the work right away. "Please try to keep it along those lines. Remember, I am a poor lieutenant colonel," said North.

"I didn't ask for a bill, and I never received one," North later told Congress. He eventually learned that Robinette billed Secord almost $14,000 for subcontractors putting up a fence, a remote-controlled gate with an intercom, and a camera. Secord reached into his briefcase and handed over the cash.[118]

Only six months later, after the Iran-Contra scandal broke, did North ask Robinette for a bill. He was in a panic. The law forbade government employees from accepting gifts in return for their services. Robinette had already been paid, but he backdated a phony bill to protect North. Then, as North admitted, "I did probably the grossest misjudgment that I have made in my life . . . sending two phony documents back to Mr. Robinette."[119] He backdated to July 7, 1986, a letter he wrote in December 1986 to cover up his acceptance of the fence from Robinette.[120] This was "an illegal gratuity," as the main prosecutor of Iran-Contra would call it, a "colorful, undisputable confirmation of criminal intent."[121]

Senator Warren Rudman (R-NH) probably best encapsulated not only that episode but all three: "One of the unintended, and I emphasize unintended, effects of this getting private businessmen involved with U.S. officials and U.S. military is the possibility of very corrupting and very corrosive effects on our government."[122] Unintended perhaps, but foreseeable.

.....

Despite Reagan claiming—in a TV address from the Oval Office, no less—that the Sandinistas were smuggling cocaine to the United States, the truth was that the Contras were doing so.[123] The US government knew it and still funded and coordinated with them.

There remains no evidence that US government employees encouraged or participated in the drug trade with the Contras.[124] But the CIA certainly looked away when it found that some Contras were drug dealers.[125] As early as 1982, Bill Casey put together a memorandum of understanding that shielded his CIA from legal scrutiny. In the 1980s, the CIA had reports that nine individual guerrillas and three companies and more than twenty pilots and others in the Contra program were moving cocaine. Out of some fifty under suspicion, the CIA kept collaborating with a few dozen. North knew that Edén Pastora was "revealed as a drug dealer," for instance. "We knew that everybody around Pastora was involved in cocaine," said the CIA's Alan Fiers.[126] After Boland II, some Contras said they had no "choice" but to raise money through trafficking, and CIA officials also cited this alleged lack of options when needing landing sites and other facilities. It certainly proved convenient to run a "guns-down, drugs-up" system in which weapons flew down to Central America and cocaine back up to the United States. In 1988, Senator John Kerry (D-MA), after a two-year subcommittee investigation, believed "beyond a reasonable doubt" that the Contras were connected to drug trafficking. "And it happened because some people in the Reagan Administration were willing to look the other way. Politics got into it. That's my conclusion."[127]

But "narcotics was not something [CIA field personnel] were looking for in the 1980s," said a chief of station.

"Not a big deal," thought Duane Clarridge.[128]

.....

In late 1986, *U.S. News* put on its cover the Iran-Contra "shadow network" resulting from the "subcontracting of affairs of state." It assessed that "few Presidents have made such heavy use of [private actors] for covert operations as Ronald Reagan." "Nowhere has the trend toward privatization of foreign policy been so apparent as in Central America."[129]

Reagan never approved specific private funding in writing, but he did approve of government employees calling on other countries and private citizens to donate to the Contras. The third-country campaign and the private donor network, taken together, the Congress's report concluded, were "an evasion of the Constitution's most basic check on Executive action—the power of the Congress to grant or deny funding for Government programs."[130]

By mid-1986, because of all the third-country and private funding, the Contras were in serviceable shape. Militarily, although they had achieved little against the Sandinistas, they remained alive and well-supplied. On October 17, largely because of misinformation from the executive, Congress approved $100 million in aid to the Contras. The president signed the legislation on October 27.[131] The privatization of the Contra war had succeeded and was no longer necessary.

3

ARMS FOR HOSTAGES FOR PROFIT

Even more than in the secret Contra funding effort, private individuals were involved in an arms-for-hostages swap with Iran that demonstrated how privatizing a foreign policy can wrest control of it away from elected representatives. The antidemocratic nature of privatization was also true because, again, those representatives kept their dealings secret from not only the American people but also Congress.

The desire for secrecy placed this Iran policy in the hands of a cabal inside the administration, headed once again by Lieutenant Colonel Oliver North, but perhaps hundreds knew about it. As with Central America, the president designed the Iran gambit and several departments and agencies collaborated. Key figures, especially from the private sector, turned Iran policy into a web of deception. The Reagan administration thus endangered truth, the separation of powers, and the representation of the people in foreign policy.

.....

As with Nicaragua, the Republican president's misconceptions and misdirected passions led his administration into a fool's errand.

In the early 1980s, Reagan faced an Iranian enemy partly of his making, and he approached it with uncompromising hostility. The overthrow of the long-ruling, US-supported Shah in 1979 had led to the storming of the US Embassy in Tehran and the bitter 444-day crisis in which the fundamentalist regime headed by Ayatollah Ruhollah Khomeini held fifty-two Americans hostage. Iran released them moments after Reagan's first inauguration because of Jimmy Carter's eleventh-hour negotiations. During the 1980 campaign, Reagan had made much of Carter's perceived weakness before the hostage-takers and benefited from the misidentification of his presidency with the freeing of the hostages.

In the wake of its revolution, Iran found itself isolated and in need of weaponry. War erupted with Iraq in 1980, and in the next two years, the Iranian regime bought weapons costing almost $2 billion per year from around thirty countries and private dealers. Of those countries, Israel was an eager seller, eyeing Iran as part of its enemy-of-my-enemy strategy against Arab states. Selling to Iran also promised to allow tens of thousands of Jews to leave it. By late 1981, Israel had sold more than $28 million in equipment to Iran, much of it originating in the United States.[1]

Reagan may have prolonged the hostages' ordeal. Never-proven allegations made in 1991 by Gary Sick, a National Security Council Middle East specialist under Carter, tied some of those Israeli weapon sales to Iran to an October 1980 secret meeting in Paris. According to Sick, Bill Casey, then Reagan's campaign manager; George Bush, Reagan's running mate; and Iranian intermediaries agreed to delay the release of the US hostages in return for US-made Israeli weapons, all so that Reagan could defeat Carter. The Reagan administration vehemently denied these allegations.[2] If true, the "October surprise" story revealed serious foreign policy treason by a presidential campaign. It also explained—again, if true—why Iran suddenly broke off negotiations with Carter in the fall of 1980, why it dropped its demand for military spare parts, and why Israeli planes full of US equipment flew to Iran just after the inauguration. But in the 1980s, the Sick accusation was not yet public.[3]

The fact remained that the Reagan administration came into office with an attitude toward revolutionary Iran that was openly antagonistic, even apocalyptic. "What's a foot high and glows in the dark?" went a dark joke amid the Republican campaign of 1980. "Iran, after Reagan takes over."[4]

Iran responded with its own hostility, protecting those who took US hostages—one by one this time, all in Beirut in 1984 or 1985: William Buckley, the CIA station chief; the Reverend Benjamin Weir; Frank Regier, a professor at American University; Father Lawrence Jenco, a Catholic Relief Services official; Terry Anderson, chief Middle East correspondent for the Associated Press; David Jacobsen, director of American University Hospital; Thomas Sutherland, dean of agriculture at the University of Beirut; and Cable News Network correspondent Jeremy Levin. These were some of the Americans taken not by Iranian government thugs but by terrorist organizations such as Hezbollah or al-Dawa al-Islamiya (a.k.a. Dawa), over whom Iran had significant—perhaps controlling—influence.[5]

Based on the premise that the United States did not negotiate with terrorists, Reagan vowed never to trade anything for hostages.[6] As of 1983, the State Department also discouraged other nations—not only Israel but also China, Italy, Portugal, and South Korea—from selling to Iran (and, nominally, Iraq) through what it called Operation Staunch. Its success proved limited, but its message was clear. In 1984, Secretary Shultz designated Iran a state sponsor of international terrorism. Such a policy was borne of not only principle but also logic: "America will never make concessions to terrorists," Reagan pledged in 1985. "To do so would only invite more terrorism. Once we head down that path, there will be no end to it."[7]

Reagan, however, would join other nations down the path. He sold to Iran and, like Israeli, French, and German officials, went back on promises not to secretly ransom hostages.[8]

.....

Much like his fondness for the Contras, the president's intense desire, in this case to free US hostages, drove the US government to a policy it would later regret. "No problem was more frustrating for me when I was president than trying to get the American hostages home," Reagan wrote in his memoirs. "Almost every morning at my national security briefings, I began by asking the same question: 'Any progress on getting the hostages out of Lebanon?' "[9] As Oliver North recalled, "the President very clearly articulated in the meetings I was in with him in the Oval Office . . . with the hostage families, it was very clear that the President wanted as many Americans home, all of them home, as fast as possible."[10]

The first American to raise the possibility of a deal with Iran was a semi-private citizen, Michael Ledeen. His past indicated a predilection against transparency and the rule of law. As a historian at Washington University in St. Louis, Ledeen was accused of plagiarism and denied tenure. After murky years in Europe, he returned to the United States in the early 1980s only to be embraced by neoconservatives. He assailed "moralistic complaints against secrecy" and favorably cited a French conservative's argument for "breaking of law from time to time" in foreign policy.[11]

In early May 1985, Ledeen was a part-time consultant to the National Security Council and proposed going to Israel. There, he asked Prime Minister Shimon Peres to share Iran intelligence. "I questioned the ability of Michael to serve in this sensitive function given his persona in public," recalled Howard Teicher of the Near East and South Asia Directorate. "He tended to be verbose and to, I would say, describe his functions in an official capacity to the maximum extent possible which might not have been accurate."[12]

Also in May, DCI Bill Casey asked for a Special National Intelligence Estimate that called for improving US-Iranian relations, partly to prevent handing the Soviets another ally in the Middle East.[13] The idea of finding moderates in Iran—amid a stalemate in its war with Iraq and economic decline—had been circulating at Langley for years.[14] Casey pushed for it to become a National Security Decision Directive (NSDD)—in other words, policy.

Shultz and Secretary of Defense Caspar Weinberger opposed Casey's proposed NSDD.[15] The secretary of state told National Security Advisor Bud McFarlane that the Ledeen jaunt to Israel was dangerous. "Israel's agenda is not the same as ours," he warned. The Israelis wanted the Iranians and Iraqis to keep fighting and thereby bleed both sides, while the United States was officially neutral while leaning toward Iraq. And why wasn't "our Ambassador in Israel being informed" of Ledeen's démarche? added the unhappy Shultz.[16] He also warned against "the fraud that seems to accompany so many deals involving arms and Iran."[17]

"This is almost too absurd to comment on," was Weinberger's handwritten response to the Ledeen idea of engaging the Iranians in talks, "like asking [Libyan leader Muammar] Qadhafi to Washington for a cozy chat."[18]

Still, McFarlane took the idea to Reagan while the president was at Bethesda Naval Hospital for abdominal surgery. He explained all the hurdles.

As with the Contras, the president pushed for a workaround. "I guess we can't do the weapons or something like that ourselves," he grudgingly told McFarlane. "But isn't there a way that we can get at trying to keep this channel going?"[19] On July 18, McFarlane returned to the hospital with a greater sense of urgency, telling White House chief of staff Don Regan, "I've just got to see the President."[20] Reagan recorded in his diary sending McFarlane to "a neutral country" to talk to two Iranian officials.[21]

In late July 1985, McFarlane found himself working in his office on a Saturday when his secure phone rang.

"Hello, Bud." It was Reagan. He had been thinking about that "Israeli thing." "Couldn't you use some imagination and try to find a way to make it work?"

"You remember Mr. President, your Secretary of State and Secretary of Defense were opposed to this."

"I know, but I look at it differently. I want to find a way to do this."

McFarlane promised to think about it. "Please do," said the president.[22]

On August 2, McFarlane met at the White House with David Kimche, a former Mossad spy and the director general of Israel's Foreign Ministry. They discussed the Israelis selling US-made weapons to the Iranians. The hope was that the weapons would show US goodwill in starting a dialogue, at least with more moderate elements of the Khomeini government.

On August 6, Reagan, still recovering from his operation in pajamas and a robe, met in his White House private quarters with Bush, Shultz, Weinberger, Regan, and McFarlane. They made no decision at the meeting. No later than August 13, however, Reagan approved the deal, which required that the United States replenish the weapons after Israel sold them, including Tube-launched, Optically tracked, Wire-guided (TOW) missiles that Tehran wanted against Iraq. The fig leaf of Israel covered what was in reality a US sale to Iran.[23] Yet Reagan saw it, in his words, as "solely between Israel and the Iranian moderates and would not involve our country, although we would have to waive for Israel our policy prohibiting any transfer of American-made weapons to Iran." He also believed the Israelis who said that their Iranian interlocutors "opposed terrorism and had fought against it."

"I said there was one thing we wanted," recalled Reagan. "The moderate Iranians had to use their influence with the Hizballah and try to get our hostages freed." Thus, two lines blurred from the start: one separating the United States from the sale of weapons, and the other between encouraging moderates in Iran and freeing hostages held by an Iran-backed terrorist organization.[24]

Shultz still called the Israel gambit a "bad idea." Weinberger, "a terrible idea. Awful."[25] "Shultz was outraged and heatedly opposed this enterprise," one former diplomat recalled. "[He] said it was crazy, stupid, illegal, and totally contrary to long standing US policy for dealing with terrorists. . . . Simple integrity, of which Shultz normally seemed to have a more than ample supply, would seem to have required him to threaten to resign over this matter long before the scandal broke in the media."[26]

When the idea of selling weapons to Iran circulated more widely, all involved were aware that it contradicted Reagan's policy of nonnegotiation. Yet North later testified to Congress that the United States welcomed Israel as an intermediary because it offered Washington "plausible deniability."

"And was there any discussion of the fact that if we started selling them arms, that once we stopped we were going to run the risk that more hostages would be taken?" asked Congress's counsel.

"Yes," answered North.[27]

Splitting hairs, North interpreted Reagan's promise of "no concessions" to terrorists as *not* meaning "no negotiations."[28]

The NSC aide, ensconced in secrecy, saw adversaries everywhere in the executive. The State Department, he wrote, had "a tendency to assume that in just about every conflict between the United States and the Third World, the Third Worlders were right and the U.S. was wrong," not to mention "a long-standing and barely hidden pro-Arab tilt."[29]

As in Nicaragua, North took his cue from Casey at CIA. As one former Bureau of Intelligence and Research official at State recalled, "I was personally involved in several cases where Casey intervened to impose his views" on the State Department. "Casey made sure that the CIA's analysis of the situation in Iran would support the illegal covert sales to Iran that President Reagan apparently later approved and which Casey and Oliver North managed."[30]

.....

One of the biggest liabilities in David Kimche's plan was the involvement of Manucher Ghorbanifar, an arms dealer and the most reckless private individual in the Iran-Contra scandal. "Gorba," as the Americans called him, was a short, burly man in his mid-forties with curly black hair and a round, puffy face encircling a pair of hooded but sparkling black eyes (see fig. 4). Most described him as charming, slick, and shrewd and as a congenital fabricator. To Dick Secord, Ghorbanifar appeared as a "stereotypical Middle-East sophisticate, with a well-trimmed Vandyke, graying temples, five-hundred-dollar shoes and thousand-dollar suits. . . . He liked the high life, including casino games like blackjack and roulette, and was a member of several private, world-class gambling clubs."[31]

FIGURE 4
Shady middleman Manucher Ghorbanifar in a cloud of smoke. (Alex Majoli/Magnum Photos)

Michael Ledeen, meanwhile, sold Ghorbanifar to McFarlane as a "genius," a "mastermind of Iranian politics," and "almost too good to be true."

He was. The national security advisor later concluded that Ghorbanifar was "a pathological liar and, when all was said and done, like a self-serving criminal, not a patriot."[32]

Everything about Ghorbanifar was hazy, and CIA cables on him remain largely redacted. He was alternatively known as Manoucheer Korbanifar, Djafar Souzani, Ja'Far Suzani, and Manuel Pereira. Those names showed up on Portuguese, Greek, Iranian, and Iraqi passports. Others knew him as Ashgari, Nicholas Kralis, Nick the Greek, or simply Roddi. He was born in Isfahan, Iran, in 1945—or 1938 or 1944. Sometimes his English was fluent, sometimes broken. Before the 1979 Revolution, he was a partner in a shipping firm and may have served as an Iranian Army officer, using his position for self-enrichment.[33] Casey believed that the Iranian Jew was secretly an Israeli agent, but he may have been a double agent for Israel *and* Iran. One thing was certain: he was a survivor, having been an informant for SAVAK, the Shah's secret police yet, by the early 1980s, working with its nemesis, the Khomeini regime.[34]

The CIA, who had used Gorba as a secret source since 1974, vetted him several times, and each time found him to be a liar.[35] On March 18, 1984, the agency subjected him to a polygraph after he "volunteered information about [the] possible location of kidnapped American diplomat William Buckley" and about supposed Libyan hit men sent to kill Ronald Reagan and Walter Mondale, opponents in the upcoming presidential election. The test "showed deception regarding several key elements" of both stories.[36] The CIA polygraphed him again on June 12. Again he failed.

On July 25, the CIA sent out a "burn notice," a warning to all not to trust Ghorbanifar. Clair George of the CIA called a burn notice "a very rare occurrence" in the spy business. "If we only served and dealt with the honest and fair, we would be out of business fairly fast."[37] But Gorba had "a history of predicting events after they happened," a CIA cable noted wryly. He was "perceived to be a rumormonger of occasional usefulness. His information consistently lacked sourcing and detail notwithstanding his exclusive interest in getting money for his questionable pursuits."[38]

On January 11, 1986, Ghorbanifar took a third CIA polygraph and again "showed deception on virtually all of the relevant questions." He lied on thirteen of the fifteen questions, and results were "inconclusive to the remaining two"—his name and nationality. "Ghorbanifar is clearly a fabricator and a wheeler-dealer who has undertaken activities prejudicial to U.S. interests," concluded the agency.[39]

In a five-hour interview after the last failed lie detector test, Ghorbanifar unloaded on the CIA, deeming his relationship with it "most unsatisfactory." He informed for it from 1980 to 1982 and claimed that "he never requested funds from the Agency." He convinced other Iranians to either end their relationship with the agency or feed it disinformation. He claimed to be part of a faction of conservatives in Iran who could be dealt with, as opposed to fundamentalists. He expected "millions of dollars" after one operation saved "the life of the Crown Prince of Bahrain."

Considering this lying, CIA minder Charlie Allen's assessment of Ghorbanifar was judicious:

> Subject is a highly energetic, excitable individual who possesses an extraordinarily strong ego that must be carefully fed. Intelligent and clearly an individual who has made a considerable amount of money in procurement of arms and in provision of "other services," he is relatively straight forward about what he hopes to get out of any arrangement with the United States. . . . He appears to have influence over or business arrangements with a substantial number of individuals in the Middle East and Europe and inside Iran itself. . . . He is impatient if one tries to pin him down on the specifics of some of the complex plots that he describes.[40]

A few weeks later, on January 26, 1986, Allen met Ghorbanifar at the Churchill Hotel in London's Portman Square. After "a lengthy diatribe" against one agency officer, Gorba still sought a relationship with the CIA and discussed "a number of terrorist plots." He claimed that his group in Iran held $100 million in assets and "control[led] the President like a chicken." He was not out to "trick" anyone, Gorba pledged, "unless he found himself dealing with deceptive individuals or organizations."[41]

"People betray me, I betray them," Ghorbanifar said was his code. "People are honest with me, I give them everything. If not, I cut their throat."[42]

Contracting an international weapons dealer for a project is common and legitimate in foreign policy. "But there is no reason the arms dealer has to know the destination and the group the arms are being delivered to," wrote Stansfield Turner, President Carter's DCI.[43] In the case of Ghorbanifar, he was both standing to profit from the deal and holding—or claiming to hold—a monopoly of information on who the purchasing party was.

Ghorbanifar was the most brazen profiteer in Iran-Contra. He said he set a markup of "only" 60 percent. He once charged Iranians $8 million for a shipment of missile spare parts worth $2 million.[44]

Another private individual involved in the Iran deals was Albert Hakim, who had brought Richard Secord on to run "the Enterprise" in Central America. Hakim had represented US firms such as Motorola and Hewlett-Packard in prerevolutionary Iran, becoming a millionaire and decamping before Khomeini took over. His manner was courtly, his appearance groomed (see fig. 5). He admitted to dealing in *baksheesh*, the Middle Eastern practice of bribing, to win government contracts.[45] When Secord worked for the US military in Iran, he had helped Hakim secure lucrative deals. Hakim, in turn, provided the CIA with intelligence.[46]

Ghorbanifar, himself Jewish, called Hakim "a real Jewish gangster."[47] About a meeting in Frankfurt in February 1986, Hakim testified that Ghorbanifar "violently rejected the idea" of Hakim as translator: "I was an enemy of the state and in no way I should get involved." More likely, with Hakim beside him, Ghorbanifar would not have been able to manipulate both sides by distorting the translation.

Hakim said to Secord, "OK, Richard, how are you going to solve this problem? I know Mr. Ghorbanifar. I have met him in the past. I am sure he will recognize me."

"Albert," retorted Secord, "you have shown that you are resourceful. Why don't you go and solve the problem?"

Hakim had a wild idea. *A wig.* With little time to spare before the meeting, he rushed to the concierge of the Frankfurt Sheraton Hotel to find out

FIGURE 5 Iranian-born Albert Hakim, the embodiment of privatization during Iran-Contra. Hakim managed most of the US missile sales to Iran. (Bettmann/Getty)

where to get one. When he did, Secord and North looked at him: "No way Ghorbanifar will recognize you."

He didn't. But Ghorbanifar did continue to translate and translate badly. "I found out that what the American delegation was saying and what the Iranian delegation was saying, they were absolutely on two different frequencies," recalled Hakim. North wanted a long-term relationship and spoke of hostages as "obstacles" to that end. In contrast, "the approach of the Iranian official was highly, if not only, focused on [the] purchase of weapons."[48]

Although no match for Ghorbanifar in mendacity, Hakim also had a reputation for profiteering. A CIA cable from 1976 reported that he had sold "unneeded oversophisticated equipment at exorbitant prices" to the Shah of Iran.[49] Hakim's own records showed that he and Secord transferred more than $250,000 of one Iran-Contra transaction to other investments, including an arms company and a timber operation.[50] On one $2.1 million sale, Hakim testified that he, Secord, and former CIA operative Thomas Clines made a profit of $861,000, a markup of 41 percent.[51]

Hakim's interest in helping North was not only immediate profit but also the greater windfall if US-Iranian relations returned to normal and the $15 billion-a-year Iranian arms market reopened.[52]

Oliver North testified that he assumed "fair, just, and reasonable compensation" would go to men such as Ghorbanifar and Hakim. "I do not believe that these funds, any of them, should be or should have been used to make anybody rich," he claimed, but, as in Central America, he remained unaware of specific profit margins.[53] John Poindexter, who succeeded McFarlane, also assumed "some compensation" to Hakim and Secord. "But I did not think in terms of large profits." Neither North nor Poindexter asked about markups. Had these private businesses contracted through the normal channels of the US government, it would have followed a competitive process of awarding contracts with some attention paid to profits. When asked "what oversight in accounting" he had over his contractors, Poindexter replied, "the trust and confidence in Colonel North and General Secord."[54]

"At the very end of this whole thing, and to this day," said North in 1987, "I still do not know how much money was under [Ghorbanifar's] control and where it was."[55]

An additional problem of privatization was that inflated prices risked infuriating the Iranians, thereby threatening the political and humanitarian goals of the Reagan administration.

So why continue working with Ghorbanifar, Hakim, and others? Clair George's explanation was that "the White House was already working it." The burn notice got lost in the urgency to ship weapons and free hostages. "It's sort of, 'Would you please get out of the way?' "

George once pleaded with Casey to drop Ghorbanifar: "Bill, I am not going to run this guy anymore."

"He has what appears to be valuable terrorist information," countered Casey. As George explained, "You have got to take terrorist information seriously even though you think who told you is crazy."[56]

According to Congress, when the Iran sales were added to those to the Contras, $48 million flowed through the Enterprise's accounts, and Hakim, Secord, and Clines took $6.6 million in profit, not to mention another $4.2 held in "reserves" for future operations and $1.2 in their Swiss bank accounts.[57] A later report specified that "Secord in 1985 and 1986 received $2 million in direct personal benefits from the Enterprise, and more than $1 million in cash payments. Hakim in 1985 and 1986 received $2.06 million in direct benefits, and more than $550,000 in cash."[58] In his autobiography, Secord minimized his and Hakim's take, saying that his partner made a "commission" of only $1.5 million "during the whole Iran and Contra support period." Secord claimed he never took a profit because he wished for "another high-level government position, perhaps as deputy director of operations for the CIA."[59]

As Senator Paul Trible (R-VA) concluded, "In the activities of Mr. Hakim and Secord, we have seen private interests riding roughshod over public motives, a cause compromised as individuals reaped enormous profits, and in my judgment the trust of Colonel North betrayed. All this demonstrates to me the sheer folly of conducting the people's business without checks and balances."[60]

"I don't agree that this was a privatization of foreign policy," countered Poindexter. "The foreign policy was clearly established by the President. . . . We are talking here about details of implementing that policy. And I still contend that the American people don't want to know those details."[61]

. . . . .

In just one arms deal with Iran and Israel, significant privatization had occurred, along with its concomitants: lying, lawbreaking, profiteering, and elected representatives' powerlessness over budgets and aims. Oliver North called the Iran deal "one of the biggest mistakes of my life."[62] Michael Ledeen also called it "a terrible mistake."[63] Congressional committees concluded that, "by permitting private parties to conduct the arms sales, the Administration risked losing control of an important foreign policy initiative. Private citizens—whose motivations of personal gain could conflict with the interests of this country—handled sensitive diplomatic negotiations, and purported to commit the United States to positions that were anathema to the President's public policy and wholly unknown to the Secretary of State."[64]

Yet more was to come. The Reagan administration would eliminate the Israeli middlemen and devise a paper trail to conceal its lawbreaking, all the while evading oversight by the legislative branch.

4

FABRICATING FINDINGS

Privatization was only part of the Iran story. The Reagan administration eventually bypassed Israel and took over the direct sale of missiles and spare parts to Iran. The deals flew in the face of the rule of law by disregarding several statutes on the books. They also snubbed the separation of powers when Reagan himself kept his "findings" from Congress, which had the legal right to them.

.....

In the first six months of the Iran sales, Israel acted as the go-between.

On August 20, 1985, ninety-six TOW missiles in sixteen wooded crates followed a secret flight path on an unmarked DC-8—with Manucher Ghorbanifar on board—from Ben Gurion Airport to Tehran. These antitank weapons marked what Iran considered to be a sign of goodwill. Their arrival freed no hostages, dashing US expectations.[1]

In a heated meeting with Americans in Paris, Ghorbanifar claimed that more missiles—about 400—would be needed to obtain the release of only one hostage. "Do you want the Iranians to send an arm and a leg of [William] Buckley as an advance?" he threatened, referring to the CIA hostage. On September 14, the DC-8 brought another 408 TOWs.

President Reagan expected to free all seven US hostages in Lebanon at the time.[2] The Americans, put in a position to "play God and choose one hostage," as one lawyer later put it, picked the CIA's man to be freed, but Ghorbanifar claimed Buckley was too sick. In truth, Buckley had died at least two months before.[3] Only Reverend Benjamin Weir, held for sixteen months, was released after the first 504 TOWs arrived.

To add to US disappointment, the missiles sent to Iran ended up in the hands of the extremist Revolutionary Guards rather than any moderate faction.

It was a poor showing, given Reagan's ambitions.

By October, Iran wanted more, this time HAWK (Homing-All-the-Way-Killer) antiaircraft missiles that could hit Iraqi bombers.[4] Again, announced Ghorbanifar, these were necessary for alleged moderates in Iran to free the rest of the hostages.

"I have a bad feeling about this whole operation," wrote McFarlane. "My intention is to shut it down." But Gorba persisted, so McFarlane sold Secretary Shultz on the shipment on a promise that another four hostages would be released. Shultz was glad about the hostages but upset to have been informed so late into the operation. McFarlane approved a shipment of 120 HAWKs. "Not one single item" should make it to Iran without first receiving "live Americans," the national security advisor insisted. Reagan's attitude was suppler: "Cross your fingers, and hope for the best."[5]

Secrecy, which begat more privatization, plagued this November 1985 HAWK shipment. To cover up its Israeli origin, the plan was for an Israeli 747 to fly the HAWKs from Tel Aviv to Lisbon, Portugal, and from there to transship them to Iran. Eighty HAWKs took off from Tel Aviv. But, receiving no clearance from Lisbon, the flight returned to Israel.

"A bit of a horror story," is how North described what occurred next. The US government found itself thrust into a starring role.

After the first attempted shipment was returned to Israel, on November 19, North sent Dick Secord a message, which he signed "Robert C. McFarlane" without telling his boss. It pleaded with the retired general to get to Lisbon and transship the missiles discreetly but quickly. "Obviously, Israel cannot deal directly with Iran."[6] Among other things, Secord tried to intercept the prime minister and foreign minister of Portugal at the Lisbon airport, eliciting "suspicions, antagonism" from authorities there.[7]

Secord proposed to use a plane belonging to his Lake Resources corporation for a flight to Iran by November 23. North described the plan to Poindexter: "So help me I have never seen anything so screwed up in my life."[8]

He was about to see worse. The Portuguese, conscious of Washington's ban on arming Iran under Operation Staunch, demanded a formal diplomatic note describing the aircraft and cargo. Wary of divulging that information, the US chief of mission in Lisbon instead rudely told the Portuguese, *never mind*. The Portuguese foreign minister called the operation "disastrous."[9]

North rang up Duane Clarridge at the CIA, who put him in touch with St. Lucia Airways, an air charter company that the CIA previously owned—"a proprietary," in agency parlance. Prodded by Clarridge, the CIA chief of station and the chargé d'affaires in Lisbon failed to get the Portuguese foreign minister out of a cabinet meeting to help them.

On November 23, the Americans decided to send a proprietary Boeing 707 from Frankfurt to Tel Aviv. It took an obscenely long twenty-four hours to load eighty missiles on it. The cargo was designated "sensitive." There was no manifest, so officials told the crew that they were loading industrial spare parts, then medical equipment, then mining equipment, then oil-drilling gear. Then, realizing that the plane was US registered and therefore could not fly to Iran, local authorities had to unload the cargo and reload it onto a plane from Western Europe with a new crew. Finally, the plane took off on November 24. From there it was to fly to Turkey, where again a Cold War ally demanded to know what the cargo was. "Sophisticated spare parts for the oil industry," lied Clarridge. Another change of plans followed.

The plane now headed to Cyprus, but it had to defuel in Tel Aviv because it proved too heavy to land on the island. There, again, it had no documentation. Local authorities insisted on inspecting its cargo before letting it proceed. The captain produced a false cargo manifest and took off.

Having to fly again over Turkey, the captain, again improvising, made up a diplomatic clearance number when the Turkish ground controllers demanded one. They refused him clearance, and the captain flew around Turkey while arguing for an hour and a half with them. He finally "talk[ed] his way through" Turkish airspace and toward Iran.

Finally landing in Iran on November 25, again the plane was not expected there. The crew unloaded the cargo under the watch of "one military and one civilian with [a] submachine gun." The civilian told the crew "to keep their mouth shut about this." After fourteen and a half hours of delays at a hotel, waiting for a car, and more, the captain and crew left Tehran safely. "The mission was poorly planned and directed by our contract partners in a [*sic*] amateurish way," concluded the airline manager, referring to the CIA and the Israelis.[10]

"The longer it went on," he added, "the more I had the feeling I am dealing here with lunatics."[11]

Clarridge explained to his boss, Bill Casey, the "rather bizarre manner" of relying on a private contractor "over which we have no direct control."[12] For instance, the proprietary airline's manager demanded a down payment of $30,000 for landing fees and fuel. The Israelis managed to cough up $8,000.[13] Secord's company ended up paying $127,000 to the proprietary, more than twice the agreed-upon $60,000.

Capping that epic series of snafus, the cargo itself turned out all wrong. The HAWKs that the Iranians received could not shoot down planes flying at 60,000 or 70,000 feet. And they were marked with Israeli Stars of David, which the Iranians detested.[14]

Ghorbanifar had been paid $42.72 million for eighty missiles, charging $300,000 per missile for which he paid the Israelis $140,000.[15] Yet he accused Reagan of "cheating us."[16] Because the missiles proved of little use, the Iranians released no hostages. As North recalled, Iranians "were absolutely furious about the November HAWK shipment."[17] Several ambassadors cursed the CIA and NSC's odd procedures and secrecy.[18]

Because of this logistical nightmare, the Reagan administration made a momentous decision to eliminate the Israeli middlemen and sell directly to Iran. The deputy director of the CIA, John McMahon, insisted that any other shipments must follow procedures, including a written "intelligence finding" by the president.[19]

.....

The November HAWK shipment proved significant also because it moved the Reagan administration further along the path of defying the rule of law and the separation of powers through convoluted, bend-the-rules presidential "findings." Since the Hughes-Ryan Amendment of the 1970s, presidential findings had been legally necessary for every covert operation. And the National Security Act of 1947 required the CIA to explain all important intelligence activities to Congress's intelligence committees—at the very least the "group of eight" specified by law, meaning the leaders of each party in the House and Senate and the chairs and ranking minority members of the SSCI and HPSCI. In addition, the Arms Export Control Act (AECA) stated that arms sales to foreign countries could occur only if the president "found"—in a "finding"—that they would strengthen the security of the United States and promote world peace. Any sale of $7 million or more had to be reported to

Congress, which could veto the sale. The AECA also banned weapons exports to countries supporting terrorism even through a third country. The weapons sold could be used only for self-defense, and the recently passed Intelligence Authorization Act also required reports to Congress for any weapons transfers of more than $1 million.

For years, lawyers sought to overcome the legal obstacles to selling US weapons to Iran—namely, informing Congress, which might veto the sales or cause a leak. State's lawyers wrote that, if the news spread, "it would be difficult to defend publicly the legal rationale for proceeding in the manner proposed." The lawyers at State, Defense, and the CIA agreed that the "President has the discretionary authority to proceed with the proposed activity," but they added that "to do so would present legal risks, chiefly that Congress might challenge his decision and enact new, restricting legislation."[20] Attorney General William French Smith followed up by suggesting that, at the least, "the House and Senate Intelligence Committees should be informed of this proposal and the President's determinations."[21]

By 1985, just about everyone at the CIA and NSC involved in the shipments was aware that they were likely illegal and that any finding barely covered them with a veneer of legality. In November 1985, amid the Portugal-Turkey-Cyprus rigamarole, when McMahon of the CIA found out that Clarridge had approved the St. Lucia Airways flight, he was furious. "Goddamn it! I told you not to get involved. For Christ's sake, we can't do that without a finding!"

He stomped down to the office of Clair George, CIA deputy director of operations. "You will not support this activity without a finding," he ordered.

Calling Stanley Sporkin, general counsel for the agency, McMahon said, "I want a finding—and I want it retroactive to cover that flight."[22] A retroactive finding went against the spirit of reporting to Congress, which all assumed had to be anticipatory—before an operation, not after. In January 1985, the Reagan administration had confirmed that findings needed to be "in writing" and follow "congressional reporting procedures."[23]

For good measure, McMahon also called Oliver North. "You know what you are?" he told North. "You're pure bullshit. You're dangerous. You're a disaster!"[24]

Sporkin drafted what he told Congress was "stiff legal advice," specifying that he agreed with McMahon and that the CIA needed a finding from Reagan.

"What is so stiff about telling the Agency that they have to comply with the law?" Senator Bill Cohen (R-ME) later asked, incredulous.

You can't ask the president for a finding covering every little thing, explained Sporkin. "You can't micromanage this country."

"It is not micromanaging," replied Cohen. "It is a question of applying the law." Cohen imagined that, if the president could retroactively sign findings, then "the CIA could hold the President hostage for a Finding in the future." If the agency helped overthrow a foreign leader, for instance, it might force the president's hand in approving the coup after the fact or else face embarrassment. "Doesn't that, in effect, undercut the very purpose of the Hughes-Ryan Act?"

Sporkin knew his finding contradicted Hughes-Ryan.[25] Yet on November 26, he delivered to Casey that very thing, justifying a straight arms-for-hostages deal, omitting anything about Iran moderates or improving relations.

On December 5, 1985, Poindexter, now national security advisor, presented the one-page draft for the president's signature. It was a sort of second edition of the late-November finding, which had never gone into effect. In it, Reagan declared, "Because of the extreme sensitivity of these operations, in the exercise of the president's constitutional authorities, I direct the Director of Central Intelligence not to brief the Congress . . . until such time as I may direct otherwise."[26]

"All prior actions taken by the U.S. Government officials in furtherance of this effort are hereby ratified," it added. That was the retroactive part. This December 5 document would become known as the first retroactive, secret finding covering the Iran deals. Poindexter declined to share it with not only the Congress but also State.

. . . . .

Ghorbanifar felt emboldened. For all the clumsiness of the arms deals he put together, they did seem to have obtained the release of Reverend Weir, so Gorba tried to shape future negotiations. As North reported in December 1985, "Gorbanifahr [*sic*] refused to return to Geneva with our message that no further deliveries would be undertaken until all the hostages were released." "While it is possible that Gorbanifahr is doubling us or simply lining his own pockets," he continued, "we have relatively little to lose in meeting his proposal, i.e., the Israelis start delivering TOWs and no hostages are recovered." He summarized: "Information is incomplete, the motivation of the various participants uncertain, and our operational control tenuous in that we have had to deal exclusively through the Israelis."

Here's an idea, North threw in at the end: "We could, with an appropriate covert action Finding, commence deliveries ourselves."[27]

. . . . .

Negotiations and deliveries went only marginally more smoothly once the Americans took direct control as 1985 turned into 1986. Concerns about legalities did not die down. Yet arms sales kept occurring, without many results in terms of hostage-freeing and zero improvement in US-Iranian relations.

On December 4, North proposed to Poindexter a sequential exchange of 3,300 TOWs and 50 HAWKs for the freeing of all remaining US hostages and one French hostage. He thought "the idea of bartering the lives of these poor men repugnant," but the pattern was set.

The idea also stood as North's effort at taking personal control of US Iran policy. Richard Armitage, the assistant secretary for defense for international security affairs, heard rumors of North's plan, suspected the Pentagon was being kept in the dark, and took him to lunch to straighten him out. "His ass was way out on a limb," Armitage communicated to North. "He ought to get everyone together quickly to discuss this problem." North needed to assemble the "elephants," as Armitage called the president's main advisors. At State, Shultz also felt cut out of cable traffic and that the proposed trade was, no less than the Israeli ones, "a very bad idea."[28]

"Ultimately," he cautioned, "the whole story will come out someday and we will pay the price."[29]

On December 7, 1985, Reagan held an NSC meeting that proved a showdown between Shultz and Weinberger on one side and Casey (represented by Deputy Director McMahon), Poindexter (replacing the also-present McFarlane), and Chief of Staff Don Regan on the other. In some ways, it was an absurd meeting, meant to certify an arms-for-hostages practice that had already flourished for half a year. Unusually, it took place in the president's family quarters, and no record was kept. Also, no one discussed the September or November shipments.[30]

Shultz was first to reiterate his opposition to any future deal as illegal and contrary to US policy.

"Cap?" the president turned to Weinberger.

"Are you really interested in my opinion?" the secretary of defense asked the president.

"Yes."

"There are legal problems here, Mr. President, in addition to all of the policy problems."[31] Among these, Weinberger had long argued, was the possibility of being blackmailed. Secrecy entails entrusting confidences to sometimes undesirable partners who might say, as Weinberger told Congress, "unless you do thus and so forth or unless you continue to send us more weapons or unless you take various policy positions, we will take steps to have this matter become public."[32]

Most attendees at the Pearl Harbor Day meeting recalled Reagan saying very little. He pulled a footstool up to the coffee table between them and sat there, listening. According to Shultz, the president grew frustrated. Reagan allegedly told Weinberger that "he could answer charges of illegality but he couldn't answer charge that 'big strong President Reagan passed up a chance to free hostages.'" Shultz confirmed that Reagan said that Americans would not understand if hostages perished because "I wouldn't break the law."

"They can impeach me if they want," said Reagan. "Visiting days are Wednesday," he joked.

"You will not be alone," retorted Weinberger.[33]

No one at the meeting pointed out that telling Congress might provide a political safety net if the story got out.[34]

It ended without a directive from the president—not uncommon for the amiable, nonconfrontational Reagan. Weinberger told his military assistant, Colin Powell, that "this baby has been strangled in its cradle," meaning that Reagan had killed the policy.[35] McFarlane tended to agree but sensed that the president "was not pleased by it." McMahon and Regan, meanwhile, thought the president leaned toward more arms sales.[36]

"Inside," Reagan later wrote, "I felt that we should proceed with the initiative on a step-by-step basis. . . . I felt a heavy weight on my shoulders to get the hostages home."[37] The most important takeaway was Poindexter's, which mirrored Reagan's: The president did see "an opportunity to get the hostages back" and vaguely ordered, "we ought to at least take the next step."[38]

Reagan's only concrete move was to send McFarlane to London to meet with Ghorbanifar and the Israeli dealmakers. It did not go well. Gorba's stock among Iranians had fallen after the botched delivery in November, and he needed more arms for hostages. McFarlane pushed his private interlocutor: "Is there real authority? Can you take decisions and change things?" On his way back to Washington, McFarlane called Ghorbanifar a "borderline moron."[39]

Hearing of "Bud M.'s" disastrous London meeting, Reagan confided to his diary on December 10, "Our plan regarding the hostages is a 'no go.'"[40]

North was not dissuaded and proposed to "deliver something." On January 7, 1986, Reagan called a meeting of his NSPG, which included Shultz, Weinberger, Regan, Casey, Poindexter, and this time, now–Attorney General Meese and Vice President Bush. Faced with the AECA, Casey came armed with a workaround: the Economy Act. The CIA would buy arms from the Pentagon and resell them, somehow without having to report. Meese had written up the rationale, resting it on his belief in executive privilege—the "President's inherent powers as Commander in Chief" and the "President's ability to conduct foreign policy." Meese and Casey also recommended not telling Congress, not even the HPSCI and SSCI. Meese consulted no experts at Justice.[41]

Shultz again declared his opposition on the same grounds as he did the month previous. To Poindexter's argument that the president would enjoy plausible deniability if this covert operation went south, he shot back, "Plausible deniability is nonsense."

But Poindexter was winning over Reagan, who drummed his fingers on the table as the national security advisor explained that, because the law required "timely" notification, the weapons would be at their destination in thirty to sixty days, and only then would Congress be notified.[42]

.....

North knew he needed another presidential finding, this time to cover direct sales to Iran. He called Sporkin, the general counsel at the CIA. Formerly chief enforcer at the Securities and Exchange Commission, Sporkin was once described as "a meddler, a stickler and a menace. His tenacity and zest for hounding people who jiggled their accounts and bribed their customers made him an ogre in the takeover set."

Yet when he moved to the agency, Sporkin applied his meticulousness to concealing other people's disdain for the rule of law. When it came to Reagan, he said, "You can't straitjacket the president. . . . Someone can go out and do it and later on you can do the paperwork."[43]

CIA lawyers thus crafted a justification to get around all the laws.[44] They agreed to using the Economy Act to get Defense weapons to the CIA at cost for resale in its covert ops. The "key issue" was having to report this to Congress, which three laws required, even though Meese's rationalization ignored them.[45] Sporkin suggested what his boss Casey wanted to hear: "not to report the activity until after it has been successfully concluded and to brief only the chairman and ranking minority members of the two Oversight Committees."[46] This lined up with Poindexter's thinking.

George Clark of CIA's General Counsel office smelled a rat. Sporkin called him on the afternoon of January 15. *What if Defense sells weapons to a CIA middleman "agent," who would pay with money from a third country?*

"I would feel more comfortable if CIA were directly involved in the activity," Clark recalled responding, "and that it would be essential that we act in furtherance of a traditional covert action objective. I said that I could foresee problems if this activity were merely intended to rotate a specific country's stock of weapons," meaning that if Israel gave Iran older missiles and took new ones from the United States.

Sporkin several times urged Clark to reconsider. Oliver North even came on the line to "clarify" the facts, then put Sporkin back on.

Clark held firm. "I will not make the legal determination you are seeking without all the facts." North would not provide Clark with the president's draft finding.[47]

Poindexter admitted that the finding was "prepared essentially by the CIA as a—what we call a CYA effort." *Cover your ass.* Casey told Reagan to sign it. Poindexter briefed him verbally, and under the word "OK," Reagan wrote "RR." The president thus signed the infamous second finding on January 17, 1986.[48] Although Reagan had allegedly signed a similar document on January 6, this time there was no misunderstanding. "Well," he said, "if we get all of the hostages out, we'll be heroes. If we don't, we'll have a problem."[49] That evening, in his diary, he wrote, "I agreed to sell TOWs to Iran."[50] He knew he had, for the first time, given the US government permission to sell arms directly to a country he had repeatedly declared a pariah.

That very day, Clair George put out a notice saying the CIA would no longer do business with Ghorbanifar. The next day, he recalled, "I was taken to the White House and given a Finding which in its practical sense said you will be doing business with Mr. Ghorbanifar."

George protested in vain. "On many occasions, I said, 'Ollie, you're out of your GD mind, I'm not taking the responsibility for that.' He would then get back to me by going to Poindexter or McFarlane and they would go to Casey and sometimes Casey would make another decision."[51]

After the January 17 finding, Weinberger and Shultz all but gave up their protests, but the military's lawyers griped about it for months.[52]

On January 19, Meese approved the sale without telling Congress, just as Sporkin had advised Casey.[53] Legally, the executive had to inform the intelligence committees in a "timely fashion."[54] Sporkin interpreted "timely" to mean not "beforehand" but rather "after it has been successfully concluded." Sporkin later testified that Reagan's decision implied that the president had no intention of notifying Congress until all the hostages presently held were freed. Not thirty days. Not sixty. There was no time limit on the goal.

"If you can delay a written Finding for 3 weeks, then there is no reason you can't delay it for 3 months," inferred Senator Sam Nunn (D-GA) later. He called this "legal gymnastics."

Senator Edward Boland (D-MA) recalled the legislative history from 1980. "When the timely fashion provision was drafted, we assumed, I think rightfully so, a degree of comity would exist between any administration and any Congress such that notice would be forthcoming in a very, very short period of time. . . . Timely fashion doesn't extend to 10 months, or when the President gets around to issuing a Finding on it."[55]

Meese "vaguely" recalled that those who drafted the finding planned that, "as soon as we got the hostages, even on our planes en route to Wiesbaden [a US base in Germany], that we would notify Congress then, before it became public generally."[56]

Other than illegality, another problem with not notifying Congress was the implication that foreign characters, such as Ghorbanifar and Hakim, were in on US state secrets while major political figures such as the speaker of the House and top Democratic and Republican leaders were out.[57]

Regardless, by January 24, 1986, North amplified his ambitions. He now had a fifty-nine-step process of obtaining all five US hostages, plus Italians, a Brit, Lebanese Jews, and fifty Shia Muslims, along with $40 million to Ghorbanifar and Secord. In return, the Iranians now wanted 4,000 TOWs, up from their original demand for 500.

On February 18, the United States delivered 500 TOWs to Iran. Nine days later, another 500 arrived. Payments passed through several hands: Ghorbanifar borrowed funds from legendary Saudi businessman Adnan Khashoggi and put them in a Swiss bank account controlled by Secord, who transferred the cost of the missiles to a CIA account. (Khashoggi took out a $22 million life insurance policy on Ghorbanifar, reflecting his dwindling confidence in the Iranian's lifespan).[58] The agency then purchased the TOWs from the US Army. Secord got a Miami-based charter company active in resupplying the Contras, Southern Air Transport, to ship the missiles from the United States to Israel. From there, an Israeli charter ferried them to Iran.[59]

To the great, impotent irritation of the White House, no hostages were freed after either of these new TOW deliveries. Silence. Poindexter had vowed that, if no hostages were let go after the first 500 TOWs, the rest of the deal was off. Yet the missiles continued to ship, and the Iranians, to haggle. Increasing the peril, Ghorbanifar was arrested in Geneva for working on a side deal that turned out to be a sting operation.[60]

By April 1986, Poindexter typed a PROFS note instructing North to tell the Iranians that "the President is getting very annoyed at their continual stalling." He was losing confidence in Ghorbanifar and becoming more rigid. "There are not to be any parts delivered until all the hostages are free in accordance with the plan that you layed [*sic*] out for me before. None of this half shipment before any are released crap. It is either all or nothing."[61]

.....

Instead, it continued to be half-measures, this time in the belly of the beast. On May 23, 1986, Bud McFarlane, now out of the White House, came back to head a US delegation to Tehran to try to hammer out a final deal. In his mind, he was reenacting Henry Kissinger's meeting with Chou En-lai before the opening to China.[62] His entourage, flown in by one of Secord's Lake Resources crews, carried HAWK spare parts despite having vowed no longer to sell to the Iranians unless all the hostages were first freed.[63]

Before they landed, Ghorbanifar made an ambitious promise to the delegation: that McFarlane would meet with "three top officials in Iran." Charles Allen, the CIA's national intelligence officer for counterterrorism, presumed that this meant the president, prime minister, and speaker of the Parliament. However, Gorba added, Iran would release only one hostage upon their arrival as a "gesture of good will."[64] The Iranians also demanded all the HAWK spare parts *and* more weapons.[65]

"I knew," testified North, "and so did the rest of us who were dealing with him, exactly what Mr. Ghorbanifar was. I knew him to be a liar. I knew him to be a cheat, and I knew him to be a man making enormous sums of money." So again the question came, Why continue to work with him? "It was difficult to get other people involved in these kinds of activities. I mean, one can't go to Mother Teresa and ask her to go to Tehran." To North, at least Ghorbanifar had gotten negotiations underway.

"We had gone too far down the line with Ghorbanifar. What was his—his process, if you will, was to tell the Iranians one thing and tell us another. Then let the two sides sit down and duke it out.[66]

"We cannot trust anyone in this game," North told Poindexter.[67] Not an auspicious attitude.

As a measure of his low expectations, North testified that Casey gave him "suicide pills" in case things went south. (Clair George called that scenario "absolutely impossible.")[68] The flight from Tel Aviv was shrouded in secrecy. "As we started our descent into Tehran," recalled North, "I prayed that our disguised Israeli 707 wouldn't be shot down by some trigger-happy pilot."[69] McFarlane entertained the notion that if he were captured, he would be tortured.[70] As a recent national security advisor, he knew his country's secrets.

For the Tehran trip, North told Secord he did not want to rely on Ghorbanifar as a translator.

"Well, I will get Albert Hakim," offered Secord.

"So," Rep. Ed Jenkins (D-GA) later asked of North, "the only representative[s] that we had . . . that spoke Farsi were two people outside the government?

"That is correct."

"Did you stop to think at all . . . that the only person negotiating for the United States of America with Iran . . . was a private citizen who had a substantial financial interest in the outcome of those negotiations?"

"It may well be, Congressman Jenkins, that I was most injudicious," North admitted. But he also rationalized privatization as a good thing: Hakim "had interests that went beyond just his next promotion or going back and getting an accolade from his boss; that in fact it offered a greater chance for ultimate success."

"The fact that he had a financial interest?"

"The fact that he saw long term the potential for a financial interest."[71]

Upon deplaning in Tehran at 8:30 a.m. on Sunday, May 25, the Americans felt themselves strangers in a strange land, aware of the consequences of relying on Ghorbanifar. The delegation "was left to cool its collective heels for about two hours," reported the CIA. "During this period the Iranian Air force put on a show in which one by one a squadron of F-4's took off from Mehrabad airport." Ghorbanifar showed up a half hour later, chiding the Americans for arriving early.[72]

During their first meeting at the *Istiqlal* or Independence Hotel that afternoon, McFarlane gamely pleaded with the Iranians to "use your influence to secure the release of captive Americans." In exchange, he was "prepared to transfer certain items."

One Iranian immediately complained about the paltry parts the delegation had brought with them. "We could not bring it all on the plane," replied McFarlane. Besides, defying the logic of US-Iran relations in the previous year, he called the arms and the hostages "separate and not related."

To complicate matters, one delegation member remained on the plane, and the Iranians wanted him off.

"We can't do that," said McFarlane, explaining that the man "performs communications functions as well as logistics accountability." *He's keeping an eye on our stuff*, meant McFarlane.[73] The CIA's version: "It was clear that the Iranians only wanted to search the plane."

When the Iranians complained again of getting less than half the hoped-for parts, McFarlane became annoyed. He got up from his seat, "very firm and stern." *At least we brought something*, he argued. "So far nothing has happened on your side." After more Iranian grumbles, McFarlane again got angry. "I have come from [the] U.S.A. You are not dealing with Iraq. I did not have to bring *anything*. We can leave now!"[74]

The Americans did, only to return the next afternoon. It went much the same way, with the exception that McFarlane, presenting himself as "a Minister," asked to speak only with "decision-makers." He ended the meeting after half an hour.[75]

The third day, Tuesday, the Iranians reported that hostage holders in Beirut now imposed "heavy conditions" for any release, including several of their own brothers freed and for Israel to withdraw from the Golan Heights and southern Lebanon. "How's that for chutzpah!!!" McFarlane wrote to Poindexter.[76] McFarlane referenced an alleged threat by Reagan to leave because "it was pointless to pursue an ineffective dialogue." He gave until 6:30 a.m. on Wednesday for the Iranians to arrange the freeing of the hostages. Behind McFarlane's back, North ordered a plane with the remaining spare parts to leave Tel Aviv. To this the Iranians countered, "If the plane arrives before tomorrow morning, the hostages will be free by noon."[77] Now McFarlane grasped the gravity of Ghorbanifar's lies: The Iranians "expected all deliveries to occur before any release took place."[78]

Later that night, North brought up Ghorbanifar's promise of meeting with three top officials. "Why did you think this?" asked the Iranians.[79]

On Wednesday morning, fed up and with no word about the hostages, the Americans were "wheels up" at 9 a.m. *Our spare parts plane is in the air*, announced McFarlane before departing, *but it will turn around if there is no word on the hostages by 9:30*. (It soon after turned around.)

Despite realizing the massive responsibility of "a dishonest interlocutor," the CIA still concluded, "We will have to lean heavily on Gorba in the future." The rationale was precisely what had gotten them in this mess to begin with—privatization: "Since both Gorba and [redacted—Hakim?] stand to make a lot of money out of this deal, they presumably will work hard to bring it off."[80]

Secord later described Ghorbanifar's role in negotiations as wanting "the game to continue. . . . He may have posed as an agent of Iran but he was really his own agent. He was a businessman, interested in making money, and that was it." After one of his checks to Secord bounced and Secord threatened to drop him from negotiations, Ghorbanifar complained to the Israelis that Secord was trying to have him killed.[81] In other words, both men threatened to derail a nominal US government negotiation based on their own financial self-interest.

After the Tehran debacle, McFarlane briefed the president: "The current state of government in Iran lacks competence. The competents were decapitated."[82] He recommended no further secret shipments of arms to Iran. But Reagan—who had called the Iranians "rug merchants"—stayed true to the initiative.[83]

.....

Ghorbanifar was on his way out of the Iran-Contra affair—finally. He was in deep debt to Adnan Khashoggi—somewhere between $4 million and $15 million and "under the threat of death from his creditors"—and angry at the Americans and the Iranians for failing to come to an agreement.[84]

Muscling him out seems to have been the initiative of Secord and Hakim. In April 1986, Hakim, boldly declaring he was "speaking for the President," informed Ghorbanifar he was no longer needed. This caused Gorba to become "emotionally upset," according to North. The CIA's Allen called him up in London, where it was 3 a.m., and Ghorbanifar answered "immediately." "I am indeed upset," said Ghorbanifar, relating Hakim's news.[85]

North, Secord, Hakim, and the rest were moving on to the so-called second channel in their negotiations with Iran. The phrase referred to a small number of Iranians led by Ali Hashemi Bahramani, a young Iranian official and the "favorite nephew" of Akbar Hashemi Rafsanjani, who was then speaker of the Parliament. Hakim described the new relationship as "day and night" compared with Ghorbanifar. The Bahramani group "was more sincere. . . . They understood that their relationship should not be limited to the United States supplying only arms. They were interested in a long-term relationship."[86] They also said all the right things to the Americans—that they, too, worried about Soviet penetration, that they opposed terrorism, and that they hated Iraqi leader Saddam Hussein.[87]

Hakim made clear to Congress that he partly pursued this second channel in the hopes of pocketing an additional commission. Then the questions came.

"Did it bother you at all that here you—and I say it respectfully—a private citizen was left with this kind of task of negotiating an agreement in which if it succeeded, you stood to benefit very substantially?" queried counsel Arthur Liman.

"Did it ever strike you as a businessman as particularly gratuitous," asked Representative Boland, "that there was a seemingly inexhaustible supply of both of the commodities in these transactions; that is, arms for hostages?"

"You increased your profits," Senator Cohen accused Hakim, "when you cut out Mr. Ghorbanifar. You thereby had an opportunity to reduce the overhead in that sense. You didn't have to pay him off?"[88]

Summarizing his colleagues' skepticism, Senator David Boren (D-OK) asked Secord, "Do you think it is strange for a private citizen to be taking an action of such importance for the foreign policy of the United States?"[89]

These were politicians' rhetorical questions, to be sure. But the doubts raised in Congress highlighted the perils of privatizing foreign policy.

North, Secord, and Hakim valued Bahramani so much that they conducted a midnight tour of the White House for his representatives. The late-night visitors to the president's mansion included one who had no security clearance, another who had been denied clearance, and a third whom the US government had branded as a terrorist.[90] According to another account, Bahramani's retinue entertained sex workers at the Tyson's Corner Sheraton while the CIA bugged the rooms.[91]

On July 26, 1986, Father Lawrence Jenco was released, apparently in a delayed response to McFarlane's mission to Tehran in May.[92] After Reagan approved North's request to send the remaining HAWK spare parts—the ones turned around in May—Secord arranged their delivery for early August. As before, the Iranians complained: Some parts were missing their own parts, others did not work, 299 were outright missing, and 63 other items were fit only to be returned.[93] Iranians also learned that the Americans had grossly overcharged them—by 270 percent—for some shipments.[94]

In September, Poindexter told North to make another deal with Bahramani as two more Americans were taken hostage. These two essentially zeroed out the freeing of Weir and Jenco.[95] Reagan's most passionate objective—ransoming hostages—was back to square one.

After delivering more missiles in October, on November 2, David Jacobsen was released. But kidnappers would take yet another hostage, again bringing to zero the net humans freed by the more than 1,000 deadly missiles sold to a nation at war.

Around the same time, North, Secord, and Hakim met with the second channel in Frankfurt. Other meetings in Washington and Germany produced multipoint plans, but they all collapsed when revelations broke open the Iran-Contra affair. The second channel, Congress concluded, "turned out to represent the same Iranian leaders as did the First Channel [Ghorbanifar]." They also hoped for bribes, and they also wanted only weapons for hostages.[96]

As anyone could have predicted, Ghorbanifar proved difficult to extricate from the Iranian deals. Despite often claiming hardship, he once offered North $1 million to be cut in on a deal. (North refused.)[97] In September 1986, feeling that he was "out of the loop" with the second channel, he threatened to go public.[98]

In early October, Charlie Allen of the CIA heard from Ghorbanifar again. He and his family were in financial and legal trouble. His mother had been denied a visa. Not surprisingly, he suffered high blood pressure and digestion problems. The "guy will not stand there," noted Allen. "Will take revenge."[99]

In his memoirs, North suggested it was Ghorbanifar's ouster that led to the taking of more hostages. The intermediary had promised no more hostage-taking—so long as he was involved. He also half-warned that "if he wasn't handled properly, the whole Iran initiative would come bashing down," suggesting also that Gorba might have leaked the talks to the Iranian press.[100]

.....

More so than in the Contra war, with Iran, President Reagan committed potentially impeachable offenses. He pursued a secret mission contrary to the policy announced to his voters. He violated the AECA by selling to a terrorist country. He never reported these covert operations to Congress because they never succeeded. And he concealed his government's steps by signing retroactive findings. In only one aspect of Iran-Contra was the president likely not involved—the diversion of profits from arms sales to Iran to the Contras. Many considered that scheme the most scandalous.

5

THE HYPHEN

Toward the end of the Reagan administration's dealings with the Contras and Iranians, the idea to fuse the two came up. The Enterprise overcharged the Iranians for some of the missiles it acquired, and Oliver North diverted the profits to the Contras. The transfer became the hyphen in *Iran-Contra*. North called it "a neat idea."[1]

It was not neat for American democracy, but instead quite messy. It redoubled the secrecy within the administration, and the scheme, of course, needed to be kept from elected representatives and the press. It was also illegal. Although North conceived of the diversion as giving Iran's money to the Contras, in fact, he took money from the sale of US government property, intended for the US Treasury, and unilaterally reappropriated it. It was US taxpayer money going directly to the Contras, which Congress had explicitly banned.

.....

It remains unclear where and when the idea took shape.

According to one tale, the place was London and the time was early December 1985. When Reagan sent outgoing National Security Advisor Bud

McFarlane to the British capital right after his contentious Pearl Harbor Day meeting, McFarlane found himself in a row house near Hyde Park. Officials were going over the books and realized they had $850,317 left over from $1 million deposited by Israel in Dick Secord's Lake Resources account during the chaotic November sale.

"What do you recommend doing with the balance?" asked Secord of North.

"Use it to support the Contras," North reportedly said, flipping his hand. "You're starting an airline and you're going to need it."[2] Secord dubbed it "a contra-bution."[3]

According to North's testimony, however, the first he heard of excess profits was from Amiram Nir, the Israeli premier's advisor on counterterrorism. In late December 1985 to early January 1986, "maybe New Year's Eve," Nir suggesting selling TOWs at a profit and using "part of that money for other operations" without specifying which.[4]

According to North's memoir, again in London, this time on January 22, 1986, it was Ghorbanifar who first suggested diverting profits to the Contras. A much greater windfall had blessed the Enterprise when a lowly major at Army headquarters flipped through a price list and mistakenly priced each TOW missile at an outdated $3,469 instead of the current $8,435. Ghorbanifar had already offered to pay $10,000, which now meant a profit of $6,531 for Secord's Enterprise. Ghorbanifar himself would sell each missile to Iran at $13,000 to $14,000.[5]

During a break in discussions with Nir at the Churchill Hotel, Gorba motioned North to follow him into the bathroom. He ran tap water to muffle what he suspected were secret tapings by the Israelis.

"Ollie," he whispered, "I know what you've been doing in your spare time. Maybe we can make some money available to your friends in Nicaragua."

Hmm, keep talking, thought North.[6]

In fact, North himself taped Ghorbanifar in that bathroom. The recording is muffled, but on it Gorba is heard to say, "We will never find such a good time again, never get such good money." He saw everything coming to them "free of charge"—the hostages, "American business," and "Central America." North agreed, seeing the two as connected by more than these funds: "w[ith] Central America, you know that there is a lot of Libyan, a lot of Libyan *and* Iranian activity with the Nicaraguans."[7] North saw poetic justice in the proposal because his information—likely exaggerated—was that Iran provided the Sandinistas with $100 million in oil per year, plus weapons.[8] Now North could make them fund the Sandinistas' enemies.

To North, Ghorbanifar's bathroom offer was an "incentive," meant to make more acceptable the risk of dealing with the Iranians.[9] Oddly, North did not take Ghorbanifar's revelation as a veiled threat to reveal his own relationship with North.

In February 1986, North returned from London to brief his boss on the Iran sales. "Near the end of the conversation," as John Poindexter recalled to Congress, North said: "Admiral, I have found a way that we can legally provide some funds to the Democratic Resistance . . . through funds that will accrue from the arms sales to the Iranians."

"Did he use the word 'legally'?" Congress's lawyer, Arthur Liman, asked Poindexter.

"My best recollection is that he did, but of course I know that Colonel North is not a lawyer and so I was taking that in a layman's sense, that that was his conclusion."

At the end of the conversation, Poindexter approved the diversion "in a broad, general way that didn't really require any further return to me to carry it out."[10] North testified to Congress that the transfers of Iranian moneys to Contra-directed accounts occurred three times—in February, May, and October 1986. "I saw that idea of using the Ayatollah Khomeini's money to support the Nicaraguan Freedom Fighters as a good one. I still do. I don't think it was wrong. I think it was a neat idea and I came back and I advocated that and we did it."

To Congress, North preferred to call the diverted funds "residuals," basing his term on "my use of Webster." Yet North's following sentence referred to a diversion: "The only thing we did was divert money out of Mr. Ghorbanifar's pocket and put it to a better use."[11] North said he also did not conceive of these funds as *diverted* because they sloshed around the same general "off-the-shelf" covert action fund. In fact, Casey conceived of this "stand-alone" set of operations as self-financed, so North looked anywhere for "revenue producers" that could fund other covert actions.[12]

.....

"I told Colonel North repeatedly not to put anything in writing on the transfer of funds to the Contras and not to talk to anybody about it," recalled Poindexter. "I told him several times."[13]

Yet on April 4, 1986, North, likely dictating to his secretary, Fawn Hall, composed for his superiors a memo titled "Release of the American Hostages in Beirut." On page 5, he briefly mentioned what he would do with a $15 million profit from a sale to Iran: After Secord's Enterprise was to pay $3.6

million to the United States for HAWK spare parts, "$12 million will be used to purchase critically needed supplies for the Nicaraguan Democratic Resistance Forces." Under "Recommendation," North wrote: "That the President approve."[14] North said he wrote five or six memoranda asking for Reagan to approve the diversion, yet no copy of the memo ever bore the president's signature. Poindexter said both that he could not remember seeing this memo and that he had probably destroyed it without showing it to Reagan. Yet five copies survived.[15]

The only mention of the diversion anywhere on paper, the April 4 missive became known as the "diversion memo."

.....

The memo mentioned no legal or political problems that might arise. To be sure, North and others aware of the diversion always understood that, if made public, it would be "politically damaging," as he said. "This had better never come out" is how Poindexter put it.[16]

But why? What exactly was wrong with the diversion that was not already wrong with the Contra or Iran parts of the Enterprise?

The illegality resided in both the diversion of US government property sales and the use of diverted funds to defy Congress's Boland Amendment specifically and, generally, Congress's prerogative to appropriate funds. Unlike their encouragement of private donors, in this case, US officials had clearly used taxpayer money to fund the Contra war. As Clair George of the CIA explained: "You do not sell U.S. Government equipment to make a profit, to engage in international activities that are neither authorized nor appropriated by the U.S. Congress. . . . You cannot take U.S. weapons and just go out and sell them for a profit and use the profits as you see fit."[17]

"On the formal level, the case is obvious," agreed Henry Kissinger, former secretary of state. "The executive branch cannot be allowed—on any claim of national security—to circumvent the congressional prerogative over appropriations by raising its own funds through the sale of government property." The issue was constitutional, said George Shultz: "You cannot spend funds that the Congress doesn't either authorize you to obtain or appropriate. That is what the Constitution says, and we have to stick to it."[18] Without the Congress's sole right to appropriate funds, the president or anyone else in the executive could sell federal property and use the funds for a private endeavor. As the congressional committees warned, "That is the path to dictatorship."[19]

The diversion was also impractical. As much as the millions might help the Contras, they could just as well torpedo relations with Iran. The Iranians' fury at being overcharged made them less likely to exchange more hostages for weapons.

Over at CIA, Charlie Allen and Bob Gates were apprehensive. "I can't prove it," said Allen, but he suspected that Secord and his partner, Albert Hakim, were involved in two separate operations that were now related. If an agency sold assets, Gates thought, profits should go to the US Treasury, not to another operation or private actors.[20] Clair George also found it "improper" to intermingle two covert actions. "You have authorized me one million dollars to [deleted]," he illustrated to Congress in redacted testimony. "I take $50,000 and take it off to [deleted] and [deleted], I have not done what I have been authorized to do either by my own leadership or the authorizing, appropriating process of the U.S. Congress."[21] Constantine Menges, a special assistant to Reagan, heard rumors of the two missions converging and judged that "it would be contrary to the need for compartmentation and secrecy."[22]

Chief of Staff Don Regan confirmed additional improprieties. First, "the normal practice when the United States sells arms to any nation is to sell them at our cost. . . . We don't sell to make a profit." Even if Poindexter authorized North and claimed that "the buck stops here with me," Regan added, nobody authorized Poindexter. "It was an unauthorized act on both of their parts."[23]

Months after the scandal broke, North did not seem to grasp whose money he was spending and whether or not he had the right to spend it. Ghorbanifar "suggested that we might want to use it to support the Contras, but that was up to us," Congress's counsel, John Nields, tried to clarify.

"Correct," said North.

"So it was our money that was going to the Contras, not Mr. Ghorbanifar's."

"You've lost me, counsel. . . . When you said our money—."

Nields moved to another issue. "And we could do with that money what we wished, as a government; isn't that true?"

"The Government of the United States was not out there dealing directly with Mr. Ghorbanifar," North countered. In other words, he arrogated the right to choose the destination for funds that he never considered were owed to the United States. Privatization, in his mind, took those founds out of public hands. "You keep saying that it was our money," he explained to Nields. "General Secord was an outside entity who had been established as an outside entity."

Nields seemed taken aback. "Are you testifying that the transaction was set up, structured in such a way that it was up to General Secord to decide how the residuals were going to be used?"

"Well, I don't want to put it all on his back," replied North. He discussed "a concert of opinion" about the destination of the funds. That concert, however, had few voices. Originally, he told only Poindexter, Casey, and Secord. "Director Casey used several words to describe how he felt about it," said North, "all of which were effusive."

Then who exactly made the decision to divert? North obfuscated with the passive voice: "The decision was made. . . . with the authority that I got from my superiors, Admiral Poindexter, with the concurrence of William J. Casey and I thought at the time the President of the United States."

North used an analogy to characterize the profit made off US public property as private: "If I were to buy a piece of land from the U.S. Park Service for $10,000 and then a year later or a week later go out and sell it for $20,000, would the Government of the United States lay claim to my $10,000 profit?" He imagined Secord to have purchased outright US weapons and therefore to enjoy the right to any profit. In truth, Secord was an intermediate, and the profit belonged to the American people.

When Nields tried to conclude that "it was our money that was going to the Contras, wasn't it?" North said no. "I disagree with your conclusion, counsel."

A final problem with the diversion was that it, too, was subject to profiteering. Of the $12 million earmarked for diversion, only about $3.5 million made it to the Contras.[24] Secord kept much of the difference.[25]

. . . . .

The diversion memo was Iran-Contra's most stunning revelation. It was a serious breach of democratic and bureaucratic practice, not to mention of the law. Yet, for an administration on the defensive, it also became a way to deflect attention from the other potential crimes and norm-busting of the scandal because the diversion, seeming not to involve the president, spared him an impeachment trial. Talk of a diversion became as much of a Republican shield for Reagan's protection as it was a Democratic cudgel to assail the administration.

The matter of who knew about the diversion was thus crucial. After North and Poindexter put it in action in February 1986, it came up again at the end of the Tehran trip in late May. The frustrated Americans had hoped to free some hostages but found themselves on the tarmac of the Iranian airport, headed back to the United States empty-handed.

North tapped McFarlane on the shoulder and grinned. "Don't worry, Bud, it's not a total loss. At least we're using some of the Ayatollah's money in Central America."[26] (It was not, of course, the Ayatollah's money but the Iranian people's.)

Oh, shit, thought McFarlane.[27] "I was a little startled," he later testified, but "I was not in the government," and he opted not to report it.[28] After Tehran, when McFarlane briefed Reagan, Bush, Poindexter, and Regan, he did not mention the diversion.[29]

Poindexter thought about whether to brief the president. He reasoned that Reagan approved of third-country and private support for the Contras, so why not this, too? Funds from Iran sales "could have been characterized as private funds or they could be characterized as third country funds. . . . I was convinced that I understood the President's thinking on this and that if I had taken it to him that he would have approved it."

Hold on, said Arthur Liman in congressional hearings. "If [the diversion] were viewed as a contribution from a private donor, who would that donor have been?

"It would have been General Secord," responded Poindexter.[30]

For his part, Secord did not know if—but believed that—Reagan was "well aware" of the diversion. If he was not aware, he still would approve of it because it advanced his policy. North joked to Secord that he told Reagan about the diversion, and Secord proved "skeptical."[31]

"Now," Poindexter explained to Congress, "I was not so naive as to believe that it was not a politically volatile issue, it clearly was, because of the divisions that existed within the Congress. . . . I made a very deliberate decision not to ask the President so that I could insulate him from the decision and provide some future deniability for the President if it ever leaked out." The national security advisor added, "I wanted the President and his staff to be able to say they didn't know anything about it."[32] Regan claimed not to know about it, and Poindexter confirmed: "[Regan] knows very little, and it's best you keep it that way," he instructed North."[33] Poindexter also denied telling Casey.[34]

At CIA, knowledge of the diversion did not seem to spread beyond Casey until soon before the scandal broke. On October 1, 1986, Charlie Allen, the CIA's specialist on Iran, went to see Robert Gates, who had succeeded John McMahon as deputy director. He told Gates of the diversion. "He was very startled at this," Allen recalled. "He started to laugh because it sounded absurd, but then he became very serious."

"Well, that would be a very serious thing," said Gates. "Operationally, you can't commingle two operations."

In a meeting with North shortly after, the lieutenant colonel cryptically referred to "Swiss bank accounts." Gates knew nothing about this. He later went to his boss Bill Casey's office.

"You know, he [North] made some strange reference or whatever to Swiss bank accounts and the contras. Is there anything there that we should be worried about?"

Casey waved off North's reference, so Gates never followed up. Gates later testified that his impression was that Casey knew nothing about the diversion.[35]

Casey "knew about the diversion," North told one reporter in 1991. "He told me how to do it. He's the guy that helped me set up the procedures to make it happen.[36]

In any case, by the third week of October 1986, the secret had grown beyond North, McFarlane, Secord, and Poindexter. Casey, Allen, Gates, and George Cave of the CIA knew. So did Robert Earl, North's chief aide. Adnan Khashoggi, Roy Furmark (a businessman who was Casey's link to Khashoggi), and Ghorbanifar knew also. This last one, angry at being ostracized from Iran deals, threatened to tell three US senators.[37]

Yet it seems that Reagan, remarkably, never learned of the diversion. When the scandal broke, Regan was the one who broke the news to the president. He testified that Reagan "visibly was shook by this and recoiled when he heard it, every manifestation of surprise and horror at what he had just heard." Regan added that Vice President Bush also did not know.[38]

Independent Counsel Lawrence Walsh remained skeptical of Reagan's denials. "The diversion was no fringe detail," he argued. "It was the lifeline for the Contras. How could Poindexter, in his daily briefings for the president, have avoided all mention of this vital link between Reagan's two highest personal priorities? Would William Casey, who met privately with Reagan from time to time, have kept him in the dark?"[39] Walsh also speculated that Reagan must have known because he kept selling arms to Iran without getting hostages freed. "Is it believable that the President went through this embarrassing charade for a year if he didn't know he was getting money for the contras?"[40]

In the end, however, Walsh could only speculate: *Reagan must have known.* The president's reputation as incurious, indecisive, and inattentive to detail played in his favor. While in the Oval Office, he wrote few memos and often signed documents without reading them, and his staff disassembled his briefing books after use, which made Walsh's reconstruction of Reagan's information impossible. The mid-1980s also might have seen the onset of what doctors later diagnosed as the president's Alzheimer's disease. Arthur Liman expressed a similar frustration in pinning down what Reagan knew. "Too many documents were shredded, too many witnesses gave inconsistent testimony, and too many of his aides wanted to protect him. Like me, many members of the committees believed he knew, but belief is no substitute for proof."

Liman nevertheless concluded that "the president, at the very least, bore the responsibility for creating a climate in the White House in which a disdain for law had flourished."[41]

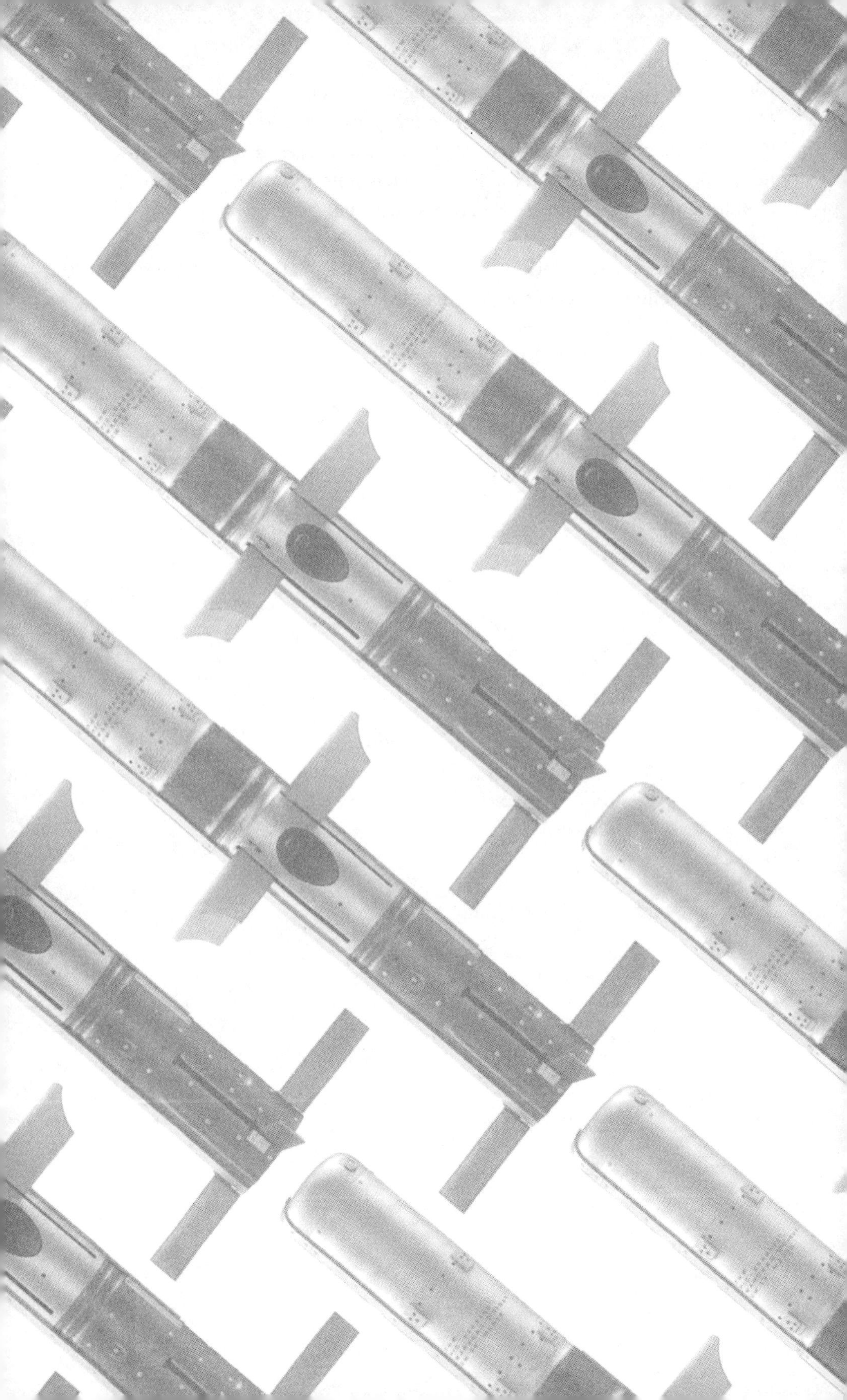

PART TWO

SCANDAL

6

CRASH AND COVER-UP

In October and November 1986, the house of cards that was the Iran-Contra initiative collapsed. Rumors percolated up from Central America, and an airplane shootdown confirmed them. Soon after, a story out of Beirut revealed the negotiations with Iran.

Those who had plotted Iran-Contra met these revelations with untruths, deceptions, and obfuscations. They lied to Congress. Ronald Reagan presided over the most disastrous press conferences of his tenure. A cabinet member broke with the White House. The attorney general showed a greater willingness to protect the president than to investigate crimes. The administration wove a tangled web that deceived few and infuriated many.

Throughout, the Republican administration demonstrated its paltry regard for three democratic norms—the primacy of the truth, the rule of law, and the unfettered processes of justice. These flaws would characterize the Reagan White House response to the rest of the scandal.

.....

In the spring and summer of 1986, cracks appeared in the wall of Iran-Contra conspiracy.

One of the most important defections stemmed from its rampant profiteering. On the morning of August 8, Félix Rodríguez walked into the office of Donald Gregg, the national security advisor for Vice President Bush. A stocky Cuban American who had fought at the Bay of Pigs and stood out as the only foreigner who talked to Che Guevara before the Argentine revolutionary's execution in Bolivia, Rodríguez had retired from the CIA to coordinate North's operation at Ilopango air base in El Salvador. Learning that Dick Secord and former CIA officer Thomas Clines, both sullied by their association with disgraced CIA officer Edwin Wilson, were involved, Rodríguez tried to quit. Gregg, whom Rodríguez knew from their Vietnam days, ushered him into a meeting with Bush and US Ambassador to El Salvador Edwin Corr, both of whom convinced him to stay.[1]

Three months later, again in Gregg's office, Rodríguez had had enough. Secord and Clines, he said, were "ripping off the Contras. Buying shoddy stuff and selling it for high prices." For example, they purchased hand grenades for $3 each and sold them for $9, "not including freight charges." *With a reasonable markup,* he thought, *the Contras could have 250,000 grenades instead of 100,000.* And the aircraft the Enterprise bought with private funds were old, poorly maintained, and cursed with broken parts. Some could not fly. "They're a piece of shit," said Rodríguez.

"It's a real fraud, a crime to profit," he ranted.[2] It was one of the reasons he had tried to quit the Contra resupply operation in the spring.[3]

Another was the fraud that occurred because of the quid pro quos with Central American nations. Rodríguez was also to deliver what he knew were forged end-user certificates. He had long had "a feeling," he later told Congress.

"You didn't trust General Secord, and you didn't trust Tom Clines; is that right?"

"For this type of operation, with that much money, no, sir."

When one of the unsafe airplanes "hit the top of a mountain," the crew wrote a letter of complaint, which Rodríguez showed to Oliver North and Colonel Robert Dutton, an associate of Secord's who managed on-the-ground operations.

"Is this a joke?" said North.

"No, I don't think it is a joke," replied Rodríguez. "The people who wrote it almost got killed the day before."

He then spoke to North alone, adding complaints about the $9 grenades. "If this is known," he warned, the resulting scandal "is going to be worse than Watergate, and this could destroy the President of the United States." North defended Clines, calling him "a patriot."

Their meeting coincided with a congressional vote on renewing Contra aid, shown on the television in the room. Just before Rodríguez left, North turned to the TV set: "Those people want me but they cannot touch me because the old man loves my ass."

The "old man" he likely referred to was President Reagan.[4]

.....

By "those people," North might have meant Congress, but he also might have been thinking of the media. Well before the scandal broke, intrepid journalists reported on the lieutenant colonel's "tactical influence" over the Contras, in defiance of Boland II. As early as April 1984, the *Washington Post* asked questions about third-country support. The HPSCI questioned CIA director Bill Casey, who denied any knowledge. Casey's liaison to the Contras, Duane Clarridge, did the same in September 1984. North encouraged private Contra resupplier John Singlaub to brag to reporters, which seemed to throw them off North's scent.[5]

In summer 1985, journalists first refrained from naming North but then identified him as an aide to National Security Advisor Bud McFarlane.[6] In December, Brian Barger and Robert Parry revealed that Contras were shipping cocaine through Costa Rica with the knowledge of many in the US government, and their story about North's private aid network came out the following June.[7] That same month, North sent an aide to threaten Alfonso Chardy of the *Miami Herald* with cutting off his access to the Contras if he "printed any derogatory comments about the FDN [Contras] or its funding sources." Chardy dropped the story. North painted another journalist as "an avowed liberal with very close connections in the Democratic party." To plug leaks, North proposed lie detector tests for the NSC staff.[8]

"Now you are getting emotional again," the always cool John Poindexter, McFarlane's successor, told North. He did suggest that North tell top Washington journalists "to call off the dogs. . . . I just want to lower your visibility so that you wouldn't be such a good target for the Libs."[9]

In October 1985, McFarlane answered questions in writing for the HPSCI. "There is no official or unofficial relationship with any member of the NSC staff regarding fund raising for the Nicaraguan democratic opposition," he flatly lied.[10]

After this initial round of press stories and denials, the NSC changed its recordkeeping. North no longer stored memos in the NSC's filing system. He instead wrote PROFS notes directly to McFarlane and Poindexter, believing that investigators would never access these computer messages.[11]

By summer 1986, North's notoriety in the press endangered congressional support. The Contra resupply operation was broadly known—and resented—in the CIA, the State Department, and elsewhere. Elliott Abrams called for an investigation to root out dissent in his own State Department.[12] McFarlane worried about leaks from private donors: "Too many people are talking to reporters from the donor community and within the administration."[13] Meanwhile, the executive branch dissembled. "Nonsense," North called reports of a private aid network. "The President never approved any such plan [to aid the Contras]," said the White House.[14]

On June 25, the House approved the White House's request for $100 million in Contra aid. Here was a great irony of the Contra affair: As it was about to blow wide open, its reason for being—Boland's aid cutoff—ceased to exist.

.....

Yet another fissure appeared in September 1986, as the secret airstrip in Costa Rica, funded by private donors but overseen by the CIA and the US Embassy, became public knowledge. The incident demonstrated the dangers of secrecy and quid pro quos.

The May election in that Central American neighbor of Nicaragua had brought in a new president, Oscar Arias, later to serve a key role in ending the war in Nicaragua. Upon taking office, Arias revoked permission to use the Santa Elena airstrip. That was bad for North but was at least secretive. On September 6, however, the Costa Rican minister of public security planned to hold a press conference to denounce the use of the airstrip as illegal. North got wind of the plan and called Abrams at State.

This is a very bad thing, said North. *It will raise all sorts of awkward questions about the previous Costa Rican government, and we ought to stop it.* Abrams agreed.[15]

North suggested that US Ambassador Lewis Tambs call Arias and threaten that he would never get to meet President Reagan and "w[oul]d never see a nickel" of a promised $80 million in Agency for International Development funds. North recognized it was "well beyond my charter in dealing w[ith] a head of state this way." Later that day, Tambs caught the president during dinner. He used a different threat: that the United States might sue Costa Rica at the International Court of Justice.[16]

I'll see what I can do, said Arias. Soon after, he said he called off the press conference.

Almost three weeks later, it occurred anyway. The minister of the interior, in North's telling, "announced that Costa Rican authorities had discovered a secret airstrip in Costa Rica that was over a mile long and which had been built and used by a Co. called Udall Services for supporting the Contras." The minister also named an associate of Dick Secord's. North promised that day that Udall Resources, a proprietary of his Project Democracy, "will cease to exist by noon today. There are no USG[overnment] fingerprints on any of the operation."[17] Five days later, North assessed "the damage done by this revelation" to be "considerable." He advised another threat/quid pro quo to Arias: "we should insist that Arias demonstrate his goodwill toward the resistance through practical steps *before* he is welcomed in the Oval Office"[18]

Arias never did have his meeting with Reagan.

.....

Storm clouds gathered. The sky cracked open when a plane fell out of it.

On October 5, 1986, a C-123 aircraft, typically used for military transport, left Ilopango base in El Salvador at 9:50 a.m. loaded with 10,000 pounds of machine guns, plastic explosives, hand grenades, mortars, and AK munitions for the Contras. The cargo never arrived at its planned drop zone. Robert Dutton reported the aircraft missing along with its three US crewmembers "with a talker," seventeen-year-old Nicaraguan radio operator Freddy Vilches.[19]

A Sandinista antiaircraft patrol had figured out the air routes of the Contras. At about 12:45 p.m., one of its soldiers, fourteen-year-old José Fernando Canales Alemán, walking near the Costa Rican border, saw the unidentified propeller plane mere minutes from landing. The Nicaraguan lifted his Soviet-made SAM-7 surface-to-air missile launcher to his shoulder, peered through the optical sight, and squeezed the trigger. He scored a rare perfect hit, and the plane started spinning.[20] Crew members were not allowed parachutes so as to leave no survivors in case of a crash, but one wore his brother's parachute and jumped out in time. As he descended, he watched the ball of flames with his fellow crew members slam into the forest. After he wandered around for a day, the Nicaraguans took him prisoner.

"My name is Eugene Hasenfus. I'm from Marinette, Wisconsin," a tall, red-headed man announced in a one-minute statement televised from the wreckage on October 7. "I was captured yesterday in southern Nicaragua." Still caked in mud, dressed in a blue cotton work shirt, blue jeans, and work boots, Hasenfus—"rabbit's foot" in German—looked bruised and swollen.[21]

He spilled the beans to his captors. He was a forty-five-year-old former Marine with a wife and three kids. From 1966 to 1974, he had worked for several CIA proprietaries in Southeast Asia: Air America, Southern Air, Civil Air Transport, and Air Asia. After a decade in construction, in July 1986, he began working out of El Salvador for Southern Air Transport, owned by Dick Secord. He made $3,000 per month as a "kicker," tying parachutes to crates of supplies and literally kicking them out.[22] He worked for Max Gómez, he said, the "CIA's overseer" at Ilopango. He meant Félix Rodríguez, for whom "Max Gómez" was an alias. In the wreckage, the Nicaraguans found documents tying the plane to Corporate Air Services from Pennsylvania, a front company for Southern Air Transport. Phone records showed the pilots had called CIA safe houses in San Salvador, including one that led to CIA Station Chief Joseph Fernandez.

As Duane Clarridge wrote, the Contra resupply effort was already "old news" in Washington. "North's operation had been discussed on the cocktail circuit for well over a year." But a US citizen was now captured, and congressional elections were coming in November.[23]

The day of Hasenfus's statement, the State Department offered "press guidance" aimed at distancing the flight from the US government. "The plane and crew in question are *not* affiliated . . . with the U.S. government . . . neither the flight, the crew, the plane, nor the cargo was financed by the U.S. government." Washington did not discourage the kind of private funding that was behind the flight, so long as it was legal.[24] The next day, the NSC tried to walk back the denial, admitting that the government was aware of such flights. Yet it called for a Contra group "to assume responsibility for the flight" and recommended that Elliott Abrams stop praising the bravery of the crew "because it contributes to the perception [that the] U.S.G[overnment] inspired and encouraged [this] private lethal aid effort."[25]

Disavowals were rife—and confusing. The CIA denied that Hasenfus worked for it but "refused to deny" knowing anything about the flight. It did not help that Hasenfus's wife in Wisconsin, Sally, "said her husband worked for the CIA."[26] Secretary of State George Shultz admitted his department knew the men involved but asserted that they were "hired by private people" who "had no connection with the U.S. government at all."[27] "There is no government connection to that at all," reiterated President Reagan himself. He said the White House was aware of private help to the Contras, but nothing about "the exact particulars of what they're doing."[28] He failed to follow Poindexter's instructions: "be careful about denying any U.S. role."[29]

Back at Ilopango, the Enterprise destroyed its remaining fleet, flying it to a remote field, dumping the planes in a large pit, and blowing them up. The Hasenfus flight would be one of its last.[30]

If a link to the US government existed, warned Senator Patrick Leahy (D-VT), "then we're in for some very serious trouble."[31] North knew it, too.

He told McFarlane they needed a "high-powered" lawyer to defend Hasenfus "to hold things together."

"There will be a fair bit of history made in the next few weeks," predicted North. He was to erase much of it. Casey had told North to "get rid of things, clean things up." Also, *get a lawyer*. North began to destroy any paper that mentioned the diversion, including a spiral ledger of all private contributions to the Contras.[32] North also delayed for six weeks an FBI investigation into the Hasenfus crash, claiming that its revelations could endanger "sensitive hostage negotiations underway" with Iran.[33] The Customs Service, also pressured by North, narrowed the scope of its own investigation. Scholar Malcolm Byrne tallied that North suppressed investigations "on at least seven occasions."[34]

Meanwhile, the Nicaraguans tried, found guilty of illegal gunrunning, and sentenced Eugene Hasenfus to thirty years in prison, but then released him weeks later on December 17.

.....

Soon after the Hasenfus crash, Reagan's director of communications, Pat Buchanan, contacted former president Richard Nixon for advice. They had gone through Watergate together when Buchanan wrote speeches for the White House.

"Get the message out," counseled Nixon. "Admit you made a mistake—you tried something, and it turned out badly. But don't cover it up."[35]

The opposite was about to happen.

On October 7, the day the Sandinistas put Hasenfus in front of cameras, Alan Fiers, chief of the Central America Task Force at CIA, answered a HPSCI staff member's question about who was running private aid to the Contras. "I can assure you that we won't touch any of that stuff," he told the staffer. He lied again to Senators John Kerry and Edward Kennedy (both D-MA) and to the Senate Foreign Relations Committee staff.[36] He again denied the same knowledge to the HPSCI on October 14.

Clair George, deputy director of operations at CIA, did much the same, lying about his knowledge of the Contra operation to the Senate Foreign Relations Committee on October 10, to the HPSCI four days later, and to the SSCI on December 3. "The CIA was not involved directly or indirectly in arranging, directing, or facilitating resupply missions conducted by private individuals in support of the Nicaraguan Democratic Resistance," he told the HPSCI in a typical disavowal. The crew of the C-123 were not CIA employees, he specified, "nor do they work for us in any way," although some had during

FIGURE 6
Elliott Abrams of the State Department fibbed and dissembled to several committees. "I want to puke," said one senator after hearing Abrams's testimony. (Bettmann/Getty)

the Vietnam War.[37] George even claimed, "We instructed our officers abroad to refrain from any contact with the individuals involved in the [Contra resupply]." He denied knowing "Max Gómez" or "Ramón Medina," aliases for Rodríguez and Luis Posada Carriles, respectively, found among documents in the Hasenfus plane. "I would never say to you that [a CIA operative] didn't work for me when I knew he did," George swore to the senators.[38]

He would later be tried for obstruction of justice, perjury, and false statements, partly for suppressing the CIA's knowledge of Gómez/Rodríguez.[39]

Abrams accompanied George before the House and went further, denying that anyone in the US government was involved in supplying the Contras (see fig. 6).

"Do you know if any foreign government is helping to supply the contras?"

"No, sir, we have no intelligence of that," said George. Abrams agreed.[40] They admitted knowing of "private Americans at Ilopango," but not who they were, whose plane Hasenfus leaped from, or who flew it.[41] It was true that Hasenfus and the rest of the crew did not work for the CIA. But Fiers, George, and Abrams knew who "Max Gómez" was, who the donors were, and that US government officials were involved.[42]

The Democratic members of the HPSCI were generally skeptical, whereas the Republicans tended to believe the deniers. Dave McCurdy (D-OK) warned, "We certainly had better be right in our categorical denials." *How could the CIA not know who flew the planes?* asked Matthew McHugh (D-NY), after Henry Hyde (R-IL) came to Abrams's defense. Dick Cheney (R-WY) "said he found [the CIA's] ignorance credible."[43]

Upon hearing George's blanket denial to the HPSCI, Joseph Fernandez, who operated under the pseudonym "Tomás Castillo," said, "I would have to disagree with that. My participation did facilitate because it provided the information" between private benefactors and the Contras with a KL-43 electronic cipher device.[44] Fernandez did not break the law by helping with communications—if he did not coordinate the Contras—but George did by lying to Congress about it.[45]

Abrams made some of the most unqualified and widely broadcast abjurations. On October 11, he was a guest on the political talk show *Evans & Novak*, hosted by two conservative pundits.

Out of the gate, Rowland Evans asked: "Mr. Secretary, can you give me *categorical evidence* that Hasenfus was not under the control, the guidance, direction, or what have you, of anybody connected with the American government?"

"*Absolutely*," responded Abrams. "*That would be illegal.* We are barred from doing that, and we are not doing it. This was not in any sense a U.S. government operation. None."

What about Bush's security aide Don Gregg, who hired Max Gómez?, asked Robert Novak, referring to the pseudonym of Félix Rodríguez.

"There's no Max Gómez," Abrams said accurately but cryptically.

Abrams denied the NSC was involved, that the United States had an air base in El Salvador, and that Hasenfus was probably not violating the Neutrality Act.

"I have to believe you, because I know you're an honest man," said Evans, astoundingly.

"You know, I've seen a lot of cover-ups in this town, Rowland," his cohost agreed. "But *this doesn't look like a cover-up*, and it doesn't because there is no equivocation."[46] Novak later said that he did not really mind that Abrams lied to him on television. "He had a tough job and there were lots of people out to get him."[47]

Abrams reiterated his assurances to the Senate Foreign Relations Committee and HPSCI. He admitted in later testimony to Congress that he failed to check with North beforehand. As the chair of the RIG tasked with overseeing North's work, "I was careful not to ask Colonel North what questions I thought I did not need to know the answers to."[48]

By October 14, Abrams's bureau at State revised its press guidance, suggesting to "kill" the "language" denying any US government ties to the downed flight. Still, it insisted, "there is not now nor has there been any U.S. government involvement in efforts to provide military assistance to the Nicaraguan Democratic Resistance since such assistance by the U.S. government was prohibited by the U.S. Congress."[49]

Abrams continued speaking untruths and accused others of lying. On October 15, a member of the House Committee on Foreign Affairs read him a news item that "U.S. Defense sources" and "an Intelligence Committee senior staff member" both said that the Hasenfus flight was "paid for by Saudi Arabian funds"—which was accurate. "I wish the Intelligence Committee would find out who that person is, because he or she is lying to the press," Abrams suggested. "I do not believe it is conceivable that such a thing could happen without my knowing about it."[50]

.....

The frustrating trip to Tehran headed by McFarlane in May 1986 did produce at least one revelation, but not one the US government hoped for. It turned out there were no "moderates" or "radicals" in the Iranian government, only devotees of Ayatollah Khomeini. Middleman Manucher Ghorbanifar told the Americans so in July. By the fall, he felt sidelined—with good reason—and he threatened to disclose the whole operation to the SSCI. "This is going to be exposed if something isn't done," Charlie Allen warned CIA Deputy Director Bob Gates.[51]

On October 15, an Iranian official angry at political rivals had more than 5 million leaflets printed, with McFarlane's image on them, denouncing the regime's agreement to buy arms from the United States. The leaflets covered Tehran University. Members of an organization that had taken American hostages in 1979 stood on street corners, handing them out.[52] The story then ran in a tiny Shiite radical newspaper in Baalbek, Lebanon. On November 2, a Hezbollah faction released hostage David Jacobsen on war-torn Beirut's seafront. The next day, the McFarlane story found its way into Beirut's *Al-Shiraa*, a small leftist weekly published in Muslim West Beirut. The editor, Hassan Sabra, was skeptical, but he trusted his two sources, secret agents within the Khomeini government.[53] The day after *that*, Speaker Rafsanjani conceded to the Parliament that the McFarlane trip had occurred (although both he and *Al-Shiraa* got the month wrong). Largely based on his speech, US newspapers featured the story on November 5.[54]

For days, President Reagan deflected. On November 6, he promised reporters that the revelation out of Beirut had "no foundation."[55] He seemed to believe it. His next day's diary entry was all about "handl[ing] the press who are off on a wild story. . . . Our message will be 'we can't and won't answer any Q's on this subject because to do so will endanger the lives of those we are trying to help."[56]

In his 1990 memoir, Reagan insisted that his White House had never done business with the government of Iran. "We had never had any contacts with the kidnappers, had seen to it that the defensive weapons that went to Iran never got into the hands of the people who held our hostages. But the press took the word of the Beirut paper over ours."[57]

In the fall of 1986, however, the heads of the congressional intelligence committees were aghast. The staff director of the SSCI drove up to Langley to confront Clair George: "How can you do this without showing us a finding?" George minimized the agency's role, saying it only gave logistical support to the NSC.[58]

The press was also not leaving this development alone. Between November 3 and 30, CBS News devoted one-quarter of its total broadcast time to the Iran-Contra story.[59] "By mid-November," recalled North, "my name was starting to show up a little too often, and I knew I was in trouble when the ABC evening news named me 'Person of the Week.' "[60]

"The cover is blown here," Chief of Staff Don Regan said he told his subordinates. "We have got to go public with it, we have got to tell the Congress, we have got to tell the American public exactly what went on so they are aware of it."[61]

Similarly, George Shultz worried about another Watergate. He had been treasury secretary under Nixon and knew how a cover-up could easily obtain: "They get in and can't get out, so they stonewall and get in deeper," he explained to his staff.[62] En route to Vienna, he wrote to Poindexter from his plane that the story was about to break. "The best way to proceed is to give the key facts to the public."[63]

"I do not believe that now is the time to give the facts to the public," answered Poindexter the next day. There were still hostages to free and intelligence committees to brief, and Iranian politics were allegedly in a state of flux. Vice President Bush, Secretary of Defense Caspar Weinberger, and Casey agreed with the national security advisor.[64]

On November 7, the White House was in full damage control mode. McFarlane, already eleven months out of his job as national security advisor, sent a note to Poindexter complaining that Chief of Staff Regan "laid the entire problem at my feet," telling journalists that McFarlane had managed a straight arms-for-hostages deal with no thought of reforming Iran. "If this is true, I will be quite mad."[65] Poindexter doubted that McFarlane had heard right, yet he got Regan to "keep his mouth shut." The current national security advisor remained defensive and secretive.[66]

Astonishingly, negotiations with Iranians continued. North, Secord, Secord's partner Albert Hakim, and CIA consultant George Cave had another meeting with Iranians in Geneva on November 8–10, again reaching no agreement.

.....

On November 10, Reagan held a late-morning Oval Office NSPG meeting to discuss how to handle the developing situation. Present were Bush, Weinberger, Shultz, Casey, Attorney General Ed Meese, Regan, Poindexter, and Poindexter's deputy, Alton Keel.

At the meeting, Poindexter gave a highly distorted overview, including that Israel had sent the first 500 TOWs without US permission and that the Rafsanjani connection through his nephew was still going strong. He mentioned only one presidential finding to justify the arms deals; there had been three. He said there were only three shipments to Iran; there had been five. He totaled all the TOWs to Iran at 1,000; the true number was 2,004.[67]

Weinberger reminded the assembled men of one democratic responsibility: "We will have to answer many questions and have Congressional hearings." President Reagan, however, kept alive his fantasy that secrecy would yield success: "We need to point out any discussion endangers our source in Iran and our plan, because we do want to get additional hostages released."[68]

Shultz brought up Reagan's main delusion: "So if the 500 TOWs plus other items have been supplied to Iran in the context of hostage releases," he asked Poindexter, "how can you say this is not an arms-for-hostages deal?"

"It's not linked!" Reagan jumped in.

"How else will we get the hostages out?" Poindexter answered, in effect contradicting the president. In his memoir, Shultz reflected that "Poindexter had unwittingly ripped away whatever veil was left to the rationale of a 'changed Iran' as the reason for our arms sales."[69]

After the meeting, the cover-up continued. Casey drafted a statement declaring "unanimous support for the President's decisions."[70]

FIGURE 7 On November 12, as the scandal unfolded, Reagan told members of Congress led by Senators Robert Dole (R-KS) and Robert Byrd (D-WV) that "We have not negotiated with terrorists. We have not broken any laws." Both expressed doubts. (Courtesy Ronald Reagan Presidential Library)

Meese and Poindexter liked the language. Shultz was disgusted. "That's a lie. It's Watergate all over again." He insisted that the word "decisions" be dropped.[71]

The White House's press statement later that afternoon vaguely denied that "no U.S. laws have been or will be violated and . . . our policy of not making concessions to terrorists remains intact."[72] The next day, a frustrated Reagan observed in his diary that the "morning press [are] largely ignoring our statement re the hostages & Iran & continuing their false stories."[73]

On November 12, two days after the NSPG meeting, Reagan and a few associates gathered congressional leaders, including Dick Cheney, in the White House Situation Room and gave them the false account the president seemed to believe himself—"the whole load," he called it (see fig. 7). He revealed the arms sales and said he could not go public for fear of endangering hostages. "We have not negotiated with terrorists. We have not broken any laws," the president insisted. "It was a covert operation . . . designed to advance our strategic interests in the Middle East."

Then he took questions. "Why do overtures to the Iranians not constitute dealing with terrorists?" asked Senator Bob Dole (R-KS), usually an ally but befuddled in this case.

"We would have continued on this track with Iran even if no hostages existed," Reagan responded, negating his single-minded focus of the previous year and a half.

"Was the State Department involved?" Senator Robert Byrd (D-WV) asked Shultz.

"The State Department had nothing to do with it," Shultz said.

"Were you opposed?"

"I never discuss the advice I give to the president," said the diplomat.

Byrd read between the lines: "You were left out."[74]

The day of the congressional leaders' briefing, Pat Buchanan, following Nixon's advice, pleaded with Regan for the White House's "full disclosure." He hated "the *appearance* . . . that we have negotiated with a terrorist regime, . . . that we violated our policy and traduced our principles, that we are now stonewalling."

"I agree," Regan wrote on Buchanan's memo. "It's late, but I hope not too late."[75]

Reagan thought it was not. "The media looks like it's trying to create another Watergate," the president wrote in his diary the same day as Buchanan's memo. "I want to go public personally & tell the people the truth."[76] He called a press conference for the following day, November 13.

Reagan's first press conference on the Iran scandal (the Contras were not yet linked) was an exercise in either self-delusion or lying. Either way, it was filled with untruths, cloaked as corrections to media distortions. "The charge has been made," said the president to the American people, "that the United States has shipped weapons to Iran as a ransom payment for the release of American hostages in Lebanon, that the United States undercut its allies and secretly violated American policy against trafficking with terrorists. Those charges are utterly false."[77] They were true.

"These modest deliveries, taken together, could easily fit into a single cargo plane," he added. Poindexter had first told Reagan that they would fit on a "small plane," but later amended it to *maybe* one C-5A, the largest cargo aircraft in the US Air Force. Maybe two.[78] North also was satisfied that 2,000 TOWs and the electronic parts would have fit.[79] Yet even this calculation omitted the HAWKs, which Israel had shipped. To Don Regan, "it was the one planeload [story] that stuck in the President's mind and stuck in the media's craw."[80]

At his press conference, Reagan also said, "It's been widely reported . . . that the Congress, as well as top executive branch officials, were circumvented. . . . All appropriate Cabinet officers were fully consulted . . . We did not—repeat—did not trade weapons or anything else for hostages nor will we."

Only 14 percent of those polled believed that Reagan had not been trading arms for hostages.[81] McFarlane figured in the majority. He found Reagan's address "frustrating to me. It showed no real change in the bunker mentality that appeared to have settled over the White House, and was just this side of an outright lie."[82] He sent a PROFS note to Poindexter warning him of another Watergate—there was that comparison again—when "well-meaning people who were in on the early planning of the communications strategy didn't intend to lie but ultimately came around to it."[83] Bush wrote in his diary that day that Reagan was "showing great tension for the first time."[84] Even North wrote in his memoirs that "President Reagan wasn't exactly lying, but he wasn't telling the truth, either. He believed what he said." The United States was not "technically" dealing directly with hostage-takers.[85]

Regan also argued that "people Ronald Reagan trusted put lies in his mouth."[86] Advisors certainly gave the commander in chief false information. But he also got more truthful information and plenty of skepticism from people he trusted, and he consistently chose to ignore it while repeating what he *wanted* to be true and what many rational people had questioned.

.....

In his diary, George Bush noted "tension between the various players"—Regan and Poindexter, for instance. Shultz, meanwhile, felt "clued out"—also by Poindexter.[87]

On November 16, the fault lines in the cabinet became public. At Regan's request, Shultz reluctantly accepted an interview with the television program *Face the Nation* to express the administration's viewpoint. After having Representative Jim Wright (D-TX) accuse the White House of violating the National Security Act with its January 17, 1986, finding, journalist Leslie Stahl asked the secretary of state, "Will there be any more arms shipments to Iran, either directly by our government or through any third parties?"

"It's certainly against our policy," responded Shultz.

"That's not an answer," retorted Stahl, and repeated her question. This time, he answered more directly, "No."

"Do you have the authority to speak for the entire administration?" Stahl wondered.

He looked her straight in the eye: "No."[88]

There the episode ended. "I need a drink," Stahl said after the cameras were off.

"I never should have come on," Shultz confessed.

"We were all amazed you did."[89]

"It was a sad day for me," Shultz later wrote of having to contradict his boss in public. "But it was the truth."[90] Bush, watching from the White House, blamed the media: "If I need something to show why the press is detested and why they hate her [Stahl?]. . . . They ought to call this show up and see it. It was rude, ugly, arrogant, and typical of the excesses that this TV journalism has caused." Yet, the vice president acknowledged, "The president's credibility is eroding."[91] Over at CIA, Casey did not care. He tried to have Shultz fired by telling Reagan he needed a "new pitcher!"[92] Humiliated on television, the president not only did not fire Shultz but he also shifted Iran policy from Poindexter to the State Department. Although the White House stated there would be no more arms for hostages, Casey continued to work on deals behind Shultz's back.[93]

.....

If the administration's intent to was improve its public image, the president's press conference on November 19, the most disastrous of his presidency, proved a giant leap backward (see fig. 8). Reagan did accept sole responsibility for the sales to Iran, but he complained again of the "mistaken perception that we have been exchanging arms for hostages." The four goals he laid out included "a negotiated end to the Iran-Iraq war" and "an end to terrorism and the taking of hostages," neither of which were ever seriously discussed at NSPG meetings let alone consistent with its decisions.[94]

After his brief statement, reporters hammered Reagan with questions. "The record shows," said Chris Wallace of NBC News, "that every time an American hostage was released—last September, this July, and again just this very month—there had been a major shipment of arms just before that. Are we all to believe that was just a coincidence?"

Bill Plante, CBS News: "How can you say, sir, that it didn't break the law, when the National Security Act of 1977 [*sic*] plainly talks about timely notification of Congress and also, sir, stipulates that if the national security required secrecy the President is still required to advise the leadership and the chairmen of the intelligence committees?"

From Trudie Fieldman of Transfeatures: "Are you telling us tonight that the only shipments with which we were involved were the one or two that

FIGURE 8 The most disastrous press conference of Reagan's presidency, November 19, 1986. (Courtesy Ronald Reagan Presidential Library)

followed your January 17th finding and that, whatever your aides have said on background or on the record, there were no other shipments with which [*sic*] the U.S. condoned?"

"That's right," responded Reagan.

When the president denied his administration was involved with Israel in shipping weapons to Iran, Andrea Mitchell of NBC News jumped in. Don Regan had told the press that the White House condoned "an Israeli shipment in September of 1985 . . . 4 months before your intelligence finding on January 17th that you say gave you the legal authority not to notify Congress. Now, can you clear that up?"

Reagan appeared lost. "Well, no, I've never heard Mr. Regan say that, and I'll ask him about that."

To Reagan's face, one journalist described "a mood in Washington tonight of a President who is very much beleaguered, very much on the defensive."

"I don't feel that I have anything to defend at all," replied Reagan.[95] Yet, within twenty minutes of the press conference, the White House press office issued a correction stating that a "third country" had indeed shipped weapons to Iran.[96] In one poll, 79 percent of Americans thought Reagan's version of the arms deals "misleading."[97] Even the usually fawning *Wall Street Journal* editors noted Reagan's "occasionally disjointed performance."[98]

Shultz had watched the president's news conference in disbelief. He immediately called for a private meeting with him—which Regan also attended.[99] There, Shultz tried to convince the president of his errors—eleven of them, to be precise, cataloged by his staff.[100] Fed CIA misinformation, Reagan thought the arms sales had somehow moderated Iran's support of terrorists. Shultz countered with, among other data, news of fresh hostage-takings in September and October.

"This is news to me," Reagan told Shultz.

Yeah, that's the point, Shultz tried to communicate. "Mr. President, you are not fully informed. You must not continue to say we made no deal for hostages. You have been deceived and lied to. I plead with you. *Don't* say that Iran has let up on terrorism."

"You're telling me things I don't know!" Reagan said.

"Mr. President, if I'm telling you something you don't know—I don't know much—then something is terribly wrong here!"[101] Regan recalled Reagan being "puzzled" by Shultz's presentation and unable to grasp what facts he had missed.[102]

.....

Another effort in the cover-up was the falsification of a chronology of the arms sales that Don Regan had requested. From November 5 to November 20, the chronology went through two dozen revisions. Its main intent was to distance the administration from the shipments of 1985, which took place before any presidential finding. The story became that the Israelis shipped missiles and told US officials that the cargo consisted of oil-drilling equipment. On November 18, 1986, Poindexter asked McFarlane to look over a draft of this fabrication. McFarlane, clearly attempting to protect Reagan, inserted the lie that the president had not given prior approval of the first sales by Israel in summer 1985. He also erased any mention of the HAWK fiasco.[103]

McFarlane recalled that evening differently. He went to North's office in the Executive Office Building at 8 p.m., he said. "The scene was chaos. In the outer office, Ollie's secretary, Fawn Hall, was typing away feverishly." North's aides were surrounded by "dozens and dozens of scraps of paper. Everyone was writing, cutting, and pasting. It looked as though a grenade had gone off in the room."

North gave him a draft chronology "put together by the agency," meaning the CIA. "Remember, Bud," North said carefully, "you and I didn't learn until January '86 about these HAWKs."

"I was hesitant to acknowledge that this was correct," wrote McFarlane, "but in all honesty I couldn't at that moment clearly recollect what had transpired more than a year ago."[104]

Later, Dick Secord checked out the chronology and saw the lie about US officials knowing nothing about the November HAWK shipment. His retelling echoed McFarlane's. While reading the chronology, "I stopped and Ollie knew I was going to stop. He was looking right at me."

"This is bullshit," said Secord. "This has been changed."

McFarlane went through it, countered North, *and he knows what the true story is.*

"I guess you guys don't need me anymore," concluded Secord. He got up and left.[105]

North later told Congress that he wrote the chronology but added that McFarlane, Poindexter, and Casey knew it was false, not to mention cabinet members who met in November and December 1985. He emphasized that he was not "a loose cannon on the gun deck of state at the NSC."[106]

.....

"Nobody is in fact being shut out of the foreign-policy process," declared confidently the *Wall Street Journal* on November 21.[107] Yet that very day, Casey complicated matters further with mendacious testimony to Congress. The previous day, about fifteen people, including North, Poindexter, and Meese, came together in Poindexter's West Wing corner office to advise the DCI. Casey planned to say, "We in the CIA did not find out that our airline had hauled HAWK missiles into Iran until mid-January [1986] when we were told by Iranians." This was already untrue because Casey and others in the CIA had known. "The CIA did not want to go on record [with] the fact that they had done an operation without a finding," recalled Poindexter's counsel Paul Thompson, who was present at the meeting.[108] North compounded the lie by revising the statement to read that "no one in the USG[overnment]" knew before January 1986.[109] No one protested the phrase. "I would call that a conspiracy," Senator William Cohen (R-ME) later said.[110]

Bob Gates called it "pandemonium." "Casey [was] going through, making changes in the testimony, updating and changing things we weren't sure of. People were passing comments and conversations and Casey was tearing off pages, and it was just mass confusion." In the midst of it, one of Casey's aides said, "Bill, not only is this chaos, there is a discussion of a diversion of Iran funds."

"I know absolutely nothing about that," Casey said, and shut down that discussion.[111]

.....

The false chronology and Casey's planned statement both made the lawyers jittery.

On November 18, White House counsel Peter Wallison called in Abraham Sofaer (pronounced "so far"), the State Department legal advisor, for a conference. That day, Sofaer found out about the January 17, 1986, finding relating to the 1985 shipments. The retroactiveness implied in the dates would "obviously raise a very serious legal question. The Finding was in January, what happened before the Finding?" *Why wasn't I told about this?* he thought. *Why wasn't Wallison?*[112]

Something else about that November deal seemed askew. In looking at Casey's proposed testimony, Sofaer saw that the CIA had agreed to help Israel by finding an airline to ship oil-drilling bits. But only once. "This made me skeptical," Sofaer recalled, "because I didn't see any reason why they would be reluctant to help Israel get the name of an airline if all they were doing was shipping oil drilling bits."[113] McFarlane had told Shultz that HAWKs were on that plane—nothing about oil drilling—but the NSC men were "sticking by their understanding."[114]

Casey was also going to discuss Southern Air Transport in his testimony. *Isn't Southern Air associated with the Hasenfus flight?* thought Sofaer. "To me, it was a red flag indicating a possible connection to Central America."[115]

Only by threatening to quit did Sofaer have Casey's statement about the CIA's ignorance of any 1985 shipments deleted from his prepared testimony. Sofaer was "satisfied" that they had avoided the issue "because at least there wasn't a lie out there and the president wasn't at risk."[116]

.....

On November 21, Poindexter and Casey gave their secret testimony before the HPSCI and SSCI. Independent Counsel Lawrence Walsh would find their presentations to be "incorrect, misleading, and at times criminally false."[117]

"When the session opened," one diplomat in the room recalled, "the question arose whether Casey should be put under oath." SSCI chair David Durenberger (R-MN) "said he knew Casey would of course tell the truth whether under oath or not, so why bother. I always wondered about that."[118]

Lying to Congress, under oath or not, is a criminal offense.[119]

Casey denied knowing of any CIA missile transfer from Israel to Iran in 1985. He also omitted the December 5, 1985, finding, which was also retroactive. He said the CIA's proprietary flight crew thought the cargo was oil-drilling equipment. And he barely mentioned the hostage rationale for selling arms.[120]

HPSCI members challenged the executive branch's decision not to notify even the eight congressional leaders. "I conceive of almost no circumstances which would warrant the withholding of prior notice except perhaps in the exceedingly rare situations where the President simply does not have sufficient time to consult with the Congress," said Durenberger. As for Casey's claim that the covert action was "too sensitive" for Congress, "such an interpretation of the statute very severely undermines the oversight role of the intelligence committees and the efficacy of the Intelligence Oversight Act." In other words, *Don't pretend this was time-sensitive, and don't presume we will leak.*

Wright agreed, stressing the democratic imperative of informing Congress. For "the integrity of the Legislative Branch," the Texan explained, "there cannot be unlimited discretion on the part of any one person as to when he will abide by the law or when he will decide to direct his appointees to withhold information that is compelled to be given under the law." Was eighteen months Casey's idea of "timely notification?" asked Bob Michel (R-IL).

Republicans sometimes criticized the "wisdom" of Casey's covert action but generally defended the president's right to sideline Congress. Henry Hyde called the "timely notification" language "weasel words, you're damn right they are. That is latitude to the President," and the fault only of those who wrote the law. Like Casey, he did not trust the Congress—his own institution—to keep a secret.[121]

"I was more concerned about cover-up than I was about anything else," Sofaer later told Congress about the chronology and the testimony. "I was not assuming that anything that had been done was illegal." This is consistent with a memo he sent to colleagues on November 21. "My main, present concern is to ensure that no one who acts or speaks for the Administration misleads us or the public as to the true facts," he wrote. "We can get through claims of illegality, but not through any disembling [*sic*]."[122]

Meanwhile, the CIA's lawyers again defended the legality of its director's keeping the Iran matter from the intelligence committees.[123] Justice's lawyers, under Meese, also tended to be unable to identify any crimes in Iran-Contra. One wrote on November 22 that arms deals with Iran were "probably" not criminal because the statues they violated carried no criminal penalties. Also, "we have no information that any *false* information was conveyed to Congress (as opposed to failure to report at all)." So breaking laws and keeping facts from Congress were legitimate because they had no "criminal implications."[124] Reagan's takeaway from Meese: "I'm in the clear legally."[125]

At the NSC, Poindexter knew he had lied, and he covered it up. He told Congress he would check his records and report back to the committees, but instead he went back to his office and destroyed the December 5, 1985, presidential finding used to approve retroactively the delivery of HAWKs.[126] His justification was that it gave the impression that the delivery was only for hostages. "I thought it was politically embarrassing. And so I decided to tear it up, and I tore it up, put it in the burn basket behind my desk."[127]

Poindexter's cover-up, however, may not have been illegal. "Obstruction of justice requires that there be some kind of proceeding already commenced," one legal analyst would explain in 1987. "It is not illegal to destroy an incriminating document. It is only obstruction of justice as of the time when the proceeding has begun." Questioning by Congress did not likely rise to the definition of a "proceeding." Yet Poindexter's intent was arguably to keep the 1985 finding from potential investigators. "That's something which can be viewed as obstruction of justice," observed another jurist.[128]

.....

On Friday, November 21, the same day Poindexter and Casey testified untruthfully to Congress, North embarked on the most manic, week-long phase of his obstruction of justice. Since the downing of the Hasenfus plane, he suspected that Casey or Poindexter would offer him up as a scapegoat. He had therefore been shredding documents "in earnest" since early October, when Casey told him to "clean up." "I didn't want some new person walking in there opening files that would possibly expose people at risk" is how he justified it to Congress. Of course, among the "people at risk" was him.[129]

Meanwhile Meese, the chief law enforcement officer in the country, was about to subordinate the process of justice to the protection of his political skipper, Ronald Reagan. As a prosecutor in California's Alameda County, Meese mostly left white-collar criminals alone while he trained his sights on antiwar protesters and Black Power militants, thus garnering Governor Reagan's admiration. He became his legal secretary, then chief of staff, then presidential campaign manager, transition head, and counselor in the first mandate before ascending to attorney general.[130] Three times in that latter post, he used his White House clout to get high-ranking federal jobs for people who had secured large loans for him and his family. In his financial disclosure forms, he had failed to include transactions required by federal law. He had been subject to three major investigations. In one, the Wedtech scandal, a manufacturer won a major military contract after Meese strongly intervened in its behalf and then became an associate of one of the company's directors. Reagan maintained that Meese was "no embarrassment to me."[131]

On that Friday, Poindexter told North that Meese was sending over aides to conduct a "factfinding inquiry," not an investigation. Meese had moved in this direction only at the instigation of Reagan, who told him to "gather the facts . . . straighten out the wrinkles"—and to do so by the following Monday, in three days.[132] Meese considered that he was interviewing colleagues "as a Presidential adviser and not the chief law enforcement officer of the country."[133] Poindexter identified another conflict of interest for Meese, who wore "two hats" as not only the attorney general but also a member of the NSPG of which Meese was now asking questions.[134]

Why not take over North's office that very Friday? It was, after all, the hub of the activity Meese was trying to clarify. "By the time I called him [Poindexter?] it was 3 o'clock," said Meese later, "and I would figure they would need at least a little time to get those documents together."[135] Meese trusted Poindexter and North to organize documents rather than destroy them. Or else he was telegraphing that it was time to turn on the shredder.

Meanwhile, North's main concern was to get rid of, as he said, "all of the documents that pertained to the residual funds being used to support the Nicaraguan Resistance."[136]

How much time do I have to shred? North asked.

Not as much as you wanted, Meese answered.[137] Still, he had until the next morning.

Meese apparently never considered sealing North's office or telling him to stay away. William Weld, from Justice's Criminal Division, suggested on November 21 that his outfit be included: "I'm not sure it makes very much sense for the Criminal Division and the FBI not to be involved in this."[138] Meese later claimed not to have attended the meeting at which Weld raised his objection.[139] Weld was not consulted until November 24, even though Justice had been looking into arms sales since November 7.[140] An experienced criminal investigator, Meese advanced a circular rationale in his congressional testimony: "There was no reason to select anyone from the Criminal Division inasmuch as there were no criminal aspects to this."[141]

For the same reason, he turned down FBI Director William Webster's offer to help gather information that same day.[142]

Meese's emissaries were instead two lawyers, William Bradford "Brad" Reynolds and John Richardson, who would follow Meese's lead and not treat their task as identifying possible crimes. Reynolds had done some national security work but was a political appointee of Reagan's in the Civil Rights Division. Richardson had worked on foreign intelligence and was Meese's chief of staff.[143]

By late afternoon on November 21, North returned to the office to shred with what he called "increased efficiency." According to McFarlane, North described what followed as a "shredding party" (North denied using the term).[144]

Fawn Hall, North's secretary, followed his directives of her own free will. She had been his secretary for years, not aware of all the details of his initiatives but fully on board ideologically and fiercely loyal. In the fall of 1986, she was even dating Arturo Cruz, a Contra leader.[145]

North and Hall began to shred documents from a five-drawer safe, apparently without telling Poindexter.[146] "As he pulled documents from each drawer and placed them on top of the shredder," she testified, "I inserted them into the shredder." She shoved them in "12, 15, 18 pages at once," so hurriedly that the shredder jammed—twice.[147]

The duo also doctored evidence. North asked Hall to revise four key NSC memos addressed to either McFarlane or Poindexter to obscure the role of North's superiors.[148] Hall did so and destroyed the marked-up originals but failed to also get rid of the corresponding file copies of the originals.[149] She understood that altering government documents was potentially obstructing justice, she later testified, but "I believed in Colonel North and there was a very solid and very valid reason he must have been doing this."[150]

The next day, Saturday, Reynolds and Richardson showed up at North's office in the Executive Office Building and began to look at documents while North remained there. Incredibly, North kept shredding with the attorney general's men in his office. "They were sitting in my office reading," recounted North, "and I would finish reading a document and say, 'We don't need that anymore.' I would walk up and I'd go out and shred it. They could hear it. The shredder was right outside the door."

"Did anyone say to you, 'Colonel, what are you doing'?" later asked the Congress's counsel, Arthur Liman.

"No, and I didn't think anything of it either. What you've got to understand, counsel, is that I didn't think I had done anything wrong."[151]

The Department of Justice, upon hearing North's testimony, would declare that it was Reynolds's and Richardson's "firm recollection that at no time while they were there did Col. North either shred any documents or turn on a shredding machine" and that "he was in view throughout the time they were there."[152]

.....

North's biographer called the news from Beirut of weapons sales to Iran "the bombshell."[153] George Shultz's assistant, Charles Hill, labeled it "the Revelation." Yet a bigger shockwave was about to rock the administration—one that connected the two halves of the Iran-Contra affair.

Before the lunch hour on Saturday, November 22, Brad Reynolds, who looked through North's documents for the attorney general, found a slim manila folder with "WH" written in red ink on the flap. He pulled out the documents and read. One was a long memo.

"I was rather bored," Reynolds later confessed. "I thought it was the third draft of a document I had seen before. I started turning the pages, and they looked the same. I damn near didn't bother to turn the next page."[154]

When he did, though, he found buried in that memo a paragraph that mentioned allocating $12 million of Iranian funds to the Contras.

"Had that paragraph not been either observed or preserved," said a senator at hearings that captivated the nation the following year, "we would not be here today."[155]

"Holy Jesus!" Reynolds murmured. North aide Bob Earl was nearby, so Reynolds kicked his partner, Richardson, under the table. He slipped over the document and pointed to the key paragraph. "It's hard to believe that happened," Richardson recalled he "probably" said. *This is too spectacular*, he thought. He paperclipped the memo for photocopying, put it back in its folder, "wiped off all my fingerprints," and stuffed it in a pile of other files to be copied.[156]

Rather than tell North, Reynolds and Richardson headed out to lunch at Old Ebbitt Grill, near the White House, where they met their boss, Ed Meese, and Charles Cooper, the assistant attorney general for the Office of Legal Counsel.

The pair told Meese about the diversion memo. "The Attorney General said something analogous to 'Oh, darn,'" recalled Cooper. "Perhaps more strenuous than that." On their way back to Justice after lunch, Meese and Cooper worried about two implications of the diversion. "It had legal significance, though its legal significance wasn't obvious to me," recalled Cooper, "and I am not sure it is still entirely clear to me, but it had political significance of a very large nature." Even after this discovery, no one brought up consulting the FBI or sealing North's office.[157]

Also back from lunch, Reynolds and Richardson continued going through North's files as he, a mere ten feet away, continued selecting top secret documents for shredding. They finally told North that Meese wanted to speak to him. North said he could not meet that Saturday afternoon. He arranged a meeting with the attorney general for the next day.

While Meese temporized, North shredded all night until 4:15 a.m. on Sunday, November 23.[158] When asked rhetorically, "Do you think Colonel North spent from 11:00 in the evening until 4:15 the next morning destroying irrelevant documents?" Meese's dumbfounding response was, "I think he probably did."[159]

Sunday morning, North again delayed his interview with Meese to go to church with his family and have lunch at McDonald's.[160] At 2:13 p.m., when Meese finally met with North, accompanied by Reynolds, Richardson, and Cooper, he did not warn him to preserve all the documents at his office. He also failed to inform him of his rights as a potential defendant. Instead, he seemed focused on appearances. I "want nothing anyone can call a cover up," he said.[161] Meese let North tell his side of the story and asked few questions. "He was basically forthright, and I didn't think, he certainly did not appear to be concealing anything," Meese recalled. He still thought "there was no hint to us of any destruction of documents."[162]

Yet, about an hour into their meeting, Meese said, "Is there anything else that can jump up and bite the President on the ass?"

"Not that I can think of," said North.

"How about this?" He handed North the diversion memo.

Oh, shit, North thought.[163] According to Reynolds, "North registered surprise."[164] "I was prepared at that point to continue not to reveal the diversion," North later recalled. "I had removed those files. . . . I thought that I had gotten them all."[165]

"Where did this come from?" North asked. Possibly to protect the recipients of the memo, he also wondered if it came with a cover sheet. It did not.

"That's not important," said Meese. "Did this happen?"

Not exactly, said North. The Contras had only gotten $3 million of the $12 million.

"Well, did anything *like* this ever take place?"

North took a moment. "This was the secret within a secret that was never supposed to be revealed," he recalled. "Yes," he admitted finally.[166] North said that, within the US government, only he, McFarlane, and Poindexter knew of the diversion, which was a lie. Toward the end of the interview, North said he hoped that the diversion "was not among the things that would have to be made known publicly."[167]

Hours after finding the memo, Meese interviewed Casey at his home but never asked him about the diversion.[168]

.....

On Monday, November 24, Meese informed Reagan, Bush, and Regan of the diversion. "The President was quite surprised and indicated he had not known anything of this."[169] Don Regan said the same: "This guy I know was an actor, and he was nominated at one time for an Academy Award, but I would give him an Academy Award if he knew anything about this when you watched his reaction to express complete surprise at this news."

Regan also told Casey, whose face betrayed no reaction. But he balked at telling the American people the facts.

"We have to get this story out," said Regan. "We can't sit on this one."

"Well," replied Casey, "do you realize the consequences of what you are doing? You are going to blow the whole Iranian thing and possibly blow the lives of these hostages."

"Be that as it may," argued Regan, "How the hell can we sit on this stuff for any longer? I mean, the thing is an absolute disgrace that we haven't put it out yet. And on top of that, now that we have this possible criminal act, how can we sit on it?"

"Well," said Casey, resigned, "I guess you got to do it."[170]

Meese then reported his findings to an NSPG meeting where Shultz, Weinberger, Casey, Poindexter, and Cave of the CIA joined. He suggested that the 1985 shipments "[m]ay be a violation of law if arms shipped [without] a finding. But [the] President did not know." At least Reagan, Regan, Shultz, Weinberger, Bush, and Poindexter knew that Reagan did know, yet no one corrected Meese.[171] The attorney general also never mentioned the diversion. According to Weinberger, the president ordered the attendees to "tell everyone in our shops to shut up. . . . Stay off air [and] say nothing. Don't answer questions." The chief of staff followed up with a memo that would become the administration's strategy: "Tough as it seems, blame must be put at NSC's door—rogue operation, going on without President's knowledge or sanction. When suspicions arose he took charge, ordered investigation, had meeting of top advisors to get at facts."[172]

Meese waited two days into his fact-finding mission before speaking with Poindexter. In response, Poindexter said something like, "Ollie has given me enough hints about this so that I generally knew, but I did nothing to follow up or stop it."

"Have you told anyone else or does anyone else in the White House know?" Meese followed up.

"No." Meese did not ask explicitly about the president. Poindexter did not recall being asked about the White House's knowledge. Meese wrote no notes. He also took no notes when interviewing Bush, Casey, Weinberger, McFarlane, and Regan, whom he interviewed alone. Before the discovery of the diversion memo, in contrast, the attorney general had taken notes and brought along witnesses.[173]

On November 24, Reagan related to his diary how Meese and Regan "told me of a smoking gun." He described it inaccurately as the fault of the Israelis and North. More accurately, he wrote, "This was a violation of the law against giving the Contras money without an authorization by Congress. North didn't tell me about this. Worst of all John Poindexter found out about it and didn't tell me. This may call for resignations."[174]

.....

It was only on Tuesday, three days after finding the diversion memo, that Meese finally ordered North's office sealed. Also only on that day did Cooper tell him of "criminal implications that couldn't be discounted."[175]

Meese was soon with Reagan and Regan in the White House, where they decided that Reagan would ask for Poindexter's resignation and transfer North back to the Marines (see fig. 9).

At 7:40 a.m., Regan walked into Poindexter's West Wing office. The national security advisor already knew he was to be fired. "He sat at the end of a polished conference table," recalled Regan, "eating breakfast alone, as was his habit."

Unblinking, Poindexter offered Regan a cup of coffee. The chief of staff refused but sat down. "Poindexter, waiting for me to speak, went on eating his eggs and toast."

"John, what the hell happened? What went on there? What did you know about all this?"

Poindexter put down his silverware and dabbed his mouth with his napkin. "I had a feeling that something bad was going on, but I didn't investigate it and I didn't do a thing about it," he said. "I really didn't want to know."

FIGURE 9 Damage control: Reagan with Weinberger, Shultz, Meese, and Regan in the Oval Office on November 25, 1986. (Courtesy Ronald Reagan Presidential Library)

"Why not?" asked Regan.

"I felt sorry for the Contras," he said. "I was so damned mad at [Speaker of the House] Tip O'Neill for the way he was dragging the Contras around that I didn't want to know what, if anything, was going on. I should have, but I didn't."[176]

Poindexter resigned that day, but not before deleting 5,012 messages from his answering machine.[177]

.....

At noon on November 25, after brief remarks by Reagan, Meese took over the White House podium and announced the firing of Poindexter, the transfer of North, and the discovery of the diversion memo (see fig. 10). He also launched—finally—a criminal investigation. Because he never asked Reagan about it, he repeated his erroneous assertion about the president not approving or knowing of the November 1985 shipment. The following week, Justice would call for the appointment of an independent counsel.

To a reporter's question, Meese admitted his own loyalty to the president: "Every member of the administration owes it to the President to stand

FIGURE 10 Reagan letting Meese handle questions at a briefing on Iran-Contra, November 25, 1986. (Courtesy Ronald Reagan Presidential Library)

shoulder to shoulder with him and support the policies that he has, the policy decisions he has made, as well as to stand by him when something has happened which the President didn't know."[178]

Senator Cohen later identified the problem with Meese's botched "fact-finding" as inappropriate "informality." "Here you have a family investigating itself. . . . You've got friends checking out friends and there was no formalization of it."[179]

.....

After hearing of his reassignment (which Reagan called being "relieved of his duties"), North headed to the Sheraton Hotel in Tyson's Corner, Virginia, to meet with Tom Green, his personal lawyer, and Dick Secord, who felt betrayed and ostracized by Meese and Reagan. North first took a phone call from Vice President Bush, who expressed his sympathy. Then Hall put Reagan through to North. In his hotel room, North stood at attention, chest puffed out.

"Ollie?" said the voice at the other end.

"Yes, Mr. President!"

"I just wanted to say I'm sorry the way things turned out."

"I understand, sir. I have nothing but the highest regard for you."

"This whole affair"—Reagan said of the diversion—"I . . . I just didn't know."

"I'm sorry this has brought you under a cloud," said North. "I just wanted to serve you, Mr. President."

"You have. You've served the country remarkably, Ollie. You're a national hero." ("I was thinking about his service in Vietnam," Reagan later said to explain his use of *hero*, but in a diary entry he wrote, "the witch hunt against him has made him a national hero.")

"That's good of you to say, sir," replied North.

"I'd say," said the former actor, "this is going to make a great movie one day."[180]

.....

In the afternoon of November 25, Hall realized that she had failed to destroy the original versions of the documents she had altered and that the PROFS notes and minutes of the May 1986 Tehran meeting were also still in North's office. Two administrators were already in there to do what Meese failed to and seal it up, preserving all its evidence.

Hall panicked. She called North.

They're closing the office, she told him. "Please come back."

North, ignorant of the new documents, said, "No, there's really no need."

"No," Hall whispered to North to not be heard by those closing the office. *I found documents you're going to want to see.* "I don't know if he quite understood," she later testified, "but he understood in my voice the urgency of coming back to the office."

He agreed to come back and told Hall to clear in Green, his lawyer. Hall had already stuffed the altered documents into her boots. Bob Earl was also present, and he offered to smuggle out some printed PROFS notes in his jacket.

Hall turned to him: "No, you shouldn't have to do this. I will do it." With no room left in her boots, she stuffed them in the back of her shirt.

"Can you see them?" she pirouetted and asked Earl.

"No," he reassured her. "At the time I removed the documents," she later recalled, "I was emotionally distraught and did not realize the severity of what I was doing."

As she walked downstairs, she encountered North and Green, and they went back up together to North's office, where she showed them that she was intending to smuggle out highly sensitive government property. No one objected. The three of them left North's office, past the NSC personnel who were inspecting briefcases—but not boots or clothes.

In the corridor, Hall offered to give the documents to North. "No, just wait until we get outside," he told her.

Once in the street, she again wanted to rid herself of the evidence. "No, wait until we get inside the car," said Green this time.

They crossed the street and got into Green's car, where Hall gave North the documents she smuggled out. Green drove them to their cars. Before Hall walked away, Green turned to her:

"And what do you say if they ask you about shredding?"

"We shred every day."

"Good," said Green. The next day, Green stopped representing North.

On November 27, two days after she stole documents, Hall applied her deception to White House counsel Jay Stephens. When he asked about any shredding, her response was, "We shred every day."

"You misled him?" she was later asked in Congress.

"Yes, sir."[181]

The next day, Hall and Earl agreed never to discuss the removal of documents if the FBI came sniffing around.[182]

Throughout his fact-finding, Meese seemed little concerned with missing documents, even after he knew of the diversion memo. On December 2, he said, "I don't know whether documents were shredded or not. I can't tell you what happened out of my sight. But I do know that we have the documents that we needed, because we had access to the files."[183] He never explained what he needed or why he had it.

.....

In late November, a *New York Times*–CBS poll revealed that Reagan's job approval had plummeted from 67 to 46 percent, the steepest ever one-month drop since such polling began in 1936.[184] Reagan and the rest of the White House may have focused on the diversion so single-mindedly because it promised to further the cover-up rather than prevent it. "We broke the story," he wrote in his diary. "I told the press what we'd learned. This headed them off from finding out about it & accusing us of a cover up."[185] The Meese press conference also kept the press focused on the diversion rather than on the wisdom and illegality of the president's Iran policy or broader assaults on democracy. As Peter Kornbluh and Malcolm Byrne argued, "the press conference to disclose the diversion amounted to a diversion of a different sort—and the public, press, and Congress took the bait."[186] North essentially agreed: "This particular detail was so dramatic, so sexy, that it might actually—well, *divert* public attention from other, even more important aspects of the story."

"Nobody from the administration *ever* asked me to tell the truth," added North. "The only message I heard was: exonerate the President. And I heard it from at least three different people."[187]

Reagan remained rancorous toward the press. He described reporters at Meese's November 25 press conference as "like a circle of sharks."[188] He admitted to a *Time* magazine reporter having "a bitter bile in my throat these days. . . . This whole thing boils down to a great irresponsibility on the part of the press," he fumed. "We got three people [hostages] back. We were expecting two others. The press has to take the responsibility for what they've done."[189]

.....

In just a few days into the criminal investigation at Justice, officials identified a slew of potential crimes. For instance, violating Boland could be charged under Title 18 Section 371 of the US Code as a conspiracy to defraud the United States. Casey and Poindexter had probably lied to Congress. And "some of the money appropriated for humanitarian aid was used to buy weapons."[190]

Any future funding of the Contras was in jeopardy. Brunei informed State that it was halting its Contra funding.[191]

And more investigations were on the way.

7

A CLOUD REMOVED

The next phase of the Iran-Contra scandal, the so-called Tower Board (or Commission) of Inquiry and resulting Tower Report that captured the nation's attention from December 1986 to February 1987, demonstrated the inability of the executive branch to investigate seriously the deterioration of American democratic norms. President Reagan appointed the investigators and gave them far too narrow a purview. The commissioners' labor was competent but far too brief, and their recommendations proved, in line with their mission, too focused on one agency, the National Security Council.

Collecting evidence for the Tower Report showed that the administration continued to disregard the growing imbalance in the separation of powers and the sanctity of truth, both of which began to have implications for the administration of justice. The result was an exoneration of the president and a whitewashing of his administration, with little reform to show for it.

.....

"My name is John Tower, but I don't," the senator from Texas used to joke when introducing himself. "Five foot five and a half," he'd specify, "but I think I've kind of sunk down to about 5′3″ now."

Tower's bit of self-deprecation would also characterize his commission's investigation into Iran-Contra, the first official word on the matter after its explosion onto the American public scene in October and November 1986. It would cast a diminutive shadow.

Tower was conservative and, by all accounts, an honest politician. The son and grandson of Methodist ministers, he chose the route of political science, teaching at Southern Methodist University until, in 1961, he became the first Republican senator from Texas since Reconstruction. He chaired the platform committee of the 1980 Republican Convention. The hawk on defense and foreign policy also served as chair of the Armed Services Committee from 1981 to 1984, rubber-stamping much of the administration's massive military buildup yet never using his position to enrich himself. After Tower retired in 1985, Reagan appointed him to negotiate with the Soviets in Geneva. "Philosophically, we're very closely attuned," he said of himself and the president.[1]

Perhaps for this reason, Tower saw no reason to question the narrow charge given him. On December 1, 1986, Reagan tasked him alongside Edmund Muskie, a former senator (D-ME) and secretary of state, and Brent Scowcroft, a former (and soon to be again) Republican national security advisor, to lead a board of inquiry (see fig. 11). "The Board shall conduct a comprehensive study of the future role and procedures of the National Security Council (NSC) staff," was the mission from Executive Order 12575 enacting the Special Review Board. It would "review the NSC staff's proper role in operational activities, especially extremely sensitive . . . missions."[2] Tower was not to ask about any other agencies or departments, uncover illegalities, or catalog lies to Congress or other improprieties.

Vice President Bush, himself briefly considered to head the board, foresaw its major obstacle: "The Commission is not supposed to find out who did what."[3] Even the conservative *Wall Street Journal* hoped Reagan's commission would "broaden its net."[4]

.....

As Tower and his team launched their investigation, the SSCI held more hearings. Elliott Abrams of the State Department was in the hot seat on November 25, the day of Ed Meese's "diversion memo" press conference. When asked about US government funds going to the Contras, Abrams answered, "We're not—you know, we're not in the fundraising business." When committee members specified whether State had approached any Middle Eastern countries for contributions, he declared, "We were talking about whether it

FIGURE 11 Reagan meeting with the Tower Commission. From left to right: John Tower, Edmund Muskie, and Brent Scowcroft. They were "thunderstruck," an aide recalled, by Reagan's abysmal memory or intent to lie. (Courtesy Ronald Reagan Presidential Library)

was possible to get any money out of the Middle East, and we all agreed that it wasn't."[5] Yet the Saudis had contributed, and Abrams had raised funds from the Sultan of Brunei. Technically, Abrams had not lied because State had not *asked* the Saudis—although the NSC and even Reagan had met with them about their contributions—and Brunei was not in the Middle East.

But, realizing he had dissembled before Congress, Abrams asked to return on December 8 and admitted that State had asked foreign governments to fund the Contras. He then engaged in what Senator David Boren (D-OK) called "splitting of hairs": "It was the impression of all of us [at State] that we were not obliged to report [solicitations] to Congress. It was a diplomatic activity, it was not an intelligence activity."

Abrams was asked if it was his "obligation to deny the information to Congress when so requested for such information?" The question led to a heated exchange.

"Well, it's the Secretary's view," replied Abrams about George Shultz, "that when we promise a foreign leader confidentiality, we ought to try to keep the promise."

"That wasn't the question," interrupted Senator Thomas Eagleton (D-MO).

"Do I—well, what was the question? Repeat it, please."

" . . . whether you would lie to us about the endeavor at all, as you did on November 25."

"Well, I resent the remark, Senator. I have never lied to this committee."

Senator Bill Bradley (D-NJ) reminded Abrams of his comment about State not being in the fundraising business. "And you have just asserted before the committee that you are in the fundraising business, but that it was a secret diplomatic fundraising effort."

Eagleton joined in: "No one intimidated that out of you. That was your answer."

"We made one solicitation to a foreign government," admitted Abrams.

Eagleton wanted to hear him say the words. "*Were you* in the fundraising *business*?"

"I would say we were in the fundraising business," conceded Abrams. "I take your point."

"Take my point?" exclaimed Eagleton. "Under oath, my friend, that's perjury. Had you been under oath, that's perjury."

"Well, I don't agree with that."

"That's slammer time," said Eagleton. He was disgusted. "'We're not in the fundraising business.' You *were* in the fundraising business, you and Ollie [North]. You were opening accounts, you had account cards, you had two accounts and didn't know which account they were going to put it into."

"You've heard my testimony," Abrams said coldly.

"I've heard it, and I want to puke."[6]

Six months later, a Senate lawyer asked Abrams, "Do you believe that the approach you took on November 25, in your sworn testimony to the Senate Intelligence Committee was compatible with keeping Congress a powerful participant in the making of foreign policy?"

"No, it was not compatible," replied Abrams.[7]

When summoned by the SSCI, the House Foreign Affairs Committee, and the HPSCI in early December, both Oliver North and John Poindexter, increasingly aware of their criminal liability, invoked their Fifth Amendment right not to testify.[8]

The SSCI was also to hear again from CIA director Bill Casey, who had lied to it on November 21. Now, on December 14, "Casey must have been sweating blood," recalled one diplomat. "He could assume Shultz was informing the Committee of everything he knew, including the diversion of illegal Iranian funds to an illegal Contra account."[9] But Casey was rushed to George Washington Hospital with what doctors would later confirm was a brain tumor.

.....

At Langley, one report for Casey contained bad and good news for the director. The bad news: The Arms Export Control Act did not authorize "the purchaser to retransfer the items sold to another party, governmental or otherwise." The agency's replacing Israeli stocks was therefore "inconsistent with the spirit of section 4 [of the] AECA." And if Israel transferred weapons to Iran without the prior consent of the president, that should have been reported "immediately" to Congress. The good news? Direct CIA sales were eligible since 1973 and the 1986 deals were made under a different authority, Section 662 of the Foreign Assistance Act of 1961. The finding of January 17, 1986, therefore, allowed transfers of more than $1 million subject to notifying Congress.[10]

Despite the ignominy of Iran-Contra, some people in the administration would not let go of its initiatives. "I had assumed that we were finished with that entire Iranian episode and so testified to Congressional Committees during last week," complained Defense's Caspar Weinberger to Poindexter's replacement on December 22, yet "United States 'negotiators' were still meeting with the same Iranians." Weinberger reiterated his "strong" objections both to the wrong-headed policy and to the "secrecy" that excluded national security primaries, such as him.[11]

.....

On January 19, 1987, while the Tower Board toiled, the SSCI issued a draft of its findings in what the *New York Times* called "a first crack at the issue."[12] Chairs David Boren and William Cohen later recalled that they had interviewed thirty-six witnesses and reviewed thousands of pages of documents. "It was never the goal or the mandate of the Intelligence Committee during this initial phase to conduct a definitive investigation," they specified. "Rather, the Intelligence Committee undertook its inquiry pursuant to its responsibility for oversight of the nation's intelligence activities."[13] Its report commended Reagan for providing the documents that Congress requested and for his aides' testimony. But otherwise, it said, the administration withheld information and misled Congress, for instance by failing to mention the diversion in its first briefings on the scandal. In what "degenerated" into an arms-for-hostages deal and "into a way to sneak money to the contras," the *Times* editorialized, "lying was an indispensable means to those ends." Casey, Abrams, and others had fibbed not only to Congress but also within the executive branch, including to the State Department.[14] This first report on Iran-Contra sent out early warnings about the separation of powers, the disregard for the truth, and the obstruction of justice.[15]

.....

Meanwhile, the Tower Board team moved swiftly. With a deadline of sixty days to deliver its report, the board could neither subpoena witnesses, compel their testimony or grant them immunity, or obtain help from the FBI. North, Poindexter, Dick Secord, Rob Earl, Albert Hakim, and Fawn Hall—not to mention the Israelis—refused to appear before it. (These first four, in addition to Robert Dutton, also declined to testify to the SSCI).[16] Reagan, as commander in chief, could have ordered his military subordinates Poindexter and North to appear, but he declined.[17] Tower's staff of twenty-one labored in a small suite of offices in the New Executive Office Building—"a boiler room type of operation," Tower called it.[18]

Within these restraints, Tower's people did interview fifty-six witnesses—although most were peripheral and had only secondary knowledge. Shultz, Weinberger, and Bush all claimed to have been excluded—often inappropriately—from Iran-Contra.[19] Abrams admitted, "I think most of us were careful not to ask lots of questions, other than once in a while, to say is this all okay, is this stuff legal."[20]

Duane Clarridge of the CIA painted an unflattering portrait of his own questioning by the trio of Tower, Muskie, and Scowcroft, whom he referred to as "the Three Stooges": "When I testified, . . . it was about two o'clock in the afternoon, and Tower, not to put too fine a point on it, seemed drunk. He could keep his head up only by staring at a picture right over my head. Muskie seemed to be there in body but not in spirit or intellect. Scowcroft looked like he was dozing half the time and appeared to have to lean on his hands to focus his attention on the proceedings." The board seemed at sea without the testimony of Poindexter, North, and Casey, who was still in the hospital from his tumor.

In contrast to his colleagues, Bud McFarlane grew uniquely troubled by Iran-Contra. He was all but alone in conceding that the Boland Amendment covered the NSC, and he seemed sincere in his belief that his staff did not raise funds for the Contras. He knew he had concealed the Saudi contributions. His two appearances before Scowcroft and Tower, two of his mentors, humiliated him.

FIGURE 12 Robert McFarlane and wife Jonda shortly after his suicide attempt. The Tower Commission, he wrote, "made it appear that I had run the renegade operation against the President's will." (Diana Walker/The Chronicle Collection/Getty)

McFarlane also emanated an aura of depression. Weinberger called him "strange, indrawn, moody . . . a man of evident limitations" and intimidated by the shadow of his former boss, Henry Kissinger.[21] "A bleak, unsmiling, poker-faced man of 48, his glum style seemed 20 years older," is how one journalist described him. "You needed strong coffee to stay awake through his press briefings."[22] One producer once told him, "Bud, you've got the most boring face ever seen on television."[23] Unsubstantiated, painful rumors circulated that he cheated on his wife of eighteen years, Jonda—"Jonny" to her "Bud."[24]

"Early one afternoon in February 1987," McFarlane wrote in his memoirs, "without telling anyone where I was going, I left my office in Washington, D.C., got into my car, and went to look for a place to die." Racked with feelings of "shame and despair," he planned to take his life two days later. "I believed the Iran-Contra scandal . . . was all my fault. . . . I was the only one talking," he recalled bitterly. He felt abandoned by everyone in the administration, who either refused to testify or distanced themselves. The Tower Board "made it appear that I had run the renegade operation against the President's will" (see fig. 12).

From his days in Japan in the 1970s, he had learned of *seppuku*, the disgraced samurai's rite of suicide to restore one's honor. "I believed I had disgraced my country," wrote McFarlane. Feeling he had dishonored his congressman father's name and dragged a cloud over his wife and kids, he felt he could "own" the problem through self-destruction.

This is likely to be the salient event of your life, McFarlane, he told himself. *Nothing will quite measure up to this sustained scandal. You're at the center of a great national loss. Had it not been for your errors, it would not have happened.*[25]

"Please, please, please forgive me for what I am doing," he wrote to Jonny and his three children. "I have prayed to God for his forgiveness; I ask yours too." He declared his love for them but admitted, "I am depressed now. And worse, it seems very clear that I will remain so forever, so deep is my sense of personal failure and remorse." Incongruously, McFarlane described a process in which he was largely innocent: Israelis proposed the Iran trade to him; he considered its goal "sensible," said he was not privy to information that "would have raised a red flag about some of the people involved," and a few months later recommended to the president that it be stopped. He again failed to dissuade Reagan when asked to return in 1986.[26]

On Sunday, February 8, at 11 p.m., McFarlane grabbed a bottle of Valium prescribed for back pain, placed a letter to Jonny next to the kitchen sink, took a deep breath, and downed "30 or more" pills with a glass of wine. He went to bed, held Jonny close to him, and fell into a deep sleep.

In the middle of the night, McFarlane's wife awoke to "my extraordinarily deep breathing and the unresponsiveness of my body," he recalled. She thought an ambulance would alert the press, so she waited for hours, likely terrified, for dawn to arrive. She then called a physician neighbor to come over. "He took one look at me and told Jonny to call an ambulance at once."[27] McFarlane survived.

The Tower Board interviewed the former national security advisor in his room at Bethesda Naval Hospital, where he underwent psychiatric therapy. "Bud was very forthcoming," reported Tower.[28]

.....

President Reagan also testified to the Tower Board—twice, on January 26 and February 11. The board took notes and apparently recorded the interview but did not transcribe it. The Reagan Library did later provide to investigators a narrative of the meeting, which showed Reagan either uninformed, confused, dissembling, or manipulated by Chief of Staff Don Regan. During his first interview, for instance, the president denied that his administration blessed the November 1985 shipment of HAWKs. He also argued that some key meeting had not discussed Iran, and he did not recall signing the January 6 finding. He repeated the "one cargo aircraft" canard.

During his second interview, Reagan walked back some admissions, claiming he had checked his notes and consulted with Regan, who somehow had a "firm recollection" of what Reagan had *not* done—authorize the August 1985 shipment in advance. "Don Regan and I have been through this on again off again," said Reagan. He swore he had "wracked his brain" about Iran-Contra, but the more he thought about it, "the more he can't recall." In contrast, his chief of staff was "very firm in his memory."

Regan's evident coaching of Reagan was not skillful enough to plug all the holes in his story. In the second interview, the president admitted he "goofed" in saying, in his first interview, that he had allowed the HAWK shipment. "Subsequently," however, he did authorize other shipments and replenishments. The narrative noted that the president "expressed continuing confusion on timing."

"So you did not authorize the November shipment?" asked Tower for instance.

"The first shipment, no," responded Reagan. November was not the month of the first shipment. Also contradicting the president was that Regan had testified that his boss had been briefed "in great detail" about the November shipment. Regan was likely protecting himself by letting the Tower Board conclude that he had fully informed his boss while the fault of not getting his *approval* was that of McFarlane.[29]

Another version has Regan prepping Reagan before even the first interview. "What is your recollection?" he asked Reagan. "Do you remember Bud [McFarlane] or John Poindexter ever telling you anything about the contras [i.e., the diversion]?"

"No."

"Well," concluded the chief of staff, "that's the story you've got to tell."

Right *after* meeting with the Tower Board, Reagan changed his mind—or didn't. "Well, it seems to me that maybe I did [know about the diversion]."

"Now wait a minute, Mr. President," said a worried Regan. "Are you absolutely sure of this, because a lot hinges on this. You've got to check your diaries carefully and check your memory carefully."

"No, I don't," Reagan finally said.

An equally shocking episode came on his second interview, in the Oval Office. When Tower asked Reagan whether he had approved the August

1985 shipment before the fact, the president rose from his chair, walked to his lawyer Peter Wallison, and said, "Peter, where is that piece of paper you had that you gave me this morning?"

Rather than read the paper before speaking, the president simply read it aloud: "If the question comes up at the Tower Board meeting, you might want to say that you were surprised."

"I was horrified, just horrified," recalled Wallison. Reagan had exposed that, at best, he did not remember major facts and that his lawyers were putting words in his mouth, and that at worst, he planned to lie. An aide recalled that Tower, Muskie, and Scowcroft returned to their offices, "slumped on the couch or in their chairs just thunderstruck by what [had] happened."[30]

"What the hell are we going to do now?" Tower asked. They could trust none of Reagan's recollections. It was also apparent that "Regan was putting his own interests ahead of those of the president" by convincing his boss that he, Reagan, had not approved the shipment in August 1985.[31]

Reagan's faulty memory gambit was not going over well. "All the testimony we got from everybody was that the president was preoccupied with this goddamn problem every day," Muskie later said. "Every day in someone's presence he said, 'What's new on the hostages?'. . . . I mean, the Israelis . . . thought that if they could transfer some of their weapons—U.S. weapons—to the Iranians, this could be used as a quid pro quo. This comes to a president who is agonizing over this thing every day, and yet he can't remember anything about it. My God!"

On February 20, Reagan wrote a note to the Tower Board: "I'm trying to recall events that happened eighteen months ago, I'm afraid that I let myself be influenced by others' recollections, not my own. . . . I have no personal notes or records to help my recollection on this matter. The only honest answer is to state that try as I might, I cannot recall anything whatsoever about whether I approved an Israeli sale in advance or whether I approved replenishment of Israeli stocks around August of 1985."[32]

The president's numerous statements, the independent counsel later concluded, were "hopelessly conflicted" and "it would be impossible to prove beyond a reasonable doubt that any misstatement was intentional or willful."[33]

The Tower Board did sift through some novel documents. As the SSCI report noted, Reagan called for his administration not to withhold documents once the scandal broke.[34] Yet Poindexter and his staff had deleted all their messages from his and North's computers, trying to throw a spoke in the wheels of justice.

As generations raised on email would realize, digital records are rarely deleted permanently. As North testified, "We all sincerely believed that when we sent a PROF message to another party and punched the button 'delete,' that it was gone forever. Wow, were we wrong."[35] On February 9, twenty-three-year-old Kenneth Krieg, a Pentagon intern who ended up on Tower's staff, happened to ask the White House if there were backup copies of emails on the computer's mainframe.

Tens of thousands of secret PROFS emails flowed out. Those messages showed, as *Newsweek* wrote, that North "was not a lone wolf who kept secrets from his superiors." Regan, Casey, and Poindexter were far more involved than they'd let on.

The Tower report "now promises to be something of a blockbuster," announced *Newsweek* breathlessly.[36]

.....

Not exactly. It certainly was highly anticipated. On Thursday, February 26, Reagan got a briefing on the report's almost 300 pages, then presented it to "hundreds of media" along with the three commissioners. "I made a statement, turned the meeting over to John Tower & left with all of them screaming Q's at me." He called the press a "lynch party."[37]

The Tower Board's conclusions, however, should have been a balm to Reagan's wounded pride. While acknowledging "mistakes," Tower himself said, "I don't believe that the president misled the American people."[38]

Muskie agreed: "I guess we couldn't bring ourselves to believe that he [Reagan] would be lying about that sort of thing. . . . I don't like to think that he was."[39] Tower called the affair "clearly an aberration."[40] The report itself declared that its role was not "to assess individual culpability or to be the final arbiter of the facts." It admitted that there might have been "violations of law," but it could not confirm that a diversion even occurred and obtained no documents from Swiss bank accounts.[41]

Despite not wanting to blame individuals, Scowcroft concluded that "the problem, at the heart, was one of people, not of process."[42] NSC leaders should have better overseen their subordinates and private contractors. They should have kept State, Defense, and the CIA in the loop. And they should have notified Congress. But the report "validates the current National Security Council system," the three men concluded. They never mentioned democracy but largely excused the affair because "covert activities place a great strain on the process of decision in a free society. . . . There is strong pressure to withhold information."

The report found that existing oversight by Congress was fine as it was, except that its intelligence committees should merge. It rejected banning the NSC—nominally an advisory body—from implementing policy. It also recommended allowing privatization of covert activities to continue, if "in very limited ways." Overall, it advised "that no substantive change be made in the provisions of the National Security Act dealing with the structure and operation of the NSC system."[43]

Under Frank Carlucci, Poindexter's successor, the NSC underwent a restructuring. National Security Decision Directive 266, which Reagan endorsed on March 4, 1987, pledged to stay clear of covert operations and better oversee the NSC staff. It abolished North's office of political-military affairs and created a new office of multilateral affairs to handle terrorism and public diplomacy. These reforms aimed to make the NSC stronger—to the chagrin of State—and did nothing to shore up the norms or institutions of democracy.[44]

.....

The press and politicos welcomed the report's release by largely dismissing the principle of separation of powers. Zbigniew Brzezinski, Jimmy Carter's neoconservative national security advisor, agreed with the board's conclusions and predicted that presidents would continue to usurp power from secretaries of state and defense—not to mention Congress.[45]

The *Wall Street Journal*, forever contemptuous of Beltway culture, ridiculed "the sense of disaster-movie melodrama that the little town on the Potomac has built up around the Tower Commission's investigation."[46] After the report's release, the paper sounded its own alarm that criticizing the president's control over foreign policy threatened executive privilege. It recalled the always handy 1936 Supreme Court opinion in *Curtiss-Wright* supposedly enshrining that privilege and concluded that "much of the blame for this fiasco goes to dangerous and perhaps unconstitutional attempts by Congress to regulate how the executive branch conducts foreign policy."[47]

Liberals disagreed. They saw in the report a confirmation of the administration's—and especially the president's—disregard for truth. Anthony Lewis of the *New York Times* saw Reagan as "extraordinarily detached from the details of government." He noted "how little he cares for facts, how easily he converts wishes into assertions."[48]

"Ronald Reagan does not emerge from the pages of the commission's report as a confused old man," countered conservative stalwart Norman Podhoretz in the *Washington Post*. Reagan was single-minded on freeing hostages and any deals struck with terrorists were worth it.[49] Podhoretz's defense only reinforced the impression that Reagan paid little heed to the damage he did to his nation's democratic values.

The public remained largely on the liberal side, suspicious of Reagan but not ready to impeach him. In early 1987, only 15 percent of those polled believed that Reagan had told everything about Iran-Contra; 75 percent believed he had not. Meanwhile, 79 percent of the public disapproved of the administration's diversion whereas 14 percent approved, yet only 19 percent thought the president should resign.[50] It helped that, on March 4, Reagan gave an error-free speech, saying that his administration had learned lessons and was ready to move on. Many conservatives concluded from the Tower phase of Iran-Contra that Reagan, unlike Nixon during Watergate, had presided over no cover-up and was on the path to political recovery.[51]

Reagan interpreted the Tower Report as exonerating him. In it, he claimed he learned "that some on the NSC staff had gone farther to help the Contras than I was aware of."[52] Yet the president actively participated in meetings with private donors and in soliciting funds for the Contras from third countries, and he knew about the contributions from Saudi Arabia, Taiwan, and Brunei. "I was definitely involved in decisions about the support to the freedom fighters," Reagan told reporters in May 1987. "I was my idea to begin with."[53]

He forgave himself easily, partly because he seemed to forget. "As president," he declared, "I was at the helm, so I am the one who is ultimately responsible. But . . . Central America was only one of many things that occupied me at the time." He admitted that the Tower Report was "frustrating for me," but "I didn't feel I had done anything to feel depressed about."

In the end, the president noted, "we were able to move on once the Tower Board had removed the cloud from over the White House."[54]

8

MONTESQUIEU VERSUS MACHIAVELLI

"We live in a world of perceptions, not reality," Oliver North once wrote to John Poindexter in a PROFS note.[1] In a sense, the joint Iran-Contra hearings held by Congress for forty-one days and at least 250 hours of testimony from May 5 to August 6, 1987, bore out his view. They privileged images, sound-bites, and superficial impressions over truth, and often did so in support of scoring partisan points. Democrats and the media deserved some of the blame for this game.

When looked at through the prism of democratic norms, however, the Iran-Contra story featured Democrats on the right side. Throughout the hearings, they sounded alarms about the disregard that a Republican administration had shown—and continued to show—for not only the sanctity of truth but also the separation of powers, the rule of law, the potential obstruction of justice, the privatization of foreign policy, and quid pro quos. To Republicans, all these precepts seemed on the table as means to an end that was dripping with irony for democracy. As Senator George Mitchell (D-ME) stated, "Many patriotic Americans are concerned that in the pursuit of democracy abroad we not compromise it in any way here at home."[2]

The resulting report from Congress encapsulated the divergent views of democracy held by Democrats and Republicans. Although the former cataloged serious and repeated departures from the norms of a democratic society, the latter dismissed them as a small price to pay for a well-intended if flawed foreign policy. Republicans laid bare what one of their own, Michael Ledeen, called "the neoconservative distrust of democracy."[3]

.....

In November 1986, after the Hasenfus crash but before the *Al-Shiraa* story hit US newspapers, the Democratic Party scored a victory in the midterm elections. It netted five seats in the House, enhancing its control. In the Senate, Democrats gained eight seats to recapture it for the first time since 1981. The damage for the Republicans would have certainly been worse if the election had taken place just a few weeks later. Still, the Democrats were all too happy to delay the Iran-Contra hearings until the 100th Congress convened after the New Year, at which time they would hold the majority on congressional committees. They also wanted to televise any hearings, because whatever emerged likely would not flatter the Republicans.[4]

In a first for the Congress, its two houses opted to investigate Iran-Contra jointly, led by Daniel Inouye (D-HI), chair of the Senate Select Committee on Secret Military Assistance to Iran and the Nicaraguan Opposition, and Lee Hamilton (D-IN), chair of the House Select Committee to Investigate Covert Arms Transactions with Iran (see fig. 13). Democrats outnumbered Republicans 6 to 5 on the Senate committee and 9 to 6 on the House side.

But Democrats wielded their power to little effect, and this, before Inouye gaveled proceedings to order. They let the White House review all internal documents for "relevance" before investigators could see them. They failed to seek out presidential calendars and phone logs and to subpoena Oval Office recordings. The CIA simply ignored document requests from Congress. Committee members never put on the stand James Radzimski, a Navy-enlisted service member who worked in the office next to North's and said he had seen two "action" memos detailing the diversion of funds that included boxes for the president to check. Radzimski could not confirm whether Poindexter had forwarded these memos to Reagan, but he qualified them as "earth-shattering." "It was a total turn around paper" that implicated the president in the most scandalous act of the scandal, he said. Radzimski left his job in October 1986. By May of the following year, a Senate committee

FIGURE 13 Daniel Inouye and Lee Hamilton led, respectively, the Senate and House committees on Iran-Contra. They hurried the process, allowed the executive too much leeway in producing documents, and focused too much on the diversion. "We did a lousy job," said one staff counsel. (Chris Wilkins/AFP/Getty)

lawyer brought him back to his office to search his old computer. The memos were gone. "I almost fell on the floor," recalled the Navy serviceman.[5]

The committees' most strategic error was to center the scandal in whether one person—the president—had known about one thing—the diversion. The question was narrow, difficult to prove or disprove, and relatively unimportant.[6] As Senator Warren Rudman (R-NH) later recalled in internal discussions, only "a conscious diversion" by Reagan—an act of commission and not just omission—would leave his colleagues "no choice" but to call for impeachment.[7] Lack of impeachment, meanwhile, spelled doom for the hearings.

Yet members of congress showed little stomach for targeting the president. Hamilton, who had also chaired the HPSCI since 1985, had "a reputation for integrity and disinterestedness," wrote journalist Mary McGrory. "We don't have any desire to cripple a president or to cripple an administration," he admitted on *Face the Nation*.[8] In the Senate, Inouye told lead counsel Arthur Liman that "he wanted a fair and nonpartisan investigation," a departure from the bitterness that the Hawai'ian recalled from his Watergate days.[9] During the hearings, conservative senator David Boren (D-OK), who supported Contra aid, stated, "I hope I never see the day when any of us stand up and say we cannot accept the word of the president of the United States, no matter what party we belong to."[10] Former Speaker of the House Jim Wright (D-TX), although not on the joint committee, later admitted he was reluctant to pursue any leads that might force an impeachment vote against Reagan. "I didn't want to focus on such a divisive subject. I may have bent over backwards in error."[11]

The tandem committees also gave themselves little time to prepare. They began work in January 1987 and set August 7 as the close of public hearings so that Congress could adjourn. After summer recess, the committees would have only two months to write their report.[12]

Liman recalled that, when Inouye interviewed him and his assistant, Mark Belnick, to head his legal team, the process seemed rushed. Liman did not consider himself on board yet. But "suddenly, without explanation, Inouye stood up, said we were late for a briefing, and led Belnick and me out to the Senate press gallery, where, to my astonishment, he publicly announced my appointment as chief counsel!"[13]

Liman had only five months to hire all his staff, have them move to Washington, find secure office space, take depositions from more than 300 witnesses, and prepare hundreds of questions based on 100,000 pages of documents (not to mention obtain security clearances to read them).[14] The time squeeze explained why the committees held joint hearings and wrote a joint report.[15] It was also why the committees' lawyers declined to have Radzimski testify.

"We did a lousy job," recalled one staff counsel years later. "It was the most awful thing I've ever gone through."[16]

.....

Among their challenges, Congress's lawyers needed to compel witnesses who had refused to testify to the SSCI and the Tower Board to somehow speak at their joint hearings. Congress could force a witness to walk through its doors, but that witnesses could invoke the Fifth Amendment's right not to testify against oneself. The Senate could hold in contempt recalcitrant witnesses but not government employees such as Oliver North.[17] A third option was to grant immunity. As early as mid-December 1986, Reagan himself asked Congress to grant North and Poindexter immunity from prosecution in exchange for their testimony to, as he wrote in his diary, "get this d—m thing over with." The Democrats refused. "They want to keep this going for a year if they can," he fumed.[18]

In the spring, the Democrats caved, granting immunity to both North and Poindexter. They did the same for Albert Hakim because, as Liman explained, "he had the records of the Enterprise; we needed those records to follow the flow of money."

Liman had gone into law because of "the abuses of due process" in the Joe McCarthy years. A New Yorker grandson of immigrant Russian Jews, he valued "tolerance, due process, and civil liberties almost as much as life itself since for many Jews they were often the same."[19] His associate lawyers now had their work cut out for them, with executive overreach, secrecy, privatization, quid pro quos, and criminality in the mix.

.....

On the second day of the hearings, May 6, CIA director Bill Casey died of brain cancer. Consternation followed. *What could he have revealed had he lived?* Many suspected that Casey mentored North and had engineered the Contra resupply around Boland II. By fall 1987, the *New York Times* assessed that Casey "would almost certainly be indicted, were he alive." Said one official, "All roads lead to Casey."[20]

Sighs of relief could be heard inside the CIA and the White House. "The secrets would be buried with him," said Reagan's deputy chief of staff, Michael Deaver. "And the President would be protected."[21]

Controversy came in September 1987, however, when Bob Woodward, the *Washington Post* reporter of Watergate fame, published a revealing book about the spy agency. In its final pages, he claimed to have walked into Casey's deathbed hospital room. Casey had had brain surgery. According to Woodward, it rendered him generally confused but with flashes of clarity.

"You knew, didn't you?" said Woodward. "The contra diversion had to be the first question: you knew all along."

Casey "nodded yes."

"Why?" asked Woodward.

"I believed."

"What?"

"I believed."

Woodward then claimed that Casey went to sleep. With no witnesses to corroborate, the star journalist swore that the DCI had copped to sharing the core secret of Iran-Contra.[22]

"He's a liar," Reagan journaled about Woodward when the book came out, "& he lied about what Casey is supposed to have thought of me."[23] Accuracy in Media, a radical, conservative media organization that peddled conspiracy theories, pushed back against Woodward with the counterclaim that Casey's wife, Sophia, and daughter, Bernadette, maintained a round-the-clock vigil and that the journalist would not have been able to enter the DCI's room without their knowledge.[24] Yet days before, Sophia admitted that CIA logs showed at least six meetings between the two men.[25]

.....

Casey or no Casey, the hearings began on May 5 with the first witness, Richard Secord. Bud McFarlane followed, and then several private citizens, a Contra leader, and secondary officials. In early July, Oliver North took up a week of the committees' time, followed by Poindexter and cabinet members George Shultz and Caspar Weinberger. The final witnesses featured the CIA's Duane Clarridge and Alan Fiers in sessions closed to the public but soon after published.

As Chair Inouye explained on the first day of hearings, "our concern in this inquiry is not with the merits of any particular policy, but with flawed policy making processes. Our hearings are neither pro-Contra nor anti-Contra, neither pro-Administration nor anti-Administration." The committees were to lay before the public the facts of Iran-Contra and present a coherent narrative of what went wrong: Who violated what statutes, "was Congress misled," did checks and balances break down, did covert policies betray public ones, and "was American foreign policy privatized"? Senator Howell Heflin (D-AL) feared that "we may well conclude, sadly, that in the course of pursuing democratic principles in foreign lands, we may have subverted them at home."[26] Representative Dante Fascell (D-FL) was even more stark in his choice of words. "I begin to feel right now that we the people, in order to form a more perfect union . . . have instead adopted the values at least temporarily of a totalitarian government in an effort to do what we feel is proper and right, and that is to encourage, enhance democracy." Right after, he corrected himself to say he meant the *methods*, not *values*, of totalitarianism. Small comfort.

.....

Superficially, it may have seemed that Republicans scored a major political victory, especially during North's charismatic, sharp testimony. On July 7, 1987, North strode into the Senate Caucus Room with his last favorability rating a 6 percent against a 35 percent unfavorability rating.[27] By his third day in front of the cameras, he drew 55 million viewers, and the three television

FIGURE 14 In the spring and summer of 1987, more than seven out of ten Americans watched the Iran-Contra hearings, including an appliance store salesman in Mississippi. (Bettmann/Getty)

networks dropped their soap operas to air the hearings instead. More than seven out of ten Americans watched (see fig. 14).[28]

"Olliemania," *USA Today* reporter Stephen Stern's term, gripped part of the nation.[29] Enterprising merchants sold Oliver North buttons, dolls, boxer shorts, and cocktails, "North for President" bumper stickers and t-shirts, and Ollieburgers—made of shredded beef, shredded lettuce, and shredded cheese.[30] There were look-alike contests. Someone wrote a rock 'n' roll parody, "Ollie B. Goode."[31]

All this attention altered the public's opinion of Iran-Contra and North. Although a majority of Americans had long opposed aid to the Contras, a White House poll said that a 60/40 against/for split on the eve of the hearings transformed into 46/48 after North's week on American TV screens.[32] Many commented on North's traditional appearance—his crew cut, broken nose, flaring ears, and crooked teeth, all of which combined with his upright bearing, occasionally quivering voice, pressed uniform, and apparent earnestness to render him a compelling witness.[33] While the camera aimed up at him—the "hero angle," in movie parlance—it looked down at the two rows of committee members, led by the frizzy-haired Liman and long-haired

John Nields, the House's chief counsel.[34] By North's fourth day, his favorability rating climbed to 43 percent, and his unfavorables sank to 14 percent.[35] Fifty-eight percent of viewers considered North believable, while 70 percent saw him as "performing well."[36] North described himself as going from being a "household name" to a "household *face*."[37]

But the public quickly turned away. Poindexter's first day of testimony seemed to confirm that no evidence existed linking Reagan to the diversion. Viewership of the hearings melted.[38] The maker of the Ollie dolls projected sales of 450,000. He sold 200.[39] "Whatever happened to Olliemania?" asked one broadcaster on Labor Day 1987.[40]

.....

The media circus helped to obscure the deeper debate about democracy. Throughout the summer of hearings, Democratic committee members voiced their concern for the violated norms of US democracy, returning to them again and again, running the risk of boring the American public with lectures.

Some Republicans joined in the finger-wagging. Senator Paul Trible (R-VA) ruminated that "anyone who values truth, the Constitution, the rule of law, must be troubled by what we've heard. . . . For when public policy is taken private, when Government attempts to operate outside of established channels, there are no checks and balances, there is no accounting or oversight, and as a consequence, people—good people—and policy get into big trouble."[41] Trible also found "troubling" the "unapologetic embrace of untruth. . . . In a free society that doesn't work."[42] Senator Orrin Hatch (R-UT) admitted that "trading arms for hostages is wrong. . . . I also don't feel that misleading or lying to Congress can ever be condoned."[43] Representatives Henry Hyde (R-IL) and Dick Cheney (R-WY) felt betrayed by Reagan's exaggeration about the single planeload.[44]

Other Republicans admitted broader errors in upholding democratic standards. Senator Rudman called the NSC's shredding and lying a "cover-up": "These actions and the attitudes they represent are antithetical to our democratic system of government. They cannot be justified by passion, patriotism, appropriate concern over the expansion of communism in Central America, or legitimate dismay over the policies enacted by the Congress."[45] Elliott Abrams of the State Department conceded that he had been "too clever" in misleading Congress. "Reliance on nongovernmental assistance to assist a governmental undertaking will always be playing with fire," he learned as another lesson, "for private individuals may not have—and may not feel—the legal and political limits placed on government officials."[46]

In theory, witnesses such as North stated their adherence to democratic standards, such as the separation of powers and the rule of law. Hatch characterized much of Iran-Contra as "the end justifying the means in its most insidious form."[47] But reality was different. In contrast to the Democrats, none of whom was a bomb-thrower, some Republicans on the committees proved willing to defend the most egregious Iran-Contra activities even at the expense of Congress. Party leaders had stacked the deck. Of the fifteen Democrats on both committees, six had recently approved Reagan's aid request to the Contras; none of the eleven Republicans had voted against.[48] The Republicans, in fact, were "specially chosen," according to one party staffer, "for their allegiance to the president and the party's policies" and for "their willingness to engage in principled combat." The party "reached down into the ranks," Cheney once explained, choosing junior House members Jim Courter (R-NJ), Mike DeWine (R-OH), and Bill McCollum (R-FL) so they would "put more into it."[49] Meanwhile, Senate minority leader Bob Dole (R-KS) granted the chairmanship of the committee to Rudman in return for the New Hampshire senator's support should Dole run for president.[50]

As a result, Republicans on the committees were generally reverent, even obsequious with witnesses, deferring to their judgment and underscoring their military records and years of service to the US government. Straying from Inouye's priorities, they *did* debate policy, reiterating the good intentions of Reagan such as—to take Hyde as an example—"help[ing] keep freedom alive in Central America," safeguarding Iran from being "Soviet-dominated," or ending the suffering of hostages.[51] Many blamed the scandal on Congress's inconsistent Boland prohibitions. Hyde called it "our on-again/off-again, limp-wristed—I grope for a word and I can only find *wimpish*—support for the Contras over the years" (see fig. 15).[52] Republicans also reveled in the fact that no material evidence of Reagan's knowledge of the diversion existed.

Republicans and the witnesses to whom they were friendly depreciated the damage done to democratic norms and excused lawbreaking and contempt for Congress as Machiavellian means to an end. Rob Owen, whom one journalist described as "North's gofer" in Central America, best described this justification by quoting the Biblical David.[53] When his brothers challenged his right and ability to fight Goliath, the shepherd boy replied, "Is there not a cause?"[54] Cheney among others felt "very, very strongly" that North be allowed to present to Congress the slideshow he had performed many times to persuade prospective donors. (The slides were made available to the press.) Cheney wanted North to put "on the public record" the "nature

FIGURE 15 Because the Boland Amendment disallowed some funding to Contras after allowing it, Representative Henry Hyde (R-IL) argued that the executive was right to disregard the "on-again/off-again, limp-wristed" legislation. Waving around the spending bill to which the short amendment was attached misleadingly suggested its complexity. (Bettmann/Getty)

and extent of the Soviet threat in Central America and Nicaragua." The evident purpose was to insist on the ends of the North initiative and minimize discussion of the means.[55]

.....

Chief among the democratic norms under duress was the separation of powers, which directly affected members of congress. Few could deny that the executive kept the legislative branch in the dark and spent money not appropriated by Congress, thus evading the checks and balances critical to the separation of powers. "There's no question the covert operation was designed to be concealed from Congress," admitted Secord.[56] Inouye opened the first day of proceedings by intoning, "The President may be the senior partner in foreign policy, but is not the sole proprietor."[57]

Some Republicans tried to bridge the chasm. Moderate Senator Bill Cohen (R-ME) recognized that Congress should display "flexibility" in the executive's notification of covert ops. "But unfortunately," he added, "flexibility is too often taken as license, and then after the fact it is rationalized as a constitutional power that cannot be diluted or diminished by congressional action. . . . I think that comity is important, but it has to run in two directions on Pennsylvania Avenue."[58]

Secretary of State George Shultz stated his dictum for Washington politics, "Trust is the coin of the realm," and proved to be the most democratically minded among the Republicans: "Sometimes it gets doggone frustrating with what the Congress does or doesn't do, and I can be critical," he allowed. "However, . . . we have this very difficult task of having a separation of powers that means we have to learn how to share power . . . And [Iran-Contra] is not sharing power, this is not in line with what was agreed to in Philadelphia."[59] Bicentennial celebrations of the Constitution had just occurred in that foundational city the previous week.

Most Republicans on the committees and among the witnesses, however, seemed to agree that the separation of powers should be largely discarded when it came to foreign policy. Poindexter considered congressional inquiries as "outside interference," believing that "the President has the constitutional right and, in fact, the constitutional mandate to conduct foreign policy." Congress's right to appropriate moneys did not "restrict what the President can do in foreign policy."[60] Hatch defined "success" for the hearings as "Congress recognizing that the President needs to be given some latitude to carry out his foreign policy without 535 Members of Congress, mini-Secretaries of State, second guessing everything the President is trying to do."[61]

Boland II was just one example of a recent tendency of the Congress to limit the president's prerogative. "We in the Congress [have] become so intrusive . . . in foreign policy," complained Hatch, "that every decision made by National Security Council people, whether in a Democratic or Republican administration, has to be questioned by the Congress."[62]

Cheney was skeptical that the president should notify the Congress in advance of covert operations: "I think lots of times demands for notification are overdone by the institution I am a part of."[63] By the same token, Hatch led Attorney General Ed Meese to claim that requiring the president to notify Congress before every covert action "could be an unconstitutional limitation on the president's authority."[64] In his concluding remarks, Cheney urged no "further restrictions on the power and flexibility of future presidents."[65]

. . . . .

Rule of law was a particularly difficult norm for Republicans to refute, presenting themselves as the party of law and order. Representative Jack Brooks (D-TX) summarized the injuries to the "rules of law": "We have been supplying lethal weapons to terrorist nations, trading arms for hostages, involving the U.S. government in military activities in direct contravention of the law, diverting public funds into private pockets and secret unofficial activities, selling access to the President for thousands of dollars, dispensing cash and foreign money orders out of a White House safe, accepting gifts and falsifying papers to cover it up, altering and shredding national security documents, lying to the Congress. Now I believe," he concluded, "that the American people understand that democracy cannot survive that kind of abuse."[66]

Boren, prone to lecturing, brought up the president's special responsibility: "The Constitution says that the President, under Article II, shall see to it that the laws shall be faithfully executed. It doesn't just say that he won't break the law, or that he will avoid technically getting around the law. It says that he shall be the guardian of the law, he shall see to it that it be faithfully executed."

Boren grilled Owen, who admitted to breaking a contract with a US ambassador that barred him from handling weapons because he considered it his "right to take off my hat working for [the NHAO] and put on my hat as Robert Owen, private citizen." Such a rationale clearly violated Boland II, said Boren. "If we embark on a course in this country where everyone can do what they think is right without regard to the law, as strongly as we may feel about it, about a particular course of policy, it is a dangerous course."

Owen tied himself up in knots. *Would the President have approved your actions?* he was asked.

"Sir, I think you are asking me a question that I am not sure I can respond to."

But the reason "you felt justified was because the President had clearly laid out this policy . . . regardless of the technical problems of the law."

"Sir," Owen replied gamely, "I think that I don't believe that the President would knowingly condone the breaking of the laws."[67]

Meanwhile, Mitchell reproved US Ambassador to Costa Rica Lewis Tambs, who had overseen the Contras' southern front despite the Boland Amendment, on government officials' "positive duty not to obey orders" they found illegal. "And that's particularly important in a democracy which exists under the rule of law." Yet Tambs not only had not read Boland; he had not even asked his legal counsel about it. "I didn't do it. What can I say?"[68]

Mitchell saw in the rule of law a democratic norm defining the United States. "Most nations derive from a single tribe, a single race; they practice a single religion. . . . The United States is different; . . . The glue of nationhood

FIGURE 16
"Sometimes you have to go above the written law," North's secretary Fawn Hall told the Iran-Contra committees. (Bettmann/Getty)

for us is the American ideal of individual liberty and equal justice. The rule of law is critical in our society. It's the great equalizer." Countering the emerging rationale of the Republican Party, he added, "We must never allow the end to justify the means where the law is concerned. However important and noble an objective, and surely democracy abroad is important and is noble, it cannot be achieved at the expense of the rule of law in our country."[69]

Republicans seemed to underappreciate the criminality that had occurred, as when Hatch once referred to "the shredding and the other activities, which I have to admit do not look very good," and the hearing room erupted in guffaws.[70] Poindexter explained that misrepresenting the truth to Congress was no "lie" and hiding facts was no "cover-up."[71]

Fawn Hall said the quiet part out loud—"Sometimes you have to go above the written law"—and immediately regretted it (see fig. 16).[72]

Mostly, Republicans and witnesses argued for disregarding the rule of law when circumstances warranted it. They insisted on restating the sometimes-heroic records and anticommunist bona fides of witnesses who might have committed crimes. Courter argued that "motive" should count less when it came to profiteering and more when it came to "principle." Hyde agreed: "There is a zeal among some to confine this inquiry to who did what, and ignore why."[73] The "why" or motivation for Reagan's policies made Hyde identify with hostages more than with his colleagues in Congress—or with the laws they passed: "A lot of us feel in a protective mode towards what we conceive to be far more important than even adhering to every jot and tittle of the law."[74]

"I just have a visceral feeling," said Hyde to Secord, "that you and Ollie North are the kind of guys that the country turns to when it is in real trouble and it has a dirty job to do and it needs some brains and some bravery."[75] Hyde never noted that "the country," defined as either the president or the Congress, had never turned to North—and certainly not Secord—for "dirty work." Instead, he compared the men to Winston Churchill, an elected head of government.

North was once asked, if a law were to be "in conflict with the President's policy, . . . which is controlling, the law or the President's policy?" After denying that "any of us are above the law," he skirted the hypothetical by stating his belief that "in this case . . . the President's policy was within the law."[76]

Finally, to the charge that the NSC should have been less cavalier with its legal justifications, Mike DeWine asked an *ad absurdum* rhetorical question: "Has Congress in its zeal to have its say in international relations created a situation where those engaged in the execution of foreign policy must have lawyers by their side 24 hours a day?"[77]

.....

The privatization of foreign policy and attendant profiteering also worried Democratic lawmakers. Republicans? Not so much.

"Privatization of foreign policy is a prescription for confusion and failure," warned Lee Hamilton.[78] "It bothers me," added Inouye, "that as we find ourselves on the 200th anniversary of our Constitution [we have] private citizens conducting a war in the name of the United States and private citizens entering into agreements in the name of the United States."[79] Privatization surrendered to individuals all of the rights of government without its attendant responsibility. "It seems to me," Senator Paul Sarbanes (D-MD) explained to Secord, "what you have done here is construct an arrangement whereby you can go completely outside of any accountability, any normal channels of procedure, where you are getting in effect the assistance of the Government, both in raising the money and in spending it, but you treat the money as though it is completely a private matter, and then proceed to engage in activities as you pick them."

One lawyer asked Secord if he found it "natural" that the Pentagon or CIA would sell him items that he could then mark up to resell to the Contras.

Secord explained that his prices were not "outrageous"; they were "the right prices." He also did not like the word "profit" or "profiteer." Yet he later admitted "taking what we regarded to be an extremely modest profit in the arms dealer business."[80] Secord claimed to have come out of Iran-Contra with "precarious" personal finances, yet he had about $8 million squirrelled away in Swiss bank accounts.[81]

Boren was especially vigilant against privatization. After Albert Hakim claimed to be both a patriot and a businessman looking for profit, Boren bored in: "You sold taxpayers' property. You sold it for $30 million, you only paid back $12 million, you had $3 million of expenses, so when can we expect you to give the taxpayers back their other $15 million?"

Hakim seemed taken aback. "Are you suggesting that the American public—

"I am asking you a very simple question, and you can answer it by saying *never*. When do you plan to give the American taxpayers back their $15 million?"[82] Boren asked four times. Hakim gave no direct response.

The Oklahoman pointed to another facet of privatization: private making of public policy. When McFarlane testified, Boren berated him for working with "people like Mr. Ghorbanifar," who ended up making "important decisions." He asserted: "And that is a terrible mistake, to bring shadowy people at the edges of any kind of accountability to the public into an important policy-making role, and again, that is what happens when you try to go around the process instead of having the people who were elected or appointed and confirmed to positions of responsibility make those decisions."[83]

Boren targeted Secord for the same norm breaking. When the NSC told the private businessman to give up a base of operations, Boren pointed out, Secord refused because the NSC staffers were "misinformed." "So, in other words," said Boren, "again we have Mr. Richard Secord, private citizen, substituting his own personal judgment on the conduct of an operation . . . , rejecting the request from the National Security Council because Mr. Richard Secord—private citizen, no appointment from the President—felt that was the wrong thing to do; is that correct?"

"That is correct, and I think the results were the correct results." The ends justified the means.[84]

Sometimes, Republicans admitted that privatization could endanger or weaken policies. As Hatch told Hakim, "I don't think you were trained or prepared to conduct foreign policy operations or foreign relations."[85]

But in general, Republicans argued for privatization. When Cheney learned that beer magnate Joseph Coors had donated to the Contras, he was delighted. “Let me assure you,” he vowed, from now on “I’ll buy nothing but Coors beer.”[86] Hatch called Secord’s work for the Enterprise “a pretty doggone thankless task.”[87] When major donors to the Contras such as Ellen Garwood testified, the Utahn thanked them.[88]

“Every President has used private citizens for important missions,” argued Hyde, citing examples from Washington to Reagan.[89] Yet all were trusted friends sent by the president himself, and none was in it for profit. Hyde used the appearance of precedent to blur these distinctions.

Hyde also sowed doubt on the idea that the Enterprise had inappropriately handled funds meant for the US Treasury. “I am not altogether convinced that those proceeds necessarily belong to the Treasury since Secord bought them from the CIA and paid whatever they wanted in front. I don’t know. I think there is an argument there.”[90]

.....

The problem of quid pro quos took up relatively little of the hearings’ time. When it did, Democrats again feared losing democratic control over foreign policy. Hamilton, for instance, lectured Abrams for having withheld the truth to the Congress on the pretext that the Sultan of Brunei wanted his contribution kept confidential. “We simply cannot let a sultan or a king undermine the established constitutional procedures of our government.”[91]

In contrast, Republicans attempted to portray quid pro quos as business as usual. “Would it surprise you if you found out that lots of countries are helping in U.S. foreign policy?” asked Jim Courter of Gaston Sigur, an East Asia specialist at State who had approached Taiwan for Contra funds. “No, no, I think lots of countries do help in our foreign policy,” replied Sigur, helping to blur the distinction between *help* and *manipulate* that lay at the core of the quid pro quo problem. Hyde, meanwhile, stuck with the means-ends logic by implying that any “quid pro quos for this sort of contribution” were balanced by strengthening Washington’s anticommunist alliances.[92]

Republicans also minimized the means that Iran-Contra had sacrificed. Hyde specified that Brunei, “an enclave on the northwest corner of the Island of Borneo with less people in it than Shreveport, LA,” contributed $10 million “to protect our interests” yet “doesn’t want anything from us. Nothing.” North himself said, “I don’t think that we have incurred liabilities by asking others to help us with the cause of democracy in Central America.”[93] Hyde was technically correct, although Brunei had inquired into quid pro quos and expected *something* in return down the line. As for the many compromises made in Central America, the airstrip in Costa Rica was the country’s quid for helping the Contras, and it grew into a liability when a new government exposed it.

.....

Obstruction of justice began in earnest before and during the hearings. North and Poindexter refused to testify until they received immunity, which banned the use of any of their testimony in any future court proceedings against them. North's lawyer was also ferociously defensive, at times shouting at the members of the committees. Poindexter refused to answer questions so often that Senator Sarbanes put it on the record: "Repeatedly when questions have been put to Admiral Poindexter he has refrained from responding and engaged in extended consultation with his counsel. . . . I think counsel is abusing the process."

In going over his lying and destruction of documents from late 1986, Poindexter freely admitted, "I intended to withhold information from Chairman Hamilton, which I did. . . . I wanted to withhold information on the NSC operational activities in support of the Contras from most everybody."[94]

Members of Congress were also annoyed with Ed Meese for his failure to collaborate. Representative Peter Rodino (D-NJ) chastised the attorney general for not providing all the documents the committees had requested in six letters since early 1987. "This non-production, delayed production, and non-compliance with committee requests over a 6-month period has made witness interviews difficult, made it possible that some witnesses will have to be reinterviewed and this has complicated our preparation for your testimony." He accused Meese of dilatory tactics, deception, and redaction of documents.

"We have provided all the information that we possibly could," retorted Meese lamely. He suggested the committee counsel talk to John Bolton, his assistant for legislative affairs.[95]

To impress upon Poindexter the importance of not tampering with evidence, Brooks of Texas brought up the Presidential Records Act, which made all staff records the property of the US government and nearly impossible to destroy. "The value of the paper that you destroyed, . . . what is at issue is not that value," Brooks explained, "but the effort of people like you and Colonel North to make the historical record conform to what you wanted it to be by tampering with that record."[96] North admitted no familiarity with the 1978 Act, so Brooks illuminated him: It was "meant to prevent the very thing you did."[97]

Republicans parried these Democratic advances with the claim that, unlike Nixon in Watergate, Reagan had so far cooperated with the investigators and Congress, producing witnesses and documents and refusing to invoke executive privilege to keep items from the committees. Contradicting themselves, however, they defended executive privilege. Courter claimed that "leading attorneys in the United States" were "concerned about its erosion."[98] They sought to protect the president's notes and documents from prying congressional eyes. "I frankly think the White House made a terrible mistake in ever releasing those PROF notes," said Poindexter. "They were intended to be private, frank communications between two staff officers, and they were not intended for public use."[99]

Hyde mocked the very principle of openness in government, philosophizing that it might be "a vulnerability of democracy" even to hold the very hearings he spoke in because "evidently nothing is in confidence anywhere in this town." He foresaw the absurdity of NSC meetings with the president becoming televised—"then we wouldn't have to go through all this paper chase." "Open covenants, openly arrived at," he snickered, invoking the first of Woodrow Wilson's fourteen points from 1918.

Mostly, Republicans engaged in pearl clutching at the suggestion that witnesses might be less than forthcoming. "I think it is grossly unfair for anyone to infer or suggest that the Attorney General of the United States and the Justice Department was involved in some effort to cover up or obstruct the discovery of the true facts in this matter," said Rudman.[100] This, after hearing a litany of unproduced documents, notes, logs, message sheets, calendars, telephone toll records, Immigration and Naturalization Service records, and more.

North tried his "lies for lives" rationale on Liman also as a reason for destroying diversion memos during the attorney general's weekend-long fact-finding in November 1986.

"Who were you protecting?" asked Liman.

"What do you mean, who was I protecting?" countered North. "I was protecting the lives and the safety of the people who were engaged in the operation."

Hold just a minute, thought Liman. "Explain to us how telling the Attorney General of the United States that Director Casey approved a diversion would jeopardize lives."

"Well, I don't know," North finally said.

Later, North also admitted destroying documents to obstruct justice, to protect operational secrets and agents, to avoid political embarrassment for his superiors, and to impede any criminal investigation against him: "I shredded. I was never told not to shred. I shredded because I thought it was the right thing to do. When I didn't have a shredder, I put it in a burn bag and they were burned."[101] During the hearings, Secord sued to block the release of his Swiss bank records.[102]

. . . . .

The truth was the most abstract yet fundamental endangered democratic norm that members of congress fought over. Inouye wished to "examine what happens when the trust which is the lubricant of our system is breached by high officials of our government. The story is not a pretty one."[103] Later recalling Watergate, Inouye found it "troubling to me . . . to see this Nation once again faced with this breakdown of trust between the important branches of government. . . . And, more importantly, between the government and the American people."[104]

By the same token, Cohen chided Poindexter: "If the administration would like to regain the strong support of the American people . . . it has to stop insulting their intelligence and tell them the direct, unvarnished truth." Poindexter would answer some version of "I can't recall" or "I don't remember" a whopping 184 times during his testimony. "If we continue to lie to each other, or withhold information, or leak information, alter or shred documents or put them in burn bags, if we continue to interrupt the flow of truth and trust between the 16 blocks that separate [Congress from the White House]," continued Cohen, "we will enter into a permanent state of guerrilla warfare."[105]

Mitchell felt he needed to explain to North the bases of democratic discourse: "In our democracy, public policy is made in public. It's the product of open, competitive debate. There are two reasons for that. The first is that the American people have a right to know what their government is doing and why. And the second is our belief that if all points of view are heard, especially opposing points of view, the person making the decision is more likely to make the right decision." Full debate in the determination of covert operations is not possible, he continued, "so the law tries to compensate for that" by requiring that at least eight members of congress be told. Because so many foreigners knew of Iran-Contra, "how much would the risk of disclosure have been increased by telling eight of the highest elected officials in the U.S. Congress"?[106]

"We cannot advance U.S. interests," added Hamilton, "if public officials who testify before the Congress resort to legalisms and word games, claim ignorance about things they either know about or should know about, and at critical points tell the Congress things that are not true." He admitted that the Congress was "not flawless," but it could not "play its constitutional role if it cannot trust the testimony of representatives of the President."[107]

To McFarlane, Hamilton worried about the erosion of trust in Congress among the executive. "If the National Security Adviser to the President of the United States and other high officials do not provide complete and accurate answers to the Congress, what can we do? How must we frame our questions to get the facts?" He saw a slippery slope. "Must we put every executive branch official under oath who comes before us? Must we regard every claim of executive privilege and every statement of explanation with great skepticism?"[108]

Representative Louis Stokes (D-OH) worried about the "chilling . . . scenario" of "officials who lied, misrepresented, and deceived. Officials who planned to superimpose upon our government a layer outside of our government shrouded in secrecy and only accountable to the conspirators. . . . It is a prescription for anarchy in a democratic society."[109]

Because of all the lying, Liman did not believe Poindexter's claim that the president did not order the diversion or the cover-up. Poindexter's destruction of a finding sank his credibility. "How could we believe anything he'd told us?" Liman suspected that Poindexter's choice to appear out of uniform—unlike North—was to safeguard his military honor when he lied. During a recess, Liman found himself talking to Senator Sam Nunn (D-GA) when a reporter asked him what he thought of Poindexter's testimony.

"It's bullshit," blurted Liman.[110]

After six weeks of hearings, Hamilton summed up his worries about the erosion of truth and trust in American democracy: "Our Government cannot function cloaked in secrecy. It cannot function unless officials tell the truth. The Constitution only works when the two branches of government trust one another and cooperate."[111] Edward Boland concluded that trust between Congress and the intelligence agencies of the executive branch had been lost. "That trust, I fear, has been one of the casualties of the Iran Contra affair."[112]

As with other norms, Republicans saw honesty as dependent on the circumstances. "There may be times when telling the truth is more immoral than failing to," declared Senator Jim McClure (R-ID), defending Poindexter and North's lies to Congress.[113] As hearings concluded, he added, "It is a difficult and dangerous world in which we live, and I am not sure that the public is best informed by telling everything that we know nor that U.S. policy is best served by an absolute revelation of the innermost negotiations of our government."[114]

Hyde was among the toughest on his own institution. On one hand, he claimed to "find it very difficult to defend the lies and the deception."[115] On the other, he asked rhetorically whether "a major reason for the weakness in the United States capability to conduct covert operations is the fact that keeping secrecy when Congress is notified is virtually impossible?"[116]

Common to Republican arguments were attacks on the press as mendacious and as secretive as any agency in government. Hyde, for instance, advanced that *secret* was "a dirty word," with "an aura of un-Americanism to it." But "if you really want to know secrecy, ask one of the reporters behind you to give you one of their sources. You will hear secrecy, you will see secrecy."[117]

Hatch, meanwhile, asked one of many rhetorical questions, aimed not so subtly at the press: "Do you think it would be a good thing if, as a result of these hearings, . . . if we reconsidered the staging of these kinds of public media shows where we disclose in great detail to our international friends and our enemies our documents, our methods, our secret plans, and the details of our own national security?"[118] Poindexter also lamented an "overreaction of the media to [Iran-Contra]."[119]

. . . . .

Oliver North's testimony put front and center the debate over truth in democracy. North was, to put it plainly, a liar. He lied often, and he lied about important things. Patriotic and dedicated he may have been, but he eroded the trust in his office—and therefore in the US government—by fabricating stories whole-cloth. And not all his lies were to advance Reagan's policies. He often lied to burnish his legend and enhance his career.

To be sure, North lived in a world of secrets. He traveled with fake passports and under assumed names, including "William P. Goode," "Mr. Johns," "Mr. West," and "Paul." He sometimes disguised himself, dying his hair, donning a wig, or wearing eyeglasses.[120] The CIA's Alan Fiers described spycraft as "a schizophrenic world, a world where we deal with the lie as a tool of the trade. We deal with deceit, deception, and manipulation in a positive and negative sense. You can't lose sight of your moral compass." North, Fiers thought, was in danger of misplacing his. "There were lots of times I suspected he was putting the spin on something that wasn't exactly the way it was. An attempt to influence the way things come out. He dropped names a lot."[121]

But mendacity in North's life preceded its requirement for the job. It also contradicted the Honor Concept of his beloved Naval Academy, which declared, "Midshipmen will not lie, cheat or steal, nor will they mislead or deceive anyone as to known facts."[122] In late 1974, North allegedly suffered a psychic breakdown, wandering through his house naked with a .45 pistol in his hand, saying he was going to kill himself. After a brief stint in Bethesda Naval Hospital's psychiatric ward, he had the episode erased from his file.[123]

Once he was assigned to the NSC, his lying really took off. "Ollie was about thirty to fifty percent bullshit," said an NSC colleague. "He was notorious for constantly exaggerating his role in things. He was always 'coming from a meeting with the vice president.' We checked once, and he hadn't been in to see the vice president at all."[124] North told of taking a map into the Oval Office and persuading Reagan to invade Grenada, one of numerous tall tales of a private meeting with the president. In his telling, he and Reagan also watched the returning US students on television deplaning on US soil from that Caribbean island.

In this fantasy, the president put his arms around North. "You see, Ollie, I told you not worry. You can trust Americans."

Maybe, but no one could trust North with that story, which the White House rebuked.

North did have nineteen meetings with the president, but none alone.[125] He once told Constantine Menges, who worked on Latin America at State, of dining the previous weekend with U.N. Ambassador Jeane Kirkpatrick. Menges checked with Kirkpatrick, who set the record straight: "I've never had dinner with Oliver North." Another time, Menges caught North on the phone pretending that he had Henry Kissinger there in his office.[126] North also lied that he had talked with Nancy Reagan. "By late 1984," Menges concluded that "North was regularly exaggerating and reshaping events, and was increasingly seeking to impress people through 'personal hype.'"[127]

North's friend, Michael Ledeen, cataloged several other deceptions: that North had escorted President Ferdinand Marcos of the Philippines from Manila to Guam; that he had masterminded the arrest of an Iranian terrorist; that the Sandinistas had attacked his helicopter; and that he had a "long, chummy conversation" with Ariel Sharon, Israel's minister of defense. None of this occurred. Ledeen excused North's lies on the grounds that North was "firmly convinced of the truthfulness of these stories."[128] Others reported North swearing that events that had occurred to others had happened instead to him, thus inflating his biography just as his hero Reagan did.[129]

The result was that those who were not already under his thrall grew to distrust him, even fear him. "Ollie North. God, the man could speak a blue haze of bullshit," recalled a CIA specialist on Latin America. "At times, I was convinced that he was mad."[130] One colleague who worked at the NSC for only "some weeks" said of North, "I've concluded that not only is [he] a liar, but he's delusional, power hungry, and a danger to the president and the country."[131]

It was no surprise that North's big mouth made his name the first government official's to be linked by the media to illicit Contra aid. He was overconfident, leading others to believe that illegal acts must have been legal or at least approved by the White House. He also believed other liars, such as Manucher Ghorbanifar, who might have exposed him.

Nor was it a shocker that North, once he realized he could be charged with crimes, chose to stay mum. He had refused to testify to the SSCI and the Tower Board, and when the congressional committees' staffs took depositions, he again balked.[132] His reticence was understandable. The press was camped outside his house every day, even on holidays. "We couldn't go to the store, or to church, or the gas station without being watched," he recalled of his family. "We couldn't get the newspaper, fetch the mail, wash the car, or mow the lawn without being observed, filmed, videotaped, photographed, tape-recorded, or written about." The press even hounded his mother, alone in upstate New York.

North grew to hate the press—not a felicitous trait for a self-appointed defender of democracy. "I try to read two things every morning," he snidely told reporters. "The Bible and the *Washington Post*. That way I know what both sides are thinking." He was convinced that the threats his family received from terrorists were due to press attention.[133] During his testimony he recalled leaks to the press by members of congress that "seriously jeopardized" covert operations.[134] In his memoir, he likened journalists to "a crowd of jackals."[135]

Because he had not yet testified, he strode into a packed Senate Caucus Room on July 7 as a largely unknown quantity. "We have no idea what he is going to say," a White House spokesperson said of North on July 6.[136] Fifty-nine percent of those polled assumed he would lie, just as 57 percent thought Reagan was lying about the diversion.[137]

.....

When he finally spoke in televised testimony for six days that captivated a nation, North told many truths, but many were admissions of lies and claims that he lied to save lives. "I came here to tell you the truth, the good, the bad, and the ugly," North pledged. "I am here to accept responsibility for that which I did."

North stated some plain truths about lying and governing. "By their very nature, covert operations or special activities, are a lie," he explained. "We make every effort to deceive the enemy as to our intent, our conduct, and to deny the association of the United States with those activities." He lied to the Iranians, for example. He even lied to Secord "to encourage him to stay with the project."

Some lies, such as the fake November 1986 chronology, he said he told to avoid political embarrassment. It was also "misleading" to write that he had not "solicited funds, facilitated contacts for prospective potential donors, or otherwise organized or coordinated the military or paramilitary efforts of the [Contra] Resistance." Some documents that were meant to deceive Congress were "erroneous, misleading, evasive, and wrong, and I did it again here when I appeared before that committee convened in the White House Situation Room, and I make no excuses for what I did."

"You denied Congress the facts," clarified John Nields, lead counsel for the House.

"I did."

Other North lies still were meant to evade the separation of powers or the process of justice. He was "exercising what I understood to be executive privilege," he said, when deciding "not to tell the Congress" about covert operations.[138]

"Watching his performance on television," wrote McFarlane of North, "I felt as though I were being stabbed, over and over again, straight in the heart. . . . When he flat-out denied raising money for the contras, he lied. Willfully and knowingly." Especially stinging to McFarlane was that North told the committees that it was McFarlane who told him to refer to the November 1985 HAWK shipments as oil-drilling parts. "It was the worst act of betrayal that I have ever experienced in my life."[139]

The former national security advisor, who had never asked for immunity, demanded to return in front of the committees to rebut North's claims. He never told North to "fix" memoranda, he swore to Congress. North did not report all his activities to him. North's interpretation of Boland as not extending to the NSC was wrong, said McFarlane, and McFarlane denied many of his subordinate's requests on those grounds. The oil-drilling lie, he added, "violates every tenet of my political beliefs, everything that I have sought throughout my career to sustain and advance. These are my beliefs in the rule of law and the doctrine of accountability."[140]

McFarlane stood out for his honesty, perhaps fortified after surviving his suicide attempt. North was at the other extreme, but closer to the Republican embrace of mendacity regardless of its impact on democracy.

.....

On November 18, 1987, more than three months after the end of the hearings, the joint committee published its 690-page report along with massive volumes of documents. It was the result of not only the hearings but also the review of more than 300,000 documents and interviews with more than 500 witnesses over ten months. All sixteen Democrats on the committees and three Senate Republicans (Cohen, Rudman, and Trible) signed the majority report. Like a Supreme Court dissenting opinion, the other two Senate Republicans (Hatch and McClure) and all House Republicans penned a minority report.

Most of the report related the actions of Poindexter, North, and company in setting up and running their schemes. Perhaps its most remarkable feature was its description of Iran-Contra's broad assault on democratic norms and not merely on the separation of powers.

"The common ingredients of the Iran and Contra policies were secrecy, deception, and disdain for the law," the report stated. "A small group of senior officials . . . viewed knowledge of their actions by others in the Government as a threat to their objectives. They told neither the Secretary of State, the Congress nor the American people of their actions. When exposure was threatened, they destroyed official documents and lied to cabinet officials, to the public, and to elected representatives in Congress. They testified that they even withheld key facts from the President. . . . Constitutional process is the essence of our democracy and our democratic form of Government is the basis of our strength."

The majority related the evils of privatization: "Funds denied by Congress were obtained by the Administration from third countries and private citizens. Activities normally conducted by the professional intelligence services—which are accountable to Congress—were turned over to Secord and Hakim." Those two men made $4.4 million in commissions and "used $2.2 million more for their personal benefit," not to mention another $4 million set aside in Swiss bank accounts.

The report also warned against quid pro quos: "The solicitation of foreign funds by an Administration to pursue foreign policy goals rejected by Congress . . . , when done secretly and without Congressional authorization, create[s] a risk that the foreign country will expect and demand something in return." Such solicitations were not unconstitutional, but if the money went to a third party yet the executive controlled it, then Congress lost its "power of the purse," and *that* "undermined a cardinal principle of the Constitution."

Why was secrecy so wrong in this instance? "The very premise of democracy is that 'we the people' are entitled to make our own choices on fundamental policies. But freedom of choice is illusory if policies are kept, not only from the public, but from its elected representatives."[141]

During the hearings, Senator Hatch had identified "a cloud over all these hearings and that cloud is nobody seems to really be able to pinpoint with great specificity the laws that are allegedly broken here."[142] Perhaps for Hatch's benefit, the report cataloged the broken laws:

- the diversion of arms profits to the Contras violated the Appropriations Clause of the Constitution *and* the Anti-Deficiency Act (31 U.S.C. Section 1341), which prohibited a U.S. officer from spending funds not appropriated by Congress;
- funding the Contras evaded "the letter and the spirit" of Boland *and* Executive Order 12333, which banned agencies other than the CIA from conducting covert operations;
- not disclosing operations to the HPSCI and SSCI violated Section 501 of the National Security Act;
- failing to produce *written* presidential findings *before* covert operations violated National Security Decision Directive 159;
- approving sales by Israel to Iran in 1985 before any finding "was inconsistent with the Government's obligations under the Arms Export Control Act";
- lying to Congress, even if not under oath, was a felony according to the false statement statute, 18 U.S.C. 1001;
- finally, destroying or altering documents or otherwise impeding a congressional inquiry was also a felony (18 U.S.C. Section 1505); it also violated the Presidential Records Act.

The committees refrained from associating individuals with specific crimes, but, it stated, "There is no place in Government for law breakers."

"The American system works well only when its branches of government trust one another," the report lectured. "The Iran-Contra Affair is a perfect example of how to destroy that trust."

The majority refused to reach one conclusion: "The role of the President in the Iran-Contra Affair. On this critical point, the shredding of documents by Poindexter, North, and others, and the death of Casey, leave the record incomplete." Yet the majority assigned to Reagan "the ultimate responsibility for the events in the Iran-Contra Affair" for failing to communicate with his advisors, neglecting to enforce the laws, and misstating facts to the public.[143]

FIGURE 17
Representative Dick Cheney (R-WY) helped write the minority report of the Iran-Contra committees, dismissing the majority's "overstatements about democracy and the rule of law." (Bettmann/Getty)

The majority report made twenty-seven recommendations, all minor fixes, such as that Congress be notified *prior to* covert actions or, in rare instances, no more than forty-eight hours after a finding; that findings be written; and that the NSC staff not engage in covert actions—all undergirded by the belief that government officials failed to follow the law, not that the law itself was faulty—essentially, the "loose cannon" reading of the scandal.

Some committee members wanted the report to recommend sanctions against Reagan but not enough to prevail. "The president has been punished very, very severely," Liman told the press when the report came out.[144]

.....

In their minority report, meanwhile, Republicans read the majority's analysis as partisan. "[Democrats] tried as desperately as they could to besmirch the administration, to put the worst light on everything," said Courter. Hatch was offended that "they do not accept the incontrovertible facts that the president did not know [about the diversion]." One Republican committee source summarized, "We felt the Democrats had overdone it."[145]

The minority report or "Section II" dismissed the majority's "overstatements about democracy and the rule of law" (see fig. 17). The scandal consisted of "mistakes in judgment, and nothing more. There was no constitutional crisis, no systematic disrespect for 'the rule of law,' no grand conspiracy, and no Administration-wide dishonesty or coverup." It also countered the majority report's agnosticism about the president's knowledge of the diversion with unwavering belief: "The evidence shows that the President did not know about the diversion."

The "mistakes" that the minority did admit to included lying to Congress, Poindexter's authorizing the diversion on his own (which conveniently exonerated the president), and Reagan's signing of the Boland Amendment instead of vetoing it (which indirectly blamed Congress).

Not surprisingly, the minority's suggestions for reform largely aimed to weaken Congress vis-à-vis the executive; for instance, by cracking down on leaks from the Capitol and fusing the intelligence committee to reduce the "gang of eight" that the president would need to notify of covert ops to a mere "gang of four." This last proposal was identical to one by John Bolton, then Meese's assistant attorney general.

Overall, the minority concluded, "We emphatically reject the idea that through these mistakes, the executive branch subverted the law, undermined the Constitution, or threatened democracy."[146]

The *Wall Street Journal* celebrated the minority report, adding that Reagan's biggest mistake "was to roll over. . . . There was no need for [Reagan] to offer up the scalps of Ollie North and John Poindexter, invite criminal and congressional investigations and encourage the criminalizing of policy differences."[147] This last phrase would become standard in Republican descriptions of Iran-Contra prosecutions. The *National Interest*, another conservative outlet, echoed the *Journal*'s antidemocratic impulse. It found Congress "increasingly obstructive" and found an "endemic conflict . . . between democracy and foreign policy."[148]

When Cheney later served as George W. Bush's vice president, he praised the minority report's "robust view of the president's prerogatives with respect to the conduct of especially foreign policy and national security matters."[149]

. . . . .

The months before, during, and after the summer of 1987 witnessed several conservatives bemoaning the inadequacies of democracy in executing US foreign policy. Scholar Samuel Huntington, for instance, noted an "excess of democracy" in US government. He called for a more "effective operation of a democratic system," one with "some measure of apathy and non-involvement on the part of some individuals and groups." A French intellectual popular with neoconservatives, Jean-François Revel, argued that democracy "is not basically structured to defend itself against outside enemies seeking its annihilation." Norman Podhoretz blamed "the imperial Congress," reiterating a shopworn argument, made more than a century earlier by Alexis de Tocqueville, about the need for elitism, at least in foreign policy: "In the control of society's foreign affairs democratic governments do appear decidedly inferior to others."[150]

.....

For all their revelations, the hearings were, if not the proverbial tip, then at least not the entire iceberg. Despite Cheney and others' defense of the Reagan White House as completely forthcoming with documents, several key sources emerged only after the hearings. In mid-1989, for instance, Senators Boren and Cohen released several files, one containing hundreds of documents not searched by the Iran-Contra committees. One, prepared for Reagan, included key memos on a secret plan to reward Honduras—a quid pro quo—for its support of the Contras. Boren was willing to entertain that these might have escaped the committees' attention by "honest mistakes," but he could not "prove [it] without a doubt."[151]

"We blew it," a top committee counsel said after the hearings. "At this point, it's up to [Independent Counsel Lawrence] Walsh to find out what really happened."[152]

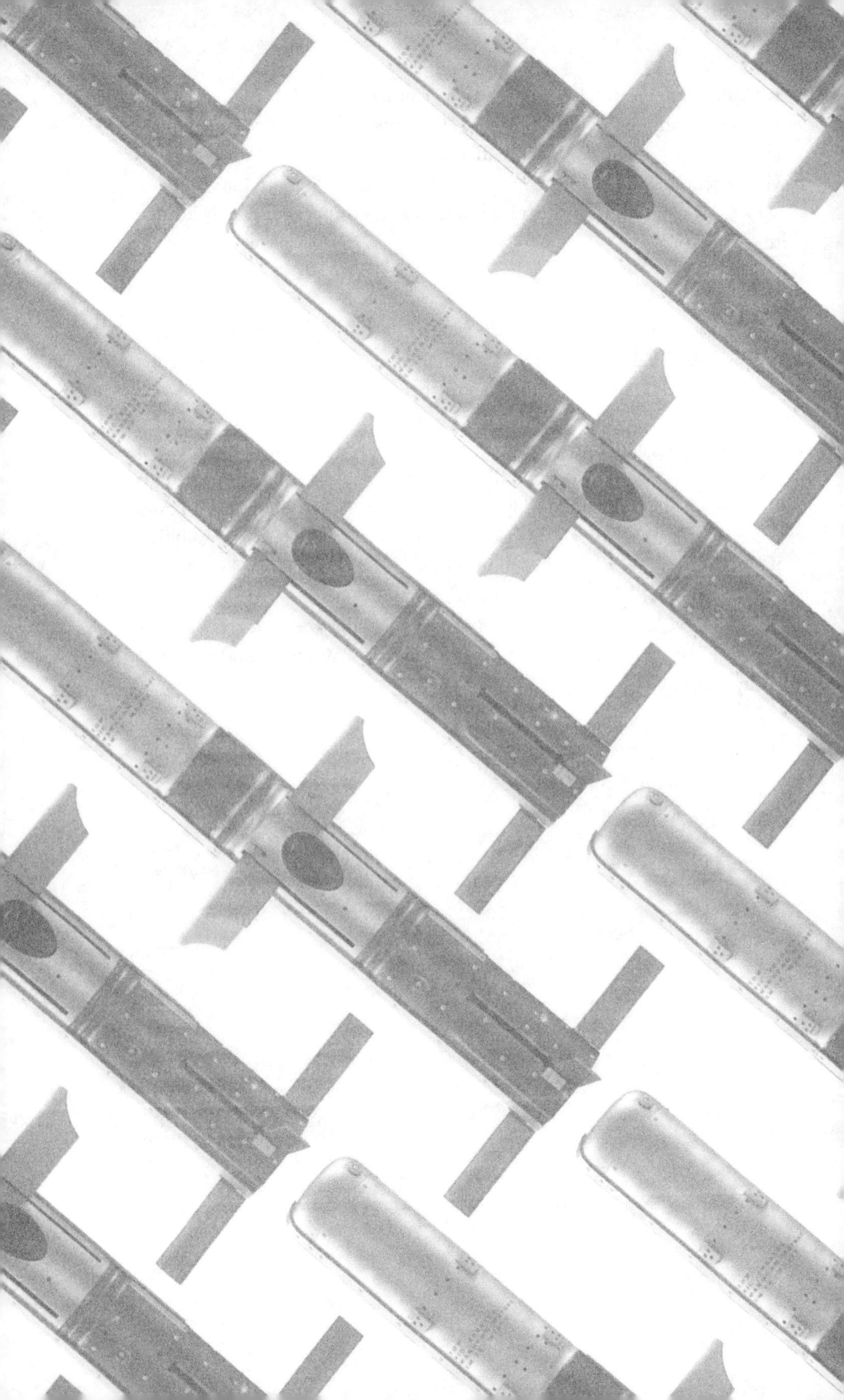

PART THREE

SCRUTINY

9

JUSTICE DEMORALIZED

Up to and during the 1987 congressional hearings, obstruction of justice remained in the background of the democratic norms and practices eroded by Iran-Contra. The separation of powers, the rule of law, privatization, the truth, and even quid pro quos were more prominent. From 1988 to 1992, however, the arena of conflict shifted to the courts, and the administration of justice would rival the separation of powers as the most salient threat to American democracy to come out of this scandal.

With the ramping up of a special prosecutor dedicated to ferreting out evidence of Iran-Contra criminality, the extent to which defendants and Republican administrations impeded the prosecutor and the courts marked a decline in American democracy's ability to punish political crimes. To be sure, defendants had a right to the best defense they could afford, and government officials retained a certain executive privilege to keep from public scrutiny documents sensitive to national security. But in Iran-Contra, both groups abused these rights, with a resulting loss of confidence in the administration of justice.

.....

The litany of how Iran-Contra plotters broke laws presented in the majority report of the congressional committees did not even run the gamut. Legal experts found that "at least 14 different areas of law, from civil statutes governing executive branch covert operations to criminal law against fraud, perjury and diversion of government funds," might apply to Iran-Contra.[1] Among the laws missing from the report's list, for instance, were the 1980 Intelligence Oversight Act, which required notifying Congress of covert ops; the 1979 Export Administration Act, which restricted exports to nations, such as Iran, that supported terrorism; the Intelligence Authorization Act (PL-99–105) that forbade aid to the Contras; and the Neutrality Act (18 U.S.C. Sec 960), which prohibited private involvement in public foreign policy.[2] Any prosecuting team had its work cut out for it.

.....

After the Hasenfus downing but before the *Al-Shiraa* story, eleven members of Congress requested an independent counsel from Attorney General Ed Meese "to investigate ongoing involvement on the part of United States officials, including George Bush, William Casey, Casper W. Weinberger, Donald Gregg, Lt. Col. Oliver L. North, Rear Adm. John M. Poindexter, Lt. Gen. Leonard H. Perroots, Vincent M. Cannistraro, and others, with the Nicaraguan rebels, commonly known as the contras, that may be in violation of U.S. law."[3]

At first, Meese resisted the request. But his chumminess with the president made the conflict of interest too glaring to ignore.[4] "My truthfullness [*sic*] seems to have become an issue," Reagan confided to his diary on December 1. The next day, Meese announced he would appoint a special prosecutor.

"I think we cooled some of the savage beasts," Reagan journaled.[5]

The law that allowed what was officially called an independent counsel was yet another response to executive overreach during Watergate. Congress introduced the institution in Title VI of the 1978 Ethics in Government Act and twice reauthorized it in the 1980s. Presidents before Richard Nixon had resorted to special prosecutors, but Nixon removed his so that he could keep White House tapes away from courts. The 1978 law allowed Congress to compel the executive to investigate its high-ranking officials through court-appointed independent counsels.

Republicans assailed the concept of an independent counsel. The *Wall Street Journal* called *independent prosecutor* "a constitutional oxymoron." The president had the power to appoint all judges, it explained, who therefore were not independent.[6] John Bolton at Justice told Congress that the president could fire the independent counsel for cause.[7] Assistant Attorney General Rudy Giuliani called the law an effort to govern "by appearance."[8] A writer for *Commentary* agreed, accusing Reagan of caving to demands for a special prosecutor "to avoid charges of a cover-up. . . . Its effects are likely to be with us for a very long time to come."[9] Meese had been the target of an independent counsel. Reagan signed the reauthorization of the Ethics in Government Act but added signing statements expressing doubts as to its constitutionality.

Equally fueling debate about the independent counsel had been the case of *Morrison v. Olson*. Independent Counsel Alexia Morrison accused Theodore Olson, an assistant attorney general for the Office of Legal Counsel, of giving false and misleading information to Congress. Before the Supreme Court, Olson argued that an independent counsel took powers away from the president and created a "fourth branch" of government. The court disagreed, irking true believers in a "unitary executive."[10]

Reagan's first attorney general, William French Smith, made the most powerful case against the independent counsel. In early 1987, he called it "cruel and devastating in its application to individuals." "Falsely destroying reputations and requiring the incurring of great personal costs," he wrote, it "has applied artificial standards unrelated to culpability and to that extent has prevented the use of normal standards of prosecutorial discretion, has been used more for political purposes and media appetite than to achieve justice, has been a nightmare to administer, and has caused a needless and substantial waste of taxpayers' money." Smith saw no historical justification for it—not even Watergate—and trusted fellow attorneys general to recuse themselves and staffs of the Department of Justice to exercise sound judgment.[11]

Despite conservative suspicions, the appointment proceeded. A three-judge panel chose Lawrence Walsh, the seventh independent counsel named since 1978. Born in Nova Scotia, raised in Queens, and educated at Columbia University, Walsh was now at the ripe age of seventy-four. He cut his political teeth working for Manhattan District Attorney and later New York Governor Thomas Dewey. As one of Dewey's "boy scouts," Walsh worked sixteen-hour days and brought down killers, racketeers, and corrupt judges and politicians. One former judge called him "very analytical, careful and objective."[12]

FIGURE 18 Lawrence Walsh, front, with three of his senior aides (left to right) Jeffrey Toobin, Clifford Sloan, and Paul L. Friedman. Toobin would write a memoir of his experience. Walsh used the word "cover-up" in the subtitle of *his* memoir. (*Washington Post*/Getty)

Walsh served on the Federal District Court in Manhattan, as deputy attorney general, and, for twenty years, as a Wall Street corporate lawyer, where governors and mayors called on him to consult, for instance on liquor industry or anticrime reforms. After student protests at Columbia in 1968, Walsh urged the university to "forthrightly attack the problem of making Harlem a self-sufficient, healthy community."[13] He knew foreign policy, having been Nixon's deputy chief of the US delegation to Vietnam peace talks in Paris. He had served as the president of the American Bar Association in 1975 and 1976.

The grandson of a sea captain, the son of a family doctor, Walsh, tall and thin, radiated what one reporter called "control and vigilance." His hair was gray; his forehead, unmarred by worry lines. He wore gray wool three-piece suits, and everyone addressed him as "Judge Walsh" (see fig. 18). He was a workhorse, with neither friends nor hobbies.[14] "One never had to worry about making small talk with Judge Walsh," recalled one of his attorneys. A half-year after setting up the office suite for Iran-Contra, it bore no pictures on the wall, no family photos on desks, no books on bookcases.[15]

"He is indefatigable," said a lawyer friend of Walsh. "There are men of 54 who would desire his stamina. He'll wear 'em all out before he's finished." Walsh could also be a perfectionist: He ordered subordinates to white out any black specks that appeared on photocopies.[16]

In 1981, rather than retire, Walsh moved to Oklahoma City, his wife's hometown, and established a practice there.[17] He stayed connected to New York firms, pushing junior lawyers relentlessly and earning a reputation for his hardball tactics. For his work in service of a drug company accused of causing birth defects, opposing lawyers dubbed him "Darth Vader."[18]

On December 6, 1986, a judge on the appointment panel called Walsh to offer the job of independent counsel in the biggest scandal of the eighties. "I felt no nostalgia for the long hours of air travel and stays in impersonal hotel rooms that had been my lot as an itinerant litigator," recalled Walsh. "And yet, a single telephone call . . . was all it took to turn me into a frequent flier again and to put me back on a diet of room-service meals."

On the first Sunday of 1987, Lawrence Walsh, a lifelong Republican, moved into Room 609 of the Watergate Hotel to investigate a Republican administration.[19]

.....

Going beyond Meese's instructions, the appointment panel gave Walsh a wide berth to investigate not only illegalities in sales of arms to Iran and the diversion of profits to Nicaragua but also *any* criminality associated with Iran-Contra. The Office of Independent Counsel would assume control of at least three ongoing Department of Justice inquiries of private Contra aid.[20] Walsh was the first independent counsel under the new statute to investigate national security crimes.[21]

"Mr. Walsh has my promise of complete cooperation," Reagan pledged, "and I have instructed all members of my Administration to cooperate fully with the investigation in order to insure full and prompt disclosure." Reagan's words reassured those who feared the president would balk, Nixon-style, at cooperating.

"I recognize the importance of what I'm being asked to do," Walsh told reporters on the steps of the Federal District Court upon being named. "We have to do it as quickly as possible." Officials assumed Walsh would take one year, maybe two, to do the job.[22] He emphasized the virtue of establishing all the facts of Iran-Contra. "The premise of democracy is that the truth is known or is ultimately knowable. The electorate functions on the basis of knowledge and a resolution of the facts."[23] Almost a year later, speaking at the Prayer Breakfast of the American Bar Association, Walsh explained how truth and the rule of law were "equally fundamental to the Judeo-Christian tradition." "Our judicial system," he continued, "is based upon the belief that truth is best developed by an adversary system in which the opposing parties advance their contentions in a trial supervised by an impartial judge. Cross-examinations, the rules of evidence, and the rules of procedure are all directed to the overriding goal of the search for truth." Truth and the rule of law also sustained the separation of powers. "If the three branches of government are to cooperate to establish a workable structure of government, they must deal candidly and truthfully with each other." In the end, truth ensured the sovereignty of the people over their rulers. "Democracy is premised upon the belief that the people as a whole can make wiser and better decisions than any aristocracy or elite. But the people can only make such decisions if they have the facts."[24]

With an unlimited budget and no time limit, Walsh hired a staff and folded in FBI agents already working on Contra cases. His top lieutenants included Guy Struve (rhymes with "groovy"), a graduate of Yale and Harvard and partner at Walsh's former law firm who kept a framed photo of his boss on his office wall.[25] Walsh valued him as a "keen analyst who could bolster or check my intuitive approach to problems." Walsh also chose John Keker, a former clerk to Chief Justice Earl Warren, because he considered him to be "the best criminal trial lawyer in San Francisco." His shoulder shot off in Vietnam, Keker, a marine like Oliver North, was "the perfect man to put up against North if a case ever came to trial."[26]

In January 1987, Walsh began to oversee an empaneled federal grand jury. By April, it was hearing testimony several days a week, and Walsh's team had conducted 800 interviews. Walsh reported having examined "hundreds of boxes" from the White House and NSC in addition to "200,000 pages of documents from the Central Intelligence Agency."[27] His staff also worked at Vice President Bush's office, the IOB, the CIA, and State, Justice, Defense, Transportation, and Treasury. Twenty-three associate counsels, thirty-five FBI agents, eleven Internal Revenue Service agents, and four US Customs agents made up the Office of Independent Counsel (OIC).[28]

Landing his first job with Walsh after clerking, one associate counsel, the future author and CNN analyst Jeffrey Toobin, was ecstatic. "The Walsh office would take on Reagan and all the president's men," he recalled thinking, "with their contempt for the Constitution, disdain for the Congress, and hostility to the truth, the qualities epitomized by the diversion scheme." Toobin was eager to prosecute "the more prosaic crimes," such as profiteering or taking bribes. "But the Boland amendment elevated the Iran-Contra affair beyond ordinary criminality. These people broke the law—brazenly, flagrantly, intentionally. Now our job was to make them pay for it."[29]

.....

Some cases against North and company would go to trial but not before overcoming countless obstacles.

The biggest impediment to trying Iran-Contra crimes came from the issue of "use immunity." To get a witness such as North, John Poindexter, or Dick Secord to testify, a 1970 law allowed Congress to confer on that witness immunity from any prosecution that would use their congressional testimony as evidence. They could say anything they wished in the Senate Caucus Room and not be tried using that testimony (unless they lied, whereupon they could be tried for perjury).[30] In 1972, the Supreme Court had ruled in favor of use immunity in its *Kastigar* case.

Walsh thus saw Congress as "a rival operation that could undo my work before it produced any results."[31] Not only did use immunity rob Walsh's own cases of evidence, but it also forced all his legal team members, potential witnesses, and jurors to abstain, monk-like, from absorbing any of the testimony given to Congress—testimony that seven out of ten Americans had watched. Only evidence obtained outside the hearings would be admissible.

The case heightened the conflict between what one legal scholar called "two concepts in our American tradition": on one hand, the checks and balances enhanced by legislative hearings; on the other, the rule of law championed by the OIC. Another source of tension: "Congress would prefer to grant immunity to the person most culpable in order to get the whole story, while an independent counsel would prefer to grant immunity to the lower-level wrongdoers in order to convict the 'big fish.' "[32]

When Walsh negotiated with leaders of Congress and of the Iran-Contra committees, he was taken aback by their queries. "How much information did the independent counsel have?" they asked. "How much would they share with congressional investigators? How soon could the cooperation begin?" Walsh was ready to cooperate but could not share some information, for instance, that presented to a grand jury: "Disclosing such evidence before trial could amount to prosecutorial misconduct." He also refused to share Swiss bank information to anyone not "prosecutorial." Dick Cheney (R-WY) of the House committee "acidly characterized our position," wrote Walsh, "as a desire for a 'one-way street,' in which they would share information with us and get nothing in return."[33]

Unable to stop Congress from holding hearings, Walsh asked that it let him finish his investigation first. No dice. Walsh then pleaded with Congress to at least delay hearings so that his OIC could gather as much evidence as possible for its cases. His FBI team discovered North and Poindexter's PROFS memos, which delayed granting immunity, but not by much. Other minor victories included getting the House committee to put off immunity for the CIA's Thomas Clines. Under law, Walsh could delay the granting of immunity for only thirty days. In March 1987, he asked for ninety.[34] Watergate prosecutor Archibald Cox, whom Nixon had fired during the so-called Saturday Night Massacre, wrote to Congress in support of Walsh. "A grant of immunity at this time," he argued, would "undermine the rule of law."[35]

The congressional committees had their own agenda and timetable, which was to inform the American people, and quickly. "The public would be ill-served," said Senator Warren Rudman (R-NH), "if we wait 12 to 18 months while Walsh investigates before we hear from [witnesses]."[36] It was not clear why. Senator Paul Trible (R-VA) made the equally spurious argument that "if Lawrence Walsh had a case of conspiracy or obstruction of justice against Poindexter and North, it exists now, and it will not be jeopardized by their testimony." He added, "The benefit our country would receive from hearing from Poindexter and North far outweighs the risks to Walsh's potential prosecution of them."[37] House members were not as rushed as senators, but both moved faster than Walsh wished. In March, the committees agreed that North and Poindexter would testify publicly in mid-summer, giving Walsh a few more months.[38]

Ultimately, the decision to grant immunity to witnesses proved "fatal to the prosecutions of North and Poindexter," Walsh wrote in his report.[39] His letters to Congress on immunity demonstrated that congressional leaders knew exactly what roadblocks they created for prosecutors. "It ought to be clear where [the immunity] problem lies. It does not lie with the independent counsel," the judge at the North trial would conclude.

During and after the hearings in summer 1987, Walsh's team found itself in an impossible situation. The massive audiences for North and Poindexter's testimony amounted to what North's lawyer called "the most extraordinary dissemination of immunized testimony" in history. Walsh faced "one dickens of a problem," he said. He considered ending his investigation.[40]

His only solution was to create two teams of legal staff—one exposed or "tainted" by the testimony whose jobs were to liaise with other agencies and the Congress and to "monitor the hearings for possible perjury," as Walsh explained; and a second team that, by hook or by crook, would avoid any television screen, newspaper, magazine, or conversation in which they might be exposed to any of the witnesses' congressional testimony.[41]

"Everybody had to stick their heads in the sand," said John Keker. Aides canceled newspaper subscriptions and asked spouses not to talk about the hearings. They changed seats on airplanes to avoid chatter. For the non-tainted, one tainted aide wrote daily news summaries of Iran-Contra developments that excluded immunized testimony.[42] Walsh swore that, when he watched television and heard the name of one of the immunized witnesses, "I turn[ed] it off."[43] Sometimes he called his wife in Oklahoma City, one time zone earlier than in Washington, for her to watch network news programs. If they had not covered Iran-Contra, he could watch.[44]

All these restrictions also applied to the twenty-three grand jurors. "The blackout had to be almost total," Walsh recalled: no electronic news of any kind, and only the local news, sports, and features in newspapers.[45]

"Are you saying," OIC staffers asked their bosses, "that when the testimony starts, we can't read newspapers?"

"You can't read any story that might make a reference to the Iran-Contra affair," was the answer.

"No television news at all?"

"That, too." *At cocktail parties*, they added, *cover your ears*.

What? That was impossible in Washington, of all places, said the lawyers. Even Walsh was flabbergasted: "How can I be the only person in America not reading the newspaper?"[46]

Accidents were unavoidable. One time, Guy Struve and his five-year-old son were strolling through Central Park when a newspaper with "something about Ollie in it" blew across their path.[47] Toobin strained to avoid sidewalk newspaper dispensers. "I found myself almost jerking my head in an attempt to avoid the giant letters that heralded the birth of a new folk hero."[48]

Walsh also had to file sealed reports to the Federal District Court in Washington that would be unsealed only after the hearings. This step would prove what evidence Walsh's team had gathered before the immunized testimony.[49]

This monasticism was to last from the start of the hearings until the end of the trials, which could be years. When Congress's report came out in November 1987, part of Walsh's team could not read it.

Also overwhelming and complicating Walsh's task were the records of private corporations. *Just send us everything*, his people told companies tied to Iran-Contra, and everything is what they seemed to get. Sometimes, "box after box after box" of documents flowed into Walsh's cramped offices.[50]

Walsh also requested documents from thirteen countries, but *their* corporations and governments were under no obligation to comply.[51] Swiss bankers appealed to Swiss courts for full hearings, which they received, and so Walsh had none of the records to prove the diversion until late 1987, after the hearings. By the time he did, Congress had already given immunity to Albert Hakim, who had moved his funds around.[52] The Israeli government also balked, even after Walsh himself offered immunity.[53] Walsh had to drop demands for four Israelis to appear before him in return for access to Swiss bank records and Israeli documents.[54] None of either country's citizens testified.

An institution that ultimately proved more of a roadblock to justice was, paradoxically, the Justice Department and the Reagan administration more broadly. Walsh made the "basic mistake," as he later called it, of asking for documents in writing rather than issuing subpoenas. "I was acting like a government lawyer who could expect honest compliance by a government agency." Subpoenas might also "invite litigation." Without subpoenas, executive officials could refuse to release or declassify documents. Walsh grew all too aware that "the administration, having been forced to retain me, regarded itself as an adversary rather than a client." Those involved in national security might not want their secrets revealed to the public in the courts, even if these were simply embarrassing rather than hazardous to national security. They certainly would not want crimes exposed. Thus, "we found ourselves between the hammer and the anvil," wrote Walsh: "Congress was trying to rush us to a superficial conclusion, while the national security community tried to delay our progress."[55]

In one instance, Walsh accused William Bradford Reynolds, one of the assistant attorneys general who found the diversion memo in November 1986, of trying to give his office details of North's testimony that could defy the immunity ruling and sabotage his case. Reynolds dismissed his information as "simply a brief, inadvertent reference" to North's television testimony. The incident indicated the landmines around which Walsh's team tiptoed.[56]

The White House and National Security Council also put up roadblocks. FBI agents asked for some documents from the former only to be "deemed irrelevant by White House counsel." Individuals produced their own notes "either late or in incomplete form, or both; in some cases, individuals falsely claimed not to have any notes at all."[57] One judge wrote in his diary: "No documents move, justice demoralized. . . . White House is the key. They continue to resist."[58]

At the CIA, Acting Director Robert Gates ordered an internal investigation. To Walsh, this was more obstruction. "No longer would we be able to question CIA witnesses while they were fresh. They would already have run their stories by the inspector general. The CIA high command—Gates and his director of operations, Clair George—would learn where the agency was vulnerable before we had a chance to uncover the truth."[59] Walsh also faulted the CIA for withholding documents until he threatened subpoenas.[60] The president's special advisor on Iran-Contra would admit that the CIA "was very slow" in producing evidence, citing a "scary dimension" in giving documents to investigators. "Conceivably, any one of them might contain a smoking gun—something incriminating of the president."[61]

A clearer statement of withholding evidence for political purposes could hardly have been uttered.

Out of its hundreds of interviews, the OIC did glean significant new information. Fawn Hall, for instance, revealed that North kept meticulous notebooks of his daily activities. Robert Earl informed the Walsh team that North said that Reagan told him that it was important that he "not know"—whatever that meant. According to Walsh, other individuals such as State's Elliott Abrams, the CIA's Alan Fiers and Duane Clarridge, and former ambassador Edwin Corr lied in their interviews.[62]

.....

One final significant problem for the OIC was choosing which crimes to prosecute. Legal experts foresaw broad impediments. First was that neither the Boland Amendment nor the Constitution clearly classified what North and others had done as a crime. The spirit, yes, but not necessarily the letter, and violating both was required in criminal law.

Walsh's chief FBI agent once lamented, "The Boland amendment? The *Boland* amendment? What the hell kind of crime is that? Sheeet."

Boland had no criminal punishment attached to it. It merely prohibited the expenditure of government funds to the Contras. Toobin thought it was still a more serious offense than lying or stealing. "History, I thought, would see the Boland amendment violations by North and the others as their most significant misdeeds. The way they flouted the will of Congress seemed to me more than a mere criminal violation, but a challenge to our constitutional system of checks and balances. They acted like they were above the law."[63]

Obstruction was also difficult to prove because, at the NSC at least, it occurred only if North and Poindexter destroyed papers or emails while knowing they were under criminal investigation. The sloppiness of Meese's November 1986 investigation left that question open.

Aware he faced "terrible legal troubles," Walsh tried instead to prove a conspiracy to defraud the government under a broad federal statute that covered a systematic abuse of power.[64] Other possible charges included "spending unappropriated funds, theft of government property (the Iran arms profits), mail fraud, personal enrichment, and obstruction—destroying records and providing false testimony."[65]

.....

In May and June 1987, the congressional testimony of the immunized witnesses crept ever closer. Walsh's assistant counsels felt more rushed. They had no time to tell worthwhile from worthless documents, so agencies felt free to withhold sensitive ones. As Walsh explained, "We accepted [Secretary of Defense] Caspar Weinberger's denial that he had relevant notes, for example, and we accepted the assurance of [Secretary of State] George Shultz's executive assistant, Charles Hill, that he had given us all of Shultz's relevant notes. The CIA, which produced thousands of documents, withheld for months the working files of Charles Allen, who had worked closely with North. As Walsh recalled, "notes of the two critical restricted interagency group meetings in August and September 1986, at which North had disclosed his activities, were also kept from us."[66]

.....

The consequences of obstruction, criminal or not, were in full view in the long run-up to the trial of Oliver North.

North's command TV performance at the 1987 hearings made prosecuting him for criminal charges challenging. As James Reston wrote in the *New York Times*, "It's hard to imagine any prosecutor putting together a jury that would convict him and even harder to imagine Mr. Reagan permitting it if any jury tried."[67] The usually routine task of finding jurors who did not know or had no opinion of a defendant proved excruciating in North's case, and the possibility of a pardon hovered over the trial. One did go forward, but not for lack of attempts by North to obstruct it.

In February 1987, one of the first moves North made against Walsh was to file suit claiming that the Ethics in Government Act was unconstitutional because it infringed on the prosecutorial powers of the executive branch. The administration had said the law violated the separation of powers by turning over prosecutions to the courts. Even though North was technically suing

Attorney General Ed Meese, some Department of Justice officials joined in North's criticism of the OIC.[68]

Walsh asked to dismiss North's suit, saying it would delay and obstruct his work by inviting "witnesses to withhold cooperation and to challenge" subpoenas.[69] He also persuaded Meese to reappoint him as an independent officer at Justice and thus render moot the accusation that Walsh was not in the executive.[70]

North responded with a second lawsuit, this time claiming that Meese lacked the authority to reappoint Walsh.[71] "NORTH DROPS BOMB ON PROBE," headlined the *New York Post*. Walsh's associate counsels greeted the news with "disbelief—and more than a little fear," recalled Toobin.

In pretrial proceedings, North's lawyer, in a voice "trembling with outrage," called the OIC "a group of what essentially are *vigilantes*, private citizens who have no authority."

At these words, the judge looked up from the lectern, directed his disbelieving gaze at North, and asked: "Who are the vigilantes you refer to?"[72] Within days, a federal district judge dismissed both North suits on procedural grounds.[73]

On May 8, just as the congressional hearings were off and running, North moved to quash a grand jury subpoena for a sample of his handwriting. A judge held North in contempt while he refused to provide even a signature.[74]

In June, North's wife Betsy invoked the Fifth Amendment and refused to testify before the grand jury.[75]

That same month, congressional investigators ordered North to hand over personal notebooks and other documents or face criminal contempt proceedings.[76]

.....

As the hearings transfixed the nation and the committees published their reports, North's team engaged in more pretrial shenanigans. By July 1987, North appealed a ruling that Walsh's authority was valid.[77] The following month, the federal appeals court upheld the authority for Walsh. North also had to give his signature or face prison.[78] In January 1988, skirmishes spilled into the Supreme Court, which North petitioned, in vain, to block the investigation.[79]

Meanwhile, both Walsh's and North's teams prepared for trial. They could review tens of thousands of classified documents only in a Sensitive Compartmented Information Facility (SCIF). Deep inside a former private law firm, at a cost of $200,000, the SCIF was transformed into a fortress of secrets. Its security officers let in only those with a special pass and a four-digit code, which changed every week. Twenty-seven experts and lawyers from the intelligence community had vetted its contents. Justice Department officers monitored all work in the SCIF. Its IBM processors and Hewlett-Packard printers featured special shielding to prevent interception of their faint electronic signals. "It had all the charm of a subway tunnel," recalled North. Rent on the room? $336,000 per year.[80]

Such security derived from a 1980 law, the Classified Information Procedures Act (CIPA). Before CIPA, many national security cases simply were not prosecuted for fear of "graymail," or the ability of the prosecution or defense to leak state secrets and thus sabotage the case. Sandra Jordan, an associate counsel on Walsh's team, explained that "a defendant could threaten to reveal secrets of the nation hoping that the government would rather forego the prosecution than risk disclosure." She called graymail "a not-so-subtle form of legal blackmail."[81] After CIPA, judges had guidelines—convoluted guidelines, but guidelines nevertheless—to determine what documents were admissible. But the threat remained, and North and other Iran-Contra defendants wielded it.

.....

On March 16, 1988, after a fourteen-month grand jury investigation, Walsh filed a 101-page, twenty-three-count indictment against North, Poindexter, Secord, and Hakim together. One observer judged it "the most sweeping case against White House operators since Watergate."[82] The criminal offenses divided into four categories: first, conspiring to defraud the United States by obstructing government functions; second, diverting public funds to so-called public ends, meaning the Contras; third, diverting public funds to private ends (i.e., profiteering); and, fourth, lying or withholding information from Congress and the attorney general. Conspiracy, diversion, theft, and cover-up: some counts applied to more than one defendant, and each defendant also had individual counts—including, for example, North for obstruction of Congress and accepting a gratuity (the security fence); Poindexter for lying to Congress; Secord for paying for North's fence and offering an illegal gratuity (the button account) to North's children; and Hakim for conspiring in Secord's gratuities.[83]

The *New York Times* took the opportunity of the indictment to mark that Iran-Contra not only "perverted democracy" but also reflected President Reagan's political values. "The defendants are the President's men. He has never repudiated their actions or called them anything but heroes.

Even now, he condones their conduct and makes light of the prosecution.[84] The *Miami Herald* also took Reagan to task for "treat[ing] the affair as a matter of politics and patriotism run amok. It is much more. Iranscam defiled the very processes by which the Government maintains its legitimacy."[85]

.....

One law enforcement official predicted what would follow the indictment: "pre-trial nuclear warfare."[86] Overseeing that battle would be US District Judge Gerhard Gesell (pronounced "gazelle"). The son of a prominent developmental psychologist, Gesell had attended Yale Law School, worked at the Securities and Exchange Commission under future Supreme Court justice William Douglas, became a leading antitrust lawyer, and, like Lawrence Walsh, was a moderate-to-liberal Republican.[87]

Lyndon Johnson appointed Gesell to a federal judgeship in 1967. There, he had dealt with the most divisive issues, including abortion and integration of the armed forces. He had struck down an order by Nixon to prevent the publication of the Pentagon Papers by the *Washington Post*. Most recently, he had presided over Watergate proceedings. "It is impossible to preserve freedom anywhere when zealots take over and the rule of law is ignored," he had said during that scandal.[88]

In 1988, Gesell, a white-haired seventy-seven-year-old, was admired as "one of the best-known and most experienced trial judges in the nation," according to the *Austin American-Statesman*.[89] In his spare time, the man with "a face like a two-year-old potato," as one admirer wrote, kept bees and made honey. No-nonsense, impartial, ethical, and energetic, Gesell promised an expeditious trial.[90]

For the case against North, Poindexter, Secord, and Hakim, Gesell began the only diary he ever kept. "If it goes to a jury all the way," he predicted in it, "it will be the greatest political trial in the history of the US and there will be many lessons learned."[91]

The indictments of North et al. shocked the conservative press. The *Wall Street Journal* judged them a worse travesty than the actual crimes of Iran-Contra. The paper did not deny the facts in the indictments but merely condemned their "frivolousness." It also valued feelings over facts. "Let's take a poll," it asked readers: "Do you feel more defrauded by Ollie North, or by Congress and this special prosecutor?"[92]

Even Ronald Reagan, inappropriately, said in public that he considered the four men not guilty. "I find it hard to think of as a scandal," he added of

Iran-Contra. Seventy percent of poll respondents disagreed with Reagan that North was a "hero."[93]

Despite the fears of conservatives, Gesell was fair to the defendants. He agreed to delay the trial until after the fall 1988 elections, preventing undue politicization and granting the defense more time to review documents. He also loosened CIPA restrictions so that defense lawyers could access Walsh's documents sooner.[94]

But Gesell sided with Walsh when North's lawyers used their client's immunity to call into question the entire trial. "Defendants will attempt to so disrupt the case it can't be tried," he confided to his diary in April 1988. "They filed several so-called motions refusing to do what I ordered."[95] In July, the American Civil Liberties Union joined North and other defendants in asking the US Court of Appeals to dismiss charges. One ACLU attorney was torn: "We believe it is critically important that constitutional rights be afforded even to those who may . . . have subverted the Constitution."[96] Gesell agreed in principle, but would not, for instance, allow the defense to examine Walsh's staff to ensure that none had been exposed to congressional testimony.[97] He repeatedly refused to dismiss the case on the immunity issue.

Sharpening the contrast between his rights to evidence as a defendant and the government's rights to keep secrets, North graymailed his former employer, demanding to see documents that potentially revealed just about every high-level national security secret since 1984. Predictably, the Justice Department refused to affirm even the most open secrets, such as the existence of the Ilopango airfield in El Salvador. Or the identity of countries that everyone knew had given aid to the Contras, such as China and Saudi Arabia. Or that the transshipment country for arms sales was to be Portugal—a fact that Secord had divulged on TV. "You have documents stamped with the highest possible classification that are just twaddle," fumed Judge Gesell.[98] North hoped that Gesell would dismiss the case, or at least some of its charges, because of the lack of evidence.[99] The judge did threaten dismissal, accusing the government of "intentional holding of documents necessary for the defense." He specified, however, that "the responsibility lies with the Attorney General and the White House," and not with Walsh.[100]

The biggest blow to Walsh's case may have come on June 8, 1988, when Gesell severed the combined case against North, Poindexter, Secord, and Hakim into four separate lawsuits. He had previously called the suggestion "ridiculous" but came around to seeing it as the best way to protect the four defendants' civil liberties.[101] As the *Los Angeles Times* explained, "North might defend himself, for example, by calling Poindexter and asking him about his testimony that he ordered the arms-for-hostages swap. But doing that in front of a jury also deciding Poindexter's fate would deny him a fair trial."[102] For Walsh, Gesell's ruling not only reduced the chances of conviction—especially for the charge of conspiracy, with a single defendant in the dock—but also created what the *New York Times* called a "logistical nightmare."[103] Walsh assessed the additional commitment needed for four trials instead of one as "at least two years" and "millions of dollars."[104] Gesell's decision was "a punch in the gut" for the OIC, wrote Toobin.[105]

Some people in Congress now wondered if granting immunity to so many witnesses had been wise. What had the congressional hearings achieved, really? Gesell felt that Congress "pushed perhaps beyond the legislative goal . . . for more selfish reasons." By June, his diary entries revealed pessimism:

> Walsh can't control gov[ernmen]t. His classified paper man not experienced and can't tell who is in charge. . . .
>
> Meese out to lunch . . .
>
> CIA will control result—Believe now case will never be tried.[106]

In mid-1988, North's graymailing resumed. Gesell ruled that the defendant could use classified documents that tended to exonerate him of conspiracy charges because they demonstrated that high-level Reagan officials knew his secrets. The interagency group declassifying documents had so far screened or censored 82,000 of 300,000 requested pages. The White House claimed it was working as fast as it could. North's lawyers then demanded to see 147 "additional categories of documents" that Walsh had not yet seen.[107] In May, Gesell refused, but then in July, he agreed to about twenty categories or programs.

Little by little, graymail by North and the government's glacial declassification forced Walsh to back off his own indictment. In late October 1988, he consented to drop one of the sixteen criminal charges against North—the cover-up of the $14,000 security system for his home. Defense argued that obstruction of justice had not occurred because the grand jury was not convened until the month after North forged backdated letters accepting the system. This technicality chipped away at North's accountability.[108]

In mid-November, however, Gesell denied a request to dismiss charges that North lied to investigators and tried to obstruct Meese's inquiry. By thinking that no government official could ask him about Iran-Contra in his NSC days, said Gesell angrily, North evinced a "skewed attitude toward our form of government." The lieutenant colonel thought "that he had the absolute right to lie, to obstruct such inquiries, and to remove or destroy official NSC records because he had not been warned that if he did so, he might be indicted." The judge added, "Ours is a country governed by the rule of law. There is nothing in the Constitution, federal statues, or applicable decisions which warrants this cynical approach."[109]

In the run-up to the trial, Gesell received what he described as "wild letters from [the] public" reflecting divisions over North's attitude toward democratic norms.[110] Most letters warned of the lieutenant colonel's criminality. "Please do not let that slimy North slither out of your grasp and get away with his thieving, shredding and perjuring," wrote Rosemary Brown of Florida. "It would set a wicked precedent for future administrations to commit any nefarious acts they please, if you allow Reagan, Bush and their co-conspirators to wrap themselves in the ridiculous excuse of 'national security.' "[111] Robert Clark of Philadelphia agreed: "*Please*, in the name of governmental honesty, truth, and plain good common sense, *don't* let Ollie North get away with the law breaking he has committed. . . . It's extremely important that our youth see that it's *wrong* to break the law."[112]

George Kehler of Tennessee, meanwhile, made the conservative case that Cold War ends justified criminal methods: "The danger is so great that any means is right and legal in this instance in order to stop communism. . . . This is not a case of law or congress, but *survival*."[113] Owen Cain of Texas made another argument common among conservatives, that popularity trumped criminal responsibility. North, Poindexter, and Secord "have already been tried before the Iran-Contra Committee Inquisition and the National Television Media." They were "found innocent by reason of patriotism and . . . by virtue of the outcry of millions of citizens."[114]

In December 1988, exasperated by blatant delay tactics and what he described in his diary as "arrogant graymailing," Gesell again restricted North's use of secret documents.[115] The judge gave him until early January to choose 3,000 pages (about 300 documents) for his defense, considerably less than the 40,000 pages, then 30,000, that North was seeking. The prosecution faced the same limit.[116] "They've got a hostage—a plane full of 300 secrets—and they're going to kill one a day until Ollie's set free," said one government official of North's lawyers.[117]

For his efforts to disclose the most relevant secret documents while keeping the case moving, Gesell was becoming "the new hero in America's strange search for a hero in the Iran-contra affair," editorialized the *Milwaukee Sentinel*.[118] One Illinois letter writer to Gesell praised him as "A MAN OF COURAGE" who upheld "the rule of law as being applicable to Presidents, to the military, and to all the president's men."[119] Heidi Lau-Sed of Vermont, meanwhile, wrote that she used to consider *North* a hero and still admired "his courage, steadfastness, intensity of conviction, his personification of devotion, loyalty and love of country." But now, she was "overwhelmed with anger" over secrecy in government. North and others were "violating my and every other American's democratic right to discuss and find consent among ourselves before decisions are made by our government." North and his codefendants "have willingly sacrificed the principles of our Democracy for the achieving of their own agenda."[120]

In January 1989, another major blow befell the prosecution. When the Reagan administration refused to make available classified documents, Walsh was forced to ask to dismiss the two broadest charges against North—conspiracy and theft. Of the documents, Gesell had merely insisted, for instance, that officials change specific names to general titles such as "CIA agent" or "South American" country.[121] But a panel of respected Republican foreign policy experts, including Shultz, Secretary of Defense Frank Carlucci, and National Security Advisor Colin Powell, said no.[122]

Walsh called this near-death knell to his case "a stunning disavowal of the president's publicly professed desire for full disclosure."[123]

Others were more cynical. "It seems clear," said Representative Jack Brooks (D-TX), "that this is a back-door way for the Administration to grant a pardon to North while hoping to avoid the political costs and damage to Ronald Reagan's place in history that an overt pardon would have exacted."[124] The *New York Times* suspected no such conspiracy but still judged the dismissal "a heavy loss for justice, denying the public a test of whether Iran-contra was a criminal conspiracy, as well as reckless and duplicitous."[125]

The remaining twelve charges against North covered lying to Congress, obstructing inquiries, and accepting an illegal gratuity. "What's left," said a Washington lawyer close to the case in a disturbing statement, "is nothing you couldn't charge a hundred other people with in this town."[126]

In February, Attorney General Richard Thornburgh asked the Supreme Court to halt the trial, claiming it was "all but certain" that sensitive secrets would be disclosed.[127] The justices agreed, pressing Walsh and the now-Bush administration to arrange for Walsh to notify Thornburgh in advance if any document was about to spill secrets in one of nine categories. If Thornburgh objected, Gesell would decide whether North could still be tried on any count related to that information.[128] The judge complained of this "cuckoo-clock" trial of constant interruptions.[129] It was indeed a procedure worthy of Rube Goldberg, but it allowed the trial to begin—finally.

.....

More than the guilt or innocence of North and his codefendants was at stake in his trial. "If the trial does not go forward," wrote Lila Lieberman of New York to Judge Gesell, "it is the end of accountable government in the U.S. and therefore the end of our democracy."[130] Such apocalyptic language was exaggerated. But the run-up to the trial of North and others demonstrated how the secretiveness of the US government had legalized obstruction of justice and delayed the rule of law.

Maybe it would also deny it.

10

DEMOCRACY ON THE DOCKET

In a first phase of Iran-Contra trials, Lawrence Walsh, leading the OIC, went after those most directly responsible—officials at the NSC and private individuals. The crimes they had committed were not grave enough to warrant lifetime sentences. But they *were* crimes that deserved to be punished, if only to deter their recurrence. Yet in almost all instances, obstruction compelled the OIC to back down from enforcing the rule of law. As a result, the punishments meted out proved negligible.

.....

Before even the congressional hearings, the OIC did score an early victory. In late April and early May 1987, Carl "Spitz" Channell and Richard Miller both pleaded guilty to conspiring "to defraud the United States of America and the IRS," in the words of their indictment, by raising funds for Contra weapons through their tax-exempt organization, the NEPL.[1]

Channell and Miller were the first to admit breaking US law during the Iran-Contra scandal, making official the erosion of the rule of law. These would also be the first convictions under the 1978 Independent Counsel law.

The two had dubbed their project "Toys," asking for tax-exempt contributions meant for Christmas gifts for the Contra rebels' children. In truth, they procured arms. To make matters worse, Congress would assess that Channell raised $10 million but that only $4.5 million reached the rebels. The rest went to salaries, fees, and expenses.[2]

With whom did you conspire? the judge asked Channell in federal court.

"Colonel North, an official of the National Security Council."[3] Thus did Oliver North enter the legal record as an unindicted coconspirator.

Channell faced a maximum penalty of five years in prison and a fine of $250,000. More than two years later, however, in July 1989, a federal district judge would place him on two years' probation, imposing no other penalty. He was forty-four years old.[4] Miller, who was thirty-six, also received two years' probation as well as 120 hours of community service.[5]

The neocon magazine *Commentary* drew no lesson from this early conviction other than that it was unfair. "No criminal law was broken," it argued. "Raising money to buy arms for the contras is probably not even a civil offense."[6]

.....

Former national security advisor Bud McFarlane also pleaded guilty relatively early in the OIC's investigation. In March 1988, he became the first Reagan administration official to admit to Iran-Contra crimes. His were four charges of withholding information from Congress, specifically in three 1985 letters to House committees and one testimony on December 6, 1986.[7]

McFarlane pleaded only after Walsh downgraded the charges from felonies to misdemeanors in return for McFarlane acting as a witness against North.[8] Advising McFarlane was his old friend, Richard Nixon. *Take the deal,* said the former president.

Congress's lawyer for the hearings, Arthur Liman, blamed Reagan for coercing McFarlane into lying. "Once the President decided the Administration would cheat on the Boland Amendment," he said, "a lot of people got caught up in deceptive conduct that was alien to their nature, and Bud is a particularly sympathetic case of that."[9]

McFarlane refused to blame Reagan, but his statement to the court noted an erosion of norms: "For the past twenty years in which I have served in Washington it has been clear that our institutions—the Presidency and the Congress—were becoming less able to work together responsibly in the formation of American foreign policy. . . . President Reagan was extremely disdainful of the Congress," he added. "The twenty-year trend continues to worsen." He expressed distress for his part in the scandal. "But most of all I regret that we don't seem to have learned from this experience as a country."[10]

McFarlane also seemed to have learned little. Despite his suicide attempt, he showed no contrition and resisted pleading guilty to any crime. For instance, he explained to investigators his logic in criminally withholding information from Congress: "You do not lie to the Congress . . . You put your own interpretation on what the truth is." Yet to Congress he had stated the following, which he knew to be false: "None of us has solicited funds, facilitated contacts for prospective potential donors, or otherwise organized or coordinated the military or paramilitary efforts of the resistance." He added: "Lieutenant Colonel North did not use his influence to facilitate the movement of supplies to the resistance." He also lied that third-country funding was "beyond my ken."[11]

Yet again, conservative media minimized the damage done. "Pardon McFarlane" editorialized the *Wall Street Journal*. "McFarlane did not confess to lies." It also claimed that the executive would be hamstrung if it could not withhold information from Congress. In a gross overstatement, it claimed that, by the standards of the trial, "every letter to Congress since George Washington's first days in office could have been crimes." Finally, it quoted Reagan admiringly to the effect that McFarlane "just pleaded guilty to not telling Congress everything it wanted to know. I've done that myself."[12]

On March 3, 1989, a year after his plea, like Channell and Miller, McFarlane received a relatively light sentence: two years' probation, $20,000 in fines, and 200 hours of community service.[13] He credited "two good friends" for organizing to help pay his fine "in very little time."[14] The far more serious damage to him were his $750,000 in legal bills.

McFarlane claimed to be the first cabinet officer in US history prosecuted for withholding information from Congress.[15]

. . . . .

On February 21, 1989, a full two years into Walsh's investigation, in courtroom six on the second floor of the US District Court in Washington, Oliver North's trial finally began. Americans were still divided over North's guilt. In a *New York Times*–CBS News poll, 43 percent said North should be tried, whereas 45 percent believed charges against him should be dropped.[16]

Unlike in 1987, the public would neither enjoy nor endure the TV spectacle of a preening witness and dueling lawyers because no cameras were allowed in the courtroom. Media interest, however, remained high. Half the seats in the courtroom were for reporters, and twenty television crews waited in the courthouse plaza to interview anyone walking through its brass doors.[17]

Some of the public followed closely the trial of "the world's most famous white-collar criminal," in the words of a columnist.[18] Only about fifteen seats were reserved for the public, who lined up outside at 5 a.m. to claim one. "A couple from San Diego has come to witness history," wrote journalist Haynes Johnson. "A lawyer from Chicago takes pride in believing that so many citizens understand the importance of the trial and what it represents to the country. A young public school teacher from Ohio wants to see how justice is applied to the powerful in America so she can report on the process to her students." One local, from the District of Columbia, carried a pocket Constitution and pointed to Article II's oath to defend it. "That's what this is all about," he said. "They didn't defend it."[19]

Throughout the trial, Judge Gesell, assuming an authoritarian mantle, kept a brisk pace by shutting down needless delays on both sides.

At one point, head prosecutor John Keker offered, "I'd be happy to approach the bench."

"I'd be happy for you not to," snapped Gesell.

"May *I* approach the bench?" asked North's lawyer, Brendan Sullivan.

"No."[20]

When Fawn Hall was on the witness stand, Keker argued with her, and Gesell broke in. When Hall continued talking, he cut her off: "Please keep your mouth shut while I am talking!"[21] When North's lawyer attempted to introduce more details of Iran arms sales, Gesell refused, saying, "I'm simply trying to limit proof so we can end this trial while I'm still alive."[22]

Most of the problems with democratic norms had been dealt with before the trial, but they popped up occasionally in front of the jury. At times, the proceedings certainly had a "cuckoo-clock" quality. When North's courier Robert Owen was on the stand and someone's name in a document came up, Gesell was forced to send the jurors home for the day and oversee a seventy-seven-minute closed-door CIPA hearing. The name turned out to be Costa Rica's former minister of security, which was already public information.[23]

The next day brought more of the same. A three-hour hearing featured Gesell's "weary, exasperated tones" that memos were being somehow reclassified. "I don't know what the rules are any more," sighed Gesell, sending the jury home for a second day in a row.[24] He faced "an absurd situation in where [*sic*] the press is accurately reporting information in the public domain while the court is confronted with representations that the same facts must never be officially acknowledged."[25]

In his diary, Gesell recorded a total of "15 *in camera* CIPA" hearings.[26]

The *Washington Post*'s editors were equally exasperated, suggesting that the Reagan administration might be "using the claim of national security to cover up for Col. North." It was outrageous that "at any point along the way the Justice Department can abort the trial" by refusing to declassify documents.[27]

.....

During North's and others' trials, conservatives confirmed their tenuous embrace of democratic values. North reiterated that, when he lied to the HPSCI in 1986 about third-country funding, he made a choice reflecting his upbringing. "I was put in a situation where—having been raised to know what the Ten Commandments were—I knew that it would be wrong to do that, but not that it would be unlawful."[28] The defense moved that North could not be prosecuted for lying about helping Nicaraguan rebels because fibbing to Congress was *de rigueur*. Prosecutors called the claim "a shocking and cynical view of the relations between the people's elected representatives in Congress and officials of the executive branch."[29] Walsh's team heard so many of North's lies that they organized them by subject in a "thick black binder," recounted Jeffrey Toobin, with documentation to refute each untruth. When Keker cross-examined North, he confronted him with lie after lie, and North admitted to each. "This, the jury could now see, was a man who lied and cheated," Toobin recalled.

North surprised everyone by recalling sitting in Poindexter's office, as the scandal broke in November 1986, watching his boss take from a safe the only copy of the finding Reagan signed in December 1985 authorizing the first shipment of missiles to Iran. *What happened to that copy?* asked Keker.

"I am told," North said, "that it was destroyed."

"Where did you learn that Admiral Poindexter had destroyed the finding?"

"I was there."

"You were present when he destroyed it?" asked Keker, incredulous.

"Yes. I was."

Keker "lost his lawyerly reserve and allowed the outraged citizen in him to surface," wrote Toobin. He imagined North thinking he was in a "den of thieves," but North would not bite.[30]

Keker suggested that North had "loosened the standards" he lived by in the Marines. "You said that, Mr. Keker, not me," North replied angrily. Yet North acknowledged that he drew on a cash reserve of up to $15,000 kept in a steel box in his home to buy a used truck, a used van, a new roof for his home, and a horse for his daughter. He claimed to have raised that amount by emptying his pockets of change every night. (The math worked out to more than $14 in small change every week, without taking out a penny, for twenty years.) North accounted for the funds in a spiral ledger that he destroyed, at the urging of CIA Director Bill Casey, when the scandal broke. "I couldn't believe I would ever be accused of doing something wrong with the money," explained North.[31]

When Ed Meese was on the stand, he seemed to agree with North that, during Meese's weekend investigation in November 1986, the lieutenant colonel was in fact not legally obligated to tell the truth. To his questions, said Meese, North "would have no obligation other than as a loyal member of the administration and a person in the White House." Meese conducted only "an administrative inquiry" in which there was no expectation of truth.[32] Gesell's diary reflected his disgust at the former attorney general: "Bright clear memory unless he didn't want to recall. . . . Political damage specialist—Saved RR [Reagan] from possible impeachment."[33]

Another lie revealed on the stand: Rafael Quintero, formerly of the CIA, confirmed that North had given the Contras military advice, despite North's many denials.[34]

In addition, witnesses and documents disclosed at the North trial demonstrated that both Reagan and Bush were far more involved in violating the Boland Amendment than the Tower Board or Congress had uncovered.[35] McFarlane, for instance, divulged that Reagan told him not to share with Congress that third countries were funding the Contras. (To McFarlane, this was not lying. From Gesell's diary: "The worst witness I've ever heard. Couldn't face facts. He lied again and again without realizing it.")[36]

The trial also revealed that Reagan telephoned Honduran president Roberto Suazo to urge a secret quid pro quo. When the Hondurans threatened to close Contra camps and block arms shipments, Reagan initialed his approval of $110 million in military, economic, and intelligence aid to the Central American country in exchange for military support to the Contras. He also approved a secret plan to air-drop to the Contras intelligence and powerful recoilless rifles intended to blow up two ships.[37] (Some at State claimed the deal was never consummated.)[38]

A forty-two-page government document released at the trial revealed a slew of quid pro quo efforts with at least ten countries, including Israel, South Korea, Taiwan, China, Guatemala, Honduras, and Panama.[39] The study also contained a "potentially momentous disclosure" for Bush, wrote the *New York Times*: The then vice president had met with Honduras's Suazo, likely as part of the tit for tat, thus giving the lie to Bush's claim of no involvement in North's wrongdoing.[40] Why the White House did not turn over such documents to Congress in 1987 remained a mystery. Its lawyers denied any cover-up.[41] Bush's chief of staff, John Sununu, explained that Bush met with Suazo to discuss aid to Honduras only, not to the Contras, although they probably discussed the Contras. "That's a step back from quid pro quo," said Sununu.[42] In May, Bush broke his silence: "No implication, no quid pro quo, direct or indirect, from me to the president of Honduras on that visit."[43] *On that visit*, he specified. And records showed that "incentives" to Honduras, as the report called the quos, did flow in right after three high-level meetings.[44]

In the *New York Times*, Anthony Lewis called Reagan offers of aid to other countries to help the Contras "about as direct an abuse of the Constitution as can be imagined, grounds for impeachment."[45]

North subpoenaed both Bush and Reagan. But Gesell ruled that no declassified documents suggested that Bush had "any specific information relevant and material" to North's case. He also doubted North's "very broad undifferentiated claim" that Reagan knew of the diversion. In any event, dismissing the conspiracy and theft charges made any testimony by Reagan irrelevant.[46]

"Government by deception is not a free government," Keker said in his summation, trying to clarify things. "Government by deception is not a democratic government. Government by deception is not a government under the rule of law." He added, "The tragedy of Oliver North is that a man who says he cared so much about freedom and democracy in Nicaragua forgot about the demands of freedom and democracy here at home."[47] "Why should anyone pay attention anymore to the Iran-contra scandal?" asked David Hoffman in the *Washington Post*. His answer: "a simple conclusion that becomes ever more apparent": "They lied to us—to the media, the Congress and the American people."[48]

After sixty-four hours of deliberation, the jury agreed—in part. On May 4, 1989, it found North guilty of three serious felonies: aiding and abetting in the creation of the false chronology, accepting an illegal security system, and shredding documents. Jurors absolved North of nine other counts, which largely involved lying to Congress and to Meese. R. W. Apple of the *New York Times* observed that the decision's logic seemed, "Why should [North] be singled out [for lying] when everyone does it?"[49] One juror, a veteran of Patton's Third Army, said he believed North, who "had to do what he was told." He said the length of the deliberations was because three women on the jury held out against finding North not guilty.[50] "Basically, on the counts of 'not guilty,' he was following orders," explained the jury foreperson. This, despite Gesell instructing jurors not to let North off the hook on this so-called Nuremberg defense.[51]

After the verdict, 69 percent of Americans polled essentially agreed with the jury that North was "well-meaning but misguided," whereas 14 percent called him "a hero and a patriot" and 11 percent "a liar and a criminal."[52] In a brief statement on the courthouse steps, John Keker claimed a limited victory: "The principle that no man is above the law has been vindicated."[53]

Conservatives, meanwhile, ignored all the withheld documents, all the secrecy, and the obstruction. They minimized the remaining rulings against North. "The government has convicted him of shredding documents, writing two paragraphs, and arranging third-party financing of an alarm system," wrote the *Richmond News Leader*. "Some Svengali. Some conspirator."[54] One Marylander writing to Gesell called the verdict "a political lynching based upon unconstitutional invasions of the Executive branch's prerogatives by Congress." He judged that the twelve black jurors from the District of Columbia did not qualify as North's "peers."[55] One journalist saw "thinly veiled racism" in the disparagement of the all-black jury.[56]

On July 5, Gesell sentenced North to a $150,000 fine, two years' probation, and 1,200 hours of community service. The judge told North he believed he was "a low-ranking subordinate working to carry out initiatives of a few cynical superiors," yet North accepted "the mistaken view that Congress couldn't be trusted," part of a larger "total distrust in some constitutional values."[57]

One scholar judged North's sentence "surprisingly lenient." Experts had suggested twenty-one to twenty-seven months in prison—not zero.[58] But even liberal newspapers such as the *San Francisco Chronicle* and the *Washington Post* assessed his punishment "about right."[59]

North also barely avoided losing his $23,000-a-year pension from the Navy. A 1974 law banned pensions for those "holding office under the United States" who were convicted of destroying government documents. North's supporters changed the definition of "holding office" just enough to protect his pension. When debate in the Senate closed, conservative firebrand Jesse Helms (R-NC) waived the bill and proclaimed, "Ollie, this one's for you!"[60]

.....

Richard Secord, whose trial Judge Gesell severed from that of North, still faced charges of conspiracy, theft, and bribing North. Like North, his conspiracy charges were dropped because of graymailing. In April 1989, he was indicted again, on nine additional criminal charges: that he committed perjury seven times during his TV testimony, which he had given without immunity; that he lied to House and Senate investigators when he said North had no financial interests in profits from the arms sales despite the $200,000 "button" account and the $14,000 security system; and that he obstructed the committees' investigation. The indictment alleged that the retired Air Force major general-turned-businessman made more than $1 million in profit from arms sales to Iran and the Contras.[61] Added to the three counts left from his original March 1988 indictment, Secord faced twelve felony counts.

Secord's legal team called the charges "false," and he pleaded not guilty. Tom Green, Secord's chief lawyer, had helped North and Fawn Hall smuggle documents out of NSC offices. Now he argued that the obstruction count was so vague as to pose the same "formidable" problems as North's conspiracy issue—namely, the need to declassify government documents.[62] In other words, he threatened graymail.

On November 8, 1989—the day before the Berlin Wall fell—Secord pleaded guilty to one count of lying to investigators about North's financial benefits. In exchange, Walsh dropped the remaining eleven charges.

"You knew your answer was untrue?" asked Judge Aubrey Robinson of Secord during his plea.

"The answer was not candid," said Secord, his wire-rimmed glasses and boyish looks making him look nothing like his reputation as a covert operative. "I was trying to shield both of us," he admitted, meaning North and himself.[63]

On the single count, Secord faced five years in prison and a $250,000 fine. But he agreed to testify in the upcoming trials of Poindexter, Hakim, and Joseph Fernandez of the CIA, and so the court delayed his sentence. In January 1990, Judge Robinson sentenced him to two years' probation—the same as North. "There has been punishment enough in this case," said Robinson. Secord expressed deep "regret" to the judge, yet, at a press conference after, called Walsh "a monster at large in our criminal justice system."[64]

Secord also lashed out at Ronald Reagan for not taking more responsibility for Iran-Contra. "Reagan has been hiding out," he said. "I think it's cowardly. . . . He could have said, 'This was done on my authority.' Instead, they built a wall around him."[65] In his memoirs, Secord identified the real scandal of Iran-Contra as "when the President's advisors set up their Chinese Wall and began lying needlessly to investigators and falsifying evidence."[66]

It was never clear how much Secord made in profits from Iran-Contra. Prosecutors said $1.5 million. He said no more than $250,000.[67] Walsh called Secord's testimony to his OIC and to Congress "generally accurate as to operational matters and blatantly false regarding his personal finances."[68] Secord called Walsh's case "financially ruinous for me." Friends, including at least one retired Air Force brigadier general, organized a fundraising campaign on his behalf. In June 1989, they claimed he had $170,000 in unpaid bills, which would probably mount to $600,000.[69] By February 1990, the *Miami Herald* totaled his debts at $800,000.[70]

Fundraisers for Secord made arguments by then common among those who minimized the erosion of democracy during Iran-Contra. First was that those accused of crimes somehow did not deserve to be tried for them because they had served honorably: "These men had dedicated their lives to serving our nation and fighting communism—why was Congress treating them like a bunch of criminals?" Second were attacks on "the libelous media."[71] Secord's wife, Jo Ann, wrote that "reporters and newsmen camped out on our doorstep for weeks on end. We could not move outside of our home without the cameras on us and obnoxious reporters hollering and yelling at us. We even had camera crews come up to our home and put their cameras to our windows to take pictures. They were like vultures."[72] Third was to catalog the $42 million of "waste" in Walsh's office, an emblem of big government spending that now included 28 lawyers, 35 FBI agents and, "almost unbelievably, a staff historian!"[73] (In July 1989, the OIC countered that it had spent only $15.9 million; by October 1990, $22.1 million.)[74]

Secord was the fourth person sentenced in Iran-Contra, after Channell, Miller, and McFarlane. (North was appealing his sentence.) None had been found guilty of selling weapons to Iran or the Contras, and none had gone to prison. The *New York Times* said the affair was "turning into a sort of crime without a perpetrator."[75]

.....

Secord's partner in the Enterprise, Albert Hakim, also had his trial severed from North's and eventually bargained down. He intensified his negotiations with the OIC when Secord pleaded guilty and promised to testify against others, including Hakim. On November 21, 1989, the Iranian American copped to a single misdemeanor charge of "supplementing the salary" of (read: bribing) North with his security system.[76] His corporation, Lake Resources, Inc., pleaded guilty to a corporate felony of theft of US government property. In early 1990, the court fined Hakim $5,000 and placed him on two years' probation. His company was dissolved.

In an unusual side settlement, Hakim gave up his right to $7.3 million out of $9 million, then in Swiss banks, in profits from Iran arms deals. The businessman would share the remaining $1.7 million with the fiduciary for the bank accounts and Hakim's lawyer. The US government thus was to recover roughly what the Enterprise had taken from it.[77] However, as Walsh noted, "although Hakim agreed to take all steps necessary to facilitate the recovery of the funds by the United States, he subsequently refused to carry out his agreement."[78]

"Why the cruel and unusual punishment?" wrote humorist Art Buchwald sarcastically, noting the light—almost nonexistent—sentences of Secord and Hakim, two of the masterminds of Iran-Contra who personified privatization.[79]

.....

Because of the government's withholding of records, the OIC assumed that the same charges of conspiracy and diversion dropped in North's case would also be dismissed in the cases of Poindexter, Secord, and Hakim, so it narrowed the charges. In July 1989, it also asked US District Judge Harold Greene to dismiss wire fraud and theft of government property charges against Poindexter. Left against the former national security advisor were charges of conspiring to obstruct congressional inquiries, two counts of obstruction, and two of making false statements to congressional investigators.[80]

At a pretrial hearing, Poindexter's lawyer accused President Reagan of directing his national security advisor to give Congress false answers.

Judge Greene asked the lawyer whether he was suggesting that "the president said, 'You go ahead and do this.' "

"Yes," said the lawyer. *I want these things done,* Reagan had said.[81]

Unlike the North trial, in which the judge refused to subpoena Reagan on the grounds that he was not the defendant's immediate superior, Poindexter's status as a presidential advisor made the chief executive's testimony more relevant.[82] In November 1989, a judge ordered the former president to surrender his diary. Not surprisingly, Reagan's lawyers countered that surrendering a private record of their client's "thoughts and reflections" while in office raised "profound constitutional concerns."[83] Poindexter, who in 1987 had painted Reagan as "not a man for great detail," now argued that the president routinely and privately gave him direction on selling arms to Iran and covertly supporting the Contras. Some of that might be in the diaries.[84] The fight over Reagan's diaries delayed Poindexter's trial. In late January 1990, when Greene finally looked at about one hundred diary excerpts, he judged twenty-nine to be "relevant to [the] defendant's claim."[85] It was the first time since Watergate that a president had to turn over private materials to a court.

A week later, Reagan's lawyers refused the judge's order, laying claim "to the constitutionally protected privacy of his diaries." They later specified what they meant: "executive privilege." A spokesperson for Reagan reasoned that "future presidents may be inhibited in maintaining personal diaries for their own reflection and personal deliberation." Bush's Justice Department helped Reagan by requesting that the production of the diary excerpts be postponed, which Greene called "nothing more than an attempt to delay."[86] The *New York Times* acknowledged the need for executive privilege. "But the privilege, especially when pleaded as loosely and vaguely as Presidents Nixon and Reagan pleaded it, must yield to the needs of justice."[87] Such language was almost identical to that used by the Supreme Court when compelling Nixon to testify: the "general interest" of executive privilege must "yield to the demonstrated, specific need for evidence in a criminal trial."[88] Besides, wrote Richard Cohen in the *Washington Post*, all presidents who keep diaries in these modern days must assume that there is some slight chance of publication. "Would [Reagan], for instance, tell his diary that he and Poindexter discussed an allegedly illegal operation? Would he tell his diary what he actually thought of some subordinate[?]"[89] When Poindexter's lawyers finally saw Reagan's files, they complained of getting "a big runaround" that turned up no notes on Iran-Contra. They believed there were "numerous other handwritten notes" not turned over.[90] During the trial, Judge Greene ruled in favor of Reagan's executive privilege, now saying the twenty-nine diary entries "offer no new insights."[91]

Greene also subpoenaed Reagan, now a private citizen, to testify and gave him the option of a videotaped deposition, which would allow the court to pause to settle any dispute over national security secrets. In February 1990, Reagan yielded. Even then, his lawyers urged Greene to bar the media in case Reagan disclosed classified information. He did so, but he soon after provided a transcript and, later, an edited version of the tape.[92]

The tape showed a diminished president who divulged no classified information but also claimed to remember little of Iran-Contra. For eight hours over two days in a sealed Los Angeles courtroom, he answered questions. He admitted for the first time to actively urging foreign leaders to fund the Contras and knowing of plans to build a secret airfield in Costa Rica. But he denied having "any inkling" that North was guiding Contra "strategy in any way."[93] He complained of leaks, saying "Washington is a sieve. . . . In eight years it was virtually impossible to find out who was doing the leaking and shut them up."[94] He displayed his hostility to Congress when shown a misleading letter sent by Poindexter to its committees: "I am in total agreement," said Reagan. "If I had written it myself, I might have used a little profanity."[95]

Otherwise, the seventy-nine-year-old said "I don't recall" more than 120 times. Reagan could not remember his own chair of the Joint Chiefs of Staff, even when given the name. He did not recall that McFarlane had admitted to lying to Congress. He even denied what the Tower Commission had confirmed—that arms sales profits were diverted to the Contras. "No one has proved to me that there was diversion," he said, astonishingly.[96] And he insisted that no arms were traded for hostages and that he had not dealt with terrorists. (Two years later, Walsh personally deposed Reagan, who could remember no Iran-Contra meeting, discussion, or diary entry at all, except to say that "yes, I would violate . . . that law" to free hostages. Two years after that, Reagan would be diagnosed with Alzheimer's disease.)[97]

The *New York Times* called Reagan's February 1990 performance "embarrassing" and "even more vague and dismaying than anticipated."[98] R. W. Apple described the former president as "smaller, older, less sure of himself." Shorn of his notecards and advisors, "his energy level seemed lower than ever."[99] "Of all Ronald Reagan's television performances, this was the least enjoyable," wryly assessed Tom Shales, the *Post's* TV critic.[100]

Unlike Secord, Poindexter reached no deal with Walsh and pleaded not guilty to all five felony charges, which included conspiracy, obstruction of Congress, and lying to Congress. He faced up to twenty-five years in prison and $1.25 million in fines.

Dan Webb, the lead prosecutor, asserted that North "lied, lied, lied" to Congress as ordered by Poindexter. Richard Beckler, chief defense counsel, countered that Poindexter himself "never lied to Congress." Yet he himself explained that the charge against his client was technically true: Poindexter said he did not know about the November 1985 shipment of HAWK missiles to Iran until January 1986. "After 30 years in the Navy, they want to nail him on a five-week mistake and call it obstruction of Congress," said Beckler, minimizing the crime based on the criminal's long service.[101]

Oliver North testified, but he was not happy about it. He repeated the story of seeing Poindexter tear up Reagan's November 1985 finding.

"You saw somebody tear it in two?" asked prosecutor Webb.

"Yes," whispered North, his face tense.

"It was John Poindexter that you saw?"

"Tear it in two, yes."

"That was in John Poindexter's office?"

"Yes."

"Near the Oval Office where the President sits?"

"Around the corner."

Webb and North's exchange was so halting that Judge Greene had to stop and answer Webb's questions. "It's like pulling teeth," he said in exasperation.[102]

Other exchanges, over North's lying, were rapid-fire and no less heated.

"You don't doubt for a moment that Congress has a right to ask questions and get accurate information if they are going to pass laws to represent the people of this country?" Webb asked North. "And the executive has the right to withhold information . . . and you suggested that to Mr. McFarlane and to Admiral Poindexter?"

"Yes." North, sitting stiffly in the witness chair, was scowling.

"And McFarlane and Poindexter, on two different occasions, they decided it was better to lie?" asked Webb.

"I don't know what they decided, but I know the consequences," replied North.

"The consequence was lies to Congress," said the prosecutor.

"Yes."

"You knew it was wrong?"

"Yes," answered Mr. North. *Wrong but not illegal,* he specified.

"You thought you could go in front of those 12 Congressmen and lie and lie and lie?" Mr. Webb shouted.

"I was not under oath," answered North. "I have never lied under oath. It was an informal meeting."

"Did you think this was a tea party going on over there in the White House situation room?"

"No, counsel, I knew it wasn't a tea party."[103]

Despite his reluctance, North revealed that knowledge of Iranian arms sales was widespread in the Pentagon and the CIA, including among senior officials. Lawbreaking and keeping it to oneself became commonplace. Even the National Security Agency, he added, was asked to provide "highly reliable intelligence"—code for electronic spying—on all US-Iran deals.[104]

Other witnesses testified to further obstruction of justice. A former White House software manager testified as to Poindexter's frantic email and phone message deletions. An FBI agent said that, on November 24, 1986, Poindexter logged on at 4:30 a.m. "By 9 a.m. there were no more messages left in his system."[105] North, meanwhile, deleted 736 emails. These were the messages investigators later found on backup tapes.[106]

Poindexter, like North, used his trial as a fundraising tool to pay legal fees. "I stand, one man, alone against the massive onslaught of liberal special interests who want to imprison me for serving my country," one of his fundraising letters said.[107]

In April 1990, Poindexter stood, rigid and expressionless, as the jury foreperson pronounced him guilty on all five charges. The *Washington Post* judged the verdict Walsh's "most important victory" because it demonstrated "that a high-level conspiracy existed within the Reagan administration to deceive the public and Congress." Poindexter failed to understand that "no small group of individuals, elected or not, in any branch of the government can develop and conduct policy without regard to the law and to the rights and responsibilities of the other branches. That is the central and solemn theme of all the Iran-Contra cases, and it has been reaffirmed and strengthened by this conviction."[108]

In urging prison time in sentencing, Walsh warned that "if . . . high-ranking officials of one branch of government feel free to feed the other branch a diet of lies, then the constitutional system will surely sicken and, eventually, die." Judge Gesell had spared North from prison because he followed his superiors' orders. But Poindexter *was* "one of his superiors."[109]

Walsh got his wish. On June 11, Judge Greene gave the former national security advisor six months in prison as "the decision-making head" of a scheme to "invalidate the decisions made by elected officials." He imposed no fine. In a retort to the arguments of conservatives, he added, "With all due respect to the distinguished military records of Adm. Poindexter, Col. North . . . and the others, they have no standing in a democratic society to invalidate the decisions made by elected officials."[110]

At this point, in mid-1990, Poindexter was the only one of the seven defendants to be sentenced to prison. He would end up avoiding it.

.....

The coda to the North and Poindexter convictions demonstrated the full impact of widespread secrecy on the administration of justice.

North appealed his conviction on all three counts. At first, Judge Gesell refused to review whether the evidence against North was tainted.[111] On July 20, 1990, however, a three-judge appeals panel, in a 2-to-1 vote, reversed North's conviction for shredding and vacated his other two convictions, saying Gesell failed to fully ensure that the witnesses had not used North's immunized testimony.

The panel ordered Gesell to hold new so-called *Kastigar* hearings, proceeding "witness-by-witness; if necessary, . . . line-by-line and item-by-item" to make absolutely sure that no immunized testimony made its way to any witnesses or trial testimony.[112] Walsh warned this would "require a complex psychological inquiry into the thought processes and memory of every witness," adding weeks or months—maybe half a year, according to Toobin—to a trial.[113]

Of the two judges in the majority, one was Laurence Silberman, a former top official in the 1980 Reagan-Bush campaign. At that time, Silberman later admitted, he had met with an arms dealer allegedly tied to the Ayatollah Khomeini of Iran to release US hostages in exchange for arms shipments—a scheme known as the "October Surprise." A former ambassador, Silberman failed to report this offer to the State Department, where wits dubbed him "our ambassador to Khomeini." He had also written that Walsh had no authority to put North on trial, even getting into a shouting match at a conference with the chief of the panel that had appointed Walsh. Silberman also hated Gesell.[114] The other judge in the two-person majority, David Sentelle, was, like Silberman, a Reagan appointee. The North Carolinian was a longtime Republican operative and supporter of segregationist senator Jesse Helms, who helped restore North's pension.

In favoring North, Silberman's logic was that some of Walsh's witnesses had heard North testify and therefore the whole trial needed to be dumped. He cared little that the prosecution had not elicited any immunized testimony, and the panel did not hold that Walsh's team had used North's testimony against him.[115] The lone dissenting judge, Patricia Wald, wrote that the majority ruling "makes a subsequent trial of any congressionally immunized witness virtually impossible."[116] She argued that the defense should at least have to find allegedly tainted evidence before the government had to disprove the taint.[117]

Walsh petitioned the Supreme Court to review the decision, but it refused.[118] Republicans in the House called for the attorney general to shut down the OIC, saying it had become too costly.[119] North accused Walsh of being "a vindictive wretch," out to "ruin my family and me."[120]

It turned out that *Kastigar* hearings would not take weeks or months. Bud McFarlane was the first witness to be called back for "line-by-line" questioning, and he admitted that his testimony in North's trial was inevitably "colored" by North's words to Congress, although he failed to point to how that testimony changed a single fact in his own testimony.[121] McFarlane told prosecutor Michael Bromwich that he wanted to both "tell the truth" and "take responsibility" for what occurred.

"Were you trying to help Col. North?" asked Bromwich.

"Yes."

"Consciously?"

"Yes."

"Repeatedly?"

"Yes." He added, "In watching four days of riveting testimony by a man who was like a son to me, how could I not have been affected?"[122]

That was all it took. Four days later, on September 15, 1991, seeing no path forward, Walsh dropped all charges against North. "This terminates the case," concluded Gesell. Outside the courthouse, North felt "totally exonerated, fully, completely, I don't have another word for it." From the White House, President Bush praised the "system of justice" as "working."[123] The *New York Times*, in a measured judgment, saw the case as an affirmation of citizens' rights against self-incrimination but also "a serious setback for another objective of democratic government: promptly to uncover the truth in high-profile cases and to prosecute them."[124]

Although he fulfilled his mandated community service in an inner-city drug prevention program, North never paid his fine because Gesell suspended it pending the outcome of North's appeal. McFarlane, for one, was bitter at North's impunity. "The man I had thought was patriotic, self-sacrificing and loyal was revealed to be devious, self-serving, self-aggrandizing and true first and foremost to himself."[125]

.....

In late 1990, six months after his sentence, Poindexter also appealed. In November 1991, another 2-to-1 Court of Appeals decision, again with two Reagan appointees outvoting a Carter appointee, reversed Poindexter's conviction on the same grounds as North's.[126] The panel did not declare him innocent; it merely found witnesses in his trial to be tainted by immunized congressional testimony.

As with North, the Supreme Court again refused to revisit the panel's decision. At the Justice Department, which could have supported Walsh's petition, Solicitor General Ken Starr, who would later become the most controversial independent counsel ever, remained silent, prompting the *New York Times* to editorialize that Justice "can share the blame for this obstruction of justice."[127] Walsh found himself forced to dismiss the Poindexter case, too.[128]

.....

In 1993, when Lawrence Walsh published his final report, McFarlane wrote him a personal letter. The former national security advisor recognized that Walsh's "was an impossible task—to define the reasons for these events and to prosecute wrongdoing successfully in the face of fatal congressional compromise of your authority." Walsh handled it "with more courage and determination than either the subjects, the Congress or the American people expected or, unfortunately, seemed to want."[129] For all its graciousness, McFarlane's letter failed to mention the obstacles put in the independent counsel's way by him and other defendants, and especially by the White House, CIA, Justice, State, and other departments. Although their obstruction was legal, it was nevertheless antidemocratic. Their motivations were to keep the US public in the dark about important national security secrets that, if divulged, in the main endangered no US interests. As scholar Malcolm Byrne assessed, the OIC trial of North and others revealed "serious impediments to the ability of the U.S. legal system to expose and remedy official wrongdoing in the national security sphere."[130]

More broadly, the Iran-Contra trials uncovered among conservative defendants, journalists, and ordinary Americans a deep well of antipathy to truth, the rule of law, the separation of powers, and the administration of justice. Over these, conservatives valued service to country, popularity, and fear of communism. Most tragically, this first round of Iran-Contra trials showed conservatives that they could disregard democratic norms with little to no consequence. Secrecy had clearly triumphed over fairness. Conservatives rejoiced. Their relief would turn to rage with the next and final round of trials.

11

THE WHOLE TRUTH AND NOTHING BUT

In late 1991, after Lawrence Walsh reluctantly dismissed the case against John Poindexter, he gave journalist George Lardner a rare interview that never became public. Despite his recent reversals, Walsh declared himself "very pleased with the last two years." He thought the crimes his team had prosecuted were serious and in need of deterrence. He praised the "thoughtful" juries and "creative" judges who had navigated the vexing issue of use immunity.[1]

A year earlier, when North and Poindexter were successfully challenging their convictions, Walsh had predicted that his investigation would end in spring 1991.[2] After three years, dozens of lawyers, 2,700 interviews, hundreds of thousands of documents, five guilty pleas and one felony conviction, he was ready to take one last year to write up his final report.[3]

Instead, his team moved to a new phase. They had so far focused on "the operating group, the group who carried out these activities," Walsh said. Now came "the group that protected them and supported them even with respect to the congressional investigation. And then you've got those whom [*sic*] have obstructed our own investigation for whatever reason." "Now," he assessed, "there's a merging between the second and third."[4]

These more peripheral defendants—some of them cabinet members—had been under investigation for years. Their cases revealed an ongoing disregard for truth, justice, and Congress among officials in the Reagan-Bush era.

Equally important, the pursuit of those whom Republican officials and their friends deemed unfairly maligned created a lasting sense of political persecution. Partisanship had always been part of the Iran-Contra scandal. But as the 1980s gave way to the next decade and Reagan to Bush, Republicans closed ranks and increasingly assaulted not only Walsh and his OIC team but also the institution of the independent counsel as a big-government waste of taxpayer funds for Democratic political purposes. Such a calcification of Republican attitudes became a mainstay of America's memory about Iran-Contra, eclipsing the crimes and improprieties that caused the scandal.

.....

Walsh's reactivated investigation, which he called "continuing," first focused on a half-dozen characters suspected of having either helped in obstructing justice or lied in the investigation—usually both. Their potential crimes resulted from the investigation itself. The OIC had hoped this final phase would be over in six months.

It took three years. Thousands more documents had to be reviewed by experts from several agencies. Several witnesses, including Oliver North and Poindexter, had to be reinterviewed.

The first group targeted were the spymasters.

The first CIA official indicted for Iran-Contra crimes had been Joseph Fernandez, back in 1988. Fernandez, known by his pseudonym "Tomás Castillo," was charged with obstructing inquiries and lying nineteen times to his superiors at CIA headquarters and to the Tower Commission.[5] Walsh was forced to drop the charges when Bush's CIA refused to declassify documents for Fernandez's defense and when Attorney General Dick Thornburgh, in October 1990, backed the spy agency. Walsh was furious, accusing the CIA of trying "to protect a fictional secret," in this case, CIA locations in Central America that reporters had already made public.[6] "We agree with the intelligence agencies 98 percent of the time," he said. "But the disagreements are over matters that the court knows, the public knows and that we know the public knows. Yet there is an effort to keep it classified."[7] The real goal of the CIA, Walsh charged, was "to preserve official deniability to avoid embarrassment of the host country."[8] He also called the attorney general's interference a conflict of interest.[9]

But to no avail. Bush's administration was less cooperative than even Reagan's. This was the first time the government blocked critical information under CIPA.[10] Walsh proposed narrowing the charges, but Judge Claude Hilton refused. As a workaround, Walsh suggested a simple code: give jurors cards with the name of the problematic CIA locations associated with a number, and everyone in the courtroom would use only the number. The CIA was open to it. Judge Hilton, however, "thought this kindergarten-like proposal too complicated," according to Walsh.[11]

"Graymail" won an early victory. Walsh warned of "the development of an enclave of important national security officers who are beyond prosecution because the intelligence agencies will not release the information necessary to their trial."[12]

.....

Walsh got a second shot at the CIA when, in February 1990, a federal grand jury indicted Thomas Clines, who had retired from the agency and worked with Secord and Hakim. The man whom Walsh called "seasoned, hard-boiled" oversaw purchases of private weapons in Europe and their delivery to the Contras.[13] For his services, he received 20 to 33 percent of Enterprise profits.[14] Known as "C. Tea" for his Swiss bank account name, Clines allegedly underreported his income in 1985 and 1986 and lied that he had no foreign financial accounts. Congress accused him of making $973,000, but he and his wife reported only $265,000 in 1985 and $402,513 in 1986. In December 1986, as the scandal broke, Clines had withdrawn $990,000 from the "C. Tea" account. He now faced twenty-one years in prison and $950,000 in fines.[15]

In September, a jury in Baltimore found Clines, now sixty-two, guilty on all charges.[16] Months later, he was sentenced to sixteen months in prison and fined $40,000 in addition to prosecution costs.[17] Walsh's prosecutor, Stuart Abrams, detailed how Clines used "sham corporations and Swiss bank accounts" to enrich himself. "This was not a case of misplaced patriotism," Abrams said. "It was purely a case of greed."[18] In February 1992, an appeals court upheld the conviction. Clines served his sentence—the only Iran-Contra defendant to ever do so.

.....

In May 1990, after Clines's indictment but before his trial, a new federal grand jury launched a criminal inquiry that now focused on mid-level Reagan officials. In the second half of 1991, the OIC first prosecuted Alan Fiers, who headed the CIA Central American Task Force, for lying to Congress. North's notebooks, obtained by the OIC only in 1990, contradicted many of Fiers's denials to Congress and the Tower Commission.[19]

In July, Fiers pleaded guilty to two misdemeanor counts of false statements and perjury to Congress, promising to cooperate with prosecutors. (False statements have a broader definition than perjury, including lying to investigators when not under oath.) It was the first time a CIA official admitted in a courtroom knowing of the diversion as early as spring 1986.[20] North had told him about his sales to Iran and "kicking dollars into the Contras' pot."[21]

The *Washington Post* admitted that, "at times we too have thought that Mr. Walsh was about at the point where he should give it up. But," it continued, "the Fiers assertions need to be pursued. The special prosecutor's license is not a threat to the balance of powers but a means of preserving the balance."[22]

In January 1992, Judge Aubrey Robinson sentenced Fiers to one year probation and 100 hours of community service. Robinson noted how, since his days as a football player under Woody Hayes at Ohio State, Fiers had burned to win. "It's the same way at the other end of the spectrum—as a nation," Robinson told him. "We want to win everything we get involved in. But what would a win mean if, in winning, we destroy the very fundamental beliefs, convictions and everything else that made us what we are?"[23]

Fiers's sentence was light because he divulged much to Walsh's team about his colleagues' crimes, mostly that they had lied to Congress because they wanted legislators to renew funding. "No other Iran/contra defendant assisted OIC with the degree of professionalism exhibited by Fiers," wrote Walsh in his final report. "Many pieces of the Iran/contra puzzle fell into place solely because of the information provided by Fiers."[24]

Many people at the CIA predicted that colleagues would be prosecuted and see their careers end for doing their patriotic duty. David Boren (D-OK) disagreed. The chair of the Senate Intelligence Committee countered that, when faced with "totally new" information such as Fiers's testimony, "you can't sit back and say, 'Well, we're not even going to ask questions about it.'" For his part, Vincent Cannistraro of the CIA regretted that his otherwise distinguished colleagues "don't put loyalty to the law as their first area of concern. . . . There is a very significant danger of betraying your own principles."

.....

Walsh's team now exuded a new vigor. Fiers's cooperation led to indictments against former CIA Deputy Director for Operations Clair George, third-in-command at the agency, and former CIA Chief of the European Division Duane Clarridge. "If Alan Fiers was not safe, then no one is safe," assessed a retired intelligence officer.[25]

In September 1991, George was indicted on ten counts of what was becoming the usual—lying and obstruction.[26] Hoping to share the graymail luck that blessed Fernandez, George's lawyer asked for millions of secret documents. This time the judge, Royce Lamberth, denied the request, refusing to let the defendant "search for a needle in a haystack of the country's most classified secrets, without the slightest indication of what the needle might be and how it might be material to his defense." George's "absurdly broad request," Lamberth added, was plainly aimed at sabotaging the trial.[27] Months later, the judge allowed George to see some classified documents but immediately seemed to regret it, accusing the Bush administration of trying to "thwart this trial from going forward" by ignoring his deadlines for declassification. A Reagan appointee, Lamberth threatened to dismiss the case.[28]

George's lawyer argued that his client "risked his life and the welfare of his family countless times in service to his country. He has not profited one iota from his labors and has always comported himself in a manner in which, this case will show, puts all Americans in debt to him."[29]

Unfortunately for George, he was not accused of being unpatriotic but rather of lying to Congress, and of that, the trial showed, he was guilty. Fiers said he told George about the diversion and that George ordered him to mislead Congress by deleting testimony language that confirmed the agency's knowledge of the arms network and the people involved.[30]

"We have to tell that story," Fiers said he pleaded with George, "because that tells what we know. It puts on record what's happened, and it will get us through the narrows that are ahead, Clair."

"No, I don't want to do that," George replied. "That will put the spotlight on either the White House, the Administration or Ollie, I can't be sure."

"Clair it's going to come out."

"No, Alan, I don't want to do that."[31]

Thus, the denials continued. "We were not aware of their identities," George lied to the Senate about those aboard the Hasenfus flight and similar ones. He also claimed he "never laid eyes" on Richard Secord when he had met him in the White House and knew his operation intimately.

Asked about the deletion (which became the obstruction charge), George at first said, "I do not recall."

When told the document was marked, "Deleted by D[eputy] D[irector of] O[perations]," and asked again if he ordered the deletion, he had insisted, "I cannot believe I did."

"Do you know who did?" the prosecutor asked.

"I do not."[32]

One former member of the Senate Intelligence Committee recalled that "Clair George had the same contempt for Congress that Bill Casey did. To give Clair his due, he was absolutely loyal to the CIA and he believed in the mission of the CIA. But there is no doubt that Clair was telling as little as he could get away with."[33]

Unlike Fiers, George refused to plea bargain, angry that he had become, as he put it, "a pawn in a continuous drama of political exploitation."[34] He pleaded not guilty. During the trial, when Fiers, sometimes in tears, testified that George ordered him to deceive Congress, George acerbically called him "my then-trusted colleague."[35] George's lawyer, Richard Hibey, highlighted Fiers's own mendacity, in the process exposing the CIA's loose definition of a lie. With Fiers on the stand, Hibey asked rhetorically if Fiers's own prosecution for withholding information from Congress meant that he, too, had lied.

No, said Fiers. "It was not a true statement," he tried to explain of one of his lies.

"It was, therefore, a lie."

"It was not a true statement," repeated Fiers.

"Do you have difficulty with the word 'lie'?" Hibey snapped.

"It's relativism gone rampant," one ex-officer said about Fiers's testimony. "What's the truth? What's a lie? Everything can be explained away in one way or another, so nothing is ever a lie and nothing is ever the truth."[36]

George, meanwhile, demonstrated his contempt for Congress. He pounded the witness stand and shouted at the prosecutor, "Congress wanted to set someone up, and I walked right into it!" He claimed the Senate committee "all knew about Ollie North as much as I did." His face turned red: "They were waiting for me to say something wrong. And goddamn it, that's hypocrisy!"[37] He was so loud that passersby in the hallway heard him.

It was a disturbing scene, not precisely for its high emotion but mostly because George, a one-time chief of congressional relations at the CIA, confirmed that he thought the CIA enjoyed the prerogative to share with

Congress only what it was willing. Of one meeting with Congress on October 14, 1986, George recalled, "If they thought I was going to come down and tell them everything I suspected or heard by rumor, they were wrong."[38]

George chafed so much at the questions asked of him and interrupted others so much that Judge Lamberth, a conservative Republican, pounded his gavel, shouting, "Mr. George!" The witness barely dodged a contempt charge.[39]

As testimony wound down, one former CIA officer said he would not trust George "even under oath." "You can be a good soldier in the Cold War and a very bad American," said Rob Simmons, referring to George. "I think the essence of being a good American is allowing the democratic system to work."[40] Prosecutor Craig Gillen told the jury that George "lived in a world where he thought he owned the secrets. He apparently forgot this is a democracy, and the United States does not belong to Clair George."[41]

In the end, the evidence presented at the trial was overwhelming. Fiers and Secord both contradicted George. An FBI expert had George's fingerprints on a document censored for Congress.[42]

In August 1992, with a majority feeling that George had been evasive but not deceptive enough, the jury first deadlocked, causing a mistrial.[43] Upon retrial, the OIC dropped two obstruction counts. The jury almost deadlocked again, but in December, it convicted George on two felony counts of perjury and false statement to Congress. He was the first senior CIA official convicted of felonies committed while he was at the agency.[44] National Security Advisor John Poindexter had long said, "The buck stops here with me."[45] But this case demonstrated that the conspiracy of Iran-Contra was not limited to the NSC and White House.

George faced ten years in prison and fines totaling $500,000. Sentencing was set for early 1993.

.....

In November 1991, shortly after George's indictment, a federal grand jury indicted Duane Clarridge on seven counts of perjury and false statements. Wearing a camo jacket to court, he pleaded not guilty.[46] Because Clarridge had told the same lies several times, the judge forced the OIC to drop "multiplicitous" or redundant charges.[47] In late 1992, he was awaiting trial.

.....

The CIA's policy was not to pay for its employees' legal costs. So, in what the *New York Times* called "a highly unusual move," former intelligence officials banded together to pay the expenses of colleagues targeted by Walsh.[48] Within three weeks, the fund had raised $40,000. The solidarity was not merely out of collegiality. Defenders of George and Clarridge shared their disdain for telling Congress the truth. "I don't think people like George should be indicted," said Ray Cline, a former deputy director of intelligence. "The only thing they have ever been accused of doing is lying to Congress, which is a very delicate issue and isn't criminal in my opinion. You don't have to tell all of your sources and methods to Congress, and you try to conceal as best as you can."[49] By the trial of Clair George, the CIA defense fund had received thousands of donations amounting to $250,000. In the courtroom, the two rows reserved for the audience were filled with retired CIA employees.[50]

Five prominent lawyers expanded the fundraising to their colleagues. "They are persons who have spent a substantial part of their lives serving their country as members of an exacting and frequently dangerous profession," said the lawyers about defendants such as George and Clarridge, suggesting that such service generated not only mitigation but also impunity. Some of the lawyers had represented clients against Walsh or were themselves subject to his probes, and they added an anti–big government arrow to their quiver: "Each of us has served in government and we are acutely aware of the overwhelming power of the government when it is arrayed against an individual."[51]

.....

Also in the 1990s, the OIC turned its attention to the State Department. This was unforeseen. Since 1986, as Walsh wrote, State Department officials, from Secretary George Shultz down, "were the emerging heroes of the Iran/contra story." They had opposed its policies and been cooperative with investigators. They "seemed to have nothing to hide."

That changed in 1991. When Fiers pleaded guilty in July, he backed North's testimony that former Assistant Secretary of State for Inter-American Affairs Elliott Abrams knew about the Contra supply network.[52] It could hardly have been otherwise, since Fiers, North, and Abrams together made up the RIG that oversaw Central American issues for Reagan. Abrams had asked the Sultan of Brunei for funding, and, in fall 1986, had lied to Congress about that, too, again so that Congress would approve the $100 million for the Contras.

Abrams expressed no remorse for misleading Congress. "Every time you testify," he rationalized, "you select what to say and what not to say, which is to say you withhold information." As he told his own kids, "When I was in the State Department I knew a lot of secrets. . . . Now, some people are saying, you should have told Congress. You had to tell. When they asked you, you had to tell, and not telling is a crime. And I am saying, no it isn't." Yet he presented no evidence that it was not. He justified withholding from Congress first, on the assumption that it would leak, and second, on the precedents set by as Franklin Roosevelt, John Kennedy, Lyndon Johnson, and Jimmy Carter—conveniently, all Democratic presidents.

In court, when Walsh and his team offered a plea bargain, Abrams thought, *Oh, fuck them.* Then it dawned on him: *My God, they are serious, they are going to do this to me. They have heard our side, our brilliant side, our perfect case, and they don't buy it.*[53] Certain of his innocence but facing one or two years of court battles and a likely $1 million in legal fees—not to mention jail time if he lost—Abrams buckled. In October, one month before the five-year statute of limitations for misleading Congress ran out, Abrams pleaded guilty to two misdemeanor counts of doing so in fall 1986. He also promised to cooperate fully in other cases.[54]

New York Times editors called the plea "a welcome admission that stonewalling Congress is a crime." "This guilty plea shames the State Department in the same way that the plea of Alan Fiers last July shamed the Central Intelligence Agency," they added. The misdemeanors were misnomers. Abrams had committed perjury—a felony—but had bargained his charge down to "withholding."[55]

In November 1991, Abrams was sentenced to two years' probation, 100 hours of community service, and a $50 fine.[56] Like other Iran-Contra convicts, he escaped a harsher punishment, which could have climbed to two years in prison and $200,000.

.....

These cases irked the ends-over-means anticommunists, the defenders of agency turf, and the factual relativists. But it was the prosecution of former secretary of defense Caspar "Cap" Weinberger that most enraged mainstream Republicans and united them against the OIC.

Weinberger was a strong believer in the limited role of Congress in foreign policy, and Iran-Contra only reinforced his conviction. In 1987, while denying any "imperial presidency" and admitting Congress's role in "helping articulate the broad goals of our nation's foreign policy," he fully entrusted the "conduct" of that policy to the president.[57]

Yet Weinberger had balanced his reverence for Reagan with warnings, especially that selling arms to Iran was bad policy and likely illegal. The president had overruled him. Defense had then collaborated with the NSC and the CIA in getting those arms to Iran. Throughout, the secretary remained informed of arms sales and third-country funding.

After the scandal, Weinberger had been interviewed and deposed before several bodies. In June 1987, the House Iran-Contra committee asked him whether he ever kept notes of his many meetings.

"Yes, occasionally, but comparatively rarely," he had answered.

In October 1990, to the FBI and OIC, he denied that it was "his habit to take notes throughout his seven years as Secretary of Defense." He was unaware of any notes not turned over to investigators. Or so he said.[58] In his memoir of that same year, he mentioned "going over . . . my own rather meager notes" on Iran-Contra.[59]

In reality, Weinberger had for years taken notes on five-by-seven-inch note pads. He had done so seven days a week, and kept them dated, labeled, and organized. It was, in essence, a diary. About 1,700 of its pages concerned Iran arms sales.[60] Upon leaving office in November 1987, the secretary somehow legally took 13,000 classified documents with him, including his diary. In 1988, he donated them to the Library of Congress.[61] There they lay undisturbed for more than two years while an archivist processed them.

A statement by Secretary Shultz that had been recorded by an aide—"Cap takes notes but . . . never had to cough them up"— tipped off a Walsh aide in August 1990. Greg Mark, a young associate counsel of Walsh's, visited the Library of Congress and inspected Weinberger's notes marked "classified." When Mark asked to see *un*classified material, Weinberger's longtime secretary and a librarian let him see only "items that specified Iran or a Central American country in the register." The diary was not among these, so Mark left. A year later, in November 1991, two aides returned for another look. This time, they were allowed to see the whole register and thus found the diary.

To Walsh's team, the diary contained "highly sensitive" material and contradicted the former secretary's claim of limited knowledge of Iran-Contra.[62] For instance, when asked if he had known of a HAWK missile sale, Weinberger had answered, "No I did not." Yet his diary allegedly showed he had discussed the deal four times with Bud McFarlane.[63] To Walsh, "Weinberger knew his notes conflicted with the positions taken by President Reagan and Vice President Bush as well as by himself and other cabinet officers. He kept them secret until after the Iran-Contra select committees concluded their hearings. He then tried to conceal them from me."[64]

Walsh recalled with bitterness how Weinberger "deliberately lied to Congress. He had their counsel in his office, four feet from the drawer where he kept the notebooks and he looked them in the eye and told them he didn't have any notes, that he wasn't like Henry Kissinger, he didn't keep notes."[65] Walsh saw Weinberger's "misconduct" as "part of a broader pattern of obstruction by the Reagan administration that had begun on November 10, 1986, and had entailed withholding information from congressional leaders; blocking our work by overclassifying documents; lying to Congress, the Tower Commission, the grand jury, and my staff; and withholding [several officials'] notes."[66]

Like Reagan, Weinberger was convinced of his own righteousness. A May 1992 lie detector test asked him whether he "ever intentionally withh[e]ld diary notes" or misled anyone in government, including the OIC, and whether he engaged in a cover-up or lied to Congress about Iran-Contra. He answered no to all questions, and he passed.[67]

On June 12, Weinberger's lawyers informed Walsh that there would be no plea from their client. *Okay*, answered Walsh, *then expect an indictment*. Weinberger's lead lawyer shook Walsh's hand and smiled, "Of course, you know this means nuclear war."[68]

Four days later, a federal grand jury charged Weinberger with one count of obstruction (withholding his notes), two of making false statements, and two of perjury.[69] He was the first Reagan cabinet member to be charged with an Iran-Contra crime. At seventy-four years old and now the publisher of *Forbes* magazine, Weinberger had refused to plead to a misdemeanor. Nor would he give what he claimed Walsh wanted—"statements which were not true about myself or others."[70] His lawyers refused to explain this vague allegation. Walsh called it "a brazen lie. We had asked in a general way about various information he might have, but we had neither asked him to give false testimony nor specified the testimony he would be required to give. We had merely wanted him, like every other potential witness, to tell the truth—the whole truth."[71] Each of the five counts carried a maximum penalty of five years in prison and fines of up to $250,000.

In a subsequent memoir, Weinberger admitted "that I had been mistaken in the chronology of some of the responses I made to various inquiries. But," he added, "that is a long country mile from perjury, which requires both criminal intent to deceive and a deliberate giving of false information." As to his diary, he recalled, "It did not occur to me that my notes, which were basically logs of phone calls, appointments, and personal matters . . . had any value or relevance for investigators." Weinberger claimed to have given written permission to researchers to see his Library of Congress papers and that Walsh failed to do so and then accused Weinberger of "concealing" the notes.[72]

Weinberger left out of his tale that he avoided an interview with the OIC until issued a grand jury subpoena and then evaded being served until an FBI agent caught him leaving his office building through a service entrance.[73]

Because Weinberger's notes had long been available, the judge threw out the obstruction charge, but four counts remained. His trial was set for January 5, 1993.[74]

.....

Republicans were up in arms about the Weinberger indictment. "Absolutely outraged," Ed Meese pronounced himself.[75] Not only did it reach up into the Reagan cabinet, but it targeted a public servant revered for his ethics. Colin Powell, then chair of the Joint Chiefs of Staff, signed an affidavit insisting that Weinberger made an honest mistake in not linking his notes to Iran-Contra investigations and called him "one of the true heroes of the Iran-Contra matter" for opposing the arms sales. He was a "straight arrow" and "one of the most honest men I have ever known."[76]

Bob Dole, the Senate Republican leader, turned defense into offense. He called Walsh and his aides "paid assassins."[77] Senator Orrin Hatch (R-UT) called the indictment "criminalizing policy differences." "We're going to wreck this country," he warned, "if we keep allowing these politically oriented . . . young prosecutors to run amok."[78] In his memoir, Abrams bitterly accused the OIC of being "primarily liberal Democratic, and motivated by a nasty mix of personal ambition, ideology, and animus. They were after scalps." He made arguments spreading among opponents of the OIC: that its budget was unlimited, its caseload out of control, and its deadlines, competition, and oversight nonexistent.[79] Weinberger accused the OIC of election-season partisanship. Outside the courthouse, after pleading not guilty, he said, "I have become a pawn in a clearly political game as is shown by the return of the indictment only days before the Presidential election."[80]

Republicans were now united against him, and some Democrats joined in. "Enough is enough," Representative William Broomfield (R-MI) of the congressional investigative committee wrote to the attorney general.[81] Senators Daniel Inouye (D-HI) and Warren Rudman (R-NH), who had headed the inquiry in 1987, stated that it was "inconceivable to us" that Weinberger "would intentionally mislead or lie to Congress."[82]

After the Weinberger indictment, one group of Republicans asked President Bush's attorney general, William Barr, to appoint an independent counsel to investigate the existing independent counsel, all the while arguing—with no hint of irony—that the institution should be abolished.[83]

Also following the indictment, Republicans fundraised for Weinberger as they had for Oliver North. One group, led by Mike Burch of McDonnell Douglass, piggybacked on the newest political fundraising methods. It used a 50,000-person database to reach out to Republican Party contributors, sent 1,000 personal letters, and prepared a mass mailing to 20,000. The *Washington Times* and *Wall Street Journal* obliged with editorial attacks on Walsh, as did William F. Buckley. The Heritage Foundation think tank sent a letter to its members. About seven weeks after the indictment, these efforts had raised $60,000, but the legal bill even before the indictment ran up to $145,000.[84] (One invoice from lawyer Robert Bennett charged Weinberger more than $300,000 for one month or 1,721 hours of legal work—an average of $175 per hour or $380 in 2024 dollars.)[85] Although many deplored the "waste" incurred by Walsh, few noted how defense attorneys padded their bank accounts.

An associated group, led by president of the Legal Affairs Council Richard Delgaudio, called itself "Friends of Caspar Weinberger" and set up a legal fund for what it assessed would be more than $1 million in legal bills.[86] On September 23, 1992, Delgaudio and friends hosted a fundraising dinner at the Mayflower Hotel in Washington. They raised seed money through "defense industry contacts, *Forbes* and Bechtels"—everywhere Weinberger had worked. They invited all former Reagan and Ford cabinet officers, all former secretaries of defense, joint chiefs, and other military dignitaries.[87] A thousand showed up to the dinner, where Republicans let loose their ire at Walsh. Senator Malcolm Wallop (R-WY) called the indictment "the revenge of a petty, small-minded man, trying to find something to salvage his career." Others called Walsh a "sleazy bounty hunter," a "witch hunter," and a "stumbling, bumbling independent counsel who couldn't keep up with his own ego."[88]

"This is the rottenest, son-of-a-bitchin'est thing that ever happened," said Senator Alan Simpson (R-WY). The crowd roared.[89]

In addition to paying the $35 for dinner, many who attended wrote out checks for $5,000 or $10,000.[90]

.....

One might be forgiven for agreeing that Walsh was out of control with all his indictments. Yet his team followed many more leads that it chose *not* to turn into indictments—and not always because the investigated were innocent. Walsh chose not to proceed for various reasons, including insufficient evidence, the granting of immunity for testimony, the low significance of one's crimes, or the lack of resources—despite accusations of lavish spending. Among the individuals investigated but never indicted were Vice President Bush; Attorney General Ed Meese; Chief of Staff Don Regan; US Ambassador to Costa Rica Lewis Tambs; Assistant Secretary of Defense for International Security Affairs Richard Armitage; CIA Deputy Director Robert Gates; Colin Powell, Weinberger's senior military assistant; Donald Gregg, national security advisor to Mr. Bush; "CIA Subject #1," a senior CIA field officer in Central America; James Adkins, chief of a CIA facility in Central America; Army Colonel James Steele, the military group commander at the US Embassy in El Salvador; North's secretary, Fawn Hall; Ambassador to El Salvador Edwin Corr; William Zucker, the Enterprise's Swiss financial manager; and various officers and employees of the NEPL.[91]

The most telling nonindictment was that of Secretary Shultz. In 1987, Charles Hill, Shultz's executive assistant, had given to Congress's investigators his notebooks about only the Iran arms sales, not the Contras. In 1990, the OIC discovered in Hill's archive at the Hoover Institution in Palo Alto, California, 12,000 new pages of Hill's handwritten notes, some verbatim dictations from his boss. (Some of Hill's writings, still at Hoover, counter that "the I[ndependent] C[ounsel] had access to all [my] notes.")[92] These notes suggested that Shultz had known far more than he had let on, for instance that arms shipments were planned and delivered to Iran.

Had the State Department misled the OIC? Yes, Walsh concluded, "Hill had willfully withheld relevant notes and prepared false testimony for Shultz in 1987."[93] Shultz's testimony to Congress had been clearly incorrect—he admitted so himself—yet Walsh suspected that a jury might reasonably doubt that Shultz had misled Congress. He also factored in the secretary's opposition to Iran-Contra policies. "I had no urge to prosecute the one voice of courage and reason among Reagan's senior foreign policy advisors."[94]

As for Ronald Reagan, when Walsh released his report in early 1994, he reserved his harshest words for a president against whom impeachment "certainly should have been considered" by Congress. A Walsh team internal memo concluded that Reagan broke the law: He "knowingly disregarded statutory restraints" in selling weapons and not telling Congress and "knowingly condoned the systematic evasion" of the Boland Amendment. This misbehavior "may have invited congressional retaliation or impeachment," it added, "but it did not present the willful disobedience to a statute carrying criminal sanctions that would be necessary to support a prosecution." The OIC also believed that the president, "as the only individual recipient of constitutional power is and should be largely free of prosecutorial harassment."[95] In his final report, Walsh reiterated that Reagan "set the stage for the illegal activities of others." He "created the conditions which made possible the crimes" linked to deviations from his own Iran policy and his instructions to keep the Contras together "body and soul" in defiance of the Boland Amendment.[96] Reagan shot back that Walsh's investigation had "become both excessive and vindictive."[97]

.....

"Secrecy, which made the Iran-contra affair possible, is now a huge obstacle to its cleanup."[98] So editorialized the *New York Times* in 1990 about Walsh's last wave of investigations, one that washed over the CIA and the Departments of State and Defense with limited success. In the process, the OIC revealed much about the state of American democracy in the aftermath of Iran-Contra.

In nearly seven years of searching, Walsh found much evidence no one else had, including notes or diaries from Bush, Hill, North, Reagan, Regan, Shultz, and Weinberger. By late 1992, results piled up: Fourteen indictments resulting in eleven convictions and no acquittals confirmed that the OIC did not indict unless it was sure to win. Two of the eleven convictions were overturned on appeal, but only due to congressional grants of immunity that Walsh thought were ill-advised. Of the other three indictments, one was dismissed because the Justice Department refused to release classified materials. Two others, of Weinberger and Clarridge, awaited trial.

The saga suggested the low estimation in which Reagan and Bush officials, both senior and middling, held key tenets of democracy, among them the separation of powers, the rule of law, the administration of justice, and the sanctity of truth and trust. NSC and State Department officials were openly disdainful of Congress. CIA officials admitted to withholding information as a matter of bureaucratic course. And the CIA, Justice, and White House denied the release of classified documents with little justification. Walsh cataloged more than fifty false statements made by Iran-Contra conspirators to investigators.[99]

There is no evidence that Republicans colluded to keep incriminating evidence from investigators. In some instances, they likely worked hard to review massive amounts of documents and still blew past deadlines. They may have been underresourced, as Walsh was. He never formally charged collusion, but, toward the end of his probe, the "lack of full disclosure . . .

sooner or later leads you to feel that it's not all individualistic action, that it was planned." Walsh also concluded that, although many defendants were "likable and dedicated" and at times protected legitimate state secrets, in the second half of his investigation, they largely resorted to "a protection of cover-up."[100] He used "cover-up" in the subtitle of his memoir.

12

IMPUNITY

On Christmas Eve 1992, outgoing President George H. W. Bush pardoned all those who, at the time, stood convicted or indicted for Iran-Contra crimes, thereby ending the work of the Office of Independent Counsel. Bush rationalized it as the nation putting to rest an excessively politicized prosecution, but his own political goals were transparent. He also communicated to fellow Republicans that crimes in the service of pursuing a foreign policy, even one repudiated by the president, would henceforth be unprosecutable.

Equally serious, Bush himself had disregarded the norms of democracy over the span of the Iran-Contra scheme. His involvement in the operations and the cover-up, from engaging in quid pro quos to withholding his notes, was deep, lengthy, and damaging to the rule of law. Right before his pardons, that involvement caught up with him, leading many to suspect that Bush, in pardoning political allies, also cut off any investigative path to himself.

.....

The framers of the US Constitution conceived of the pardon power, as laid out in Article II, Section 2, Clause 1, as practical statecraft rather than self-protection or political favor-granting. The president enjoyed the "Power to grant Reprieves and Pardons for Offenses against the United States, except in Cases of impeachment." When the legal system failed to yield moral or political fairness, the president could commute or vacate what he considered to be an excessive punishment for a federal crime. A pardon was not a pronouncement of innocence, nor did it reverse a conviction, although it could precede even an indictment. In *Federalist No. 74*, Alexander Hamilton called the power a "benign prerogative."[1] The framers trusted that presidents would exercise restraint in the use of pardons, if only to avoid retribution in the next election.

Most presidents issued pardons to heal political wounds. Abraham Lincoln pardoned draft evaders and deserters during the Civil War, as did Jimmy Carter and Gerald Ford in the Vietnam years. Other presidents used the pardon, as scholar Margaret Love wrote, "for reasons of state, and to override or preempt unpopular or inconvenient laws." Thomas Jefferson released those imprisoned under the Alien and Sedition Acts. William Henry Harrison and Grover Cleveland pardoned Mormon polygamists as Utah was about to be admitted as a state. Woodrow Wilson released more than 500 violators of liquor laws after Congress overrode his veto of the Volstead Act. John Kennedy and Lyndon Johnson pardoned more than 200 drug offenders.[2]

To ensure legitimate pardons, the Justice Department almost universally vetted petitions and presented them to the president. One of the few exceptions was Ford's pardon of former president Richard Nixon for his cover-up of Watergate. That precedent allowed Ronald Reagan, in 1981, to bypass Justice and pardon two FBI officials who authorized the illegal surveillance of radicals.

Pardons were also supposed to be routine. Until 1980, presidents granted about two per week, and rarely during holidays or before departing office—timing that would arouse suspicion about intent.[3]

Finally, implicitly denied in the Constitution was the self-pardon. Adjacent to a self-pardon was the pardoning of political allies who could inform on crimes by the president.[4]

For all its normative restraints, the pardon remained fraught with danger, being among the few unchecked powers in the Constitution. Only the president could issue one, he could do so without even his own bureaucracy, and neither the Congress nor the Supreme Court could check or balance him.

.....

The question of the pardon for Iran-Contra crimes came up often during the Reagan years, but the president never issued one. In the middle of the

Iran-Contra hearings in summer 1987, Oliver North was so popular a witness that it seemed a no-brainer for the president to eventually pardon him. Senate committee member Orrin Hatch (R-UT) said he would support a pardon for North and John Poindexter. In the House committee, Dick Cheney (R-WY) agreed that Reagan "may have to consider" a pardon even though he thought it premature because no criminal charges were forthcoming at the time.[5] In March, Poindexter's lawyers "came over," Bush wrote in his diary, "pressing for a pardon" before a Reagan speech on Iran-Contra, "not a threat to have Poindexter say something, exactly, . . . to counterdict [*sic*] the President, but saying this would be a good time to pardon John."[6]

Rumors proved baseless. Thanksgiving 1987—supposedly "a time for forgiveness and healing," said the *New York Times*—seemed like an opportunity, but it came and went without a word from Reagan.[7]

"Mr. President, Pardon Oliver North Today," read a full-page ad in the *Washington Times* on Veterans Day 1988, as North, Poindexter, Richard Secord, and Albert Hakim awaited trial. Its sponsor was the Legal Affairs Council, a conservative research group that had flooded the Iran-Contra hearings with telegrams and would fundraise for Caspar Weinberger's legal fees. The council's president, Michael Boos, recounted walking up to Reagan.

"Mr. President, please take care of Ollie North, please don't leave him hanging," Boos allegedly said.

The president looked back at Boos, winked, smiled, and said, "I will."[8]

Thanksgiving 1988 saw intensified calls for pardoning North and company. Republican strategists had advised Reagan to avoid pardons during his vice president's campaign to succeed him, but now the election was over. The *Wall Street Journal* called for a pardon, as did thirty retired admirals and generals.

Senator George Mitchell (D-ME), meanwhile, warned against setting "the precedent that any future president's advisors may act outside the law, that they may break the law with impunity and that if they are caught, they need not even stand trial and be judged for their actions." A pardon would set a "dual standard of justice": "one for the powerful, another for all other citizens."[9]

Reagan noted in his diary on November 29, 1988, that the Reverend Jerry Falwell had submitted to the White House a petition of 2 million signatures "demanding a pardon for Ollie."[10] Falwell was using the appeal to fundraise for himself, selling $25 videotapes of "the inspiring Ollie North story" and $15 color photographs of North alongside his calls for signatures.[11] On his weekly TV broadcast, the evangelist would flash a toll-free phone number for viewers to add their name to the "Master Pardon Petition." As chancellor of Liberty University, he turned its graduation into a political rally for North. He compared the lieutenant colonel to Jesus Christ, both "indicted and convicted and crucified."[12]

Others followed suit. Beverly LaHaye of Concerned Women for America tied her fundraising among its 500,000 members to a pardon for North. The American Freedom Coalition—on whose board sat John Singlaub, the private Contra fundraiser—planned a TV program, newspaper ads, and pro-North rallies in all fifty states. Within twenty minutes of North's indictment, the Conservative Victory Committee led by Brent Bozell launched a pardon drive.[13]

"I can't do that before the trial," Reagan had written on November 28 of a pardon for North and Poindexter. "It would leave them under a cloud of guilt for the rest of his [*sic*] life." A few days later, Reagan ruled out the possibility in public.[14] First Lady Nancy Reagan was allegedly opposed to any pardon and "forbade the subject to be raised."[15]

Attorney Jeffrey Toobin, for one, thought this spoke to Reagan's "fundamentally ungenerous" nature. "Granting a pardon would expose him to calumny and attack because of an action on behalf of those who served him. Reagan did not go for that sort of thing."[16] To journalist Carl Rowan, Reagan gave his "cloud of guilt" rationale, but he also predicted that, by the time the trials run, "I won't have to face that issue."[17]

.....

So the decision passed to George H. W. Bush, who strode into the Oval Office one month before Oliver North walked into a Washington, DC, courtroom for his trial.

As vice president, Bush had been as incensed as any other Republican by what he saw as an arrogant Congress and zealous independent counsel. The Founding Fathers did not intend "that our foreign policy should be conducted and reviewed by grand juries," Bush said to a conservative lawyers' group in early 1987. He decried "the erosion of presidential authority" in the previous twenty years.[18]

Bush also denied almost any knowledge of or involvement in Iran-Contra affairs. In August 1987 to the *Washington Post*, he denied royally, "We were not in the loop."[19] In his 1988 campaign autobiography, he claimed he was "deliberately excluded" from arms sales discussions.[20] "Not in the loop" is how he again described himself on *Nightline*, the ABC News program, in 1992.[21] He rejected three times to journalist David Broder the suggestion that he had heard the objections to Iranian arms sales from Secretary of State

George Shultz and Secretary of Defense Caspar Weinberger, leading Broder to compare the episode to the Biblical Denial of Peter.[22]

When Weinberger heard the "in the loop" comment, he called Shultz.

"That's terrible. He was on the other side," said Weinberger, meaning that Bush favored the arms sales. "It's on the record. Why did he say that?"[23]

Weinberger's lost-in-the-archives 1,700 pages of notes showed that Bush was in the room when the secretary of defense voiced his opposition to the arms sales. It confirmed the testimony by Shultz and a note by Charles Hill, Shultz's aide.[24] Richard Secord also wrote that he was convinced that Bush "knew virtually all the tactical details of the Iran initiative."[25]

Indeed, in private interviews with the FBI in 1986 and OIC in 1988, Bush acknowledged knowing about much of the arms sales.[26] On November 5, 1986, he inserted in his diary, "I'm one of the few people that know fully the details [of the arms-for-hostages swap], and there is a lot of flak and misinformation out there. It is not a subject we can talk about." Then follow four redacted lines.[27] On December 18, to the Tower Commission, Bush admitted knowing of Israeli sales to Iran and about TOWs, but not about HAWKs or HAWK parts, Contra aid, "North's contra activities," the diversion, or even "how shady Ghorbanifar was."[28]

In early 1988, standing in subfreezing temperatures outside a farm research lab in Iowa, presidential candidate Bush said he could not recall any objections by senior cabinet members such as Shultz and Weinberger during the January 7, 1986, National Security Council meeting, which he attended and at which they were vociferous in those protestations. A former official said Bush may have left the meeting early.

What about the meeting ten days later when Poindexter briefed Reagan about revising a finding for arms sales that had already taken place? The former national security advisor's notes placed the vice president at that meeting. "I don't recall a finding being signed and I think I'd remember that," Bush said. "Now, the president may have signed the finding, but there was no discussion of a finding in front of me."

On the notion of trading arms for hostages, Bush claimed to be as unable to connect scandal-size dots as was Reagan: "I sensed that we were sending arms. And I sensed that we were trying to get hostages out. But not arms for hostages."[29] Yet memos showed that Bush had "intensive discussions" about arms and hostages while in Israel in 1986.[30] "Mr. Bush Had to Know" was the title of the *New York Times* editorial in response.[31]

On the Contras, finally: "I knew nothing of the shipments by the so-called private network of arms to the contras," declared Bush.[32] Yet in November

1984, the vice president was given a CIA analysis detailing the financing of the Contras by private and government sources.[33] North's private notebooks also showed meetings with Bush alone and with Bush and Donald Gregg, his national security advisor, both in 1986.[34]

Bush certainly was involved in the quid pro quo with Honduras by traveling there in March 1985 to offer "incentives" in return for President Roberto Suazo's help to the Contras. In April 1989, during the North trial, the forty-two-page document detailing the tit for tat saw the light of day. Nine months before his trip, Bush had warned against making promises to third parties that "some people might interpret . . . as some kind of an exchange," yet he later became the emissary of $110 million in aid.[35]

Senator Mitchell said the quid pro quo agreements "were clearly inappropriate, possibly illegal, and involved the United States in a way in which our country should not be involved."[36] "Explain, Mr. President," editorialized the *Miami Herald*. Bush stated only that he did not want to upset the trial of North. "As soon as the trial ends, however, President Bush owes the American people a thorough and open discussion of his role in that seedy affair and of his campaign denials of that role."[37]

Bush claimed that documents showing his secret involvement with the Central American country had always been "available" to the Iran-Contra committees. Yet a House panel asked to see all the documents from North's office, only to be turned down. The White House insisted that only the FBI could search the documents, and its procedure tended to limit the number of batches.[38]

.....

Bush's denials overlapped with a presidential election year and dogged him throughout the primaries and general election. Republican and Democratic opponents alike blasted his dodginess.

One of Bush's strategies to evade the truth was to attack the media that sought to uncover it. In an interview that one scholar dubbed "the day the politicians began to win the war against the media," Bush confronted legendary *CBS Evening News* anchor Dan Rather.[39] On January 25, 1988, the program began with a five-minute report demonstrating how Bush's Iran-Contra comments contradicted the record.[40] Cut to a live interview, where Rather asked about those contradictions and the vice president cut him off, reading off a cue card held by none other than Roger Ailes, a campaign manager who would go on to run Fox News.

"You've impugned my integrity by suggesting . . . that I didn't tell the truth," Bush accused Rather. "It's not fair to judge my whole career by a rehash on Iran. How would you like it if I judged your career by those seven minutes when you walked off the set in New York?" he added, referring to when Rather had stormed off his own show when a sports event preempted it.[41]

After the interview, Bush knew he had a victory. "He didn't lay a glove on me," he said of Rather, demeaning him with what one journalist described as "an off-color slang term for the female anatomy."[42] "I meant *pussycat*," he wrote in his diary, "the way he came on like a tiger." He called CBS "dirty [redacted] in their approach."[43]

"It's going to help me," Bush told supporters about the interview. To ensure that it did, Bush's campaign telephone banks poured calls in to CBS stations complaining of Rather's impetuousness, creating the impression of one-sided public outrage.[44] Bush had successfully deflected the effort to clarify his role by attacking the "liberal media" during an election in which the accusation carried weight.[45]

He won the election.

.....

Four years later, the contest would not go so smoothly. In September 1992, the notes by Weinberger, Shultz, and Secord contradicting Bush's denials dropped like bombshells in what was a close general election. Bush's opponent, Arkansas Governor Bill Clinton, pounced on the revelations. "It's time for George Bush to come clean," said George Stephanopoulos, Clinton's communications director.[46] "Since his current story is now different from his original alibi," Stephanopoulos charged, "Bush either told the American people one thing in public and told investigators another in private—or misled both."[47]

Bush's answers to these allegations were confusing. He said he answered 4,000 questions about the Iran-Contra affair, "450 by me, some under oath, some to the news media, [and] 3,500 by staff." At another point, he said, "I've testified 450 times under oath." He had testified under oath once, on January 11, 1988, and the proceeding was never made public. He also appeared before the Tower Board, but not under oath.[48] More documents—some new, some reexamined—kept linking Bush to the scandal during the final weeks of the election.[49] In September, one poll revealed that 65 percent of Americans believed Bush had not told the truth on Iran-Contra; another, that 55 percent were dissatisfied with his explanations.[50]

Then came Independent Counsel Lawrence Walsh's supplementary indictment of Weinberger on October 30, the Friday before Election Tuesday. It quoted a note from Weinberger that the "VP favored" the swap of hostages for arms during the January 7, 1986, meeting that he long denied attending.[51] The Clinton campaign called it "the smoking gun that George Bush lied to the American people about his role in the arms-for-hostages affair."[52]

Bush denied there was any news in this item and claimed "a big witch hunt" by Walsh timed to hurt his reelection chances. Bush was right that the January 7 meeting was public knowledge, but the Weinberger note was its first documentary evidence. Again, Bush deflected by attacking the media. When a host on CNN pressed him on the revelations, Bush charged back, "Do you plan to spend the whole time on Iran-Contra? Because I don't." Even some Republicans admitted that the news was costing Bush votes.[53] From a dead heat, after the indictment, the polls nudged Clinton's way.[54] Vice President Dan Quayle called Walsh's move "the last nail in the coffin."[55]

Republicans were angriest at Walsh after the election. Senator Bob Dole (R-KS) led colleagues in their surreal call for an independent counsel to investigate the independent counsel. They also demanded that both the Senate judiciary committee and Attorney General Bill Barr investigate the OIC, alleging improper ties to the Clinton campaign.[56] Dole's central accusation was that the OIC was "a hotbed of Democratic activist lawyers" because one of them and his firm had donated to the party before he joined Walsh's team. (Meanwhile, Dole had received campaign contributions from Weinberger's attorneys.)[57]

In 2020, when Barr was again attorney general, this time under Donald Trump, one former colleague recalled that he had "always had a broad view of executive power."[58] Conservative Catholics, Barr's Upper West Side Manhattan family rooted for Barry Goldwater in 1964. His parents worked in education, instilling in him a love of intellectual combat wedded to a fear of what their son would call "social pathology." In the 1970s, Barr supported Nixon and resented the Congress that curtailed the abuses of the CIA. In 1982, he joined the White House's legal team, "devising a legal armature for the executive branch as it tried to restore its power," explained one journalist. The team advised the president to veto more laws and refuse to enforce those that encroached on his power. Independent prosecutors were part of the problem—a Democratic ploy to weaken Republican executives.

Under Bush, Barr first ran the Office of Legal Counsel at Justice, where he argued for fighting against legislative encroachment. He chaired meetings at which general counsels of executive branch departments strategized against Congress. In foreign policy, he wrote rationales for Bush to arrest Panamanian strongman Manuel Noriega. As deputy attorney general, he argued that the president could go to war whenever he wanted—for instance invading Iraq. Even Dick Cheney, then secretary of defense, expressed shock at an attorney general giving the president political advice.

As attorney general, he would recall in 2001, Barr considered Walsh "a—I don't know what to say in polite company."[59]

In response to Dole's demand for an investigation of Walsh, Barr rejected appointing another special prosecutor, but he referred the matter to his department's Criminal Division and said, "I think people in the Iran-contra matter have been treated very unfairly, many of them." He added that his Justice Department would not have brought up the kinds of charges Walsh did. Although Walsh could finish his investigation and report, the law that oversaw him had expired a few days before. "Good riddance," said Barr.[60]

.....

Like Reagan, Bush long resisted pardoning Iran-Contra defendants, and the country, too, was of two minds. Early in Bush's tenure, in May 1989, 51 percent of respondents supported a pardon for Oliver North (see fig. 19).[61] When a jury convicted Poindexter in April 1990, the pressure once again mounted on Bush to pardon him and North. Even a liberal such as journalist Daniel Schorr, who had figured on Nixon's infamous "enemies list," called for a pardon "out of concern for the country rather than the culprits."[62] Dole came out publicly in favor of pardons, and Walsh rebuked him: "I can recall no case where a Senate leader has so directly intruded himself in a pending lawsuit."[63] The *New York Times* also warned of the obvious: "A pardon now would prompt widespread suspicion that Mr. Bush was shielding himself as well as others."[64]

After Bush's loss to Clinton, however, momentum built toward a pardon. Rumors flew that Weinberger's well-connected attorney, Robert Bennett, was in discussions with Vice President Quayle, White House aides such as William Kristol, and senior Republicans.[65] One Senate aide explained how Weinberger's indictment and the election results were the final straws. "Cap's considered so straight it's almost incredible," he said. "And there's the indignity of Walsh indicting a guy who was against this stuff from the start. A lot of people think that Bush, having destroyed himself, ought to do something nice for the party by closing up this matter."[66] At this point, 59 percent of Americans considered a pardon a bad idea.[67]

FIGURE 19 During the trial of Oliver North, supporters increased the pressure for a pardon. (Mark Reinstein/Corbis/Getty)

Yet it came on December 24, no doubt timed to hit the news cycle on Christmas Day, when few watched TV news or read papers.[68] In a stroke of his pen, Bush annulled one conviction (of Clair George), three guilty pleas (Elliott Abrams, Alan Fiers, and Robert McFarlane), and two pending cases (Duane Clarridge and Weinberger).[69] His statement mostly noted Weinberger's long and distinguished service to the United States and his and his wife's age and illnesses. The others he pardoned were all patriots who had "already paid a price—in depleted savings, lost careers, anguished families." He also decried "a profoundly troubling development in the political and legal climate of our country: the criminalization of policy differences."[70]

The move canceled the trial of Weinberger, set for January 5, making Bush the first president to pardon someone on the eve of a proceeding. For the former secretary of defense, the Christmas Eve news was a godsend. "For the first time in nearly a year," Weinberger recalled, "I slept well and awoke happily. That Christmas was one of the best I could remember" (see fig. 20). His legal bills still totaled $2.3 million, of which his legal defense fund paid only $600,000.[71] Once again, the only clear winners in Iran-Contra were the defense lawyers.

"The Christmas pardons were . . . a triumph for the unitary executive," wrote Steven Calabresi and Christopher Yoo a generation later. "They allowed

FIGURE 20 On January 18, 1993, a few weeks after pardoning him and in the last days of his presidency, Bush greeted Weinberger warmly as he bestowed the Presidential Medal of Freedom to his predecessor, Ronald Reagan. (Robert Giroux)

the president to reassert executive power over the Walsh investigation that the Ethics in Government Act had wrongly taken away from him."[72] One of the prosecutors for Walsh, James Brosnahan, made the same point, but disapprovingly. "If you listen to the philosophy being advanced in the United States today, you will hear royalists," he wrote after the pardon, which was "an ancient royal prerogative." Its philosophy belonged to "a person who believes above all in strong, central authority, unencumbered by excess democratic devices." "Iran-contra," he concluded, "radiated a profound disdain for Congress and through it, for the people."[73]

To no one's surprise, Walsh agreed. "President Bush's pardon of Caspar Weinberger and other Iran-contra defendants undermines the principle that no man is above the law," he said in an angry response. "The Iran-contra cover-up, which has continued for more than six years, has now been completed." He saw Weinberger's "concealment" of his notes as "part of a disturbing pattern of deception and obstruction that permeated the highest levels of the Reagan and Bush Administrations."[74]

Although a few Democrats backed the pardons, most were crestfallen. They saw Bush's decision as opportunistic, timed to carry no political risk for the lame-duck president. Arthur Liman, Congress's lawyer in the 1987 hearings, called them "a kind gesture to an old friend but a terrible precedent, since it said that a cabinet officer could lie to a prosecutor and the Congress with impunity."[75] President-elect Clinton worried that the pardon "sends a signal that if you work for the Government, you're beyond the law, or that not telling the truth to Congress under oath is somehow less serious than not telling the truth to some other body under oath." Senator Mitchell also warned, "If members of the executive branch lie to the Congress, obstruct justice and otherwise break the law, how can policy differences be fairly and legally resolved in a democracy?"[76]

. . . . .

After the pardons, Bush remained vulnerable to prosecution. His Christmas Eve proclamation was not technically a self-pardon because Bush could still have been sued, and several figures from the scandal would have been required to testify against him because they were immune from prosecution and could not invoke the Fifth Amendment.[77]

The very day of the pardons, Walsh told a news program that Bush was a "subject" in his investigation.[78] He vowed "appropriate action" against the recent revelation that Bush, too, had failed to disclose personal notes.[79] Walsh asked Bush's personal lawyers about his failure to produce the tapes that were the basis of a diary he kept in his vice presidential years. They responded that Walsh's team had not asked for the tapes specifically, that they were just "personal campaign thoughts," that Bush was too busy with his campaign to comply, and that he thought they had nothing to do with Iran-Contra.[80]

Yet no accusation of Bush lying implied criminal conduct. Walsh never investigated him for trading arms for hostages, violating Boland, obstructing any investigation, or even lying to Congress—because Congress had never questioned him. Bush gave one deposition, taken, in Walsh's words, "primarily to eliminate him as a witness for North."[81]

Walsh concluded that Bush indeed "was fully aware of the Iran arms sales" yet found no evidence of his knowing of the diversion or that he or his staff violated the Boland Amendment. (Congress found the same.) If anything, the delayed documents exculpated Bush. But the process of getting them suggested a cover-up. In 1987 and again in early 1992, Walsh had asked for any Bush notes on Iran-Contra, to no avail. On December 11, 1992, the White House told Walsh, out of the blue, that Bush had failed to produce diaries on Iran-Contra. In one entry of his diary, Bush fumed that Shultz had turned over 700 pages of personal notes, adding, "I would never surrender such documents."[82] Walsh agreed to interview Bush only after his 1992 reelection bid, yet Bush refused to discuss anything but the failure to produce his diaries.

In January 1993, after the pardons, Bush released the full transcripts of his recorded diary from fall 1986, which showed that he was informed of Iran-Contra but was not a key decision-maker. None of it proved incriminating: It showed a cautious candidate-in-waiting helping his administration minimize the political fallout, including to his electoral chances.[83] "They did not justify reopening the investigation," Walsh recalled of the diary entries.[84] All avenues to prosecution closed, Walsh closed up shop and wrote his final report.

.....

Many people at the time pronounced that Bush's pardons would ultimately be judged by "history."[85] Iran-Contra "was investigated long and through a difficult process with jillions of dollars and people and money and all that," said Marlin Fitzwater, Bush's spokesperson. "And if there are unanswered questions, my vote would be to leave them to the historians."[86] Fitzwater's advice was another way of saying that the matter should be forgotten—at least for the moment.

It was. As historian Malcolm Byrne observed, "the story faded into history without much lasting impact upon the U.S. public. The lack of significant penalty for any of the major players contributed to that outcome."[87]

One of those judgments must address their consequences on American democracy, and perhaps the most damaging of these was the disregard for the rule of law. The pardons undid most of Walsh's decimated victories. In the end, two of Walsh's eleven convictions were reversed on appeal even before six others were pardoned. And he never tried anyone for the main lawbreaking of Iran-Contra—that is, violating the Arms Export Control Act with the Iran arms sales and the Boland Amendment in funding the Contras. The only person who ended up in prison was Thomas Clines, and that was for cheating on his taxes.

Bush had established the dangerous precedent of using the pardon for personal—or at least party—political use. As the *New York Times* editorialized of the unchecked power of the pardon, "the abuse of that ultimate power may be the ultimate abuse of office."[88] Journalist Carl Bernstein of Watergate fame compared that scandal to Iran-Contra, underscoring the seriousness of the latter. The legacy of the Reagan-Bush years was the "unchecked constitutional violence that has been more damaging to the rule of law than Watergate ever was. It will surely haunt future generations. The official response to Watergate was characterized by responsible leadership in both Republican and Democratic Parties," wrote Bernstein. "This has not happened on the Reagan-Bush watch."[89]

"We have failed as a society," wrote David Broder in the *Washington Post*, "to express our contempt and disgust for those who violate their oaths of office with such impunity."[90]

CONCLUSION

ONGOING ASSAULT

This scandal is clearly not going to be the last of its kind.

SCHOLAR ROBERT WILLIAMS, 1995

Scholar Robert Busby helpfully categorized the historiography of Iran-Contra as divided into two camps. The "aberrationists" believe the scandal to have been caused by "men of zeal," individual bad apples in "what is essentially a workable system of government." Such was the conclusion of, among others, the congressional majority report in 1987. "The Iran-Contra Affair," it states, "resulted from the failure of individuals to observe the law, not from deficiencies in existing law or in our system of governance."[1] The "legalists," meanwhile, blame the system itself for incentivizing good apples into bad behavior—or bad into worse. They call for "widespread institutional reform to control the abuse of power by the units of the federal government." Lawrence Walsh and his OIC were of this persuasion, refusing to call Iran-Contra "an aberrational scheme carried out by a 'cabal of zealots.'"[2]

The evidence in this book warrants a third interpretation: that Iran-Contra was a result—and what's more, a motor—of a broader erosion of democratic *norms and behaviors*, and not merely the fault of individuals or institutions.[3] To be sure, the aberrationists and legalists make valid points. There *were* many who abused the system of government, and that system *was* in need of reform. Yet norms operate parallel and somewhat independently of persons and structures, filling in the gaps, regulating, and coordinating.[4] They drive individual behavior as much as institutions do. A problem common to norms is that they must be enforced by public opinion—through socialization, shaming, or elections, for instance—and not necessarily by laws.

The Republican Party, especially, showed that Iran-Contra did not chasten it in the least. It continued its abhorrent disregard for the unwritten rules and conventions of a just and egalitarian society. It felt no shame and socialized itself not to—through editorials, fundraising dinners, cocktail parties, and more. It paid a paltry price come election time.

In early 1994, the *New York Times* reported that, among those charged, convicted, or pardoned in Iran-Contra, "almost all are unrepentant."[5] Clair George of the CIA said that "the lesson" from the scandal "is that your government will not stand behind you when trouble comes your way." Also of the agency, Donald Gregg recalled Iran-Contra as being akin to "living with snakes in the cellar for seven years" even though the OIC never charged him. Most bitter among private entrepreneurs was Richard Secord, who called the affair "just a pack of lies and counterlies and distortions, and it started out that way with President Reagan saying he knew nothing about it." Most, like Gregg, were angry at Lawrence Walsh and his team. Elliott Abrams called them "filthy bastards" and "bloodsuckers." John Poindexter concluded that Walsh "had this theory he was trying so hard to prove"—that Reagan was guilty—"and it was never correct in the first place." Poindexter also proclaimed that he was "upset with the hypocrisy of Congress."

"If I had it to do over again," reflected the former national security advisor, "I would probably do things just about exactly the same way I did then."[6]

Those who designed and ran Iran-Contra and committed crimes to protect themselves after its revelation—not to mention those who defended them in both literal courts and courts of public opinion—violated democratic norms in six distinct and overlapping ways. Violations got more egregious after the 1980s, fragmenting the bedrock of American democracy, and one political party was the overwhelming culprit. "America's great democratic experiment is under assault," wrote Jacob S. Hacker and Paul Pierson in their 2005 study of the Republicans.[7] By 2012, among other scholars, Thomas

Mann and Norman Ornstein noted that the fraying of democracy had worsened, whether Republicans occupied the White House or obstructed government from their seats in Congress: "The Republican Party has become an insurgent outlier—ideologically extreme; contemptuous of the inherited social and economic policy regime; scornful of compromise; unpersuaded by conventional understanding of facts, evidence, and science; and dismissive of the legitimacy of its political opposition."[8] The accelerated erosion became impossible to ignore during the presidency of Donald Trump.

SEPARATION OF POWERS

In the decades after Iran-Contra, presidents—especially Republicans—continued to arrogate power away from the legislature. As Malcolm Byrne noted, "the congressional and independent counsel processes failed to create a disincentive for future administrations against ill-conceived exercises of presidential power."[9] If believers in the unitary power of the executive had learned anything from Iran-Contra, it was not about executive overreach but rather about congressional *interference* with the president's conduct of foreign policy. A unitary executive would seek to prevent such meddling by affirming authoritarian powers for the president.

Some reforms did follow from Iran-Contra. Reagan shook up his staff, replacing so-called loose cannons and turf warriors with more collaborative leaders: Howard Baker as chief of staff and Frank Carlucci as national security advisor.[10] Diplomats, meanwhile, won a Presidential Decision Memorandum that required, for every covert action, that State spell out US interests and objectives, do a cost-benefit analysis, and declare them legal and constitutional. State would also sign off on renewals of each op.[11] In summer 1987, Reagan also reorganized the interagency review process under the National Security Council. Yet its added levels of bureaucracy would likely not prevent another Iran-Contra-like cabal like the RIG in Central America.[12]

The president's reform was called National Security Decision Directive (NSDD) 276. On his next to last day of congressional testimony in July 1987, Secretary of State George Shultz wrote to Reagan, "I realized that we are too far along in your Administration to undertake major structural changes." Yet, he complained, "this NSDD 276 worsens the situation by further aggrandizing the NSC staff rather than cutting it back." Shultz hated the "turf fight" between State and NSC, yet he also saw he was losing ground and asked to be invited to the national security advisor's morning briefing with Reagan.[13]

The congressional committees, meanwhile, failed to create the expectation of new legislation when they ascribed the scandal to individuals failing to follow the law.[14] They recommended only minor adjustments in conducting and reporting covert ops.[15] Against the wishes of the White House, the 1988 Intelligence Oversight Act incorporated some of these recommendations: that Congress be notified within forty-eight hours after a covert action finding; that there be no retroactive covert findings; and that all findings be in writing. It passed the Senate 71–19, but the House took no action and the bill died.

In 1990, Congress added to an intelligence authorization bill the forty-eight-hour rule that Republican White Houses had opposed. This time, President Bush killed it by not signing it—a so-called pocket veto. Bush also opposed Congress's suggestion that the executive inform Congress when it planned to use private citizens or third parties in covert operations. Only when Congress agreed that notification be merely "timely" and that Congress would know only "whether" third parties might be involved did the president sign the bill. This would have been a full return to the *status quo ante* Iran-Contra, save for making findings written and not retroactive.

These largely fruitless negotiations spoke of the lingering tug-of-war in the separation of powers. "A spirit of comity . . . must exist if the Legislative and Executive branches of the government are to work together in this complex area," one staff director of the House Intelligence Committee explained. "Iran-contra destroyed this spirit of comity."[16] Although the limited changes may have helped prevent some of the specific abuses of Iran-Contra, Congress and the White House remained miles apart on oversight.

Beyond Iran-Contra, separation-of-powers comity weakened in other ways. In his last months in office, Reagan issued an executive order adding to his emergency powers, including the right to use military personnel in civilian law enforcement. Almost anything that "threatene[d] the national security of the United States," loosely conceived, could trigger the exercise of such powers.[17] After the 1980s, war powers continued to drift to the president. Congress played virtually no part in decisions to send troops abroad—in Panama, Iraq, Somalia, Haiti, Bosnia, Afghanistan, and again Iraq.[18] The end of the Cold War rendered the executive no more compliant with Congress's constitutional prerogatives. Those seeking to abuse executive power found new justifications—weapons of mass destruction, terrorism, and more.[19]

Republicans in the 1990s, especially under House leader Newt Gingrich (R-GA), attacked Congress even when they ruled it, thus undermining the public's trust in the people's institution—and getting more Republicans elected to further undermine it. One Republican staffer explained the strategy: "By sabotaging the reputation of an institution of government, the party that is programmatically against government would come out the relative winner."[20]

The George W. Bush administration brought into the executive branch several officials interested in applying negative lessons from Iran-Contra. Now–Vice President Dick Cheney pointed to the minority report of his 1987 Iran-Contra committee to explain his embrace of the unitary executive. In 2001, the Justice Department argued that "the Constitution secures all federal executive power in the President to ensure a unity in purpose and energy in action." The Bush II administration seized additional executive power to torture terrorism suspects, approve warrantless wiretaps, create military commissions, and mislead the public into the Iraq War.[21]

In recent decades, presidents also increasingly abused their removal power, which Alexander Hamilton had advised should be shared by the executive and legislative. The unitary executive crowd argued that Congress could not limit the president's removal authority over officers in the executive by creating independent commissions or special prosecutors.[22]

Presidents have also increasingly misused clemency and pardons for partisan gain, as Bush the Elder had in 1992. On his departure from the White House, Clinton pardoned Marc Rich, a fugitive financier and Democratic donor. In 2007, Bush the Younger commuted the thirty-month sentence of Scooter Libby, Cheney's chief of staff, for obstruction of justice, perjury, and making false statements. In doing so, he bypassed the Department of Justice's clemency process as his father had done.[23]

That idea saw full fruition during the Trump years. In 2018, Trump fully pardoned Libby. Later, he commuted the sentence of "dirty trickster" Roger Stone; unlike a pardoned person, a commuted person keeps his Fifth Amendment right not to testify. This communicated to others with likely knowledge of Trump's alleged crimes to stay silent to win his forgiveness.[24] Trump also pardoned conservative political allies such as anti-immigration Arizona sheriff Joe Arpaio, former Trump campaign chair Paul Manafort, former New York police commissioner Bernard Kerik, and former national security advisor Michael Flynn among other Republicans.[25] Besides Flynn, Trump pardoned two others convicted of crimes related to the president's ties to Russia. As he left office, he pardoned former advisor Stephen Bannon, charged with fraud and money laundering. The director of the Office of Legal Counsel under Bush Jr. concluded that "no president in American history comes close to matching Trump's systematically self-serving use of the pardon power."[26] Framer George Mason had warned against the pardon for the very reason that a corrupt man "may frequently pardon crimes which were advised by himself. It may happen," added Mason, "at some future day, that he will establish a monarchy, and destroy the republic."[27]

Trump repeatedly blasted away at the separation of powers. In making foreign policy, he said, "I am the only one that matters."[28] During the coronavirus pandemic, Trump claimed that his power—in this case to lift restrictions—was "total." "I have the ultimate authority," he told the press. "When somebody is the president of the United States, the authority is total and that's the way it's got to be."[29] (When the pandemic caused havoc, however, Trump changed his tune: "I don't take responsibility at all.")

Partly because of this norm-busting, one organization that tracks democracy around the world found that, from 2015 to 2020, the Liberal Democratic Index of the United States dropped from 0.85 to 0.72, largely because of "weakening constraints on the executive under Donald Trump." The country fell from seventeenth to twenty-ninth in global democracy rankings, barely registering anymore as a liberal democracy.[30]

As Republican presidents assaulted norms, norms shifted. By 2020, 43 percent of Republicans believed that "presidents could operate more effectively if they did not have to worry so much about Congress and the courts." Before Trump took office, only 14 percent had agreed with the statement. Journalist George Packer concluded that "the separation of powers turned out to be a gentleman's agreement."[31]

RULE OF LAW

"The spirit of Nuremberg has withered," wrote one scholar near the end of the Iran-Contra trials. By that he meant that the norm of refusing to carry out unlawful orders, enshrined in the persecution of former Nazis, had disappeared along with Oliver North and others' claims to have merely followed the orders of their superiors. "If the record of the Iran-contra affair shows anything, it is that this spirit is being slowly strangled by secrecy, deceit, and ideological arrogance."[32] Democratic operative Sidney Blumenthal added that placing "extreme anticommunism . . . above the rule of law" ironically "violated the fundamental tenets of classical conservatism."[33]

Watergate had led to a host of new laws to promote accountability, but Iran-Contra produced next to zero.[34] Its schemers were never even indicted for their most important criminal acts—selling weapons to terrorists, violating Boland, and diverting funds.

Iran-Contra reflected a broader disregard for law in the Reagan administration. In 1988, one subcommittee counted more than 225 of the president's appointees who had faced allegations of criminal wrongdoing.[35] No wonder Lawrence Walsh said the administration had "no feeling for the rule of law."[36]

George W. Bush was ushered into office in a nasty assault on the rule of law. In 2000, the Supreme Court stopped a vote recount in Florida, handing the presidency to the Republican. The majority's reasoning, outside the bounds of jurisprudence, was so flawed that it made a mockery of the rule of law. With many judges on the Right formed in ideologically distorted law programs, the country's "confidence in the judge as an impartial guardian of the Rule of Law" was evaporating, wrote one scholar.[37]

Even the otherwise scandal-free administration of Barack Obama yielded to lawbreaking in its foreign policy. Despite opposing his predecessor's Iraq War, Obama kept kidnapping and torture as tools to deal with enemy combatants, and he ordered countless assassinations of foreigners with drone strikes—all crimes under US law. "I don't believe that anybody is above the law," the president rationalized. "On the other hand, I also have a belief that we need to look forward as opposed to looking backwards." His Justice Department declined to prosecute CIA torturers on the theory that they followed bad advice from Bush's lawyers—a modified Nuremberg defense. All the while, the detention center at Guantánamo Bay, Cuba, remained populated by deterritorialized "enemy combatants" who often were denied trials or detained even after they had been acquitted. "It is difficult to imagine a greater contempt for the rule of law than this refusal to abide by the judgment of a court," wrote one legal scholar.[38] In federal courts, judges, mostly appointed by Republican presidents at the urging of the Federalist Society, dismissed civil suits over torture because trials could disclose state secrets—echoes of North and Poindexter graymailing.

When Trump entered the Oval Office, all rule of law seemed to vanish. "Blah, blah, blah," answered White House Counselor Kellyanne Conway when asked if she had violated the Hatch Act, which forbade government employees from campaigning in their official capacity.[39] The Office of Special Counsel found nine senior Trump aides in violation of the law, but the president refused to ask them to resign.[40] He himself held political events on the South Lawn of the White House, against longstanding tradition. He hired and promoted his relatives—incompetent ones at that. He pressured and cajoled foreign governments to help his reelection campaign. He urged the Postal Office to discourage voting against him. He even suggested to the FBI director that he drop an investigation against him. On many issues, the Trump administration was dismissive: whistleblower protections, the emoluments clause, protections for minority religions, and the treatment of migrant families, to name but a few.[41]

Attorney General Bill Barr backed Trump's disregard for the law in his insistence that the president be an autocrat in all but name. In a likely audition for returning to the post he had held under Bush I, in June 2018, Barr sent a memo to the deputy attorney general arguing that Article II of the Constitution rendered the president incapable of obstructing justice. After he got the job, Barr ignored Justice Department norms and flew around the world collecting evidence to exonerate Russia from interference in US elections. He worked to keep Trump's tax returns secret, in effect acting as another lawyer for the president. When Special Counsel Robert Mueller released his report on Trump's ties to Russia, Barr minimized its findings and called the investigation "intrusive."[42] He formally determined that Trump had committed no crimes.[43] Barr went on Fox News to call the investigation a "witch hunt," a "hoax," and "a politically motivated fishing expedition." He claimed, without evidence, that his own FBI was "spying" on the 2016 Trump campaign.[44] He recommended a reduced sentence for Roger Stone (before Trump pardoned Stone). He also interfered in the Flynn case, moving to dismiss it. In mid-2020, Barr ousted the Manhattan US attorney who was looking into Trump's business affairs.

Inside the halls of Justice, Barr was known as "The Buffalo." "He just stampedes around and he's a big powerful creature, better not get in his way," said one former official. Two open letters by thousands of former Justice Department lawyers called on Barr to resign. "I believe that William Barr poses the greatest threat in my lifetime to our rule of law and to public trust in it," one former Justice official who had served with Barr under Bush testified to Congress.[45]

Mueller's investigation produced a few more abuses—blocking testimony, shielding grand jury testimony from Congress, and directing a private citizen not to discuss his conversations with the president. Trump, enraged, spoke to aides of wanting to fire the man investigating him. The *New York Times* was horrified: "The president is not above the law." The UK's *Guardian* proclaimed Trump "at war with the rule of law."[46]

TRUTH

Regard for the truth has probably been the most seriously abused norm since Iran-Contra.

The breadth and depth of mendacity, secrecy, and hypocrisy in Iran-Contra seemed to make the American public more cynical toward government. "We're told by our leadership to be resolute against terrorism, yet they make deals," one writer told the *New York Times*. "People have lost trust in reality and they're looking for something else."[47] In the wake of the scandal, one joke went, "Washington couldn't tell a lie, Nixon couldn't tell the truth, and Reagan couldn't tell the difference."[48] A secret such as Iran-Contra, shared by dozens if not hundreds of individuals inside the US government for years, fired the imaginations of conspiracy theorists, including terrorist Timothy McVeigh on the right and filmmaker Oliver Stone on the left. One writer told the *New York Times* that Iran-Contra convinced him that Washington could be concealing evidence of extraterrestrial beings.[49]

The term "post-truth" emerged in the early 1990s just as new media recast the norms of veracity.[50] The Internet emerged as a potent tool of mass communication, and its absence of gatekeepers made propagating lies easy and profitable. So too did cable TV, which multiplied the number of channels that needed to be filled 24-7 with "content," encouraged niche audiences whose biases programmers could cater to, and benefited from the Reagan-era lifting of the so-called Fairness Doctrine for those with broadcast licenses. By 2024, there existed more than 2,500 cable channels in the United States and nearly 2 billion websites on the Internet. "No lie is too extreme to be published, aired, and repeated, with little or no repercussion for its perpetrator," reported authors Mann and Ornstein. "The audiences that hear them repeatedly believe the lies." In 2011, for instance, 41 percent of South Carolina Republicans believed that President Obama was "probably" or "definitely" born outside the United States—the big lie that launched Trump into politics.[51] Five years later, when Trump claimed to win the popular vote—which he lost by millions—52 percent of Republicans believed him.[52]

The growth of the federal government did not allay fears about lying in politics. By the late 1990s, it was creating perhaps 17,000 new "classified" documents every day. No penalty existed for overclassification. The CIA put together the Task Force on Greater CIA Openness and then *classified its report*.[53]

The George W. Bush administration reversed one major practice about secrecy: declassification now needed to be justified; classification became the norm. In 2001, Bush issued Executive Order 13233, creating new barriers to accessing former presidents' White House materials and effectively nullifying the 1978 President Records Act.[54] In its first few years, the administration invoked the "state secrets privilege" 245 times in court, winning almost every time the right to keep documents sealed.[55]

More tragic still, Bush led the country into the 2003 Iraq War on bogus claims—repeated 935 times, by one count—that the Middle Eastern nation harbored weapons of mass destruction.[56] Another mendacious rationale for the war was that Iraqi leader Saddam Hussein was closely allied with 9/11 mastermind Osama bin Laden. In 2002, Secretary of Defense Donald Rumsfeld claimed he had "bulletproof" evidence. Two years later, he admitted having none. Colin Powell, then secretary of state, spoke of a "sinister nexus" between the two men and later admitted also having no proof. When the war began, half the American public believed Hussein was responsible for the attacks of September 11.[57]

Republican presidential aspirants, candidates, and running mates continued to far outpace Democrats in their mendacity, including whoppers from John McCain, Sarah Palin, Mitt Romney, Carly Fiorina, and Ben Carson. In the run-up to the 2016 campaign, most of what Republicans stated was untrue. Carson earned an 84 percent rating for "false," "mostly false," or "pants on fire" statements. Trump's was 75 percent. Hillary Clinton's, meanwhile, stood at 28 percent. "The fact is," a journalist wrote in the *Boston Globe*, "one political party (Republicans) lies a lot more than the other major political party (Democrats)."[58]

Conservatives disproportionately listened to small or alternative radio stations, whose talk shows shaped insular worlds often bereft of facts or logic.[59] A populist ideology plagued these forums, in which wealthy media owners and hosts portrayed "corrupt" elites arrayed against "the people." In this atmosphere, journalistic standards of accuracy and balance in reporting and editing were dissolving.[60] From 1994 until at least 2012, Gingrich made an art out of attacking mainstream media while exploiting its coverage of him. In 2016, Donald Trump called journalists "the most dishonest people on earth . . . disgusting, dishonest human beings" while he earned endless free coverage that helped him win the presidency.[61] Elsewhere he called the press "enemies of the people."[62] The *Columbia Journalism Review* study combed through 1.25 million election-year media stories to conclude that Republicans absorbed information within "a distinct and insulated media system, using social media as a backbone to transmit a hyper-partisan perspective to the world." Although Democrats did follow some partisan media, they also were mainstream in their tastes. Trump voters, meanwhile, swallowed "disinformation."[63] Aide Conway coined the phrase "alternative facts" early in Trump's presidency to indicate how the administration would relentlessly lie through the media.[64] As president, Trump even admitted to *60 Minutes* that he demonized the media "to discredit you all and demean you all so when you write negative stories about me, no one will believe you."[65]

"The most mendacious president in U.S. history" is how fact-checker and writer Glenn Kessler assessed Trump.[66] From one inauguration day to the next, the president made 30,573 "false or misleading claims," according to Kessler, accelerating his pace from six per day his first year to thirty-nine per day in his last.[67]

Trump's lies were so withering and effective because their number and cynicism undermined the very notion of truth. His lies were often not "spin" but blatant untruths whose very brazenness appealed to his partisans.[68] Republican-aimed TV news and the blogosphere created what historian James Kloppenberg described as "a fact-free world in which there are only opinions, the louder and more melodramatically shouted, the better."[69] A linked strategy was what scholars called "censorship through noise" or the drowning out of truth with lies and nonsense.[70] In an Orwellian turn, Trump called his postpresidency social media network "TRUTH social."

After Trump's "big lie" of having won the 2020 presidential election that he had lost turned into a political litmus test for Republicans, it was not clear whether the United States would ever recover its ability to digest facts over fantasy. Historian Timothy Snyder equated this "post-truth" position to "pre-fascism" and warned of the slippery slope. "When we give up on truth, we concede power to those with the wealth and charisma to create spectacle in its place. Without agreement about some basic facts, citizens cannot form the civil society that would allow them to defend themselves."[71]

PRIVATIZATION

Despite the scandalous nature of Iran-Contra profiteering and policymaking by private arms dealers, such outfits gained in legitimacy and prominence in the decades that followed.

In the 1990s, privatized militaries hired by states operated in war zones in every continent save Antarctica. The end of the Cold War seemed to prompt this intensification, perhaps because it revived long-dormant ethnic and religious conflicts between factions and small nation-states that relied on professional soldiers rather than standing armies. By the mid-1990s, there were five times more civil wars than during the midpoint of the East-West struggle.[72] The end of the Cold War also spread privatization in the former Soviet bloc. Throughout the world, private armies evaded oversight and bred corruption. Their estimated income grew from $55.6 billion in 1990 to $244 billion in 2016.[73]

In the United States, private militaries needed only an export license from the State Department to operate. No one needed to notify the Congress unless their contracts were for more than $50 million. They were under no obligation to divulge information to Congress or the press.[74] They also skyrocketed in importance. In 1995, the Clinton administration had them train the Croatian army.[75] In the first Gulf War in 1991, one found a single contractor for every fifty active-duty US military personnel. By the invasions of Iraq and Afghanistan in the 2000s, private soldiers outnumbered their active-duty peers, peaking in 2008 as 67 percent of the US force in Afghanistan. By the 2010s, the US government was the largest employer of private soldiers in the world.

Many Iran-Contra figures—not just those already in the private sector—found themselves in the private contractor world after the Cold War. Alan Fiers, Clair George, Robert McFarlane, John Poindexter, and Richard Secord all joined—or remained in—the private side of international affairs. Even Oliver North co-owned, with Joseph Fernandez, a body armor business.

Contractors could certainly perform services efficiently, but US officials rarely controlled them, so their behavior could become reckless, operating by their own rules and unconcerned with state sovereignty. Some killed innocent civilians.[76] Others tortured prisoners. One-third of such incidents at Iraq's Abu Ghraib prison involved private contractors, who lacked formal training as interrogators.[77]

As in Iran-Contra, private firms served their bottom line, not the American people. In Iraq, the Pentagon awarded nearly $15 billion in no-bid contracts to Halliburton, more than double the cost to the United States of the entire Gulf War of the previous decade. In several theaters, meanwhile, the KBR corporation earned $1.7 billion a year from military work, "dogged," according to one scholar, "by charges of preferential treatment, overbilling, cost overruns, and waste."[78] By 2019, in contracts supporting immigration, corrections, and detentions, Trump had given away $2.32 billion to ten corporations, more than double the $942 million spent in 2013. Many of these firms had made campaign contributions, 88 percent of them going to Republicans in 2018. Privatization failed to achieve significant cost savings for the government.[79]

Military firms shaped public policy if it promised more profit. Some of the tasks private firms did were banal: laundry, cuisine, and truck driving. But others had long been the exclusive province of government: not only interrogation but also intelligence gathering, military training, postconflict reconstruction, and even combat-related missions. Anyone who followed Iran-Contra could see how taking over government functions could slip into policy formulation. In Iraq, a private firm came up with a plan to remove thousands of land mines and sold it to the Pentagon. Debt-rating agencies influenced fiscal policy, private arbitrators replaced the judiciary, and corporate lobbyists manipulated intellectual property rights.[80]

Under Trump, the war in Afghanistan dragged on, and Congress's Commission on Wartime Contracting noted dozens of reports on waste and corruption in privatization. Most interviewed low-skill workers from Asia who risked their lives on US bases, paid bribes to get jobs, and faced exploitation by their contractors. Again in 2018, the Pentagon had more contractors than members of the US military in Afghanistan.[81]

Amid this criticism, Trump's administration explored a radical idea. In 2017, top aides Stephen Bannon and Jared Kushner recruited Erik Prince and Stephen Feinberg, both notorious military contractors, to pitch the privatization of the Afghan war to Secretary of Defense Jim Mattis. The plan included sending 5,500 contractors to embed with the Afghan Security Forces and appointing a "viceroy" to manage them. There would also be a private air force. Finally, they proposed that the CIA's paramilitary units take over operations in Afghanistan, thus incurring less oversight than the military.[82]

"Have [Bannon and Kushner] so quickly forgotten all the fiscal, operational and diplomatic headaches contractors caused in Iraq and Afghanistan?" asked a shocked journalist. "All the instances of contractor fraud and overbilling, to the tune of tens of billions of dollars? All the abuses, irksome and monstrous? . . . Have they forgotten all the ways in which an outsourced war is a perniciously unaccountable one, divorced from our democratic military and its long-inculcated values and commitments?"[83] One suspects they had not but also did not care.

Mattis and others listened politely to Prince and Feinberg. Luckily, they were not open to the idea of outsourcing core government functions of a democracy. National Security Advisor H. R. McMaster "hates it," Prince said of his plan. "The adults hate it," specified a congressional aide, meaning Mattis, McMaster, and John Kelly, Trump's secretary of homeland security and then chief of staff. "I think it will make Erik Prince billions of dollars while he loses the war for us."[84]

In 2018, Prince resumed his push for privatization. This time, Afghan President Ashraf Ghani was the loudest opponent: "Under no circumstances will the Afghan government and people allow the counterterrorism fight to become a private, for-profit business."[85] Trump backed off again, but he still made Feinberg the head of his Intelligence Advisory Board.

OBSTRUCTION OF JUSTICE

When it came to obstructing justice, Iran-Contra carried similar messages to that of Watergate: Don't get caught, don't tape conversations, keep the paper trail to a minimum, and either destroy incriminating evidence or keep it from the courts by claiming executive privilege or national security concerns.[86]

One legal change that resulted from Iran-Contra was, tellingly enough, the elimination of the independent counsel. North lost his challenge to the constitutionality of Walsh's job, but the idea that the special prosecutor was illegitimate had been planted.[87]

One of the first struggles in Congress over the special prosecutor law emerged in the summer of 1987. The Justice Department and White House advised Reagan to veto any congressional extension of the Ethics in Government Act—the law's formal name—due to expire in January 1988. A key proponent of killing the law was John Bolton, at the time assistant attorney general for legislative affairs. He made the same constitutional points as North, saying for instance "that the law creates an opportunity for abuse of prosecutorial power that our constitutional system cannot and must not tolerate."[88] Journalist Anthony Lewis countered that the Constitution did give courts the power to appoint "inferior officers" and that private individuals had indeed often brought criminal prosecutions.[89]

Bolton added complaints against the OIC—overspending, politicization—that echoed Republican talking points. In Congress, Representative Barney Frank (D-MA) shot back, "An attack on Walsh for spending too much money is an attack for too much investigating. . . . Walsh is clearly too diligent for them." He projected that Congress would "absolutely override" any veto.[90] Senator Carl Levin (D-MI), cosponsor of the reauthorization, added that Bolton and "the [Justice] department would have us return to the days of Watergate and Nixon's 'Saturday night massacre' when public trust in our criminal justice system hung in the balance."[91] Levin pointed out that Reagan had extended the law just four years before—in the pre-Iran-Contra era. "It sure looks bad," said the senator, suggesting that Reagan's administration only targeted a prosecutor when the prosecutor targeted the administration.[92]

Days after these exchanges, a federal judge upheld the constitutionality of the Ethics in Government Act, and the Justice Department later filed a court challenge. In October 1987, the House voted 327 to 87 to extend the law.[93] In January 1988 came a setback: A federal appeals court ruled the law unconstitutional, agreeing with the Reagan White House. Judge Ruth Bader Ginsburg was the dissenting voice in the 2-to-1 decision.[94]

The debate headed to the Supreme Court (which Ginsburg joined in 1993) in the *Morrison v. Olson* case. There, the court ruled 7 to 1 against the Reagan administration, with Justice Antonin Scalia the lone dissenter.[95] Scalia called the independent counsel a "mini-Executive . . . operating in an area where so little is law and so much is discretion." Expressing the concerns of the "unitary executive" crowd—he used those very words for the first time in an opinion—Scalia intoned, "How frightening it must be to have your own independent counsel and staff appointed, with nothing else to do but to investigate you until investigation is no longer worthwhile. . . . I fear the Court has permanently encumbered the Republic with an institution that will do it great harm."[96]

Four years later, the debate came up again as Republicans pointed to the Caspar Weinberger trial as an abuse of the independent counsel's power. This time, Attorney General Bill Barr led the charge at a lunch with reporters, stating that the Ethics in Government Act led to "injustices" and threatening he would recommend President Bush veto it.[97] As attorney general, Barr refused to seek the appointment of an independent counsel three times. Again, the law was to expire—this time in late 1992—yet some Democrats were willing to let it. "This is an extraordinarily politicized year," said Representative Frank, changing his tune from four years earlier. "Too many people have come to think of this as a Democratic weapon against Republican Presidents."[98] When candidate Bill Clinton seemed on his way to winning the White House, however, Democrats grew less fearful of being accused of attacking the presidency.[99] Yet Republicans threatened a filibuster and the law expired.[100]

Another twist came in November 1993. With Democrats in the White House, the Senate voted 76 to 21 to revive the law and Clinton signed it, this time with new restraints: Investigations needed to be reauthorized by the court after two years or when they cost more than $2 million. Bob Dole, the Republican leader of the Senate who railed against Walsh, also eliminated the independent counsel's reporting requirement.[101]

Clinton would come to regret giving the law a second life. Dole, deaf to charges of hypocrisy, called for a special prosecutor to delve into Clinton's prepresidential dealings. The court appointed Ken Starr who, unlike Walsh, was a longtime enemy of the president's party.[102] His investigation eventually overlapped with a sexual harassment suit against the president in which Clinton denied having an affair with an intern. Starr seized on this statement to charge Clinton with perjury and obstruction of justice, leading to his impeachment. Scholars agreed that Starr's reckless pursuit of Clinton "thoroughly discredited the institution."[103] After the Starr debacle, both parties agreed that the independent counsel law was too politically hazardous for any president. From enjoying broad support in late 1997, the law had no fans left a year later.[104] It was allowed to die.

With such safeguards against abuse crumbling, Trump's obstruction of justice was, again, a norm eroded by qualitative leaps beyond that of his predecessors. He obstructed openly, repeatedly, and for his own political gain. Trump publicly mocked federal judges and declared the criminal justice system a "laughingstock." He called some FBI officials "scum" and stated, "we have a lot of dirty cops."[105] He also denied the independence of law enforcement. Trump declared himself "the chief law enforcement officer," in effect declaring his control over Barr. "I have absolute right to do what I want to do with the Justice Department."[106] (The attorney general is nominated by the president but otherwise is independent.)

Trump also brazenly abused executive privilege. Many presidents had fought battles with Congress over executive privilege—including Democrats such as Clinton who fought the Whitewater investigation and impeachment, and Bush II who tried to keep classified the documents of previous presidents. Yet executive privilege does not exist in the Constitution. Trump's claims dwarfed them all, both in number and boldness. He made a blanket assertion of privilege for anything related to Mueller's report, far beyond the norm of protecting the confidentiality of a top aide's advice. For his assertion, Trump also gave no rationale such as national security. He called it "protective," and it betrayed its self-serving purposes.[107] Trump claimed "absolute immunity" for himself and his close aides. As a result, Don McGahn, Mick Mulvaney, and Bolton among twelve political appointees disregarded either subpoenas or demands for testimony from Congress.[108] Congress also subpoenaed more than seventy categories of materials, and Trump ignored them all. This "unprecedented" refusal led to the House impeaching Trump, in part, on charges of "Obstruction of Congress."[109] Republicans in the Senate voted against conviction.

Expanding on the arguments used against Walsh during Iran-Contra, Trump's personal lawyer argued that only the executive could investigate crimes—including Trump's corruption—and that, therefore, congressional investigations were unconstitutional.[110]

Under Secretary of State Mike Pompeo, the State Department joined in obstructing justice in Congress. It dismissed summonses from House Democratic committee chairs for five current—and even former—diplomats to testify on Trump's efforts to get Ukraine to find political dirt on his eventual rival, Joe Biden. It also blocked former ambassador to the European Union Gordon Sondland from testifying.[111]

On and on it went. Trump refused to turn over his tax returns to Congress, which federal law required him to do if asked. His White House blocked the release of documents about Trump's prepresidential accountants and bankers, the executive security-clearance process, the decision to add a citizenship question to the 2020 Census form, and a House inquiry into . . . obstruction of justice. The administration refused to provide information more than a dozen times, whereas most past administrations had complied.[112]

Through many of these decisions, again Attorney General Barr backed Trump. After serving Bush Sr. in the same position, he criticized Clinton for his claims of executive privilege, yet he then turned around and argued for "maximum power" in national security for Bush. Barr was in favor of military tribunals, the Patriot Act, and sweeping surveillance of Americans. One conservative litigator called Barr's work for Trump "building and extending on a foundation . . . popularized and very robustly advanced by the [Ed] Meese Justice Department [under Reagan]." Trump gave Meese the Presidential Medal of Freedom.[113]

The most serious obstruction came in the president's bid to protect himself. On Valentines' Day 2017, Trump cleared the Oval Office and instructed FBI Director James Comey, "I hope you can see your way clear to letting this go, to letting Flynn go." In May, when Comey refused to state that Trump was not under investigation, the president fired him.[114] Days later, Attorney General Jeff Sessions recused himself, and Special Counsel Robert Mueller was appointed.

"Oh my God," said Trump in response. "This is terrible. This is the end of my Presidency. I'm fucked. . . . Everyone tells me if you get one of these independent counsels it ruins your presidency." (Mueller was not formally an independent counsel.) "It takes years and years and I won't be able to do anything."[115]

Like Walsh's investigation, Mueller's probe grew and lasted largely because of the obstruction it faced. At its height, Mueller's team had nineteen attorneys and about forty staffers. It cost $25 million and led to 199 criminal counts, 37 indictments, 7 guilty pleas, and 1 conviction at trial.[116] The president himself committed ten acts of obstructing the investigation. These included attempting to stop, limit, or redirect the investigation; seeking to fire Mueller; getting others to create false evidence; and trying to prevent and dissuade witnesses from cooperation with the investigation. Mueller agreed to let Trump give written answers—a rare occurrence—in which the president repeatedly claimed he could not recall events.[117] Trump repeated asked Sessions to "unrecuse" himself.[118]

When Trump's pressure on Comey became public, at least one person saw connections to Iran-Contra. John Yoo, the lawyer notorious for penning a 2003 "torture memo" for George W. Bush, advised Trump to "look to the example of his predecessor Ronald Reagan," who "cleaned house and agreed to reforms of government oversight of covert action." Nowhere did Yoo acknowledge the resistance that the Reagan and Bush I administrations presented to investigators.[119]

The Mueller report would find that Trump's campaign knew that the Kremlin worked to get him elected. Like Walsh, Mueller had abandoned several lines of investigation for lack of resources. He chose not to subpoena Trump for an interview because it would take too long, not because Trump was innocent.[120]

Upon leaving the White House in early 2021, Trump took with him at least 300 classified documents, many marked "top secret."[121] In 2023, the Department of Justice charged him with forty criminal counts.[122] Trump's taking the documents communicated his assumption that state files were his private property.[123]

QUID PRO QUOS

"I would like you to do us a favor though." So asked Donald Trump of Ukrainian President Volodymyr Zelensky in a phone call on July 25, 2019.[124] That "favor" was to announce on TV a Ukrainian investigation into the Biden family, warranted or not. In return, Trump would unblock $391 million in congressionally approved military aid.[125] In addition to brazen extortion, the president's threat was a violation of the Impoundment Control Act.

There was "no doubt" that Trump was offering a quid pro quo to Ukraine, said Lieutenant Colonel Alexander Vindman, who listened in on the call along with many others.[126] William Taylor Jr., the top envoy to Ukraine, confirmed to the House Intelligence Committee that "security assistance would not come until [Zelensky] committed to pursue the investigation."

"So if they don't do this, they are not going to get that, was your understanding?" asked Representative Adam Schiff (D-CA), the committee chair.

"Yes, sir."

Schiff asked him whether Taylor was aware that *quid pro quo* literally means "this for that."

"I am," replied Taylor.[127]

Gordon Sondland made the quid pro quo even more explicit to a top Ukrainian. "Was there a quid pro quo?" he asked rhetorically. "The answer is yes."

"Everyone was in the loop. It was no secret."[128]

Acting White House chief of staff Mick Mulvaney confirmed: "Absolutely. No question about that," he said. "That's why we held up the money."[129]

Thus occurred the most infamous quid pro quo in US foreign policy history—the second leg on which Trump's 2019 impeachment stood. Less well known were other offers of quid pro quos. In 2018, Trump apparently asked the US ambassador to the United Kingdom to get Britain to hold the British Open golf tournament to his resort in Turnberry, Scotland.[130] Trump also pleaded with Chinese President Xi Jinping to use his economic might to ensure a Republican victory in 2020.[131]

The failure to learn from Iran-Contra was partly responsible for Trump's abuse of the quid pro quo. In July 1989, the Senate adopted the so-called Moynihan amendment, which criminalized quid pro quos and solicitations on behalf of foreign causes or governments barred from receiving US aid. But a conference committee diluted its impact, and President George H. W. Bush vetoed the bill, citing "serious constitutional problems" and "an unacceptable risk that it will chill the conduct of our Nation's foreign affairs." Bush finally accepted another amendment that barred only explicit quid pro quo agreements, had no criminal sanctions, and said nothing about solicitations.[132]

.....

Scholar Louis Fisher has described Iran-Contra as "a stunning collapse of democratic government."[133] Taking together the six norms that this book followed through Iran-Contra's scheme, scandal, and scrutiny, that judgment seems reasonable. Those who designed, executed, and covered up Iran-Contra occasionally pledged their adherence to some of the guardrails of democracy, and they certainly declared spreading democracy as a foreign policy goal in Central America and even Iran. Yet when it came to acting to defend democracy at home, dozens of officials in the NSC, CIA, and White House, as well as in the State, Justice, and Defense Departments, along with pockets of secretive businessmen in both regions, proved ready to suspend their supposed loyalty to the people's will and run their own foreign policy against the will of Congress, out of sight of the American people, and against the processes of justice.

Iran-Contra was not the first time that US foreign policymakers disregarded the democratic norms meant to restrain them, but it was arguably the most holistic such episode in American history—to that point. The Reagan-Bush assault on democracy ran far deeper, wider, and longer than the 1987 TV clash between the White House and Congress has suggested to history. During these televised hearings, House committee chair Lee Hamilton rejected the analogy of a baseball game between the executive and legislative. "We are not engaged in a game with winners and losers," he said. In Iran-Contra, "we all lost."[134] The collective loss found its measure in the erosion of the will of the people, of national sovereignty, of justice, of law, and of truth. That erosion helped to warp these concepts in Republicans' minds in the decades that followed, culminating in even grosser abuses of all six norms by President Trump, an individual with zero concern for his nation or for democracy and elected by voters who had diminished appreciation for its norms. Iran-Contra took a major step toward the deterioration of American democracy.

NOTES

ABBREVIATIONS USED IN THE NOTES

AP	Associated Press
CHP	Charles Hill Papers, Hoover Institution, Stanford University, CA
DNSA	Digital National Security Archive, Iran-Contra Affair Collection
EMP	Edwin Meese Papers, Hoover Institution, Stanford University, CA
GGP	Gerhard Gesell Papers, Manuscripts Division, Library of Congress, Washington, DC
GLP	George Lardner Papers, Manuscripts Division, Library of Congress, Washington, DC
LAT	*Los Angeles Times*
LGP	Leonard Garment Papers, Manuscripts Division, Library of Congress, Washington, DC
LOC	Library of Congress, Washington, DC
MD	Manuscripts Division
memcon	memorandum of conversation
MH	*Miami Herald*
NYT	*New York Times*
PRLB	Papers of Robert L. Bartley, Hoover Institution, Stanford University, CA
RG 449	Records of Independent Counsel Lawrence Walsh, National Archives, College Park, MD
WP	*Washington Post*
WSJ	*Wall Street Journal*

INTRODUCTION

1. Wroe, *Lives*, 45.

2. Editorial, "Something More Serious?," *WSJ*, December 19, 1986, 22.

3. *Report of the Congressional Committees*, xv.

4. Walsh, *Firewall*, 531.

5. Christopher Ingraham, "The United States Is Backsliding into Autocracy under Trump, Scholars Warn," *WP*, September 18, 2020; Dean and Altemeyer, *Authoritarian Nightmare*.

6. "Tempered Expectations."

7. "Threats to American Democracy."

8. Cited in Pfiffner, "Donald Trump and the Norms," 97.

9. Steven Levitsky and Daniel Ziblatt, "Is Donald Trump a Threat to Democracy?," *NYT*, December 16, 2016.

10. "Democracy."

11. Diamond, "What Is Democracy?"

12. See, for instance, Schmitter and Karl, "What Democracy Is," 76; Hollyer, Rosendorff, and Vreeland, "Democracy and Transparency," 1202; and Haque, *Surveillance, Transparency, and Democracy*, 122.

13. Nicolescu-Waggonner, *No Rule of Law*, 194.

14. Zakaria, "Rise of Illiberal Democracy," 22.

15. Blachman and Sharp, "De-Democratising."

16. Fisher, "Foundations of a Scandal," 157.

17. Draper, "Forward," in Kornbluh and Byrne, *Iran-Contra Scandal*, xiii. Draper's own book is *Very Thin Line*.

18. Walsh, *Firewall*, xiii; Mayer and McManus, *Landslide*, x; Draper, *Very Thin Line*, 580.

19. Marshall, Scott, and Hunter, *Iran Contra Connection*, 5.

20. These were "the right of Congress to participate in the formulation and implementation of United States foreign policy, its right to be kept informed of foreign policy initiatives proposed and implemented by the White House, and its right to oversee and check Executive Branch conduct of foreign relations," in Timbers, "Legal and Institutional," 31. See also Nichols, "Of Arms and the Man."

21. See, for instance, perhaps the only historiographical article of the scandal, James F. Siekmeier, "The Iran-Contra Affair," in Johns, *Companion to Ronald Reagan*, 321–38.

22. Koh, *National Security Constitution*, 2 (emphasis added).

23. Byrne, *Iran-Contra Scandal*.

24. Newland, "Faithful Execution," 673–86; Thompson, "Democratic Secrecy," 181–93.

25. Landon-Murray and Mujkic, "Disinformation," 512–22; Robinson and Kohut, "Believability and the Press," 174–89; Wroe, *Lives*.

26. Dickinson, "Outsourcing Covert Activities," 521–37; Glabe, "Original Privatization of Intelligence"; Marshall, Scott, and Hunter, *Iran Contra Connection*.

27. Jordan, "Classified Information and Conflicts," 1651–98.

28. Other examples include Persico, *Casey*; Currie, "Iran-Contra and Congressional Oversight," xii; Cavender, Jurik, and Cohen, "Baffling Case of the Smoking Gun," 152–66.

29. Seib, *We Should Have Seen It Coming*, 56, 57.

30. Weinberger, *Fighting for Peace*, 353.

31. *Report of the Congressional Committees*, 437.
32. Richard Cohen, "What Did Bush Know?," *WP*, September 22, 1992, A21.
33. Dabis, *Only Murders in the Building*, "The Tell."
34. Wood, *Creation of the American Republic*, 151.
35. Vile, *Constitutionalism*, 2.
36. Montesquieu, *Spirit of Laws*, 174.
37. Fairlie, "Separation of Powers," 393, 394.
38. Locke, *Second Treatise of Government*, 146, 143, 147.
39. Hamilton, Madison, and Jay, *Federalist Papers*, 239.
40. Cited in Wood, *Creation of the American Republic*, 152.
41. Cited in Vile, *Constitutionalism*, 131.
42. Hamilton, Madison, and Jay, *Federalist Papers*, 256.
43. Turner, "Constitution and the Iran-Contra Affair," 83–127.
44. Cited in Calabresi and Yoo, *Unitary Executive*, vi.
45. George, "Tocqueville's Caveat."
46. Elkin, "Contempt of Congress," 742.
47. Shendow, "Analysis of Foreign Affairs," 177.
48. Fisher, "Congressional Checks on Military Initiatives," 741.
49. Cited in Susan Hennessey, and Benjamin Wittes, "The Disintegration of the American Presidency," *The Atlantic*, January 21, 2020.
50. Hamilton, Madison, and Jay, *Federalist Papers*, 252.
51. Garret Epps, "Congress Should Go to the Supreme Court Right Away," *The Atlantic*, October 1, 2019.
52. Marshall cited in Shendow, "Analysis of Foreign Affairs," 180.
53. Cited in Arkes, "On the Moral Standing," 638.
54. Sutherland cited in Shendow, "Analysis of Foreign Affairs," 183.
55. Weaver and Pallitto, "State Secrets," 93.
56. Cited in Shendow, "Analysis of Foreign Affairs," 179.
57. Elkin, "Contempt of Congress," 1–15.
58. Epps, "Congress Should Go to the Supreme Court."
59. Sharpe, "Post-Vietnam Formula under Siege" 551.
60. Currie, "Iran-Contra and Congressional Oversight," 185.
61. Silverberg, "Separation of Powers and Control," 575–622, 595–96.
62. Koh, *National Security Constitution*, 39.
63. Ledeen, *Perilous Statecraft*, 84.
64. McCormick and Smith, "Iran Arms Sale," 30.
65. Cited in Currie, "Iran-Contra and Congressional Oversight," 188, 190.
66. Vile, *Constitutionalism*, 391.
67. Calabresi and Yoo, *Unitary Executive*, 4.
68. Vile, *Constitutionalism*, 388.
69. McCormick and Smith, "Iran Arms Sale," 30.
70. Koh, *National Security Constitution*, 49.
71. Johnson, "Contemporary Presidency," 834.
72. Calabresi and Yoo, *Unitary Executive*, 13.
73. Byrne, *Iran-Contra*, xviii–xix.
74. Reagan, *American Life*, 483.

75. Calabresi and Yoo, *Unitary Executive*, 382, 376.

76. Reagan, *American Life*, 483, 484.

77. Tamanaha, *On the Rule of Law*, 1, 3.

78. Aristotle, *Politics*, chap. 16, 1287a.

79. Cited in Hayek, *Constitution of Liberty*, 233.

80. Maravall and Przeworski, *Democracy and the Rule of Law*, 2, 3.

81. Dicey, *Introduction to the Study of the Law*, 183, 189, 191.

82. Cited in Hayek, *Constitution of Liberty*, 242.

83. Raz, *Authority of Law*, 210–17.

84. Tamanaha, *On the Rule of Law*, 7, 10–28, 48.

85. Cited in Tamanaha, *On the Rule of Law*, 52.

86. Crovitz, "Crime, Constitution," 29.

87. Goodman, "Reforming U.S. Intelligence," 125.

88. Perlstein, *Reaganland*, 103, 104.

89. Cited in Doyle, "End of Secrecy," 34.

90. Pfiffner, "Contemporary Presidency," 904.

91. Cited in "The Art of Lies? The Bigger, the Better," *CE Noticias Financieras English*, January 11, 2021.

92. Cited in Jay, *Virtues of Mendacity*, 4.

93. Ledeen, "Secrets," 49, 50.

94. Mervin, "Deception in Government," 25; Cliffe, Ramsay, and Bartlett, *Politics of Lying*, 4–11.

95. Galeotti, "Liars or Self-Deceived?," 887.

96. Cliffe, Ramsay, and Bartlett, *Politics of Lying*, 12–13; Mearsheimer, *Why Leaders Lie*, 10.

97. Cliffe, Ramsay, and Bartlett, *Politics of Lying*, 35.

98. Solomon, *War Made Easy*, 26.

99. Pfiffner, "Contemporary Presidency," 904.

100. Cited in Nichols, "Of Arms and the Man," 25.

101. Green, "Uncovering the Cover-Up Crimes," 12–14.

102. Quinta Jurecic, "Trumpelstiltskin," *WP*, January 29, 2017, B4.

103. Jay, *Virtues of Mendacity*, 6.

104. Wallenfelt, "Did George Washington Really Say?"

105. Green, "Uncovering the Cover-Up Crimes," 29.

106. Mervin, "Deception in Government," 25, 26.

107. Pfiffner, "Contemporary Presidency," 905; Mearsheimer, *Why Leaders Lie*, 46–47.

108. Pfiffner, "Contemporary Presidency," 911; Mearsheimer, *Why Leaders Lie*, 48.

109. Cited in Pfiffner, "Contemporary Presidency," 913.

110. Perlstein, *Nixonland*, 573–75.

111. Olmsted, "Truth Is Out There," 671.

112. Cliffe, Ramsay, and Bartlett, *Politics of Lying*, 56.

113. Davis, "Out-of-Sight Oversight," 629.

114. "Public Trust in Government, 1958–2022."

115. Pfiffner, "Contemporary Presidency," 906.

116. Cited in Perlstein, *Reaganland*, 6.

117. Hyde, "'Leaks' and Congressional Oversight," 25, 27.

118. Meitl, "Perjury Paradox," 548, 559–60.
119. Crawford, *Attack the Messenger*, 62.
120. Cited in Perlstein, *Nixonland*, 61.
121. Cited in Maddow and Yarvitz, *Bag Man*, 33, 35.
122. Crawford, *Attack the Messenger*, 23.
123. Perlstein, *Reaganland*, 108, 502, 751, 775, 880.
124. "Judicial Independence," Annenberg Classroom.
125. US Constitution, art. III.
126. Shapiro, "Citizen Trust," 1477.
127. Green, "Uncovering the Cover-Up Crimes," 17.
128. Eksterowicz and Roberts, "Specter of Presidential Pardons," 386.
129. Cited in Weaver and Pallitto, "State Secrets," 98.
130. Doyle, "End of Secrecy," 37.
131. Maddow and Yarvitz, *Bag Man*, 118, 124, 127.
132. Brandes, *Warhogs*, 7.
133. Cited in Singer, *Corporate Warriors*, 8.
134. Dickinson, "Government for Hire," 137.
135. Singer, *Corporate Warriors*, 28, 20–25.
136. Cited in Brandes, *Warhogs*, 1.
137. Eckert, *Outsourcing War*, 6.
138. Brandes, *Warhogs*, 3, 9, 5.
139. William L. Chaze with Steven Emerson, Carla Anne Robbins, Stewart Powell, Charles Fenyvesi, Melissa Healy, Dennis Mullin, Maureen Santini, Lisa J. Moore, and Deborah Kalb, "Inside the Shadow Network," *U.S. News*, December 15, 1986, 26.
140. Voß, "Plausibly Deniable," 48.
141. Wiltz, *In Search of Peace*.
142. Cohen and Küpçü, "Privatizing Foreign Policy," 35.
143. Cited in Brandes, *Warhogs*, 6.
144. Marshall, Scott, and Hunter, *Iran Contra Connection*, 27.
145. Friedman, *Covert Capital*, 234, 294–95.
146. Mayer and McManus, *Landslide*, 249, 250.
147. Chaze et al., "Inside the Shadow Network," 26.
148. Nincic, "International Relations," 139.
149. Clough, "*Quid Pro Quo*," 601.
150. George, "Tocqueville's Caveat," 439.
151. Clough, "*Quid Pro Quo*," 605.
152. Levy, "Advice for Sale," 64.
153. Whiting, "Controlling Tin Cup Diplomacy," 2053.
154. Whiting, "Controlling Tin Cup Diplomacy," 2046.
155. Liman with Israel, *Lawyer*, 347.

CHAPTER 1

1. *Testimony of John M. Poindexter*, 162.
2. Draper, *Very Thin Line*, 16.

3. LeoGrande, *Our Own Backyard*, 115.

4. Draper, *Very Thin Line*, 16.

5. *Report of the Congressional Committees*, 35.

6. Cited in Burns, *War in Nicaragua*, 26.

7. Cited in Karen Elliott House, "Reagan's World: Republican Policies Stress Arms Buildup, a Firm Line to Soviets," *WSJ*, June 3, 1980, 1.

8. Cited in Woodward, *VEIL*, 93.

9. Cited in Blachman and Sharp, "De-Democratising," 283.

10. Reagan, *American Life*, 473.

11. Reagan, *Diaries*, 162.

12. Cited in Blachman and Sharp, "De-Democratising," 1281, 1304.

13. Gerald M. Boyd, "Reagan Terms Nicaraguan Rebels 'Moral Equal of Founding Fathers,'" *NYT*, March 2, 1985, 1.

14. Citations in Burns, *War in Nicaragua*, 62 and 70.

15. Bruce Cameron, Department of State, statement, April 20, 1987, DNSA.

16. Persico, *Casey*, 362.

17. Reagan, *Diaries*, 150.

18. Richard Wirthlin cited in Mayer and McManus, *Landslide*, 15.

19. Cited in Byrne, *Iran-Contra*, 15.

20. Both cited in Blachman and Sharp, "De-Democratising," 1289.

21. Blachman and Sharp, "De-Democratising," 1296.

22. *Testimony of John M. Poindexter*, 162.

23. Marshall, Scott, and Hunter, *Iran Contra Connection*, 100. See also Armony, *Argentina*, and Schmidli, *Freedom*.

24. Byrne, *Iran-Contra*, 15.

25. Wroe, *Lives*, 21; North and Novak, *Under Fire*, 181.

26. Perlstein, *Reaganland*, 754.

27. Persico, *Casey*, 516.

28. Woodward, *VEIL*, 35–37; Perlstein, *Reaganland*, 753.

29. Marshall, Scott, and Hunter, *Iran Contra Connection*, 163.

30. Woodward, *VEIL*, 148, 50.

31. William Casey to George Shultz, CIA, memo, March 1, 1986, DNSA.

32. William Casey to Kenneth Dam, Arthur Moreau, and William Clark, NSC, memo, September 21, 1983, DNSA.

33. Taylor, interview, 102.

34. Reagan, *American Life*, 477.

35. Clarridge with Diehl, *Spy for All Seasons*, 23.

36. Friedman, *Covert Capital*, 249.

37. Clarridge with Diehl, *Spy for All Seasons*, 203.

38. North and Novak, *Under Fire*, 221.

39. Cited in Persico, *Casey*, 265, 266; Byrne, *Iran-Contra*, 18.

40. Woodward, *VEIL*, 187, 190, 242, 277, 281.

41. Bud McFarlane cited in *Testimony of Richard V. Secord*, 157.

42. Woodward, *VEIL*, 277, 282. On Contra failures, see also Armony, *Argentina*, 114, and LeoGrande, *Our Own Backyard*, 309–11.

43. Oliver North and Constantine Merges, memo to Robert McFarlane, March 2, 1984, folder Files of the Office of the Vice President Bush, George, box 2, Records of John Q. Barrett Attorney Files, RG 449.

44. Woodward, *VEIL*, 320,

45. Currie, "Iran-Contra and Congressional Oversight," 192.

46. Cited in Woodward, *VEIL*, 321, 333.

47. Persico, *Casey*, 373.

48. Cited in Woodward, *VEIL*, 338.

49. Barry Goldwater to William Casey, SSCI, letter, April 9, 1984, DNSA.

50. Cited in Draper, *Very Thin Line*, 21, 22.

51. Cited in Glabe, "Original Privatization of Intelligence," 116.

52. Cited in Persico, *Casey*, 277.

53. Cited in Draper, *Very Thin Line*, 22.

54. All three cited in Persico, *Casey*, 333–34.

55. Barry Goldwater, Daniel Moynihan, and William Casey, SSCI, document, June 6, 1984, DNSA; Currie, "Iran-Contra and Congressional Oversight," 193.

56. Persico, *Casey*. Dave Durenberger cited on 378, Casey on 379.

57. Cited in Woodward, *VEIL*, 388, 389; Persico, *Casey*, 417.

58. Clarridge with Diehl, *Spy for All Seasons*, 231.

59. *Testimony of Regan and Weinberger*, 79.

60. Cited in Public Law 98–473, US Congress, law, October 12, 1984, DNSA.

61. Cited in Persico, *Casey*, 392.

62. "Representative Boland," CIA, cable, October 19, 1984, DNSA.

63. H.R. 5399, CIA, memo, August 23, 1984, DNSA.

64. Cited in Draper, *Very Thin Line*, 24.

65. Abrams, *Undue Process*, 6.

66. H.R. 5399, CIA, memo, August 23, 1984, DNSA.

67. "Representative Boland," CIA, cable, October 19, 1984, DNSA.

68. The Boland Amendment, Executive Office of the President IOB, report, April 6, 1983, DNSA.

69. D. Wallace Jr., and A. Gerson, "The Dubious Boland Amendments," *WP*, June 5, 1987.

70. William Casey to Edward Boland, CIA, letter, December 19, 1984, DNSA.

71. Edward Boland and Lee Hamilton to William Casey, HPSCI, letter, January 14, 1985, DNSA.

72. Currie, "Iran-Contra and Congressional Oversight," 195.

73. Persico, *Casey*, 403.

74. *Testimony of Clarridge*, 268.

75. David Halevy, and Neil C. Livingstone, "The Ollie We Knew," *The Washingtonian*, July 1987, 77–78, 140–58.

76. North and Novak, *Under Fire*, 64, 66, 67, 68.

77. John Sinclair citing North in Bradlee, *Guts and Glory*, 48.

78. Cruz, Memoirs of a *Counterrevolutionary*, 179.

79. Brian Duffy et al., "Out of the Shadows," *U.S. News & World Report*, July 13, 1987, 20.

80. Bradlee, *Guts and Glory*, 80, 58.

81. Persico, *Casey*, 395.

82. North and Novak, *Under Fire*, 75, 98.

83. Bradlee, *Guts and Glory*, 127, 107–09.

84. Ledeen, *Perilous Statecraft*, 78.

85. *Testimony of Robert C. McFarlane*, 400.

86. Cited in Wroe, *Lives*, 123.

87. Blumenthal, "Dateline Washington," 183.

88. North and Novak, *Under Fire*, 173.

89. Liman with Israel, *Lawyer*, 344.

90. Steven Berry to Henry Hyde, August 8, 1986, *Appendixes to Parts I and II*, 488. On Reagan, see Michael Barnes to Robert McFarlane, August 16, 1985, *Appendixes to Parts I and II*, 493.

91. Executive Order 12333, cited in Steven Berry to Oliver North and Vincent Cannistraro, HPSCI, memo, August 8, 1985, DNSA.

92. Cited in Draper, *Very Thin Line*, 24–25.

93. Michael Barnes to Robert McFarlane, August 16, 1985. *Appendixes to Parts I and II*, 493.

94. Timbers, "Legal and Institutional," 32.

95. *Continued Testimony of North and McFarlane*, 124.

96. Robert McFarlane, HPSCI, testimony, December 10, 1986, DNSA.

97. Robert McFarlane, biography, folder 1, box 31, LGP.

98. Jonathan Scharfen to Robert Pearson, NSC, memo, August 23, 1985, DNSA.

99. Cited in Walter Pincus, and Joe Pichirallo, "Memo on Honduran Deal Cites Bush," *WP*, April 12, 1989, A1.

100. Crovitz, "Crime, Constitution," 25. See also the Intelligence Authorization Act, Congressional Record, transcript, October 11, 1984, DNSA.

101. Berry to North and Cannistraro, August 8, 1985, DNSA.

102. IOB, memo to Robert McFarlane, September 12, 1985, *Testimony of Elliott Abrams*, 1158.

103. *Testimony of Elliott Abrams*, 398.

104. Bretton Sciaroni to Robert McFarlane, IOB, memo, September 12, 1985, DNSA.

105. Oliver North to John Poindexter, August 19, 1985, *Appendixes to Parts I and II*, 495.

106. *Testimony of Oliver L. North*, 278.

107. *Testimony of John M. Poindexter*, 205.

108. *Testimony of Oliver L. North*, 205; Byrne, *Iran-Contra*, 44.

109. *Testimony of Regan and Weinberger*, 7, 78.

110. Cited in Mayer and McManus, *Landslide*, 172.

111. Ledeen, *Perilous Statecraft*, 82.

112. On Poindexter, Persico, *Casey*, 482; on North, Bradlee, *Guts and Glory*, 65.

113. R. Murphy, US Navy, report, March 23, 1971, DNSA.

114. Cited in Wroe, *Lives*, vii.

115. North and Novak, *Under Fire*, 192.

116. Cited in Mayer and McManus, *Landslide*, 174.

117. *Testimony of John M. Poindexter*, 165.

118. North and Novak, *Under Fire*, 193.

119. *Testimony of John M. Poindexter*, 379.

120. Cited in Walsh, *Final Report*, 204.

121. Michael Barnes to Robert McFarlane, August 16, 1985, *Appendixes to Parts I and II*, 493.

122. *Testimony of Oliver L. North*, 207.

123. Adolfo Calero cited in *Testimony of Adolfo P. Calero*, 18–19, 40, 79.

124. Victor Johnson to Michael Barnes, House Foreign Affairs Committee, memo, September 17, 1985, DNSA.

125. Bob Pearson to John Poindexter in *Testimony of John M. Poindexter*, 430.

126. Brenda Reger to John Poindexter, NSC, memo, August 20, 1985, DNSA.

127. Donna Sirko to Paul Thompson and Robert Pearson, NSC, memo, August 23, 1985, DNSA.

128. Robert McFarlane to Michael Barnes, September 12, 1985, *Appendixes to Parts I and II*, 497, 496.

129. Robert McFarlane to Michael Barnes, November 8, 1985, *Testimony of Robert C. McFarlane*, 557; see also McFarlane to Lee Hamilton, September 5, 1985, 560, and Questions and Answers, September 12, 1985, 564–77.

130. Cited in Mayer and McManus, *Landslide*, 148.

131. *Report of the Congressional Committees*, 124.

132. North cited in Bradlee, *Guts and Glory*, 287.

133. Office of Independent Counsel, report of interview with Alan Fiers, July 31, 1991, folder CIA Investigative Files Alan D. Fiers 1991 Statements (1 of 3), box 6 CIA Investigative Files, John Q. Barrett Attorney Files, RG 449.

134. Robert Parry, AP, September 22, 1985.

135. *Testimony of Oliver L. North*, 210, 211; *Report of the Congressional Committees*, 133; Wroe, *Lives*, 251.

136. John Poindexter letter to Lee Hamilton, July 21, 1986, *Appendixes to Parts I and II*, 551.

137. *Testimony of Elliott Abrams*, 12.

138. Tull, interview.

139. Kris Littledale cited in Parry and Kornbluh, "Iran-Contra's Untold Story," 22.

140. Parry and Kornbluh, "Iran-Contra's Untold Story," 13, 17, 19; Kenworthy, "Where Pennsylvania Avenue Meets," 112; Alterman, *When Presidents Lie*, 270.

141. Reich cited in Parry and Kornbluh, "Iran-Contra's Untold Story," 17, 12.

142. Alterman, *When Presidents Lie*, 270.

143. *Report of the Congressional Committees*, 6.

144. Jacobowitz, "Public Diplomacy Action," March 12, 1985, in Kornbluh and Byrne, *Iran-Contra Scandal*, 23.

145. Parry and Kornbluh, "Iran-Contra's Untold Story," 4.

146. *Testimony of Elliott Abrams*, 34–35.

147. Wroe, *Lives*, 189–90.

148. Byrne, *Iran-Contra*, 176.

149. Wroe, *Lives*, 184.

150. Cited in Walsh, *Final Report*, 6.

151. Duemling to Abrams, Department of State NHAO, memo, April 1, 1986, DNSA.

152. "Central America: Problems in Controlling Funds for the Nicaraguan Democratic Resistance," Michael Barnes, Government Accountability Office, report, December 5, 1986, DNSA.

153. Reagan, *Diaries*, 148, 403.

154. Cited in Wroe, *Lives*, 185.

155. *Testimony of Robert C. McFarlane*, 5.

CHAPTER 2

1. Alfonso Chardy, "How U.S. Officials Created a Network for Contra Funding," *MH*, October 28, 1986, 1.

2. *Testimony of Adolfo P. Calero*, 375.

3. Bradlee, *Guts and Glory*, 206.

4. *Testimony of Adolfo P. Calero*, 70.

5. Marshall, Scott, and Hunter, *Iran Contra Connection*, 196.

6. Cited in Richard Goldstein, "John K. Singlaub, 100, General Who Clashed with Jimmy Carter, Dies," *NYT*, February 1, 2022.

7. Grandin, *Empire's Workshop*, 93.

8. Cited in Perlstein, *Reaganland*, 293, 795.

9. *Testimony of Adolfo P. Calero*, 175, 179–80, 197.

10. Shultz to Ambassador Lewis Tambs, c. April 1986, in *Testimony of Adolfo P. Calero*, 605.

11. Deposition of Richard H. Melton, May 27, 1987, in *Testimony of Elliott Abrams*, 862.

12. Bradlee, *Guts and Glory*, 201, 202.

13. Draper, *Very Thin Line*, 45–47.

14. "National Security Planning Group Meeting June 25, 1984: 2:00–3:00 p.m. Situation Room—Subject: Central America," NSC, minutes, June 25, 1984, DNSA; Walsh, *Final Report*, 2.

15. Stanley Sporkin, CIA, memo, June 26, 1984, DNSA.

16. "H.R. 5399—Section 107, Prohibition on Covert Assistance for Military Operations in Nicaragua," to Stanley Sporkin, CIA, memo, August 23, 1984, DNSA.

17. *Testimony of George P. Shultz and Edwin Meese*, 17.

18. Cited in Byrne, *Iran-Contra*, 83.

19. Reagan, *American Life*, 484.

20. Cited in Draper, *Very Thin Line*, 71.

21. Wroe, *Lives*, 17; Reagan, *Diaries*, 301.

22. *Testimony of Oliver L. North*, 76.

23. McFarlane to Friedersdorf, NSC, memo, March 12, 1985, DNSA.

24. *Testimony of Robert C. McFarlane*, 25, 202, 240.

25. In addition to those discussed in this chapter, the list includes South Africa, South Korea, Singapore, Chile, Venezuela, and Great Britain.

26. "U.S. Government Stipulation on Quid Pro Quos with Other Governments as Part of Contra Operations," April 6, 1989, in Kornbluh and Byrne, *Iran-Contra Scandal*, 85.

27. *Testimony of Adolfo P. Calero*, 73, 74, 171, 184, 186.

28. *Testimony of Robert C. McFarlane*, 287, 289, 291, 300, 301.

29. Draper, *Very Thin Line*, 84.

30. Byrne, *Iran-Contra*, 90.

31. "Meeting with the National Security Planning Group," May 15, 1986, *Testimony of John M. Poindexter*, 577.

32. *Testimony of George P. Shultz and Edwin Meese*, 19.

33. *Testimony of Elliott Abrams*, 184.

34. Cited in Wroe, *Lives*, 17.

35. *Testimony of Robert C. McFarlane*, 6.

36. Reagan, *American Life*, 485.

37. Casey, memo to McFarlane, March 27, 1984, in *Testimony of Robert C. McFarlane*, 456.

38. Memo, "Meeting with Bud McFarlane," July 16, 1984, in *Testimony of Robert C. McFarlane*, 460.

39. North, memo to McFarlane, September 2, 1984, in *Testimony of Robert C. McFarlane*, 461.

40. Oliver North to Robert McFarlane, NSC, memo, September 2, 1984, DNSA.

41. McFarlane, HPSCI, testimony, December 10, 1986, DNSA.

42. Bradlee, *Guts and Glory*, 223; Robert Pear, "North Described as Central Figure in a Contra Fund," *NYT*, February 26, 1987, A1.

43. Warren Rudman, cited in *Testimony of Adolfo P. Calero*, 151.

44. Jane McLaughlin to René Anselmo, NEPL, telegram, February 28, 1986, DNSA.

45. *Testimony of Oliver L. North*, 90, 91, 92, 93.

46. Garwood in *Testimony of Adolfo P. Calero*, 113.

47. Bradlee, *Guts and Glory*, 227.

48. Cited in *Testimony of Adolfo P. Calero*, 137, 147.

49. Bradlee, *Guts and Glory*, 225, 226–27.

50. Draper, *Very Thin Line*, 67.

51. *Testimony of Regan and Weinberger*, 76.

52. Oliver North to John Poindexter, NSC, PROFS, May 16, 1986, DNSA.

53. *Testimony of Adolfo P. Calero*, 116, 117, 118, 121, 144, 139.

54. *Report of the Congressional Committees*, 85.

55. Oliver North letter to "Bill," January 24, 1986, in *Appendixes to Parts I and II*, 910.

56. Cited Jane McLaughlin in Bradlee, *Guts and Glory*, 227.

57. Byrne, *Iran-Contra*, 138; Draper, *Very Thin Line*, 67; Bradlee, *Guts and Glory*, 247. The Congress's report cited a total of $10 million, of which $4.5 million went to the Contras: *Report of the Congressional Committees*, 85.

58. *Report of the Congressional Committees*, 98; Bradlee, *Guts and Glory*, 227.

59. *Testimony of Adolfo P. Calero*, 137, 131–32.

60. Bradlee, *Guts and Glory*, 250.

61. *Report of the Congressional Committees*, 98.

62. *Testimony of Regan and Weinberger*, 59.

63. Ellen Garwood to Ronald Reagan, letter, August 23, 1985, folder Iran-Contra Affair Correspondence, box 410, GLP.

64. "Steelhammer," aka Oliver North, letter to "My Friend," undated, in *Testimony of Robert C. McFarlane*, 782.

65. "Announcing Highlights of Meeting of Senators David Durenberger and Patrick Leahy with Robert McFarlane," SSCI, press release, September 5, 1985, DNSA.

66. Cited by Rep. Dave McCurdy in McFarlane, HPSCI, testimony, December 10, 1986, DNSA.

67. Richard Durbin to Robert McFarlane, House, letter, October 21, 1985, DNSA.

68. Cited in *Report of the Congressional Committees*, 139.

69. *Report of the Congressional Committees*, 141, 142.

70. Cited in Byrne, *Iran-Contra*, 140.

71. Cited in Draper, *Very Thin Line*, 37.

72. *Testimony of Oliver L. North*, 317–18.

73. William L. Chaze et al., "Inside the Shadow Network," *U.S. News*, December 15, 1986, 26.

74. Bradlee, *Guts and Glory*, 196–97.

75. "FBI Closing Memo regarding Richard Secord and Tom Clines," FBI, memo, January 7, 1986, DNSA; Draper, *Very Thin Line*, 36.

76. The words are the FBI's, not Secord's: "Secord Interviews," FBI, document, June 1982, DNSA.

77. *Testimony of Clarridge*, 243.

78. Draper, *Very Thin Line*, 37.

79. Cited in Secord and Wurts, *Honored and Betrayed*, 204.

80. Secord and Wurts, *Honored and Betrayed*, 201, 206.

81. Markups vary depending on the source: Draper, *Very Thin Line*, 39; investigators cited in Byrne, *Iran-Contra*, 53; *Testimony of Adolfo P. Calero*, 58.

82. Adolfo Calero in *Testimony of Adolfo P. Calero*, 59, 58, 14.

83. Secord and Jay Wurts, *Honored and Betrayed*, 209.

84. North and Novak, *Under Fire*, 252.

85. *Testimony of Oliver L. North*, 126.

86. Adolfo Calero and Owen cited in Mayer and McManus, *Landslide*, 145.

87. North and Novak, *Under Fire*, 252.

88. *Testimony of Richard V. Secord*, 205.

89. Mayer and McManus, *Landslide*, 145–46.

90. Byrne, *Iran-Contra*, 138.

91. "TC," memo to "BG," February 10, 1986, in *Testimony of Robert C. McFarlane*, 816.

92. "TC," memo to "BG," March 17, 1986, in *Testimony of Robert C. McFarlane*, 820 (emphasis in the original).

93. *Report of the Congressional Committees*, 59.

94. Kornbluh and Byrne, *Iran-Contra Scandal*, 129; *Report of the Congressional Committees*, 59.

95. Kornbluh and Byrne, *Iran-Contra Scandal*, 61.

96. CIA interview of Joseph Fernandez, January 24, 1987, in Kornbluh and Byrne, *Iran-Contra Scandal*, 154–61.

97. Tull, interview.

98. *Testimony of Adolfo P. Calero*, 400.

99. "UNO/South Resupply Drop," CIA, cable, August 18, 1986, DNSA.

100. *Testimony of Adolfo P. Calero*, 202, 229, 230, 235, 243, 276.

101. Mayer and McManus, *Landslide*, 200.

102. Cited in Wroe, *Lives, Lies and the Iran-Contra Affair*, 192, 188.

103. Woodward, *VEIL*, 195.

104. Oliver North to Robert McFarlane, NSC, memo, January 15, 1985, DNSA.

105. Oliver North to Robert McFarlane, NSC, memo, March 5, 1985, DNSA.

106. *Testimony of Richard V. Secord*, 110, 165. See also Oliver North, Memo for Robert McFarlane with Attachments, "Guatemalan Aid to the Nicaraguan Resistance," March 5, 1985, in Kornbluh and Byrne, *Iran-Contra Scandal*, 100.

107. Cited in Robert McFarlane to George Shultz, NSC, memo, February 15, 1985, DNSA. See also Oliver North and Raymond Burghardt to Robert McFarlane, NSC, memo, February 11, 1985, and Alan Fiers to North, CIA, memo, February 13, 1985, both in DNSA, and Robert McFarlane, memo for the president, "Approach to the Hondurans Regarding the Nicaraguan Resistance," February 19, 1985, in Kornbluh and Byrne, *Iran-Contra Scandal*, 83–84.

108. Cited in Walsh, *Final Report*, 450.

109. "U.S. Government Stipulation on Quid Pro Quos with Other Governments as Part of Contra Operations," April 6, 1989, in Kornbluh and Byrne, *Iran-Contra Scandal*, 89, 96.

110. *Testimony of Oliver L. North*, 152.

111. Mayer and McManus, *Landslide*, 252.

112. Walsh, *Firewall*, 62.

113. Toobin, *Opening Arguments*, 130.

114. *Testimony of Oliver L. North*, 139.

115. *Testimony of Elliott Abrams*, 216, 217, 229, 230, 348; *Testimony of Oliver L. North*, 126, 128.

116. *Testimony of Oliver L. North*, 136.

117. Walsh, *Firewall*, 98.

118. *Testimony of Oliver L. North*, 137, 129, 130, 131, 132; *Testimony of Glenn A. Robinette*, 8.

119. *Testimony of Oliver L. North*, 132; *Testimony of Glenn A. Robinette*, 15–16.

120. Benjamin Chatham to Glenn Robinette, letter, July 7, 1986, DNSA.

121. Walsh, *Firewall*, 98.

122. *Testimony of Elliott Abrams*, 363.

123. Mayer and McManus, *Landslide*, 211.

124. Bradlee, *Guts and Glory*, 409. For the Gary Webb/*San José Mercury News* allegations of Contras importing crack cocaine into the United States, see Heyboer, "A Furor over the CIA and Drugs" and Kornbluh, "Crack, Contras, and the CIA."

125. McCoy, "Covert Netherworld," 860.

126. Joseph Fernandez, CIA, memo, April 1986, DNSA; "Allegations of Drug Trafficking and the Nicaraguan Democratic Resistance," to House, Department of State, report, July 26, 1986, DNSA; Bradlee, *Guts and Glory*, 402.

127. Kerry cited in Bradlee, *Guts and Glory*, 404, 402.

128. Cited in Byrne, *Iran-Contra*, 132, 133.

129. Chaze et al., "Inside the Shadow Network," cover and 26.

130. *Report of the Congressional Committees*, 4–5.

131. Draper, *Very Thin Line*, 332.

CHAPTER 3

1. Byrne, *Iran-Contra*, 34, 36.

2. Walter Pincus and Dan Morgan, "New Allegations Link Reagan Campaign to Arms-Hostages Deal," *WP*, April 16, 1991.

3. For details on the "October surprise" controversy, see Cohen, "Who Will Unwrap," 32–34, Weinberg, "October Surprise," 33–41, and Berlet, "Big Stories, Spooky Sources," 67–71.

4. Lou Cannon, "Gary Sick's Lingering Charges," *WP*, May 13, 1991.

5. Byrne, *Iran-Contra*, 38; Meese, *With Reagan*, 259.

6. *Testimony of Richard V. Secord*, 259.

7. Cited in Walsh, *Firewall*, 4.

8. Ledeen, *Perilous Statecraft*, 126.

9. Reagan, *American Life*, 490, 492.

10. *Testimony of Oliver L. North*, 289.

11. Cited in Blumenthal, "Dateline Washington," 176–78.

12. Cited in Draper, *Very Thin Line*, 138.

13. Draft National Security Decision Directive, "U.S. Policy toward Iran," ca. June 11, 1985, with cover note by Robert McFarlane, June 17, 1985, in Kornbluh and Byrne, *Iran-Contra Scandal*, 220.

14. Robert McFarlane, memo for George Shultz, "Israeli-Iranian Contact," July 13, 1985, in Kornbluh and Byrne, *Iran-Contra Scandal*, 225.

15. Walsh, *Final Report*, 11.

16. Cited in Draper, *Very Thin Line*, 140.

17. George Shultz, cable to Robert McFarlane, July 14, 1985, in Kornbluh and Byrne, *Iran-Contra Scandal*, 261.

18. Caspar Weinberger and Colin Powell, Department of Defense, memo, June 18, 1985, DNSA.

19. Cited in Mayer and McManus, *Landslide*, 127.

20. Cited in Regan, *For the Record*, 20.

21. Reagan, *Diaries*, 343.

22. Cited in McFarlane and Smardz, *Special Trust*, 31.

23. Walsh, *Final Report*, 12.

24. Reagan, *American Life*, 505, 506, 507.

25. Cited in McFarlane and Smardz, *Special Trust*, 35.

26. Taylor, interview.

27. *Testimony of Oliver L. North*, 288, 285.

28. *Continued Testimony of North and McFarlane*, 33.

29. North and Novak, *Under Fire*, 154, 155.

30. Taylor, interview, 102.

31. Secord and Wurts, *Honored and Betrayed*, 225.

32. Cited in McFarlane and Smardz, *Special Trust*, 25, 26, and in Chief, CIA Near East Division, memo to William Casey, "Meetings with Michael Ledeen/Manuchehr [*sic*] Ghorbanifar," ca. December 23, 1985, DNSA.

33. "Early Background Report on Manucher Ghorbanifar," CIA, report, September 1, 1981, DNSA; Wroe, *Lives*, 10; Draper, *Very Thin Line*, 132.

34. Persico, *Casey*, 446–47.

35. Woodward, *VEIL*, 413.

36. CIA, "Intelligence Report on Manucher Ghorbanifar's Information on Kidnapping of William Buckley and on Iran-Sponsored Plot to Assassinate U.S. Presidential Candidates," March 21, 1984, DNSA; Woodward, *VEIL*, 413.

37. *Testimony of Clarridge*, 190.

38. CIA, "Iranian Terrorist Threat Information," cable, December 27, 1985, DNSA.

39. CIA, "Ghorbanifar Polygraph Examination," memo, January 12, 1986, and Ghorbanifar Polygraph—Date (1985) Incorrect," CIA, memo, January 13, 1986, both in DNSA.

40. Charles Allen, CIA, memo, January 29, 1986, DNSA. Written after a five-hour interview on January 13, 1986.

41. CIA, "Interview with Subject, 26 January 1986," memo, February 18, 1986, DNSA.

42. Cited in Mayer and McManus, *Landslide*, 118.

43. Cited in Charles Mohr, "Former U.S. Intelligence Aides Ask: Was a Lesson of the 70's Forgotten?," *NYT*, December 22, 1986.

44. Wroe, *Lives*, 96.

45. Mayer and McManus, *Landslide*, 142.

46. Marshall, Scott, and Hunter, *Iran Contra Connection*, 157.

47. "Conversation with G on 23 February 2010 Hours," transcript, February 23, 1986, DNSA.

48. *Testimony of Elliott Abrams*, 224, 225.

49. CIA, "Albert Hakim's Sale of Unneeded Communications Equipment to Iran," cable, August 18, 1976, DNSA.

50. *Testimony of John M. Poindexter*, 261.

51. *Continued Testimony of North and McFarlane*, 54.

52. *Report of the Congressional Committees*, 8.

53. *Continued Testimony of North and McFarlane*, 54, 55.

54. *Testimony of John M. Poindexter*, 260, 262.

55. *Testimony of Oliver L. North*, 121.

56. *Testimony of Clarridge*, 196, 211, 212.

57. *Report of the Congressional Committees*, 9.

58. Walsh, *Final Report*, 171–72.

59. Secord and Wurts, *Honored and Betrayed*, 208.

60. *Continued Testimony of North and McFarlane*, 57.

61. *Testimony of John M. Poindexter*, 263.

62. North and Novak, *Under Fire*, 31.

63. Ledeen, *Perilous Statecraft*, ix.

64. *Report of the Congressional Committees*, 9.

CHAPTER 4

1. Mayer and McManus, *Landslide*, 133; Kornbluh and Byrne, *Iran-Contra Scandal*, 214.

2. Reagan, *Diaries*, 350.

3. Arthur Liman cited in *Testimony of Robert C. McFarlane*, 50; Walsh, *Final Report*, 13.

4. Kornbluh and Byrne, *Iran-Contra Scandal*, 215.

5. Cited in Mayer and McManus, *Landslide*, 166.

6. Cited in Draper, *Very Thin Line*, 185, 187.

7. "Deposition of (CIA CHIEF)," Select Committee to Investigate Covert Arms Transactions with Iran, April 13, 1987, in *Testimony of Glenn A. Robinette*, 764–83.

8. Cited in Draper, *Very Thin Line*, 191.

9. NSC Mission," to CIA Immediate Director, CIA, cable, November 23, 1985, DNSA.

10. CIA, "Mission TLV/THR," memo, November 30, 1985, DNSA.

11. Cited in Wroe, *Lives*, 8.

12. Duane Clarridge, cable to Director of Central Intelligence, November 25, 1985, DNSA.

13. CIA, "Mission TLV/THR," memo, November 30, 1985, DNSA.

14. Walsh, *Final Report*, 15.

15. Draper, *Very Thin Line*, 196.

16. Cited in Mayer and McManus, *Landslide*, 168.

17. *Testimony of Oliver L. North*, 29.

18. CIA, "NSC Request," cable to CIA Flash Director, November 25, 1985, DNSA.

19. Mohr, "Former U.S. Intelligence Aides Ask."

20. Davis Robinson, Department of State Office of the Legal Advisor, memo, October 2, 1981, DNSA.

21. William Smith, letter to William Casey, Department of Justice, October 5, 1981, DNSA.

22. John McMahon, deposition to Congress, June 1, 1987, DNSA.

23. Cited in Draper, *Very Thin Line*, 208.

24. Cited in Persico, *Casey*, 474.

25. *Testimony of Glenn A. Robinette*, 122, 181, 182, 184, 185, 124.

26. Draft of finding, November 25, 1985, in *Testimony of Glenn A. Robinette*, 424.

27. Oliver North, memo to Robert McFarlane and John Poindexter, December 9, 1985, in *Testimony of Glenn A. Robinette*, 429–31.

28. Cited in Draper, *Very Thin Line*, 223, 224, 225.

29. "George Shultz Expression of Opposition to NSC Operation with Iran," Department of State, memo, December 7, 1985, DNSA.

30. Meese testimony to Tower Commission, January 20, 1987, folder EM III testimony (redacted) Jan 20, 1987, box 568, EMP.

31. Cited in *Testimony of George P. Shultz and Edwin Meese*, 31, 32.

32. *Testimony of Regan and Weinberger*, 140.

33. Cited in Byrne, *Iran-Contra*, 106, 107.

34. *Testimony of George P. Shultz and Edwin Meese*, 207.

35. *Testimony of Regan and Weinberger*, 140.

36. Cited in Draper, *Very Thin Line*, 229.

37. Reagan, *American Life*, 513.

38. *Testimony of John M. Poindexter*, 25.

39. Cited in Draper, *Very Thin Line*, 231, 232.

40. Reagan, *Diaries*, 375.

41. Byrne, *Iran-Contra*, 156.

42. Cited in Persico, *Casey*, 491.

43. Cited in Mary McGrory, "The Takeover of Stanley Sporkin," *WP*, June 25, 1987.

44. George Clarke to Stanley Sporkin, CIA, memo, January 7, 1986, DNSA.

45. The Arms Control Export Act, the Hughes-Ryan Agreement, and the National Security Act of 1947.

46. Stanley Sporkin to William Casey, CIA, memo, January 15, 1986, DNSA.

47. George Clarke, CIA, memo, January 15, 1986, DNSA.

48. *Testimony of John M. Poindexter*, 17. The finding is given in Exhibit SS-19, *Testimony of Richard V. Secord*, 465.

49. Cited in Mayer and McManus, *Landslide*, 185–86.

50. Draper, *Very Thin Line*, 257.

51. *Testimony of Clarridge*, 212, 216.

52. Susan Crawford to John Marsh, US Army Office of the General Counsel, memo, February 13, 1986, DNSA.

53. Mayer and McManus, *Landslide*, 184.

54. National Security Act, Sections 501(b) and 501(a)(1)(B).

55. Cited in Draper, *Very Thin Line*, 255–56. See also *Testimony of Glenn A. Robinette*, 195–96, 198, 204, 214.

56. Meese testimony to Tower Commission, EMP.

57. *Testimony of Glenn A. Robinette*, 197.

58. Draper, *Very Thin Line*, 450.

59. Cannon, *President Reagan*, 583.

60. Mayer and McManus, *Landslide*, 198, 220.

61. John Poindexter to Oliver North, PROFS, "Private Blank Check," April 16, 1986, in Kornbluh and Byrne, *Iran-Contra Scandal*, 294.

62. *Report of the Congressional Committees*, 237.

63. *Testimony of Oliver L. North*, 293.

64. Cited in Charles Allen, CIA, memo, April 16, 1986, DNSA.

65. Walsh, *Iran-Contra*, 21.

66. *Testimony of Oliver L. North*, 220, 229.

67. Oliver North to John Poindexter, NSC, PROFS, May 5, 1986, DNSA.

68. *Testimony of Clarridge*, 273.

69. North and Novak, *Under Fire*, 35.

70. *Testimony of Richard V. Secord*, 185.

71. *Continued Testimony of North and McFarlane*, 4, 5, 7.

72. George Cave, CIA, memo, May 30, 1986, DNSA.

73. Howard Teicher, NSC, memcon, May 25, 1986, DNSA.

74. George Cave, CIA, memo, May 30, 1986, and Howard Teicher, NSC, memcon, May 25, 1986, both in DNSA.

75. Howard Teicher, NSC, memcon, May 26, 1986, DNSA.

76. Cited in Draper, *Very Thin Line*, 321.

77. Howard Teicher, NSC, memcon, May 27, 1986, DNSA.

78. Robert McFarlane, cable to John Poindexter, NSC, May 27, 1986, DNSA.

79. Howard Teicher, NSC, memcon, May 26, 1986, DNSA.

80. George Cave, CIA, memo, May 30, 1986, DNSA.

81. *Testimony of Richard V. Secord*, 93, 105.

82. Memcon, May 29, 1986, in *Testimony of Regan and Weinberger*, 355.

83. Reagan, *Diaries*, 414.

84. North cited in Draper, *Very Thin Line*, 382; North and Novak, *Under Fire*, 286.

85. Charles Allen, CIA, memo, April 2, 1986, DNSA.

86. *Testimony of Elliott Abrams*, 261.

87. Memcon, Washington, September 19, 1986, folder Iran-Contra Affair Ghorbanifar Operation, box 415, GLP.

88. Liman cited in *Testimony of Elliott Abrams*, 295; see also 355, 356.

89. *Testimony of Richard V. Secord*, 207.

90. *Testimony of Regan and Weinberger*, 60.

91. Bradlee, *Guts and Glory*, 438.

92. Reagan, *American Life*, 522.

93. Draper, *Very Thin Line*, 397.

94. Cannon, *President Reagan*, 586.

95. Walsh, *Iran-Contra*, 22.

96. *Report of the Congressional Committees*, 245, 8.

97. *Continued Testimony of North and McFarlane*, 167.

98. Unauthored, undated, "Rundown of Visitor's Comments on 19/20 Sept 86," in *Appendixes to Parts I and II*, 791.

99. Charles Allen, CIA, personal notes, October 9, 1986, DNSA.

100. North and Novak, *Under Fire*, 281.

CHAPTER 5

1. *Testimony of Oliver L. North*, 109.

2. Cited in Secord and Wurts, *Honored and Betrayed*, 229. See also Joel Brinkley, "Birth of a Scandal and Mysteries of Its Parentage," *NYT*, December 25, 1992, A23, and Draper, *Very Thin Line*, 199.

3. Mayer and McManus, *Landslide*, 190.

4. *Testimony of Oliver L. North*, 298.

5. Draper, *Very Thin Line*, 277.

6. North and Novak, *Under Fire*, 19, 20.

7. Cited in Draper, *Very Thin Line*, 273.

8. *Appendixes to Parts I and II*, 8.

9. *Testimony of Oliver L. North*, 122.

10. *Testimony of John M. Poindexter*, 35, 118.

11. *Testimony of Oliver L. North*, 109, 13.

12. Alterman, *When Presidents Lie*, 277.

13. From a deposition cited in *Testimony of John M. Poindexter*, 116.

14. North, "Release of American Hostages in Beirut," April 4, 1986, in *Appendixes to Parts I and II*, 5.

15. Draper, *Very Thin Line*, 301.

16. *Testimony of Oliver L. North*, 142, 300.

17. *Testimony of Clarridge*, 222, 223.

18. Mayer and McManus, *Landslide*, 191.

19. *Report of the Congressional Committees*, 390.

20. Persico, *Casey*, 564, 524.

21. *Testimony of Clarridge*, 223.

22. Menges, *Inside the National Security Council*, 315.

23. *Testimony of Regan and Weinberger*, 51–52, 38. Poindexter is in *Testimony of John M. Poindexter*, 38.

24. *Testimony of Oliver L. North*, 114, 115, 116, 118, 142, 123.

25. Oliver North, interview with George Lardner, 1991, folder 6, box 177, GLP.

26. Cited in McFarlane and Smardz, *Special Trust*; North tells substantively the same story in North and Novak, *Under Fire*.

27. Walsh, *Final Report*, 21.

28. *Testimony of Richard V. Secord*, 64.

29. Walsh, *Iran-Contra*, 21.

30. *Testimony of John M. Poindexter*, 36, 37, 48, 49.

31. *Testimony of Richard V. Secord*, 288.

32. *Testimony of John M. Poindexter*, 37, 118.

33. *Testimony of Regan and Weinberger*, 38.

34. Fisher, "Foundations of a Scandal," 162.

35. Draper, *Very Thin Line*, 438, 443.

36. Oliver North, interview with George Lardner, 1991, folder 6, box 177, GLP.

37. Draper, *Very Thin Line*, 449.

38. *Testimony of Regan and Weinberger*, 63, 127.

39. Walsh, *Firewall*, 24.

40. Cited in Scott Spencer, "Walsh's Last Battle," *NYT Magazine*, July 4, 1993, 30.

41. Liman with Israel, *Lawyer*, 349, 350.

CHAPTER 6

1. David Binder, "Ex-C.I.A. Officer Testifies about Arming Contras," *NYT*, August 5, 1992, A16.

2. Cited in Samuel Watson, Office of the Vice President, memo, December 17, 1986, DNSA. See also *Testimony of Adolfo P. Calero*, 339–40.

3. Donald Gregg, Office of the Vice President, memo, August 8, 1986, DNSA.

4. *Testimony of Adolfo P. Calero*, 298, 305, 306.

5. *Report of the Congressional Committees*, 118.

6. Joanne Omang, "White House Defends Legality of NSC Contact with Contras," *WP*, August 9, 1985, A1; Joanne Omang, "McFarlane Aide Facilitates Policy in Latin America," *WP*, August 10, 1985, A1; Joel Brinkley, "White House Aid to Nicaraguan Rebels Reportedly Worried C.I.A.," *NYT*, August 10, 1985.

7. Barger and Parry, untitled wire story, *Associated Press*, December 20, 1985; Barger and Parry, "U.S. Allegedly Ran Private Network," *Baltimore Sun*, June 11, 1986, 1A.

8. Oliver North, memo to John Poindexter, June 3, 1986, in *Appendixes to Parts I and II*, 750.

9. Cited in Draper, *Very Thin Line*, 336.

10. Cited in Draper, *Very Thin Line*, 118.

11. Kornbluh and Byrne, *Iran-Contra Scandal*, 189.

12. Morton Abramowitz, memo to Elliott Abrams, May 24, 1986, in *Testimony of Elliott Abrams*, 796.

13. Robert McFarlane to John Poindexter, NSC, PROFS, June 12, 1986, DNSA.

14. Both cited in Draper, *Very Thin Line*, 334.

15. *Testimony of Elliott Abrams*, 24.

16. Oliver North to John Poindexter, NSC, PROFS, September 6, 1986, DNSA.

17. Oliver North to John Poindexter, NSC, PROFS, September 25, 1986, DNSA. See also Draper, *Very Thin Line*, 346–349.

18. Oliver North, memo for John Poindexter, "Press Guidance re Costa Rican Airstrip," September 30, 1986, in Kornbluh and Byrne, *Iran-Contra Scandal*, 181, 182.

19. Robert Dutton, KL-43, October 6, 1986, DNSA; Draper, *Very Thin Line*, 353.

20. Byrne, *Iran-Contra*, 1, 234; Norman Stockwell, "The Exposure of Eugene Hasenfus," *The Tico Times*, October 6, 2014, https://ticotimes.net/2014/10/06/the-exposure-of-eugene-hasenfus.

21. Julia Preston, "Captured American Presented by Nicaragua: Crash Survivor Described as Adviser in El Salvador," *WP*, October 8, 1986, A1.

22. "Informaciones Obtenidas sobre el Prisionero Eugene Hasenfus," personal notes, October 8, 1986, DNSA.

23. Clarridge with Diehl, *Spy for All Seasons*, 363.

24. "Nicaragua: Sandinistas Shoot Down USG Aircraft?," Department of State Bureau of Inter-American Affairs, press guidance, October 7, 1986, DNSA.

25. Robert Earl to Craig Coy, NSC, PROFS, October 8, 1986, DNSA.

26. Cited in Joanne Omang, "Captured American Presented by Nicaragua: Reagan Administration Denies U.S. Link to Plane," *WP*, October 8, 1986, A1.

27. Cited in Draper, *Very Thin Line*, 355.

28. Cited in Bradlee, *Guts and Glory*, 446.

29. Cited in Mayer and McManus, *Landslide*, 274.

30. Byrne, *Iran-Contra*, 253.

31. Cited in Omang, "Captured American," A1.

32. Woodward, *VEIL*, 483; Persico, *Casey*, 531.

33. FBI, "Unknown Subjects; Possible Neutrality Violation Concerning a C-123 Aircraft Shot Down by Nicaraguan Military Forces, October 7, 1986; Neutrality Act—Nicaragua," memo, December 5, 1986, DNSA.

34. Byrne, *Iran-Contra*, 217.

35. Cited in Busby, *Reagan and the Iran-Contra Affair*, 73, 76.

36. Currie, "Iran-Contra and Congressional Oversight," 196.

37. US House, "Statement of Clair George, Deputy Director for Operations, Central Intelligence Agency," October 14, 1986, in *Testimony of Clarridge*, 669.

38. SFRC, "The Situation in Nicaragua," October 10, 1986, folder F, Master Congressional, Vol. 3, 1992, box 5, Master Congressional Correspondence 1992, RG 449.

39. Indictment, *United States v. Clair E. George*, folder F, Master Congressional, Vol. 3, 1992, box 5, Master Congressional Correspondence 1992, RG 449.

40. "Briefing on Downed Plane," HPSCI, transcript, October 14, 1986, DNSA.

41. Patricia Taylor, CIA, memcon, October 14, 1986, DNSA.

42. Walsh, *Iran-Contra*, 10.

43. Patricia Taylor, CIA, memcon, October 14, 1986, DNSA.

44. *Testimony of Tomas Castillo*, 48.

45. George James, memo to General Counsel, March 2, 1987, in *Testimony of Tomas Castillo*, 131.

46. Cited in "Evans and Novak," *Cable News Network*, 629–41.

47. Cited in Eric Alterman, "Democracy's Lies," *NYT*, November 4, 1991.

48. *Testimony of Elliott Abrams*, 68.

49. "El Salvador/Nicaragua: U.S. Involvement in Contra Supply Flights?," Department of State Bureau of Inter-American Affairs, press guidance, October 14, 1986, DNSA.

50. "Saudi Arabia Involvement in Private Funding of Contras," House Foreign Affairs Committee, hearing, October 15, 1986, DNSA.

51. Cited in Mayer and McManus, *Landslide*, 285.

52. Persico, *Casey*, 525.

53. Brinkley, "Birth of a Scandal and Mysteries of Its Parentage," A23; Mayer and McManus, *Landslide*, 293.

54. Cannon, *President Reagan*, 600–601.

55. Walsh, *Firewall*, 8.

56. Reagan, *Diaries*, 448.

57. Reagan, *American Life*, 528.

58. Cited in Persico, *Casey*, 526.

59. Brody and Shapiro, "Policy Failure and Public Support," 361.

60. North and Novak, *Under Fire*, 308.

61. *Testimony of Regan and Weinberger*, 21.

62. Shultz, *Turmoil and Triumph*, 787.

63. George Shultz, cable to John Poindexter and Nicholas Platt, Department of State, November 4, 1986, DNSA.

64. Poindexter, memo to George Shultz, White House Situation Room, November 5, 1986, in *Testimony of George P. Shultz and Edwin Meese*, 566.

65. Robert McFarlane to John Poindexter, NSC, PROFS, November 7, 1986, DNSA.

66. John Poindexter to Robert McFarlane, NSC, PROFS, November 7, 1986, DNSA.

67. Cannon, *President Reagan*, 604.

68. Caspar Weinberger, memo, "Meeting on November 10, 1986, with the President, Vice President, Secretary Shultz, DCI Casey, Attorney General Meese, Don Regan, Admiral Poindexter, and Al Keel, in the Oval Office," n.d., in Kornbluh and Byrne, *Iran-Contra Scandal*, 316.

69. Shultz, *Turmoil and Triumph*, 813.

70. Kornbluh and Byrne, *Iran-Contra Scandal*, 305.

71. Shultz, *Turmoil and Triumph*, 815.

72. Cited in Walsh, *Final Report*, 23.

73. Reagan, *Diaries*, 449.

74. Cited in Mayer and McManus, *Landslide*, 300.

75. Patrick Buchanan to Donald Regan, Executive Office of the President, memo, November 12, 1986, DNSA.

76. Reagan, *Diaries*, 450.

77. All citations from this press conference are from "Address to the Nation, November 13, 1986," *Appendixes to Parts I and II*, 1298–300.

78. *Testimony of Regan and Weinberger*, 25.

79. North and Novak, *Under Fire*, 311.

80. Regan, *For the Record*, 33.

81. *Los Angeles Times* poll cited in Draper, *Very Thin Line*, 474.

82. McFarlane and Smardz, *Special Trust*, 95.

83. Robert McFarlane, PROFs note to John Poindexter, November 13, 1986, in *Testimony of Robert C. McFarlane*, 636, 637.

84. George H. W. Bush diary extracts, November 4, 1986–January 2, 1987, folder Iran-Contra, box 107, GLP.

85. North and Novak, *Under Fire*, 311.

86. Regan, *For the Record*, 32, 33.

87. George H. W. Bush diary extracts, GLP.

88. "Face the Nation," transcript, November 16, 1986, *Testimony of George P. Shultz and Edwin Meese*, 599.

89. See also Shultz, *Turmoil and Triumph*, 823.

90. *Testimony of George P. Shultz and Edwin Meese*, 43.

91. November 16 entry, Bush diary, folder Files of the Office of the Vice President Bush—VP Diary, box 2, Records of John Q. Barrett Attorney Files, RG 449.

92. Cited in Walsh, *Iran-Contra*, 215.

93. Charles Hill handwritten notes, [1992?], folder Iran Contra—the Independent Counsel, box 69, CHP.

94. "The President's News Conference of November 19, 1986," in *Weekly Compilation of Presidential Documents*, 22, vol. 47 (November 24, 1986): 1583–91, DNSA.

95. "The President's News Conference of November 19, 1986," in *Appendixes to Parts I and II*, 1301–308.

96. "Statement by the President, November 19, 1986," in *Appendixes to Parts I and II*, 1310.

97. Mayer and McManus, *Landslide*, 316.

98. Editorial, "The Purpose of Presidents," *WSJ*, November 21, 1986, 32.

99. George H. W. Bush diary extracts, GLP.

100. "Briefing Paper for George Shultz's Meeting with President Reagan on November 20, 1986, concerning the Iran Initiative," Department of State, November 20, 1986, DNSA.

101. Shultz, *Turmoil and Triumph*, 828.

102. Cited in Cannon, *President Reagan*, 614.

103. Byrne, *Iran-Contra*, 265.

104. McFarlane and Smardz, *Special Trust*, 95, 96.

105. Cited in Bradlee, *Guts and Glory*, 461.

106. *Testimony of Oliver L. North*, 36, 30–33.

107. Editorial, "Purpose of Presidents," 32.

108. Cited in Mayer and McManus, *Landslide*, 318.

109. *Testimony of Glenn A. Robinette*, 242.

110. Nicholas C. McBride, "Meese Is Sucked Deeper into the Iran-Contra Vortex," *Christian Science Monitor*, July 2, 1987, 6.

111. Cited in Mayer and McManus, *Landslide*, 319.

112. Cited in Draper, *Very Thin Line*, 481.

113. "The Deposition of Abraham D. Sofaer," June 18, 1987, in *Testimony of Glenn A. Robinette*, 886.

114. *Testimony of Glenn A. Robinette*, 248, 249.

115. "The Deposition of Abraham D. Sofaer," in *Testimony of Glenn A. Robinette*, 874.

116. Cited in Mayer and McManus, *Landslide*, 321; *Testimony of Glenn A. Robinette*, 250.

117. Walsh, *Final Report*, 24.

118. Taylor, interview.

119. Laura Jarrett, "Lying to Congress Can Put You in Jail, Even if You're Not under Oath," CNN, July 24, 2017, www.cnn.com/2017/07/24/politics/penalty-for-lying-to-congress/index.html.

120. Casey testimony to joint Congressional committees, November 21, 1986, *Appendixes to Parts I and II*, 164–71.

121. "Closed Testimony of Bill Casey to Congressional Committee," November 21, 1986, in *Testimony of Glenn A. Robinette*, 670, 676, 678, 686, 687.

122. Abraham Sofaer, memo to Nicholas Platt, Charles Hill, Paul Bremer, and Arnold Raphel, Department of State, November 21, 1986, DNSA.

123. Kathleen Watson, memo to George Clarke, CIA Office of the General Counsel, November 19, 1986, DNSA.

124. Jo Ann Farrington, memo to Gerald McDowell, Department of Justice, November 22, 1986, DNSA.

125. Reagan, *Diaries*, 453.

126. *Report of the Congressional Committees*, 10.

127. *Testimony of John M. Poindexter*, 20.

128. John C. Coffee Jr. and Paul P. Puccio cited in Ruth Marcus, "Testimony Raises a Crucial Question; Was Poindexter Aware of Probe When He Destroyed 'Finding'?," *WP*, July 17, 1987, A16.

129. *Testimony of Oliver L. North*, 16, 19.

130. Perlstein, *Reaganland*, 754; Mayer and McManus, *Landslide*, 324.

131. John B. Oakes, "Meese's Record of Failure," *NYT*, November 17, 1987, A35.

132. Charles Cooper cited in Kim Eisler, "Bungling and Heroes Emerge in Iran Probe," *Legal Times*, June 29, 1987, 13; "Attorney General's Interview with Independent Counsel Staff re Iran Investigation," folder AG's interview with Independent Counsel Iran investigation, July 6, 1987, box 575, EMP.

133. *Testimony of George P. Shultz and Edwin Meese*, 279.

134. *Testimony of John M. Poindexter*, 395.

135. *Testimony of George P. Shultz and Edwin Meese*, 227.

136. *Testimony of Oliver L. North*, 22.

137. "North Obstruction: Chronology," House, November 24, 1986, *Appendixes to Parts I and II*, 687.

138. Cited in *Testimony of George P. Shultz and Edwin Meese*, 283.

139. Sara Fritz and Karen Tumulty, "Meese Defends His Iran Inquiry," *LAT*, July 29, 1987, 1.

140. Eisler, "Bungling and Heroes Emerge in Iran Probe," 1.

141. *Testimony of George P. Shultz and Edwin Meese*, 226.

142. Cannon, *President Reagan*, 617.

143. *Testimony of George P. Shultz and Edwin Meese*, 282.

144. *Testimony of Oliver L. North*, 22, 149; *Testimony of Robert C. McFarlane*, 214.

145. Cruz, *Memoirs of a Counterrevolutionary*, 199.

146. *Testimony of John M. Poindexter*, 118.

147. *Testimony of Elliott Abrams*, 497, 499.

148. George Lardner Jr. and Bob Woodward, "4 Memos Said Altered by North's Secretary," *WP*, February 24, 1987, A1.

149. "North Obstruction: Chronology," House, November 24, 1986, *Appendixes to Parts I and II*, 687.

150. *Testimony of Elliott Abrams*, 552.

151. *Testimony of Oliver L. North*, 256.

152. Cited in Susan Page and Alison Mitchell, "Oliver North, Shredder," *Newsday*, July 10, 1987, 5.

153. Bradlee, *Guts and Glory*, 454; Charles Hill handwritten notes, CHP.

154. Cited in Mayer and McManus, *Landslide*, 331.

155. Senator William Cohen, cited in *Testimony of George P. Shultz and Edwin Meese*, 326.

156. Cited in Wroe, *Lives*, 38, 39.

157. *Testimony of Glenn A. Robinette*, 258.

158. *Testimony of Oliver L. North*, 260.

159. *Testimony of George P. Shultz and Edwin Meese*, 338.

160. *Testimony of Glenn A. Robinette*, 260.

161. [Author?], handwritten notes, November 23, 1986, folder Weekend investigation notes, box 571, EMP.

162. *Testimony of George P. Shultz and Edwin Meese*, 246, 247.

163. North and Novak, *Under Fire*, 327.

164. "Notes of Interviews with William Bradford Reynolds by Congressional Iran-Contra Investigators," memcon, April 24, 1987, DNSA.

165. *Testimony of Oliver L. North*, 246.

166. North and Novak, *Under Fire*, 327.

167. *Testimony of Glenn A. Robinette*, 264, 295.

168. *Testimony of George P. Shultz and Edwin Meese*, 236, 237. See also *Testimony of Oliver L. North*, 254.

169. *Testimony of George P. Shultz and Edwin Meese*, 251–52.

170. *Testimony of Regan and Weinberger*, 29–30, 32.

171. Walsh, *Final Report*, 526.

172. Cited in Byrne, *Iran-Contra*, 277.

173. *Testimony of George P. Shultz and Edwin Meese*, 254, 281; *Report of the Congressional Committees*, 11.

174. Reagan, *Diaries*, 453.

175. *Testimony of Glenn A. Robinette*, 268, 269.

176. Regan, *For the Record*, 41–42.

177. Draper, *Very Thin Line*, 540.

178. Cited in *Testimony of George P. Shultz and Edwin Meese*, 279.

179. McBride, "Meese Is Sucked Deeper into the Iran-Contra Vortex," 6.

180. Cited in Bradlee, *Guts and Glory*, 11; Reagan, *American Life*, 541; and Reagan, *Diaries*, 514.

181. *Testimony of Elliott Abrams*, 504, 505, 506, 530, 507.

182. "North Obstruction: Chronology," House, November 24, 1986, *Appendixes to Parts I and II*, 687–689.

183. Cited in Bob Woodward and Walter Pincus, "North Destroyed Data, Aide Says," *WP*, February 22, 1987, A1.

184. Busby, *Reagan and the Iran-Contra Affair*, 7.

185. Reagan, *Diaries*, 454.

186. Kornbluh and Byrne, *Iran-Contra Scandal*, 310.

187. North and Novak, *Under Fire*, 7, 15.

188. Reagan, *Diaries*, 454.

189. "An Interview with the President," *Time*, December 8, 1986, 18.

190. Ralph Martin, memo to William Weld, Department of Justice, November 28, 1986, DNSA.

191. United States Embassy in Brunei, cable to Department of State, December 4, 1986, DNSA.

CHAPTER 7

1. Mary Battiata, "John Tower & His Arduous Mandate," *WP*, February 26, 1987, B1.

2. "Executive Order 12575."

3. George H. W. Bush diary extracts, GLP.

4. Editorial, "A President's Trouble," *WSJ*, November 26, 1986, 20.

5. "Briefing on Nicaragua," SSCI, hearing, November 25, 1986, DNSA.

6. Elliott Abrams, "Testimony of Elliott Abrams," SSCI, hearing, December 8, 1986, DNSA.

7. *Testimony of Elliott Abrams*, 78.

8. Busby, *Reagan and the Iran-Contra Affair*, 112.

9. Taylor, interview.

10. Jerome Silber to Defense Security Assistance Agency Office of the Director, Defense Security Assistance Agency Office of the General Counsel, memo, January 21, 1987, DNSA.

11. Weinberger, memo to Acting Principal Deputy to the National Security Advisor Alton Keel, December 22, 1986, in *Testimony of George P. Shultz and Edwin Meese*, 643.

12. Editorial, "Stonewalling by Any Other Name," *NYT*, January 20, 1987.

13. David Boren and William Cohen, letter to Daniel Inouye, January 29, 1991, folder Iran-Contra Select Committee on Intelligence Report, box 331, Papers of the Committee on the Present Danger, Hoover Institution, Stanford University, CA.

14. Editorial, "Layers of Lies on Iran," *NYT*, February 1, 1987.

15. Currie, "Iran-Contra and Congressional Oversight," 198.

16. Boren and Cohen to Inouye, January 29, 1991, Papers of the Committee on the Present Danger, Hoover Institution, Stanford University, CA.

17. Tower, Muskie, and Scowcroft, *Tower Commission Report*, 17.

18. Battiata, "John Tower & His Arduous Mandate," B1.

19. "[Tower Commission Interview with George Shultz]," Tower Commission, transcript, January 22, 1987, DNSA; Alterman, *When Presidents Lie*, 286.

20. Elliott Abrams, Tower Commission, deposition, February 19, 1987, DNSA.

21. Weinberger, *Fighting for Peace*, 360.

22. Sandy Grady, "McFarlane Took the Heat While His Boss and Other Aides Kept Silent," *MH*, February 11, 1987, 17A.

23. Sandy Grady, "McFarlane's Testimony Painful, Tearful," *MH*, May 13, 1987, 21A.

24. Cannon, *President Reagan*, 552.

25. McFarlane and Smardz, *Special Trust*, 3, 6, 7, 8, 11.

26. "Bud" and "Dad," letter to "Jonny, Laurie, Scott, and Melissa," February 6, 1987, folder 13, box 30, LGP.

27. McFarlane and Smardz, *Special Trust*, 14–15, 337, 338.

28. Battiata, "John Tower & His Arduous Mandate," B1.

29. All from the Reagan Library's narrative cited in Chris Spaulding, memo to Lawrence Walsh, July 22, 1992, folder Reagan Tower Commission Testimony, box 39, General Investigative Files, Records of John Q. Barrett Attorney Files, RG 449.

30. Cited in Cannon, *President Reagan*, 631, 632.

31. Cited in Tower, *Consequences*, 283, 284.

32. Cited in Cannon, *President Reagan*, 632, 634.

33. Walsh, *Final Report*, 469.

34. "The Summer of 1987," *Foreign Affairs*, 4.

35. *Testimony of Oliver L. North*, 27.

36. Russell Watson, with Thomas M. DeFrank and John Barry, "Break Point," *Newsweek*, February 23, 1987, 18.

37. Reagan, *Diaries*, 478.

38. Cited in Busby, *Reagan and the Iran-Contra Affair*, 120, 78.

39. Cited in Cannon, *President Reagan*, 634–35.

40. Cited in Koh, *National Security Constitution*, 13.

41. Tower, Muskie, and Scowcroft, *Tower Commission Report*, 2, 1, 51.

42. Cited in Koh, *National Security Constitution*, 14.

43. Tower, Muskie, and Scowcroft, *Tower Commission Report*, 15, 98, 94.

44. Michael R. Gordon, "N.S.C. Being Restructured to Give More Focus to Coordinating Policy," *NYT*, December 22, 1986, 1; Kiehl, "Seduced and Abandoned," in *Affairs of State*, ed. Marcella, 321–70, 350; Abraham Sofaer, memo to Shultz, Washington, March 25, 1987, folder NSC Staff and Iran-Contra, box 17, CHP.

45. Brzezinski, "NSC's Midlife Crisis," 93.

46. Editorial, "The Tower Inferno," *WSJ*, February 25, 1987, 28.

47. Editorial, "The President's Speech," *WSJ*, March 4, 1987, 30.

48. Anthony Lewis, "The Man Responsible," *NYT*, February 24, 1987.

49. Norman Podhoretz, "What Reagan Knew, and When," *WP*, March 5, 1987.

50. Busby, *Reagan and the Iran-Contra Affair*, 119, 125.

51. Rozell, "Executive Privilege in the Reagan Administration," 769.

52. Reagan, *American Life*, 485.

53. Cited in Cannon, *President Reagan*, 636.

54. Reagan, *American Life*, 487, 532, 540.

CHAPTER 8

1. July 15, 1986. Cited in Wroe, *Lives*, 1.

2. *Continued Testimony of North and McFarlane*, 44.

3. Cited in Leon Wieseltier, "Democracy and Colonel North," *New Republic*, January 26, 1987, 22–25, 23.

4. Regan, *For the Record*, 59.

5. Seymour M. Hersh, "The Iran-Contra Committees: Did They Protect Reagan?," *NYT*, April 29, 1990, A46, A61; Stephen Engelberg, "Lingering Questions on Iran-Contra May Arise in Court—Or May Not," *NYT*, September 18, 1988, A5.

6. Wroe, *Lives*, iv.

7. Hersh, "Iran-Contra Committees," A61.

8. Mary McGrory, "Reverence for the Process," *WP*, December 23, 1986.

9. Liman with Israel, *Lawyer*, 304.

10. Cited in Alterman, *When Presidents Lie*, 273.

11. Cited in AP, "Iran-Contra Revisited: Fears of Impeachment," *NYT*, October 27, 1993," A16.

12. Hersh, "Iran-Contra Committees," A46.

13. Liman with Israel, *Lawyer*, 304.

14. David E. Rosenbaum, "Congress Draws a Bead on the Iran-Contra Affair," *NYT*, April 26, 1987, A4.

15. David E. Rosenbaum, "Congress Panels Merge Inquiries into Iran Affair," *NYT*, March 19, 1987, A1.

16. Cited anonymously in Hersh, "Iran-Contra Committees," A46.

17. Liman with Israel, *Lawyer*, 313.

18. Reagan, *Diaries*, 460.

19. Liman with Israel, *Lawyer*, 310, 3.

20. Philip Shenon, "Walsh Makes His Move," *NYT*, October 25, 1987, A46.

21. Persico, *Casey*, 557.

22. Woodward, *VEIL*, 506.

23. Reagan, *Diaries*, 534.

24. Inquirer Staff, "AIM: Woodward Story a 'Fake,'" *Washington Inquirer*, October 9, 1987, 1.

25. AP, "Casey Meetings Acknowledged by Widow," *WP*, October 3, 1987.

26. *Testimony of Richard V. Secord*, 3, 18.

27. Busby, *Reagan and the Iran-Contra Affair*, 144.

28. Thelen, *Becoming Citizens*, 18.

29. Thelen, *Becoming Citizens*, 26.

30. Wroe, *Lives*, 51.

31. Fried, *Muffled Echoes*, 116.

32. Tom Wicker, "Don't Count on Ollie," *NYT*, July 22, 1987.

33. North and Novak, *Under Fire*, 345; Walsh, *Firewall*, 135.

34. Liman with Israel, *Lawyer*, 336.

35. Busby, *Reagan and the Iran-Contra Affair*, 162.

36. Busby, *Reagan and the Iran-Contra Affair*, 161.

37. North and Novak, *Under Fire*, 344.

38. Wroe, *Lives*, 53.

39. Thelen, *Becoming Citizens*, 39–40.

40. Fried, *Muffled Echoes*, 119.

41. *Continued Testimony of North and McFarlane*, 59, 60, 46–47.

42. *Testimony of John M. Poindexter*, 264.

43. *Continued Testimony of North and McFarlane*, 63.

44. *Testimony of John M. Poindexter*, 210, 245.

45. *Testimony of Regan and Weinberger*, 266.

46. *Testimony of Elliott Abrams*, 144, 191.

47. *Testimony of John M. Poindexter*, 294.

48. Bradlee, *Guts and Glory*, 486.

49. Byrne, *Iran-Contra*, 281.

50. Bush diary, January 5, 1987, entry, RG 449.

51. *Testimony of John M. Poindexter*, 213–19, 224.

52. *Testimony of Adolfo P. Calero*, 192.

53. Sandy Grady, "Hearings Are Turning into a Sitcom Still, It Hurts Too Much to Laugh," *MH*, May 22, 1987, 29A.

54. *Testimony of Robert C. McFarlane*, 324.

55. *Continued Testimony of North and McFarlane*, 143, 144. The material appears in Appendix B.

56. *Testimony of Richard V. Secord*, 174.

57. *Testimony of Richard V. Secord*, 2.

58. *Testimony of Glenn A. Robinette*, 310.

59. *Testimony of George P. Shultz and Edwin Meese*, 75.

60. *Testimony of John M. Poindexter*, 159, 372.

61. *Continued Testimony of North and McFarlane*, 65.

62. *Testimony of Robert C. McFarlane*, 228.

63. *Testimony of Glenn A. Robinette*, 180.

64. *Testimony of George P. Shultz and Edwin Meese*, 395.

65. *Testimony of Regan and Weinberger*, 263.

66. *Continued Testimony of North and McFarlane*, 122–23.

67. *Testimony of Robert C. McFarlane*, 276, 375, 377, 390.

68. *Testimony of Adolfo P. Calero*, 424, 425.

69. *Continued Testimony of North and McFarlane*, 45.

70. Cited in Mary McGrory, "The See-No-Evil Senator," *WP*, June 11, 1987.

71. James Reston, "The Buck Stops There!" *NYT*, July 19, 1987.

72. Cited in Wroe, *Lives*, 199.

73. *Testimony of Adolfo P. Calero*, 350, 353.

74. *Testimony of Elliott Abrams*, 557.

75. *Testimony of Richard V. Secord*, 323.

76. *Continued Testimony of North and McFarlane*, 32.

77. *Testimony of Richard V. Secord*, 36.

78. *Testimony of Elliott Abrams*, 568.

79. *Testimony of Adolfo P. Calero*, 393.

80. *Testimony of Richard V. Secord*, 299, 150, 181, 314.

81. Mary McGrory, "The Noose Tightens," *WP*, May 10, 1987, B1.

82. *Testimony of Elliott Abrams*, 371.
83. *Testimony of Robert C. McFarlane*, 275.
84. *Testimony of Richard V. Secord*, 210, 365.
85. *Testimony of Elliott Abrams*, 375.
86. *Testimony of Adolfo P. Calero*, 153.
87. *Testimony of Richard V. Secord*, 243.
88. *Testimony of Adolfo P. Calero*, 161.
89. *Testimony of John M. Poindexter*, 222.
90. *Testimony of George P. Shultz and Edwin Meese*, 368.
91. *Testimony of Elliott Abrams*, 185–86.
92. *Testimony of Robert C. McFarlane*, 312, 320.
93. *Continued Testimony of North and McFarlane*, 98, 13.
94. *Testimony of John M. Poindexter*, 392, 95.
95. *Testimony of George P. Shultz and Edwin Meese*, 287, 288.
96. *Testimony of John M. Poindexter*, 297.
97. *Continued Testimony of North and McFarlane*, 121.
98. *Testimony of George P. Shultz and Edwin Meese*, 387.
99. *Testimony of John M. Poindexter*, 119.
100. *Testimony of George P. Shultz and Edwin Meese*, 83, 302.
101. *Testimony of Oliver L. North*, 246–47, 264.
102. *Testimony of Adolfo P. Calero*, 109.
103. *Testimony of Richard V. Secord*, 1.
104. *Testimony of George P. Shultz and Edwin Meese*, 5.
105. *Testimony of John M. Poindexter*, 254, 255; Tom Wicker, "Where the Buck Stops," *NYT*, July 29, 1987.
106. *Continued Testimony of North and McFarlane*, 34–35.
107. *Testimony of Elliott Abrams*, 186.
108. *Testimony of Robert C. McFarlane*, 282.
109. *Continued Testimony of North and McFarlane*, 161.
110. Liman with Israel, *Lawyer*, 332, 335, 336.
111. *Testimony of Elliott Abrams*, 568.
112. *Continued Testimony of North and McFarlane*, 181.
113. *Testimony of John M. Poindexter*, 334.
114. *Testimony of Regan and Weinberger*, 258.
115. *Testimony of John M. Poindexter*, 209.
116. *Testimony of Richard V. Secord*, 322.
117. *Testimony of Robert C. McFarlane*, 391.
118. *Continued Testimony of North and McFarlane*, 68.
119. *Testimony of John M. Poindexter*, 276.
120. Halevy and Livingstone, "The Ollie We Knew," 140; Wroe, *Lives*.
121. *Testimony of Clarridge*, 171.
122. Bradlee, *Guts and Glory*, 43.
123. Persico, *Casey*, 396.
124. Cited in Mayer and McManus, *Landslide*, 68.
125. Bradlee, *Guts and Glory*, 545, 482.
126. Persico, *Casey*, 397.

127. Constantine C. Menges, "The Sad, Strange Mind of Col. North," *WP*, November 27, 1988, D4.

128. Ledeen, *Perilous Statecraft*, 80.

129. Lynch and Bogen, *Spectacle of History*, 29.

130. Cited in LeoGrande, *Our Own Backyard*, 399.

131. Jacqueline Tillman cited in Menges, "Sad, Strange Mind of Col. North," D4.

132. Anthony Lewis, "Accounting for Power," *NYT*, June 19, 1987, A35.

133. North and Novak, *Under Fire*, 332, 334.

134. *Continued Testimony of North and McFarlane*, 132.

135. North and Novak, *Under Fire*, 351.

136. Cited in Busby, *Reagan and the Iran-Contra Affair*, 151.

137. "Poll: Reagan, North Liars," *MH*, July 5, 1987, 15A.

138. *Testimony of Oliver L. North*, 10, 9, 233, 173, 180.

139. McFarlane and Smardz, *Special Trust*, 350.

140. *Continued Testimony of North and McFarlane*, 205, 208, 209.

141. *Report of the Congressional Committees*, 11, 15, 16, 17, 423.

142. *Testimony of John M. Poindexter*, 9.

143. *Report of the Congressional Committees*, 18, 19, 387, 390, 406, 21.

144. Alfonso Chardy, "Counsel: Ultimate Failure is Reagan's," *MH*, November 19, 1987, 28A.

145. Cited in Walter Pincus, "Iran-Contra Panels Approve Report," *WP*, November 6, 1987, A6.

146. *Report of the Congressional Committees*, 437, 439, 441, 585, 624, 449.

147. Editorial, "Reagan's Hard Lesson," *WSJ*, November 18, 1987, 32.

148. Tucker, "Fouling Up," 93.

149. Cited in Byrne, *Iran-Contra*, 304.

150. All cited in Wieseltier, "Democracy and Colonel North," 22–25, 23, 24.

151. Walter Pincus, "New Reagan File Uncovered by Senate Intelligence Panel Data Not Reviewed by Iran-Contra Panel," *WP*, June 24, 1989, A1.

152. Walter Pincus and Bob Woodward, "Iran-Contra Report Won't Tell Whole Story," *WP*, November 5, 1987, A1.

CHAPTER 9

1. Jane Mayer and Andy Pasztor, "Deciding What Laws Apply to Iran-Contra May Be as Difficult as Finding Who Broke Them," *WSJ*, December 15, 1986, 60.

2. McCormick and Smith, "Iran Arms Sale," 29; William Weld, memo to Edwin Meese, Department of Justice, November 14, 1986, DNSA.

3. John Conyers et al., letter to Ed Meese, October 17, 1986, in *Testimony of George P. Shultz and Edwin Meese*, 1254.

4. Toobin, *Opening Arguments*, 5.

5. Reagan, *Diaries*, 455.

6. Editorial, "Independent Oxymoron," *WSJ*, March 12, 1987, 32.

7. George Lardner Jr., "Reagan Can Fire Walsh, Hill Told," *WP*, May 29, 1987, A16.

8. Cited in Eastland, "Independent-Counsel Regime," 73.

9. Crovitz, "Crime, Constitution," 23.

10. Alvis, Bailey, and Taylor, *Contested Removal Power*, 196, 199, 201.

11. William French Smith to Carl Levin, February 23, 1987, folder Independent Counsel 1987–1988, box 749, EMP.

12. George Lardner Jr., "Lawrence Walsh, Taking Pains," *NYT*, May 11, 1987, A1; Shenon, "Walsh Makes His Move," 66–70, 101.

13. Cited in Linda Greenhouse, "A Look at the Prosecutor," *NYT*, December 20, 1986, 1.

14. Crovitz, "Crime, Constitution"; Spencer, "Walsh's Last Battle," 29; Toobin, *Opening Arguments*, 19.

15. Toobin, *Opening Arguments*, 123.

16. Cited in Lardner, "Lawrence Walsh, Taking Pains," A1.

17. Wayne King and Warren Weaver Jr., "Briefing; Concern about the Counsel," *NYT*, December 17, 1986, B10.

18. Shenon, "Walsh Makes His Move," 66–70, 101.

19. Walsh, *Firewall*, 25, 34.

20. Philip Shenon, "Walsh Is Widening Inquiry of Contras," *NYT*, February 12, 1987, A9.

21. Kornbluh and Byrne, *Iran-Contra Scandal*, 331.

22. Cited in Philip Shenon, "Counsel Selected in Iran Arms Case," *NYT*, December 20, 1986, 1.

23. Cited in Mary McGrory, "A Magisterial Presence," *WP*, June 18, 1987, A2.

24. Lawrence Walsh, "Truth and the Rule of Law," San Francisco, August 9, 1987, folder Iran-Contra Affair Miscellany, box 415, GLP.

25. Shenon, "Walsh Makes His Move," 66–70, 101.

26. Walsh, *Firewall*, 28, 29.

27. Lawrence Walsh, interim report, April 28, 1987, folder Iranamok, box 106, PRLB.

28. George Lardner Jr., "Counsel Sees 'Ample Basis' for Wide Iran-Contra Probe," *WP*, April 29, 1987, A1.

29. Toobin, *Opening Arguments*, 17, 35.

30. Ghio, "Iran-Contra Prosecutions," 229.

31. Walsh, *Firewall*, 31.

32. Dormer, "Not-So Independent Counsel," 2391, 2407.

33. Walsh, *Firewall*, 49, 50; "Excerpts from Committee Hearing," March 11, 1987, folder Iran-Contra Affair Miscellany (3 of 3), box 415, GLP.

34. Philip Shenon, "The White House and the Prosecutor: Preparing for Hearings in Congress," *NYT*, April 27, 1987, B6; Joe Pichirallo, and Dan Morgan, "Walsh Asks Delay of Immunity," *WP*, March 11, 1987, A1.

35. Cited in David Rosenbaum, "Delay on Immunity for North Is Seen," *NYT*, March 11, 1987, A21.

36. Walter Pincus, and Dan Morgan, "Immunity Vote Likely for Poindexter, North," *WP*, March 7, 1987, A1.

37. Paul Trible, "Grant Immunity to North and Poindexter-Now," *WP*, March 11, 1987, A19.

38. David Rosenbaum, "Panels in Senate and House Differ on Immunity Tactic," *NYT*, March 10, 1987, A17.

39. Walsh, *Final Report*, 555.

40. Cited in Joe Pichirallo and George Lardner Jr., "Justice Aide Tried to Provide Prohibited Data, Walsh Says," *WP*, April 28, 1988, A1.

41. Lawrence Walsh, interim report, April 28, 1987, folder Iranamok, box 106, PRLB.

42. George Lardner Jr. and Joe Pichirallo, "Iran Probers Building Case," *WP*, November 15, 1987, A1.

43. Cited in Shenon, "White House and the Prosecutor," B6.

44. Philip Shenon, "Where No News Is Good News," *NYT*, July 10, 1987, A14.

45. Walsh, *Firewall*, 125.

46. Cited in Toobin, *Opening Arguments*, 60–61.

47. Lardner and Pichirallo, "Iran Probers Building Case," A1.

48. Toobin, *Opening Arguments*, 72.

49. Shenon, "White House and the Prosecutor," B6.

50. Philip Shenon, "Prosecutor in Iran Arms Case Gathers Heaps of Documents," *NYT*, March 11, 1987, A20.

51. Lawrence Walsh, interim report, April 28, 1987, folder Iranamok, box 106, PRLB.

52. AP, "Legal Snag on Swiss Records," *NYT*, March 19, 1987, A10; Walsh, *Final Report*, 31.

53. Special to the *New York Times*, "Walsh Talks with Israel Stall," *NYT*, August 7, 1987, A8.

54. George Lardner Jr. and Walter Pincus, "Walsh Gains Access to Israeli Records," *WP*, March 29, 1988, A6.

55. Walsh, *Firewall*, 55, 32, 47.

56. Pichirallo and Lardner, "Justice Aide Tried to Provide Prohibited Data," A1.

57. Walsh, *Final Report*, 28.

58. Gerhard Gesell diary, April 25, 1988, entry, folder 1, box 56, GGP.

59. Walsh, *Firewall*, 68.

60. Walsh, *Final Report*, 28.

61. Byrne, *Iran-Contra*, 312.

62. Walsh, *Final Report*, 29, 30.

63. Cited in Toobin, *Opening Arguments*, 35, 37.

64. Aaron Epstein, "Criminal Case Likely, Perilous," *MH*, July 17, 1987, 1A.

65. Byrne, *Iran-Contra*, 309.

66. Walsh, *Firewall*, 112.

67. James Reston, "A Pardon for North?," *NYT*, July 12, 1987.

68. Philip Shenon, "North Files Suit That Challenges Iran Prosecutor," *NYT*, February 25, 1987, A1.

69. Cited in Philip Shenon, "White House Overhaul," *NYT*, March 3, 1987, A10.

70. Lawrence Walsh, memo to David Abshire, Washington, February 25, 1987, folder Independent Counsel 1987–1988, box 749, EMP; Philip Shenon, "Walsh Status Changed to Undercut Challenge," *NYT*, March 6, 1987, A19.

71. Philip Shenon, "Second North Suit Assails Administration Role for Prosecutor," *NYT*, March 7, 1987, 8.

72. Cited in Toobin, *Opening Arguments*, 7, 9–10.

73. Philip Shenon, "Court Rejects Bid by North to Upset Prosecutor Law," *NYT*, March 13, 1987, A1.

74. George Lardner Jr., "North Reported in Contempt," *WP*, June 9, 1987, A1.

75. Walter Pincus and Dan Morgan, "North's Wife Refuses to Testify," *WP*, June 17, 1987, A16.

76. Dan Morgan and Walter Pincus, "Iran Probers Order North to Provide Papers by Tuesday," *WP*, June 20, 1987, A1.

77. AP, "U.S. Appeals Court Expedites Hearing on Walsh's Authority," *NYT*, July 18, 1987, 7.

78. Mary Thornton, "Walsh's Iran-Probe Authority Upheld," *WP*, August 21, 1987, A14.

79. Stuart Taylor, Jr, "Justices Refuse to Hear North's Plea to Block Walsh Inquiry," *NYT*, January 20, 1988, A19.

80. North and Novak, *Under Fire*, 385; George Lardner Jr., "A Special Place for Iran-Contra Secrets," *WP*, May 23, 1988, A9; Lardner and Pichirallo, "Iran Probers Building Case," A1.

81. Jordan, "Classified Information and Conflicts," 1651, 1652.

82. Sandy Grady, "Look Out, George—'Cause Ollie's Back in Town," *MH*, March 19, 1988, 27A.

83. Philip Shenon, "North, Poindexter and 2 Others Indicted on Iran-Contra Fraud and Theft Charges," *NYT*, March 17, 1988, A1.

84. Editorial, "The Case Against the President," *NYT*, March 18, 1988, A34.

85. Editorial, "Iranscam Redux," *MH*, March 18, 1988, 24A.

86. Cited in Shenon, "North, Poindexter and 2 Others Indicted," A1.

87. John Lichfield, "Ghost at the Republican Feast," *Independent*, January 5, 1989.

88. Cited in Sam Meddis, "Jurist for a Scandal," *USA Today*, March 23, 1988, F.

89. Jim Mann, "Judge Could Have Profound Impact on Trial's Mood, Pace," *Austin American-Statesman*, March 20, 1988, D8.

90. Lichfield, "Ghost at the Republican Feast"; Marcia Coyle, "A Logical Choice," *National Law Journal*, May 3, 1988, 1, 26–28; Editorial, "Character of a Good Judge," *Los Angeles Daily Journal*, June 22, 1988.

91. Gesell diary, first page, GGP.

92. Editorial, "No Pardon for Walsh," *WSJ*, March 18, 1988.

93. Cited in Julie Johnson, "Reagan Asserts Iran-Contra Defendants Are Not Guilty," *NYT*, March 26, 1988, 5.

94. Stephen Engelberg, "Judge Bars Trial in Fall in the Iran-Contra Case," *NYT*, April 13, 1988, A16.

95. Gesell diary, April 19, 1988, GGP.

96. Joe Pichirallo, "ACLU Joins Contesters of Iran-Contra Charges," *WP*, July 21, 1988, A1.

97. Stephen Engelberg, "Iran-Contra Trial Gets Witness List," *NYT*, April 23, 1988, 9.

98. Cited in William Prochnau, "Sketches at a Prosecution," *WP Magazine*, June 18, 1989, 15–19, 32–35, 17.

99. George Lardner Jr., "Safeguarding Secrets-and More," *WP*, December 5, 1988, A21; Walter Pincus and George Lardner Jr., "Some 'Secrets' in North Case Already Disclosed," *WP*, December 12, 1988, A8.

100. Philip Shenon, "Judge in Iran-Contra Case Says Administration Is Withholding Data," *NYT*, April 28, 1988, A16.

101. AP, "Judge Has Doubt About Charge in Iran-Contra Trial," *NYT*, May 27, 1988, A12.

102. Cited in Editorial, "Character of a Good Judge."

103. David E. Rosenbaum, "Immunity Decision: A Prosecutor's Nightmare," *NYT*, June 20, 1988, B6.

104. Walsh, *Firewall*, 168.

105. Toobin, *Opening Arguments*, 169.

106. Gesell diary, April 25 and June 25, 1988, GGP.

107. Charlotte Low Allen, "The Many Hurdles to Taking the Iran-Contra Case to Court," *Insight*, July 18, 1988, 18–19.

108. Philip Shenon, "Prosecutor Would Drop an Iran-Contra Count," *NYT*, October 25, 1988, B8.

109. "Gesell 'Rejects Totally' North's Approach," *Legal Times*, November 14, 1988, 20.

110. Gesell diary, November 14–20, 1988, GGP.

111. Rosemary Brown, letter to Gerhard Gesell, Ft. Myers Beach, Florida, December 2, 1988, folder 5, box 53, GGP.

112. Robert Clark, letter to Gerhard Gesell, Philadelphia, December 11, 1988, folder 5, box 53, GGP.

113. George Kehler, letter to Gerhard Gesell, Johnson City, Tennessee, December 3, 1988, folder 5, box 53, GGP.

114. Owen E. Cain, letter to Gerhard Gesell, Joshua, Texas, January 31, 1989, folder 7, box 53, GGP.

115. Gesell diary, November 21, 1988, GGP.

116. Gesell cited in George Lardner Jr., "Judge Rebukes North on Documents," *WP*, December 13, 1988, A6.

117. Cited in Michael Wines, "U.S. Presses for Curbs on North Trial," *NYT*, February 7, 1989, A14.

118. Editorial, "North Judge May Be Hero," *Milwaukee Sentinel*, December 14, 1988.

119. George A. Lindsley, letter to Gerhard Gesell, Cantrall, Illinois, January 9, 1989, folder 7, box 53, GGP.

120. Heidi Lau-Sed, letter to Gerhard Gesell, Brattleboro, Vermont, January 12, 1989, folder 7, box 53, GGP.

121. Joe Pichirallo and Ruth Marcus, "Walsh Seeks to Drop 2 of North's Counts," *WP*, January 6, 1989, A1; Michael Wines, "Prosecutor Asks for Dismissal of Key Charges Against North," *NYT*, January 6, 1989, A1.

122. Michael Wines, "Top Reagan Aides Knew North Case Faced Collapse,'" *NYT*, January 7, 1989, 1.

123. Walsh, *Firewall*, 180.

124. Susan F. Rasky, "Twist in North Case Isn't a Surprise in Congress," *NYT*, January 6, 1989, B4.

125. Editorial, "Oliver North: Still Accountable," *NYT*, January 6, 1989, A30.

126. Cited in R. W. Apple, Jr, "Who Knew What May Remain Unknown," *NYT*, January 8, 1989, A1.

127. Cited in George Lardner Jr., and Ruth Marcus, "High Court Is Asked to Halt North Trial," *WP*, February 12, 1989, A1.

128. Michael Wines, "Accord on Secrets for North's Trial," *NYT*, February 16, 1989, A32.

129. Cited in AP, "Security Controversy Threatened North Trial," *Naples Daily News*, February 19, 1989, 6A.

130. Lila Lieberman, letter to Gerhard Gesell, New York, January 13, 1989, folder 7, box 53, GGP.

CHAPTER 10

1. Lawrence Walsh, OIC, criminal information, April 28, 1987, DNSA; Walsh, criminal information, April 29, 1987, DNSA; [OIC?] press release, April 29, 1987, folder Iranamok, box 106, PRLB.

2. David Johnston, "Probation for a Fund-Raiser in Tax Fraud for Contra Aid," *NYT*, July 8, 1989, 6.

3. Richard L. Berke, "Key Figure Admits Fraud Conspiracy on Contra Funds," *NYT*, April 30, 1987, A1.

4. Johnston, "Probation for a Fund-Raiser in Tax Fraud," 6.

5. David Johnston, "Consultant Is Placed on Probation for His Role in Iran-Contra Affair," *NYT*, July 7, 1989, B4.

6. Crovitz, "Crime, Constitution," 26.

7. Lawrence Walsh, "United States of America v. Robert C. McFarlane," OIC, criminal information, March 11, 1988, DNSA; Joe Pichirallo, "McFarlane Enters Guilty Plea Arising from Iran-Contra Affair," *WP*, March 12, 1988, A1.

8. Walter Pincus and Joe Pichirallo, "Lack of Witnesses, Documents Troubles Walsh's Iran Inquiry," *WP*, March 14, 1988, A1.

9. Cited in Stephen Engelberg, "McFarlane's Struggle with Himself and the Special Prosecutor," *NYT*, March 14, 1988, B6.

10. Robert McFarlane, statement for the courts, undated, folder 1, box 31, LGP.

11. Cited in Walsh, *Final Report*, 87, 102, 103.

12. Editorial, "Pardon McFarlane," *WSJ*, March 17, 1988.

13. Walsh, *Final Report*, xxiv.

14. McFarlane and Smardz, *Special Trust*, 361.

15. Robert McFarlane, letter to Lawrence Walsh, September 2, 1993, folder 13, box 30, LGP.

16. "Public Split Evenly on Whether North Should Face a Trial," *NYT*, February 21, 1989, A19.

17. Michael Wines, "North Trial Courtroom Is a Stop on Capital's Must-See Circuit," *NYT*, February 27, 1989, A17.

18. Mary McGrory, "Ollie: Felon and Fall Guy," *WP*, May 7, 1989, B1.

19. Haynes Johnson, "Is North Trial Pointing the Finger at the Wrong Man?," *Pittsburgh Press*, April 3, 1989, B3.

20. Cited in Prochnau, "Sketches at a Prosecution," 15–19, 32–35, 34.

21. David Johnston, "Tearful North Secretary Backs Ex-Chief," *NYT*, March 24, 1989, A12.

22. Cited in Steve Goldberg, "Gesell Steers Steady Course in North Trial's Legal Morass," *Tampa Tribune*, March 13, 1989, 1A.

23. George Lardner Jr., "North's Trial Encounters 'Roadblock,' " *WP*, February 28, 1989, A1.

24. George Lardner Jr., "North Trial Sidetracked by 'Secrets,' " *WP*, March 1, 1989, A4.

25. Cited in David Johnston, "Judge in North Case Assails U.S. Over Handling of Secret Material," *NYT*, March 8, 1989, A18.

26. Gesell diary, April 17, 1989, GGP.

27. Editorial, "One Man's Secret Is . . . ," *WP*, March 2, 1989, A22.

28. Cited in George Lardner Jr., "North Says He Did Not Know Lying to Congress Was Crime," *WP*, April 8, 1989, A1.

29. Cited in James Rowley, "North's Assertion About Lying to Congress Derided," *WP*, October 25, 1988, A5.

30. Toobin, *Opening Arguments*, 296, 308, 309, 311.

31. Cited in David Johnston, "Ex-Marines Are Enemies," *NYT*, April 11, 1989, A1.

32. Cited in Mary McGrory, "Standard Meese,'" *WP*, March 30, 1989, A2.

33. Gesell diary, March 28–30, 1989, GGP.

34. David Johnston, "Court Told North Aided Rebels in '85," *NYT*, March 3, 1989, A14.

35. David Johnston, "Memo Hints Reagan Backed '85 Contra Supplies," *NYT*, March 17, 1989, A16; David Johnston, "North Trial Challenges Image of Aloof Reagan," *NYT*, March 20, 1989, A15.

36. David Johnston, "North Trial Told of Reagan Order," *NYT*, March 11, 1989, 1; Gesell diary, March 16, 1989, GGP.

37. Aaron Epstein, "North Seeks Reagan as First Defense Witness," *MH*, March 25, 1989, 1A.

38. Stephen Engelberg, "North Trial Document Called Faulty," *NYT*, April 26, 1989, A19.

39. Ruth Marcus, "North Trial Raises New Questions," *NYT*, April 9, 1989, A19.

40. Stephen Engelberg, "North Trial Casts Light on Reagan and Raises New Shadow for Bush," *NYT*, April 9, 1989, A1.

41. Stephen Engelberg, "Documents That Got Away: Now, to Unravel the Mystery," *NYT*, April 30, 1989, A24.

42. Cited in David Hoffman, "Sununu Defends Bush '85 Honduras Meeting," *WP*, May 1, 1989, A1.

43. Cited in David Hoffman, "Bush Says Honduras Trip Wasn't a Contra Aid Deal," *WP*, May 5, 1989, A1.

44. Joe Pichirallo, and Walter Pincus, "Key Parts of 1985 Honduras Deal Carried Out," *WP*, May 2, 1989, A1.

45. Anthony Lewis, "Why Not Watergate?," *NYT*, May 11, 1990, A35.

46. Editorial, "Tough Case, Tough Judge," *LAT*, February 1, 1989, 6; David Johnston, "Judge Won't Order Reagan Testimony," *NYT*, April 1, 1989, 1.

47. Walsh, *Firewall*, 204.

48. David Hoffman, "Official Lies: The Real Issue Behind the North Trial," *WP*, April 16, 1989, B1.

49. R. W. Apple, Jr, "Measured Judgment," *NYT*, May 5, 1989, A18.

50. Cited in Joe Pichirallo, "Some Jurors Express Sympathy for North, Say Prayer Aided 'Hardest' Decision," *WP*, May 5, 1989, A12.

51. Joe Pichirallo, and Michael Rezendes, "Jurors Found North Convincing," *WP*, May 6, 1989, A1.

52. "North Is Viewed as Misguided," *NYT*, May 9, 1989, A28.

53. Cited in David Johnston, "North Guilty on 3 of 12 Counts," *NYT*, May 5, 1989, A1.

54. Editorial, "Semper Fi?," *Richmond News Leader*, May 5, 1989, 8.

55. Charles Hellmuth, letter to Gerhard Gesell, Potomac, Maryland, May 9, 1989, folder 6, box 54, GGP.

56. Haynes Johnson, "What Saved North," *WP*, July 7, 1989, A2.

57. "Sentencing Transcript Excerpt," July 5, 1989, in Gesell, "United States v. Oliver North," 62.

58. Koh, *National Security Constitution*, 36.

59. Editorial, "The Sentencing of Oliver North," *San Francisco Chronicle*, July [?], 1989; Editorial, "A Sentence for Oliver North," *WP*, July 6, 1989, A16.

60. Cited in Keeley, *Reagan's Gun-Toting Nuns*, 209.

61. Joe Pichirallo, "Secord Faces 9 New Charges in Iran Affair," *WP*, May 12, 1989, A1.

62. Cited in George Lardner Jr., "Judge Consolidates Secord's Indictments," *WP*, June 10, 1989, A4.

63. Cited in David Johnston, "Secord Is Guilty of One Charge in Contra Affair," *NYT*, November 9, 1989, A24.

64. Cited in David Johnston, "Secord Is Put on Probation for Lie on Iran-Contra Role," *NYT*, January 25, 1990, A16.

65. Sandy Grady, "Stand by His Man? Reluctant Reagan Pulls a Nixon," *MH*, February 10, 1990, 31A.

66. Secord and Wurts, *Honored and Betrayed*, 356.

67. Cited in Johnston, "Secord Is Put on Probation," A16.

68. Walsh, *Final Report*, 175.

69. Harry Aderholt, fundraising letter, Rockville, Maryland, June 1989, folder 9, box 117, GLP.

70. Grady, "Stand by His Man?," 31A.

71. Aderholt letter, GLP.

72. Jo Ann Secord, fundraising letter, June 1989, folder 9, box 117, GLP.

73. Aderholt letter, GLP.

74. OIC, fact sheets, September 1989 and October 1990, both folder 11, box 178, GLP.

75. "Headliners; 5 Trials Down, 3 to Go," *NYT*, November 12, 1989, A7.

76. David Johnston, "Hakim Pleads Guilty to One Misdemeanor," *NYT*, November 22, 1989, A18.

77. Michael Wines, "Hakim on Probation in Iran-Contra Deal but Shares Proceeds," *NYT*, February 2, 1990, A1.

78. Walsh, *Final Report*, 179.

79. Art Buchwald, "Bargain Basement Sentences," *WP*, February 15, 1990, B1.

80. AP, "Prosecutors Move to Narrow Charges in Poindexter Case," *WP*, June 25, 1989, A5.

81. AP, "Lawyer Says Reagan Told Aide to Give False Data," *NYT*, September 7, 1989, A21.

82. Neil A. Lewis, "Poindexter Wins Access to Papers Kept by Reagan," *NYT*, October 25, 1989, A1.

83. David Johnston, "Reagan Asks Court to Kill Subpoena," *NYT*, December 7, 1989, A27.

84. David Johnston, "Poindexter Aiming to Show Reagan Knew of Iran Plot," *NYT*, December 11, 1989, A1.

85. Cited in David Johnston, "Reagan Is Ordered to Provide Diaries in Poindexter Case," *NYT*, January 31, 1990, A1.

86. Cited in Joe Pichirallo, "Reagan Ordered to Give Iran-Contra Testimony," *WP*, February 6, 1990, A1.

87. Editorial, "Ronald Reagan, Still Hiding," *NYT*, February 7, 1990, A24.

88. Cited in Anthony Lewis, "Not by Divine Right," *NYT*, February 16, 1990, A35.

89. Richard Cohen, "Lying to Your Diary," *WP*, February 9, 1990.

90. Cited in Joe Pichirallo, "No Notes on Iran-Contra Found in Reagan Files," *WP*, February 14, 1990, A18.

91. Cited in Walter Pincus, "Judge Says Diaries Not Needed in Poindexter Trial," *WP*, March 22, 1990, A4.

92. David Johnston, "Iran-Contra Judge Is Urged to Bar Public at Questioning of Reagan," *NYT*, February 14, 1990, A20; David Johnston, "Reagan Testifies in the Poindexter Case," *NYT*, February 17, 1990, 11.

93. Cited in David Johnston, "Reagan Testifies He Did Not Order Any Illegal Acts," *NYT*, February 23, 1990, A1.

94. Jeff Gerth, "Reagan as Witness: Friendly but Forgetful," *NYT*, February 23, 1990, A19.

95. Cited in Walsh, *Final Report*, 133.

96. Cited in Walsh, *Firewall*, 228.

97. Reagan, deposition, July 24, 1992, folder General Investigative Reagan—7/24/92 Interview 1, box 39 General Investigative Files, Records of John Q. Barrett Attorney Files, RG 449.

98. Editorial, "What Mr. Reagan Remembers," *NYT*, February 24, 1990, 24.

99. R. W. Apple, Jr, "The Star Flickers, but Just Dimly," *NYT*, March 23, 1990, A12.

100. Tom Shales, "The Raw Treatment of Ronald Reagan," *WP*, March 22, 1990, C1.

101. Cited in David Johnston, "Blunt Arguments by Lawyers Open Poindexter Trial," *NYT*, March 9, 1990, A1.

102. Cited in David Johnston, "North Tells of Document Destruction," *NYT*, March 13, 1990, A22.

103. Cited in David Johnston, "North, Ending Testimony, Speaks Softly and Haltingly of His Lies," *NYT*, March 15, 1990, A21.

104. Cited in Joe Pichirallo, "Arms Sales Widely Known, North Says," *WP*, March 14, 1990, A4.

105. Ellen Glasser cited in David Johnston, "5,000 Files Erased from Poindexter's Computer," *NYT*, March 16, 1990, A16.

106. Walsh, *Final Report*, 124.

107. John Poindexter, fundraising letter, folder 2, box 115, GLP.

108. "The Poindexter Conviction," *WP*, April 10, 1990, A22.

109. Cited in Joe Pichirallo, "Iran-Contra Prosecutors Urge a Prison Term for Poindexter," *WP*, June 7, 1990, A13.

110. Cited in Joe Pichirallo, "Poindexter Gets 6 Months in Prison," *WP*, June 12, 1990, A1.

111. George Lardner Jr., "North Denied Hearing on Trial Evidence," *WP*, May 27, 1989, A9.

112. Cited in George Lardner Jr., "The North Ruling," *WP*, July 23, 1990, A10.

113. David Johnston, "Prosecutor Asks Justices to Restore North Verdicts," *NYT*, February 27, 1991, B10.

114. Garry Emmons, "Judge in North's Appeal Tainted Justice," *NYT*, August 24, 1990, A28; Walsh, *Firewall*, 249, 250.

115. Walsh, *Firewall*, 250, 256.

116. Cited in Walsh, *Final Report*, 122.

117. Editorial, "White House Crime: Punish or Expose?," *NYT*, August 1, 1990, A20.

118. David Johnston, "North Conviction in Doubt as Court Lets Ruling Stand," *NYT*, May 29, 1991, A1.

119. "15 Republicans Ask End to Walsh Inquiry," *NYT*, May 31, 1991, A16.

120. Cited in "Special Prosecutor Is Accused by North of Being Vindictive," *NYT*, June 1, 1991, 10.

121. Cited in Michael Wines, "Iran-Contra Witness Imperils North Case with New Responses," *NYT*, September 12, 1991, A1.

122. Cited in George Lardner Jr., "87 Hill Hearings 'Colored' Testimony at North Trial," *WP*, September 12, 1991, A3.

123. David Johnston, "Judge in Iran-Contra Trial Drops Case Against North after Prosecutor Gives Up," *NYT*, September 17, 1991, A1.

124. Editorial, "Oliver North Beats the Rap," *NYT*, September 17, 1991, A20.

125. McFarlane and Smardz, *Special Trust*, 362.

126. David Johnston, "Poindexter Wins Iran-Contra Case in Appeals Court," *NYT*, November 16, 1991, 1.

127. Editorial, "Justice Obstructed in the Poindexter Case," *NYT*, December 8, 1992, A24.

128. Linda Greenhouse, "Iran-Contra Appeal Refused by Court," *NYT*, December 8, 1992, A22

129. Robert McFarlane, letter to Lawrence Walsh, September 2, 1993, folder 13, box 30, LGP.

130. Byrne, *Iran-Contra*, 307.

CHAPTER 11

1. Lawrence Walsh, interview with George Lardner, December 17, 1991, folder 9, box 118, GLP.

2. "Iran-Contra Chief Says Inquiry May End Soon," *NYT*, September 28, 1990, A12.

3. Walsh, *Firewall*, 222.

4. Lawrence Walsh, interview with George Lardner, December 17, 1991, folder 9, box 118, GLP.

5. AP, "Iran-Contra Deceptions by Ex-Agent Charged," *NYT*, June 6, 1989, A20.

6. Cited in Joe Pichirallo, "Court Halts Iran-Contra Trial of Ex-CIA Official," *WP*, July 25, 1989, A10.

7. Cited in George Lardner Jr., "Walsh Says Attorney General Has Conflict in Iran-Contra Case," *WP*, September 20, 1989, A7.

8. Cited in Joe Pichirallo, "Walsh Asks to Open Hearing on Secrets," *WP*, August 11, 1989, A5.

9. Lardner, "Walsh Says Attorney General Has Conflict in Iran-Contra Case," A7.

10. Joe Pichirallo, "U.S. to Block Disclosures in Fernandez Case," *WP*, July 22, 1989, A1.

11. Walsh, *Firewall*, 217.

12. Cited in David Johnston, "Iran-Contra Prosecutor Says Secrecy Issue Blocks Justice," *NYT*, December 2, 1989, 12.

13. Walsh, *Firewall*, 63.

14. Walsh, *Final Report*, 181.

15. George Lardner Jr., "Iran-Contra Arms Broker Indicted on Tax Charges," *WP*, February 23, 1990, A14; "CIA Ex-Agent Must Stand Tax Trial," *WP*, August 25, 1990, A4.

16. David Johnston, "Ex-C.I.A. Agent Is Convicted in Iran-Contra Affair," *NYT*, September 19, 1990, A18.

17. Michael Wines, "Iran-Contra Aide Gets Prison Term," *NYT*, December 14, 1990, A36.

18. Cited in Paul W. Valentine, "Clines Given Prison Term Of 16 Months," *WP*, December 14, 1990, A4.

19. George Lardner Jr. and Walter Pincus, "Iran-Contra Prosecutors Concentrate on a Former CIA Task Force Chief," *WP*, July 7, 1991, A4.

20. David Johnston, "Ex-C.I.A. Aide Says He Misled Inquiry on Aid to Contras," *NYT*, July 10, 1991, A1.

21. "Excerpts From Statement on Former C.I.A. Aide," *NYT*, July 10, 1991, A16.

22. Editorial, "The Iran-Contra Thread," *WP*, July 11, 1991, A14.

23. Cited in George Lardner Jr., "Fiers Sentenced to Probation in Iran-Contra Coverup," *WP*, February 1, 1992, A9.

24. Walsh, *Final Report*, 45, 263.

25. Cited in Benjamin Weiser, "Plea Ripples Through CIA," *WP*, August 31, 1991, A1.

26. Indictment, September 6, 1991, folder Iran-Contra Affair, box 106, PRLB.

27. Judge Royce Lamberth cited in David Johnston, "Iran-Contra Defendant Told He Cannot See C.I.A. Files," *NYT*, March 6, 1992, A16.

28. George Lardner Jr. and Walter Pincus, "Assailing Delay, Judge Sees Effort to 'Thwart' CIA Ex-Aide's Trial," *WP*, July 14, 1992, A4.

29. David Johnston, "Former No. 3 Official with C.I.A. Is Indicted in Iran-Contra Affair," *NYT*, September 7, 1991, 1.

30. David Johnston, "An Unwelcome Spotlight for a Spymaster," *NYT*, July 13, 1991, 1.

31. Cited in David Johnston, "Subordinate Gives Inside Account of Casey's Intrigues at C.I.A.," *NYT*, September 20, 1991, A1.

32. Indictment, September 6, 1991, PRLB.

33. David Holliday cited in Johnston, "An Unwelcome Spotlight for a Spymaster," 1.

34. Cited in Benjamin Weiser, "Ex-CIA Operative Chooses to Stand and Fight Charges," *WP*, September 8, 1991, A27.

35. Cited in Neil A. Lewis, "Ex-C.I.A. Official Takes Stand in His Own Defense," *NYT*, August 13, 1992, A16.

36. Cited in Benjamin Weiser, "Where the Truth Lies among Spies," *WP*, August 22, 1992, D1.

37. Cited in Neil A. Lewis, "C.I.A. Man Erupts in Anger at Iran-Contra Prosecutor," *NYT*, August 14, 1992, A12.

38. George Lardner Jr., "Ex-CIA Official Charges He Was 'Set Up' by Hill 'Hypocrites,'" *WP*, August 14, 1992, A3.

39. Cited in Neil A. Lewis, "C.I.A. Man Threatened with Contempt in Trial," *NYT*, August 15, 1992, A5.

40. Cited in George Lardner Jr., "CIA Ex-Aide Cites Distrust of George," *WP*, August 18, 1992, A4.

41. Cited in Weiser, "Where the Truth Lies among Spies," D1.

42. George Lardner Jr. and Walter Pincus, "George's Prints Found on Portion of Iran-Contra Paper, FBI Expert Says," *WP*, August 7, 1992, A6.

43. David Johnston, "Iran-Contra Trial of an Ex-C.I.A. Man Ends in a Deadlock," *NYT*, August 27, 1992, A1.

44. Walsh, *Firewall*, 446.

45. Cited in Editorial, "The Iran-Contra Thread," *WP*, July 11, 1991, A14.

46. George Lardner Jr., "Former CIA Official Pleads Not Guilty to Perjury Charges," *WP*, December 7, 1991, A2.

47. George Lardner Jr., "Iran-Contra Prosecutors Told to Drop 2 Charges Against Ex-CIA Official," *WP*, December 11, 1992, A21.

48. David Johnston, "Ex-C.I.A. Officials Start Legal Fund," *NYT*, August 14, 1991, A10.

49. Cited in Elaine Sciolino, "Scrutiny for Spies," *NYT*, September 7, 1991, 10.

50. Neil A. Lewis, "At C.I.A. Trial, Some Say Loyalty Is in the Dock," *NYT*, August 3, 1992, A12.

51. Cited in Benjamin Weiser, "5 Lawyers Seek Donations for Iran-Contra Defendants," *WP*, February 26, 1992, A2.

52. Walsh, *Final Report*, 325, xix.

53. Abrams, *Undue Process*, 11, 38, 8, 85, 91, 59, 62.

54. David Johnston, "Elliott Abrams Admits His Guilt On 2 Counts in Contra Cover-Up," *NYT*, October 8, 1991, A1.

55. Editorial, "Elliott Abrams Is Guilty," *NYT*, October 11, 1991, A30.

56. George Lardner Jr., "Abrams Sentenced to 2 Years' Probation, Fined $50," *WP*, November 16, 1991, A20.

57. Weinberger, "In Defense of the Presidency," 18. This was reprinted from a November 13, 1987, speech.

58. Carl Levin, press release, January 18, 1994, folder Iran-Contra Affair Walsh, Lawrence E. General, box 430, GLP.

59. Weinberger, *Fighting for Peace*, 381.

60. Carl Levin, press release, GLP.

61. Martin Tolchin, "On Leaving Office, Weinberger Took Along 13,000 Documents," *NYT*, June 18, 1992, B10.

62. Walsh, *Firewall*, 340, 319.

63. David Johnston, "Case Against Weinberger: Written in His Own Hand," *NYT*, June 18, 1992, A1.

64. Walsh, *Firewall*, 395.

65. Transcript, "This Week with David Brinkley," ABC News, December 27, 1992.

66. Walsh, *Firewall*, 396.

67. Paul Minor, Caspar Weinberger polygraph examination report, May 5, 1992, folder Iran-Contra Affair Weinberger, Caspar W. For Their Eyes Only, box 430, GLP.

68. Cited in Walsh, *Firewall*, 410.

69. Indictment, October 30, 1992, folder Iran-Contra Affair, box 106, PRLB.

70. Cited in David Johnston, "Weinberger Faces 5 Counts in Iran-Contra Indictment," *NYT*, June 17, 1992, A1.

71. Walsh, *Firewall*, 416.

72. Weinberger and Roberts, *In the Arena*, 354–55.

73. Walsh, *Firewall*, 338.

74. David Johnston, "Crucial Charge Is Dismissed in Weinberger Perjury Case," *NYT*, September 30, 1992, A14.

75. Both cited in Walsh, *Firewall*, 440.

76. Colin Powell Affidavit, April 21, 1992, folder Iran Contra Documents, box 36, Papers of Jim Mann, Hoover Institution, Stanford University, CA.

77. Cited in Stuart Taylor Jr., "Keep the Special Counsel," *NYT*, June 22, 1992, A17.

78. Cited in Walsh, *Firewall*, 417.

79. Abrams, *Undue Process*, 12, 212.

80. Cited in David Johnston, "Weinberger Calls His Indictment a Political Move," *NYT*, November 25, 1992, A14.

81. Cited in Johnston, "Iran-Contra Prosecutor," A24.

82. Cited in Walter Pincus and George Lardner Jr., "Weinberger Passes Lie Detector Test," *WP*, May 21, 1992, A4.

83. Author unknown, title unknown, *California Lawyer*, January 1993, 39–42, 91.

84. Mike Burch, chairman of the Caspar W. Weinberger Legal Defense Trust Fund, letter to William Clark, Arlington, Virginia, August 7, 1992, folder 6, box III: 144, Caspar Weinberger Papers, MD, LOC.

85. Robert S. Bennett, invoice to Caspar Weinberger, Washington, November 25, 1992, folder 6, box III: 144, Caspar Weinberger Papers, MD, LOC.

86. "Weinberger Friends to Help Pay Legal Fees," *NYT*, September 24, 1992, A19.

87. "Notes of Meeting at Heritage Foundation," Cap Weinberger Reception, July 28, 1992, folder 4, box III: 144, Caspar Weinberger Papers, MD, LOC.

88. Cited in Anne Gowen, "Weinberger Friends Tip Caps, Dip into Wallets," *Washington Times*, September 25, 1992, E2.

89. Cited in Lloyd Grove, "Republicans Come to the Defense of Cap Weinberger," *WP*, September 24, 1992, C1.

90. Paul Weyrich, letter to Caspar Weinberger, Washington, October 5, 1992, folder 4, box III: 144, Caspar Weinberger Papers, MD, LOC.

91. All the investigations not producing indictments are in Walsh, *Final Report*.

92. Charles Hill handwritten notes, [1992?], folder Iran Contra—the Independent Counsel, box 69, CHP.

93. Walsh, *Final Report*, xix.

94. Walsh, *Firewall*, 335.

95. C. J. Mixter, "New Draft of Final Report," September 14, 1992, folder General Investigative Reagan: CJM 3/91 Memo re Criminal Liability 1, box 41 General Investigative Files, Records of John Q. Barrett Attorney Files, RG 449.

96. Cited in Walter Pincus and George Lardner Jr., "Iran-Contra Report Castigates Reagan," *WP*, January 19, 1994, A1.

97. Theodore Olson et al., "Response of Former President Ronald W. Reagan to Final Report of the Independent Counsel for Iran/Contra Matters," Washington, DC, December 3, 1993, folder 14, box 30, LGP.

98. Editorial, "Iran-Contra: Secrecy's Victim," *NYT*, October 30, 1990, A24.

99. Hinson, "Negative Information Action," 836.

100. Cited in Reske, "Walsh Winds Up Probe," 16.

CHAPTER 12

1. Hamilton, *Federalist No. 74*, Library of Congress.

2. Love, "Reinventing the President's Pardon," 6; Johnson, "President Donald J. Trump."

3. Love, "Reinventing the President's Pardon," 7; Edward Lempinen, "How Donald Trump Has Tested the Ethical Limits of Presidential Pardons," *Berkeley News*, December 18, 2020.

4. Kalt, "Pardon Me?," 781.

5. Nathaniel C. Nash, "Some in Congress Express Support on Pardons for Ex-Reagan Aides," *NYT*, July 20, 1987, A1.

6. March 4, 1987, entry, Bush diary, folder Files of the Office of the Vice President Bush—VP Diary, box 2, Records of John Q. Barrett Attorney Files, RG 449.

7. Philip Shenon, "Rumors Abound of Thanksgiving Pardons," *NYT*, November 23, 1987, A18.

8. Philip Shenon, "Time Is Running Out for a Decision on Pardons," *NYT*, November 23, 1988, B5.

9. Hyde and Mitchell, "Pardoning Ollie North."

10. Reagan, *Diaries*, 671, 670.

11. Jerry Falwell, mass mailings, 1988, folder 3, box 53, GGP.

12. Cited in Beth Tuttle, letter to "Dear Journalist," June 16, 1988, folder 12 box 90, Mary McGrory Papers, MD, LOC.

13. Beth Tuttle, letter to "Dear Journalist," June 16, 1988, folder 12 box 90, Mary McGrory Papers, MD, LOC.

14. Stephen Engelberg, "President Rules Out a Pardon for North," *NYT*, December 2, 1988, B6.

15. Mary McGrory, "For Reagan, Mum's the Word," *WP*, March 21, 1989, A2.

16. Toobin, *Opening Arguments*, 126.

17. Beth Tuttle, letter to "Dear Journalist," June 16, 1988, folder 12 box 90, Mary McGrory Papers, MD, LOC.

18. Al Kamen, "Bush Urges Lawmakers, Judges Not to Interfere in Foreign Policy Series," *WP*, January 31, 1987.

19. Cited in David Corn, "Where Was George?," *The Nation*, August 3–10, 1992, 16.

20. Cited in Pfiffner, "Contemporary Presidency," 907.

21. Transcript, ABC News Nightline Show #2959, September 24, 1992, folder 11, box II: 511, Anthony Lewis Papers, MD, LOC.

22. David S. Broder, "The 'Possible Truth,'" *WP*, September 2, 1992, A21.

23. Cited in Shultz, *Turmoil and Triumph*, 809.

24. Walter Pincus, "Bush 'Out of the Loop' on Iran-Contra?," *WP*, September 24, 1992, A1.

25. Cited in Michael Wines, "Iran-Contra Figure Points to Wider Role for Bush," *NYT*, September 25, 1992, A12.

26. Walsh, *Final Report*, 473.

27. November 5 entry, Bush diary, folder Files of the Office of the Vice President Bush—VP Diary, box 2, Records of John Q. Barrett Attorney Files, RG 449.

28. Ken Roth, memo to White House File, July 29, 1987, folder Files of the Office of the Vice President Bush, George, box 1, Barrett Attorney Files, RG 449.

29. Cited in David Hoffman, "Not Given Iran Details, Bush Says," *WP*, January 8, 1988, A1.

30. Anthony Lewis, "The Cover-Up Crumble," *NYT*, October 5, 1992, A21.

31. Editorial, "Mr. Bush Had to Know," *NYT*, October 5, 1992, A20.

32. Cited in "'There Never Was a Formal NSC Meeting' On Iran Initiative," *WP*, January 14, 1988.

33. David Hoffman, "Bush Carried 1985 Tradeoff Deal to Hondurans," *WP*, April 7, 1989, A1.

34. David Johnston, "North's Notes Show He Met Bush Soon After Lying to Congress in '86," *NYT*, May 9, 1990, A14.

35. Hoffman, "Bush Carried 1985 Tradeoff Deal," A1.

36. Cited in Joe Pichirallo, "Bush Joined Efforts by Reagan, Aides to Solicit Arms for Contras During Ban," *WP*, April 7, 1989, A1.

37. Editorial, "Explain, Mr. President," *MH*, April 9, 1989, 2C.

38. Joe Pichirallo and David Hoffman, "Iran-Contra Panels Never Saw Some White House Documents," *WP*, April 20, 1989, A1.

39. Crawford, *Attack the Messenger*, 1.

40. Fleegler, *Brutal Campaign*, 114.

41. Transcript, CBS Evening News with Dan Rather, January 25, 1988, folder 3, box II: 883, Anthony Lewis Papers, MD, LOC.

42. Crawford, *Attack the Messenger*, 4.

43. Redacted in the original. January 25–26 entry and January 27 entry, both 1988, Bush diary, folder Files of the Office of the Vice President Bush—VP Diary, box 2, Records of John Q. Barrett Attorney Files, RG 449.

44. Crawford, *Attack the Messenger*, 5, 10.

45. Fleegler, *Brutal Campaign*.

46. Cited in Sam Vincent Meddis, "Secord: Bush a 'Close' Adviser on Iran-Contra," *USA Today*, September 25, 1992.

47. Cited in Walter Pincus and George Lardner Jr., "Bush Bristles at Queries on Iran Initiative," *WP*, October 14, 1992, A9.

48. Pincus and Lardner, "Bush Bristles," A9.

49. David Johnston, "Iran-Contra Document Says Bush Favored Secrecy in Hostage Affair," *NYT*, October 21, 1992, A14; David Johnston, "A Secret Memo Hints Bush Was Close to Hostage Deals," *NYT*, October 23, 1992, A14.

50. Meddis, "Secord: Bush a 'Close' Adviser."

51. Cited in Robert Pear, "'86 Weinberger Notes Contradict Bush Account on Iran Arms Deal," *NYT*, October 31, 1992, 1.

52. Clinton-Gore campaign, press release, October 30, 1992, folder Iran-Contra Affair Weinberger, Caspar W. General, box 430, GLP. See also Ann Devroy and Walter Pincus, "GOP Calls Release of Weinberger Papers a Political 'Low Blow,'" *WP*, November 3, 1992, A10.

53. Cited in Dan Balz, "Bush, Perot Lash Clinton; Democrat Upbeat as Race Draws to Close on Negative Note," *WP*, November 2, 1992, A1.

54. Devroy and Pincus, "GOP Calls Release of Weinberger Papers," A10.

55. Cited in Walsh, *Firewall*, 463.

56. Bod Dole, press releases, November 11 and 20, 1992, folder Iran-Contra Affair Weinberger, Caspar W. General, box 430, GLP.

57. Cited in Walsh, *Firewall*, 470, 471, 483.

58. Jack Goldsmith cited in David Rhode, "Sword and Shield," *New Yorker*, January 20, 2020, 32.

59. Cited in Rhode, "Sword and Shield," 32.

60. Cited in Sam Vincent Meddis, "Barr Rips into Iran-Contra Cases," *USA Today*, December 17, 1992; Walter Pincus, "Barr Rejects Counsel for Walsh Probe," *WP*, December 12, 1992, A6.

61. "51% Support North Pardon," *NYT*, May 7, 1989, A30.

62. Daniel Schorr, "Pardon North, Poindexter and the Rest," *NYT*, April 23, 1990.

63. Cited in AP, "Prosecutor in Iran-Contra Case Rebukes Dole," *NYT*, November 11, 1992, D20.

64. Editorial, "A Bush Pardon Now: Unforgivable," *NYT*, November 12, 1992, A24.

65. Ann Devroy and Walter Pincus, "Bush Urged to Grant Pardons," *WP*, November 7, 1992, A1.

66. Cited in David Johnston, "Pardon Is Sought for Weinberger," *NYT*, November 8, 1992, A31.

67. Walsh, *Firewall*, 476.

68. R. W. Apple Jr., "The President as Pardoner: A Calculated Gamble," *NYT*, December 25, 1992, A23.

69. David Johnston, "Bush Pardons 6 in Iran Affair, Aborting a Weinberger Trial," *NYT*, December 25, 1992, A1.

70. "Text of President Bush's Statement on the Pardon of Weinberger and Others," *NYT*, December 25, 1992, A22.

71. Weinberger and Roberts, *In the Arena*, 369, 370.

72. Calabresi and Yoo, *Unitary Executive*, 390.

73. James Brosnahan, "Pardoning Weinberger Belittles Democracy," *National Law Journal*, January 18, 1993, 17–18.

74. "Independent Counsel's Statement on the Pardons," *NYT*, December 25, 1992, A22.

75. Liman with Israel, *Lawyer*, 348.

76. Cited in Johnston, "Bush Pardons 6 in Iran Affair," A1.

77. Kalt, "Pardon Me?," 799.

78. Johnston, "Bush Pardons 6 in Iran Affair," A1.

79. "Independent Counsel's Statement on the Pardons," *NYT*, December 25, 1992, A22.

80. King and Spalding, report to President Bush, January 15, 1993, folder Iran-Contra Affair Pardons, box 428, GLP.

81. Walsh, *Firewall*, 464.

82. July 20, 1987, entry, Bush diary, folder Files of the Office of the Vice President Bush—VP Diary, box 2, Records of John Q. Barrett Attorney Files, RG 449.

83. "Was Vice President Bush in the Loop? You Make the Call," *WP*, January 31, 1993, C6.

84. Walsh, *Final Report*, xviii, 477, 48; *Report of the Congressional Committees*, 21.

85. Examples include Editorial, "Mr. Bush's Unpardonable Act," *NYT*, December 25, 1992, A30; Apple, "President as Pardoner," A23; and Walsh, *Firewall*, 476.

86. Cited in Stephen Engelberg, "On the Big Questions, the Jury Is Still Out," *NYT*, May 7, 1989, A1.

87. Byrne, *Iran-Contra*, 4.

88. Editorial, "Mr. Bush's Unpardonable Act," A30.

89. Carl Bernstein, "Conspiracy without End: The Legacy of Watergate," *LAT*, January [?], 1993.

90. David S. Broder, "Breaches of Trust," *WP*, January 3, 1993, C7.

CONCLUSION

1. *Report of the Congressional Committees*, 423. Joining the Congress in this interpretation are many of those touched by the scandal who want to minimize its impact, for instance, Meese, *With Reagan*, 301.

2. Busby, *Reagan and the Iran-Contra Affair*, 15; Walsh, *Final Report*, 562. Byrne's excellent *Iran-Contra* belongs to both groups at once. As he explains, "the book does not just scrutinize the Reagan administration and individual players, it points out structural issues that continue to be a factor in our system of government and makes it clear the scandal was not just an aberration," 5. See also Elkin, "Contempt of Congress," 1–15.

3. Some scholars have connected the many threads of political norms in Iran-Contra but either did not flesh them out or dismissed them. Ray Nichols called them "clichés" in "Of Arms and the Man: The Iran-Contra Affair as 'Representative Anecdote,'" 32. He included among these "the 'rule of law,' executive initiative, congressional will and understanding, the long associations of the right and of covert operatives, electioneering, hostages, 'national security,' 'privateers.'"

4. For more on norms, see Azari and Smith, "Unwritten Rules."

5. Joel Brinkley and Tim Weiner, "The Cast; Soldiers, Secretaries and Politicians, Now United in Bitterness," *NYT*, January 19, 1994, A8.

6. Cited in Brinkley and Weiner, "Cast; Soldiers, Secretaries and Politicians," A8.

7. Hacker and Pierson, *Off Center*, 2.

8. Mann and Ornstein, *It's Even Worse Than It Looks*, xxiv. See also Kabaservice, *Rule and Ruin*; Dionne, *Why the Right Went Wrong*; Seib, *We Should Have Seen It Coming*; and Hemmer, *Partisans*.

9. Byrne, *Iran-Contra*, 338.

10. Koh, *National Security Constitution*, 21.

11. Taylor, interview.

12. See the National Security Decision Directive 276.

13. Draft of memo, Shultz to Reagan, July 28, 1987, folder Speeches and writings 1987 Geo. Shultz to Ronald Reagan on Iran/Contra, box 35, CHP.

14. Cited in Kornbluh and Byrne, *Iran-Contra Scandal*, 331.

15. Koh, *National Security Constitution*, 21.

16. Cited in Currie, "Iran-Contra and Congressional Oversight," 199–200, 202, citation on 203.

17. Cited in Lobel, "Emergency Power and the Decline of Liberalism," 1421.

18. Fisher, "Congressional Checks on Military Initiatives."

19. Elkin, "Contempt of Congress," 1–15.

20. Mann and Ornstein, *It's Even Worse Than It Looks*, 42.

21. Cited in Byrne, *Iran-Contra*, 338; Meiers, "Return of the Imperial Presidency?," 249.

22. Bailey, "New Unitary Executive and Democratic Theory," 453, 458.

23. Love, "Reinventing the President's Pardon," 5.

24. David Frum, "Last Exit from Autocracy," *The Atlantic*, October 14, 2020.

25. Editorial, "As He Left Office, Donald Trump Abused Pardon Power," *Orlando Sentinel*, January 22, 2021, A10.

26. Jack Goldsmith cited in Pfiffner, "Donald Trump and the Norms," 111.

27. Kiran Stacey, "Trump Pardoning Spree Reignites Constitutional Debate about Scope of Presidential Authority," *Financial Times*, December 24, 2020, 6.

28. Cited in Pfiffner, "Donald Trump and the Norms," 96.

29. Cited in Meagan Flynn and Allyson Chiu, "Trump Says His 'Authority is Total,'" *WP*, April 14, 2020.

30. V-Dem Institute, *Democracy Report 2022*, 37.

31. George Packer, "The President is Winning His War on American Institutions," *The Atlantic*, March 2, 2020.

32. Canham-Clyne, "Business as Usual," 630.

33. Blumenthal, "Dateline Washington," 166.

34. For example, Byrne, *Iran-Contra*, 337.

35. Busby, *Reagan and the Iran-Contra Affair*, 17.

36. Spencer, "Walsh's Last Battle," 11, 28–30, 33, 30.

37. Waldron, "Is the Rule of Law an Essentially Contested Concept (in Florida)?," 138.

38. Cited in Pyle, "The Law: Barack Obama and Civil Liberties," 868, 876.

39. Michael Gerson, "Public Integrity? Blah, Blah, Blah," *WP*, November 8, 2019, A21.

40. Frum, "Last Exit from Autocracy."

41. Pfiffner, "Donald Trump and the Norms," 110.

42. Cited in David Rhode, "Sword and Shield," *New Yorker*, January 20, 2020, 32.

43. Paul Rosenzweig, "Trump's Defiance of the Rule of Law," *The Atlantic*, June 3, 2019.

44. Cited in Steve Denning, "How Trump's Cabinet Now Undermines the Rule of Law," *Forbes*, May 19, 2019.

45. Cited in Kadhim Shubber, "The Lawyer Who Has Trump's Back," *Financial Times*, July 1, 2020, 21.

46. Editorial, "The President Is Not Above the Law," *NYT*, April 16, 2018, A20; Rebecca Solnit, "President Trump Is at War with the Rule of Law. This Won't End Well," *The Guardian*, October 9, 2019.

47. Cited in Olmsted, "Fringe Paranoia Goes Mainstream," 244.

48. Cited in Jay, *Virtues of Mendacity*, 15.

49. Olmsted, "Truth Is Out There," 688, 689.

50. Myres, "Post-Truth as Symptom," 392.

51. Mann and Ornstein, *It's Even Worse Than It Looks*, 58–60, 62.

52. McGranahan, "Anthropology of Lying," 245.

53. Doyle, "End of Secrecy," 35, 36.

54. Montgomery, "Source Material," 789.

55. Weaver and Pallitto, "State Secrets," 86.

56. Jay, *Virtues of Mendacity*, 14.

57. Mearsheimer, *Why Leaders Lie*, 50, 52.

58. Michael A. Cohen, "Donald Trump Is a Liar," *Boston Globe*, November 30, 2015.

59. Berlet, "Big Stories, Spooky Sources," 70.

60. Hameleers, "My Reality Is More Truthful Than Yours," 1136.

61. Cited in Seib, *We Should Have Seen It Coming*, 84, 201.

62. Cited in Editorial, "Our Dishonest President," *LAT*, April 2, 2017, A17.

63. Benkler, Faris, Roberts, and Zuckerman, "Study: Breitbart-Led Right-Wing Media."

64. Cited in Jurecic, "Trumpelstiltskin," B4.

65. Cited in James Kloppenberg, "How Republican Strategies Undermine Democracy," *WP*, October 28, 2018, B7.

66. Colbert King, "All the President's Lies," *WP*, May 23, 2020, A17.

67. Glenn Kessler, "Trump Made 30,573 False or Misleading Claims as President," *WP*, January 23, 2021.

68. Jurecic, "Trumpelstiltskin," B4.

69. Kloppenberg, "How Republican Strategies Undermine Democracy," B7.

70. McKay Coppins, "The Billion-Dollar Disinformation Campaign to Reelect the President," *The Atlantic*, February 6, 2020.

71. Timothy Snyder, "The American Abyss," *NYT*, January 17, 2021, 30.

72. Singer, *Corporate Warriors*, 50.

73. Eckert, *Outsourcing War*, 7.

74. Singer, *Corporate Warriors*, 214.

75. Cohen and Küpçü, "Privatizing Foreign Policy," 34.

76. Eckert, *Outsourcing War*, 11, 17, 18, 19–20.

77. Cohen and Küpçü, "Privatizing Foreign Policy," 42; Dickinson, "Government for Hire," 139.

78. Dickinson, "Government for Hire," 139, 150, 153.

79. Alan Zibel, "Detained for Profit: Spending Surges Under U.S. Immigration Crackdown," *Public Citizen*, September 18, 2019.

80. Cohen and Küpçü, "Privatizing Foreign Policy," 40.

81. Noah Coburn, "Trump's Disastrous Plan to Increase Contracting in Afghanistan," *The Diplomat*, August 25, 2018.

82. Mark Landler, Eric Schmidtt, and Michael R. Gordon, "Trump Aides Recruited Businessmen to Devise Options for Afghanistan," *NYT*, July 10, 2021.

83. Jon D. Michaels, "Jared Kushner and Steve Bannon Want to Re-privatize the Military. That Would Be a Big Mistake," *LAT*, July 20, 2017.

84. Rosie Gray, "Erik Prince's Plan to Privatize the War in Afghanistan," *The Atlantic*, August 18, 2017,

85. Reuters Staff, "Afghan Government Rejects Proposals to Privatize War," *Reuters*, October 5, 2018.

86. Fisher, "Starr's Record as Independent Counsel," 546.

87. Philip Shenon, "North's Challenge to Prober Dismissed," *NYT*, March 13, 1987, A1.

88. Cited in George Lardner Jr., "Justice Dept. Attacks Special Counsels,'" *WP*, June 17, 1987, A1.

89. Lewis, "Accounting for Power," A35.

90. Leslie Maitland Werner, "Justice Dept. Says Prosecutor Law Should Be Vetoed," *NYT*, June 17, 1987, A1.

91. Cited in Lardner, "Justice Dept. Attacks Special Counsels," A1.

92. Cited in Clifford D. May, "A Case Against Special Prosecutors?," *NYT*, June 21, 1987, A4.

93. Kenneth B. Noble, "House Votes to Make Permanent Law Covering Special Prosecutors," *NYT*, October 22, 1987, B9.

94. Stuart Taylor, Jr, "U.S. Court Upsets Law on Appointing Key Prosecutors," *NYT*, January 23, 1988, 1.

95. Stuart Taylor, Jr, "Supreme Court Vote Upholds Law on Special Prosecutors," *NYT*, June 30, 1988, A1.

96. Justice Antonin Scalia, dissenting, Morrison v. Olson, 487 U.S. 654 (1988).

97. Cited in Sharon LaFraniere, "Barr Urges 'Fundamental Changes' in Independent Counsel Statute," *WP*, April 8, 1992, A5.

98. David Johnston, "Weinberger Case Livens Debate on Counsel Law," *NYT*, June 28, 1992, A15.

99. Sharon LaFraniere, "In Switch, Democrats to Seek Extension of Independent Counsel Statute," *WP*, August 15, 1992, A5.

100. Bretton G. Sciaroni, "Law That Deserved to Die," *WP*, October 25, 1992, C7.

101. Helen Dewar, "Independent Counsel Law Resurrected," *WP*, November 19, 1993, A27; Editorial, "Let the Independent Counsel Speak," *WP*, December 25, 1993, 30.

102. Fisher, "Starr's Record as Independent Counsel," 547.

103. Alvis, Bailey, and Taylor, *Contested Removal Power*, 215. See also Miller and Elwood, "Independent Counsel Statute."

104. Calabresi and Yoo, *Unitary Executive*, 400–03.

105. Joan Biskupic, "Trump's Unbroken Pattern of Disdain for the Rule of Law," CNN, February 22, 2020, www.cnn.com/2020/02/22/politics/trump-justice-barr-rule-of-law/index.html/.

106. Cited in Pfiffner, "Donald Trump and the Norms," 108.

107. Zachary B. Wolf, "Why Trump's Claim of Executive Privilege Is Different," CNN, May 8, 2019, www.cnn.com/2019/05/08/politics/donald-trump-executive-privilege/index.html.

108. Jeannie Suk Gersen, "The Supreme Court Confronts Trump's Challenge to the Separation of Powers," *New Yorker*, May 2, 2020.

109. Pfiffner, "Donald Trump and the Norms," 107.

110. Denning, "How Trump's Cabinet Now Undermines the Rule of Law."

111. Solnit, "President Trump Is at War."

112. Epps, "Congress Should Go to the Supreme Court."

113. Cited in Rhode, "Sword and Shield," 32.

114. Cited in Azari, *Unprecedented*, 107.

115. Cited in "Mueller Report: Here Are the Key Revelations," *Financial Times*, April 18, 2019.

116. Azari, *Unprecedented*, 96.

117. "Mueller Report: Here Are the Key Revelations."

118. Cited in Azari, *Unprecedented*, 125.

119. John Yoo, "Forget Watergate: Think Iran-Contra," *NYT*, May 18, 2017, A27.

120. "Mueller Report: Here Are the Key Revelations."

121. Maggie Haberman, Jodi Kantor, Adam Goldman, and Ben Protess, "Trump Had More Than 300 Classified Documents at Mar-a-Lago," *NYT*, August 22, 2022, www.nytimes.com/2022/08/22/us/politics/trump-mar-a-lago-documents.html.

122. Charlie Savage, "The Trump Classified Documents Indictment, Annotated," *NYT*, July 27, 2023, www.nytimes.com/interactive/2023/06/09/us/trump-indictment-document-annotated.html?searchResultPosition=1.

123. Maggie Haberman, "Another Trump Mystery: Why Did He Resist Returning the Government's Documents?," *NYT*, August 18, 2022.

124. "Full Document: Trump's Call with the Ukrainian President," *NYT*, October 30, 2019, www.nytimes.com/interactive/2019/09/25/us/politics/trump-ukraine-transcript.html.

125. Editorial, "The Disorienting Defenses of Donald Trump," *NYT*, November 10, 2019.

126. Shane Harris, Mike DeBonis, Elise Viebeck, and Michael Kranish, "'No Doubt' about a Quid Pro Quo, Official Testified," *WP*, November 9, 2019, A1.

127. Cited in Editorial, "The Disorienting Defenses of Donald Trump," *NYT*, November 10, 2019.

128. Cited in Demetri Sevastopulo, "The Facts Pile Up against Trump," *Financial Times*, November 23, 2019, 6.

129. Cited in Editorial, "The Disorienting Defenses of Donald Trump."

130. Pfiffner, "Donald Trump and the Norms," 100.

131. Bolton, *Room Where It Happened*, 301.

132. Whiting, "Controlling Tin Cup Diplomacy," 2049.

133. Williams, "The Last Word on the Iran-Contra Affair?," 380.

134. *Continued Testimony of North and McFarlane*, 196.

BIBLIOGRAPHY

ARCHIVES

Hoover Institution, Stanford University, California
- Charles Hill Papers
- Edwin Meese Papers
- Papers of the Committee on the Present Danger
- Papers of Jim Mann
- Papers of Robert L. Bartley

Manuscripts Division, Library of Congress, Washington, DC
- Anthony Lewis Papers
- Caspar Weinberger Papers
- Gerhard Gesell Papers
- George Lardner Papers
- Leonard Garment Papers
- Mary McGrory Papers

National Archives, College Park, Maryland
- RG 449, Records of Independent Counsel Lawrence Walsh

DOCUMENT COLLECTIONS AND GOVERNMENT RESOURCES

Appendixes to Parts I and II: Joint Hearings before the Senate Select Committee on Secret Military Assistance to Iran and the Nicaraguan Opposition and the House Select Committee to Investigate Covert Arms Transactions with Iran: July 7, 8, 9, 10, 13, and 14, 1987. 100th Congress, 1st Session, no. 100-7, Part 3, Washington, DC: Government Printing Office, 1988.

*Continued Testimony of Oliver North and Robert C. McFarlane: Joint Hearings before the Senate Select Committee on Secret Military Assistance to Iran and the Nicaraguan

Opposition and the House Select Committee to Investigate Covert Arms Transactions with Iran: July 10, 13, and 14, 1987. 100th Congress, 1st Session, vol. 100-7, Part 2, Washington, DC: Government Printing Office, 1988.

Kornbluh, Peter, and Malcolm Byrne, eds. *The Iran-Contra Scandal: The Declassified History*. New York: New Press, 1993.

Report of the Congressional Committees Investigating the Iran-Contra Affair, with Supplemental, Minority, and Additional Views, U.S. House of Representatives Select Committee to Investigate Covert Arms Transactions with Iran and U.S. Senate Select Committee on Secret Military Assistance to Iran and the Nicaraguan Opposition. 100th Congress, 1st Session, S. Rep. 100-216, Washington, DC: Government Printing Office, 1987.

Testimony of Adolfo P. Calero, John K. Singlaub, Ellen C. Garwood, William B. O'Boyle, Joseph Coors, Robert C. Dutton, Felix I. Rodriguez, And Lewis A. Tambs: Joint Hearings before the Senate Select Committee on Secret Military Assistance to Iran and the Nicaraguan Opposition and the House Select Committee to Investigate Covert Arms Transactions with Iran: May 20, 21, 27, and 28, 1987. 100th Congress, 1st Session, vol. 100-3, Washington, DC: Government Printing Office, 1988.

Testimony of Dewey R. Clarridge, C/CATF, and Clair George: Joint Hearings in Executive Session as Declassified before the Senate Select Committee on Secret Military Assistance to Iran and the Nicaraguan Opposition and the House Select Committee to Investigate Covert Arms Transactions with Iran: August 4, 5, and 6, 1987. 100th Congress, 1st Session, vol. 100-11, Washington, DC: Government Printing Office, 1988.

Testimony of Donald T. Regan and Caspar W. Weinberger: Joint Hearings before the Senate Select Committee on Secret Military Assistance to Iran and the Nicaraguan Opposition and the House Select Committee to Investigate Covert Arms Transactions with Iran: July 30, 31, and August 3, 1987, 100th Congress, 1st Session, vol. 100-10, Washington, DC: Government Printing Office, 1988.

Testimony of Elliott Abrams, Albert Hakim, David M. Lewis, Bretton G. Sciaroni, and Fawn Hall: Joint Hearings before the Senate Select Committee on Secret Military Assistance to Iran and the Nicaraguan Opposition and the House Select Committee to Investigate Covert Arms Transactions with Iran: June 2, 3, 4, 5, 8, and 9, 1987. 100th Congress, 1st Session, vol. 100-5, Washington, DC: Government Printing Office, 1988.

Testimony of George P. Shultz and Edwin Meese, III: Joint Hearings before the Senate Select Committee on Secret Military Assistance to Iran and the Nicaraguan Opposition and the House Select Committee to Investigate Covert Arms Transactions with Iran: July 23, 24, 28, and 29, 1987. 100th Congress, 1st Session, vol. 100-9, Washington, DC: Government Printing Office, 1988.

Testimony of Glenn A. Robinette, Noel C. Koch, Henry H. Gaffney, Jr., Stanley Sporkin, and Charles J. Cooper and Presentation by W. Neil Eggleston: Joint Hearings before the Senate Select Committee on Secret Military Assistance to Iran and the Nicaraguan Opposition and the House Select Committee to Investigate Covert Arms Transactions with Iran: June 23, 24, and 25 1987. 100th Congress, 1st Session, vol. 100-6, Washington, DC: Government Printing Office, 1988.

Testimony of John M. Poindexter: Joint Hearings before the Senate Select Committee on Secret Military Assistance to Iran and the Nicaraguan Opposition and the House Select

Committee to Investigate Covert Arms Transactions with Iran: July 15, 16, 17, 20, and 21, 1987. 100th Congress, 1st Session, vol. 100-8, Washington, DC: Government Printing Office, 1988.

Testimony of Oliver L. North: Joint Hearings before the Senate Select Committee on Secret Military Assistance to Iran and the Nicaraguan Opposition and the House Select Committee to Investigate Covert Arms Transactions with Iran: July 7, 8, 9, and 10, 1987. 100th Congress, 1st Session, vol. 100-7, Part 1, Washington, DC: Government Printing Office, 1988.

Testimony of Richard V. Secord: Joint Hearings before the Senate Select Committee on Secret Military Assistance to Iran and the Nicaraguan Opposition and the House Select Committee to Investigate Covert Arms Transactions with Iran: May 5 through May 8, 1987. 100th Congress, 1st Session, vol. 100-1, Washington, DC: Government Printing Office, 1987.

Testimony of Robert C. McFarlane, Gaston L. Sigur, Jr. and Robert W. Owen: Joint Hearings before the Senate Select Committee on Secret Military Assistance to Iran and the Nicaraguan Opposition and the House Select Committee to Investigate Covert Arms Transactions with Iran: May 11, 12, 13, 14, and 19, 1987. 100th Congress, 1st Session, vol. 100-2, Washington, DC: Government Printing Office, 1987.

Testimony of Tomas Castillo: Joint Hearings in Executive Session as Declassified before the Senate Select Committee on Secret Military Assistance to Iran and the Nicaraguan Opposition and the House Select Committee to Investigate Covert Arms Transactions with Iran: May 29, 1987. 100th Congress, 1st Session, vol. 100-4, Washington, DC: Government Printing Office, 1988.

Tower, John G., Edmund S. Muskie, and Brent Scowcroft. *The Tower Commission Report: The Full Text of the President's Special Review Board.* New York: Bantam Books, 1987.

US Constitution. *National Constitution Center.* https://constitutioncenter.org/interactive-constitution/article/article-iii.

Walsh, Lawrence E. *Iran-Contra: The Final Report.* New York: Times Books, 1994.

INTERVIEWS BY THE ASSOCIATION FOR DIPLOMATIC STUDIES AND TRAINING, ARLINGTON, VIRGINIA

McCormack, Richard T. Interviewed by Charles Stuart Kennedy, January 2, 2002, transcript. www.adst.org.

Taylor, John J. (Jay). Interviewed by Charles Stuart Kennedy, April 25, 2000, transcript. www.adst.org.

Tull, James L. Interviewed by Raymond Ewing, May 31, 2001, transcript, www.adst.org.

MEMOIRS AND PUBLISHED DIARIES

Abrams, Elliott. *Undue Process: A Story of How Political Differences Are Turned into Crimes.* New York: Free Press, 1993.

Abshire, David M. *Saving the Reagan Presidency: Trust Is the Coin of the Realm.* College Station: Texas A&M University Press, 2005.

Bolton, John. *The Room Where It Happened: A White House Memoir.* New York: Simon and Schuster, 2020.

Clarridge, Duane R., with Digby Diehl. *A Spy for All Seasons: My Life in the CIA.* New York: Scribner's, 1997.

Cruz, Arturo, Jr. *Memoirs of a Counterrevolutionary.* New York: Bantam Doubleday Dell, 1989.

Ledeen, Michael A. *Perilous Statecraft: An Insider's Account of the Iran-Contra Affair.* New York: Charles Scribner's Sons, 1988.

Liman, Arthur L., with Peter Israel. *Lawyer: A Life of Counsel and Controversy.* New York: Public Affairs, 1998.

McFarlane, Robert C., and Zofia Smardz. *Special Trust.* New York: Cadell and Davies, 1994.

Meese, Edwin III. *With Reagan: The Inside Story.* Washington, DC: Regnery Gateway, 1992.

Menges, Constantine C. *Inside the National Security Council: The True Story of the Making and Unmaking of Reagan's Foreign Policy.* New York: Simon and Schuster, 1988.

North, Oliver L, and William Novak. *Under Fire: An American Story.* New York: HarperCollins, 1991.

Reagan, Ronald. *An American Life.* New York: Threshold Editions, 1990.

Reagan, Ronald. *The Reagan Diaries*, ed. Douglas Brinkley. New York: Harper Perennial, 2007.

Regan, Donald T. *For the Record: From Wall Street to Washington.* San Diego, CA: Harcourt Brace Jovanovich, 1988.

Secord, Richard, and Jay Wurts. *Honored and Betrayed: Irangate, Covert Affairs, and the Secret War in Laos.* Toronto, Canada: Wiley, 1992.

Shultz, George P. *Turmoil and Triumph: My Years as Secretary of State.* New York: Charles Scribner's, 1993.

Toobin, Jeffrey. *Opening Arguments: A Young Lawyer's First Case: United States vs. Oliver L. North.* New York: Viking, 1991.

Tower, John. *Consequences: A Personal and Political Memoir.* New York: Little, Brown, 1991.

Wallison, Peter J. *Ronald Reagan: The Power of Conviction and the Success of His Presidency.* Boulder, CO: Westview, 2003.

Walsh, Lawrence E. *Firewall: The Iran-Contra Conspiracy and Cover-Up.* New York: Norton, 1997.

Weinberger, Caspar W. *Fighting for Peace: Seven Critical Years in the Pentagon.* New York: Warner Books, 1990.

Weinberger, Caspar W., and Gretchen Roberts. *In the Arena: A Memoir of the 20th Century.* Washington, DC: Regnery, 2001.

NEWS PUBLICATIONS

Associated Press
The Atlantic
Austin American-Statesman
Berkeley News
Boston Globe
California Lawyer

CE Noticias Financieras English
Christian Science Monitor
The Diplomat
Financial Times
Forbes
The Guardian
The Independent (UK)
Insight (Minnesota)
Legal Times
Los Angeles Daily Journal
Los Angeles Times
Miami Herald
Milwaukee Sentinel
Naples Daily News
The Nation
National Law Journal
New Republic
Newsday
Newsweek
The New Yorker
New York Times
New York Times Magazine
Orlando Sentinel
Pittsburgh Press
Public Citizen
Reuters
Richmond News Leader
San Francisco Chronicle
Tampa Tribune
The Tico Times (Costa Rica)
Time
U.S. News
U.S. News & World Report
USA Today
Wall Street Journal
The Washingtonian
Washington Inquirer
Washington Post
Washington Post Magazine
Washington Times

BOOKS, JOURNAL ARTICLES, AND DISSERTATIONS

Alterman, Eric. *When Presidents Lie: A History of Official Deception and its Consequences.* New York: Viking, 2004.

Alvis, David J., Jeremy D. Bailey, and F. Flagg Taylor IV. *The Contested Removal Power, 1789–2010.* Lawrence: University Press of Kansas, 2012.

Aristotle. *Politics: A Treatise on Government.* Project Gutenberg. Updated January 22, 2013. www.gutenberg.org/files/6762/6762-h/6762-h.htm.

Arkes, Hadley. "On the Moral Standing of the President as an Interpreter of the Constitution: Some Reflections on Our Current 'Crises.'" *Political Science and Politics* 20, no. 3 (Summer 1987): 637–42.

Armony, Ariel. *Argentina, the United States, and the Anti-Communist Crusade in Central America, 1977–1984.* Athens: Ohio University Center for International Studies, 1997.

Azari, Julia R., and Jennifer K. Smith. "Unwritten Rules: Informal Institutions in Established Democracies." *Perspectives on Politics* 10, no. 1 (2012): 37–55.

Azari, Sara. *Unprecedented: A Simple Guide to the Crimes of the Trump Campaign and Presidency.* Lincoln: University of Nebraska Press, 2020.

Bailey, Jeremy D. "The New Unitary Executive and Democratic Theory: The Problem of Alexander Hamilton." *American Political Science Review* 102, no. 4 (November 2008): 453–65.

Benkler, Yochai, Robert Faris, Hal Roberts, and Ethan Zuckerman. "Study: Breitbart-Led Right-Wing Media Ecosystem Altered Broader Media Agenda." *Columbia Journalism Review* March 3, 2017.www.cjr.org/analysis/breitbart-media-trump-harvard-study.php.

Berlet, Chip. "Big Stories, Spooky Sources." *Columbia Journalism Review* 32, no. 1 (May 1, 1993): 67–71.

Blachman, Morris J., and Kenneth Sharp. "De-Democratising American Foreign Policy: Dismantling the Post-Vietnam Formula." *Third World Quarterly* 8, no. 4 (October 1986): 1271–308.

Blumenthal, Sidney. "Dateline Washington: The Conservative Crackup." *Foreign Policy* 69 (Winter 1987–1988): 166–88.

Bradlee, Ben. *Guts and Glory: The Rise and Fall of Oliver North.* New York: D. I. Fine, 1988.

Brandes, Stuart D. *Warhogs: A History of War Profits in America.* Lexington: University Press of Kentucky, 1997.

Brody, Richard A., and Catherine R. Shapiro. "Policy Failure and Public Support: The Iran-Contra Affair and Public Assessment of President Reagan." *Political Behavior* 11, no. 4 (December 1989): 353–69.

Brzezinski, Zbigniew. "The NSC's Midlife Crisis." *Foreign Policy* 69 (Winter, 1987–1988): 80–99.

Burns, Edward Bradford. *At War in Nicaragua: The Reagan Doctrine and the Politics of Nostalgia.* New York: Harper and Row, 1987.

Busby, Robert. *Reagan and the Iran-Contra Affair: The Politics of Presidential Recovery.* London: Macmillan, 1999.

Byrne, Malcolm. *Iran-Contra: Reagan's Scandal and the Unchecked Abuse of Presidential Power.* Lawrence: University of Kansas Press, 2014.

Calabresi, Steven G., and Christopher S. Yoo. *The Unitary Executive: Presidential Power from Washington to Bush.* New Haven, CT: Yale University Press, 2008.

Canham-Clyne, John. "Business as Usual: Iran-Contra and the National Security State." *World Policy Journal* 9, no. 4 (Fall-Winter 1992): 617–37.

Cannon, Lou. *President Reagan: The Role of a Lifetime.* New York: Public Affairs, 1991.

Cavender, Gray, Nancy C. Jurik, and Albert K. Cohen. "The Baffling Case of the Smoking Gun: The Social Ecology of Political Accounts in the Iran-Contra Affair." *Social Problems* 40, no. 2 (May 1993): 152–66.

Cliffe, Lionel, Maureen Ramsay, and Dave Bartlett. *The Politics of Lying: Implications for Democracy.* London: Macmillan, 2000.

Clough, Chris. "*Quid Pro Quo*: The Challenges of International Strategic Intelligence Cooperation." *International Journal of Intelligence and CounterIntelligence* 17, no. 4 (2000): 601–13.

Cohen, Julie. "Who Will Unwrap the October Surprise?" *Columbia Journalism Review* 30, no. 3 (September 1, 1991): 32–4.

Cohen, Michael A., and Maria Figueroa Küpçü. "Privatizing Foreign Policy." *World Policy Journal* 22, no. 3 (Fall 2005): 34–52.

Crawford, Craig. *Attack the Messenger: How Politicians Turn You against the Media.* Oxford: Rowman and Littlefield, 2006.

Crovitz, L. Gordon. "Crime, Constitution, and the Iran-Contra Affair." *Commentary* 84, no. 4 (October 1987): 23–30.

Currie, James T. "Iran-Contra and Congressional Oversight of the CIA." *International Journal of Intelligence and CounterIntelligence* 11, no. 2 (1998): 185–210.

Davis, Robert V. "Out-of-Sight Oversight: The U.S. Congress and Classified Technologies." *Journal of Policy History* 26, no. 4 (2014): 625–43.

Dean, John W., and Bob Altemeyer. *Authoritarian Nightmare: Trump and His Followers.* Brooklyn, NY: Melville House, 2020.

Dicey, A. V. *Introduction to the Study of the Law of the Constitution.* 6th ed. London: Macmillan, 1902.

Dickinson, Laura A. "Government for Hire: Privatizing Foreign Affairs and the Problem of Accountability under International Law." *William and Mary Law Review* 47, no. 135 (2005): 135–237.

Dickinson, Laura. "Outsourcing Covert Activities." *Journal of National Security Law and Policy* 5 (2012): 521–37.

Dionne, E. J. *Why the Right Went Wrong: Conservatism from Goldwater to Trump and Beyond.* New York: Simon and Schuster, 2016.

Dormer, Stephen G. "The Not-So Independent Counsel: How Congressional Investigations Undermine Accountability under the Independent Counsel Act." *Georgetown Law Journal* 86, no. 6 (July 1998): 2392–419.

Doyle, Kate. "The End of Secrecy: U.S. National Security and the Imperative for Openness." *World Policy Journal* 16, no. 1 (Spring 1999): 34–51.

Draper, Theodore. *A Very Thin Line: The Iran-Contra Affairs.* New York: Hill and Wang, 1991.

Eastland, Terry. "The Independent-Counsel Regime." *Public Interest* 100 (Summer 1990): 68–80.

Eckert, Amy E. *Outsourcing War: The Just War Tradition in the Age of Military Privatization.* Ithaca, NY: Cornell University Press, 2016.

Eksterowicz, Anthony J., and Robert N. Roberts. "The Specter of Presidential Pardons." *White House Studies* 6, no. 4 (2006): 377–89.

Elkin, Stephen L. "Contempt of Congress: The Iran-Contra Affair and the American Constitution." *Congress and the Presidency* 18, no. 1 (Spring 1991): 1–15.

Fairlie, John A. "Separation of Powers." *Michigan Law Review* 21, no. 4 (1922–1923): 393–436.

Fisher, Louis. "The Foundations of a Scandal." *Corruption and Reform* 3 (1988): 157–69.

Fisher, Louis. "Congressional Checks on Military Initiatives." *Political Science Quarterly* 109, no. 5 (Winter 1994–1995): 739–62.

Fisher Louis. "Starr's Record as Independent Counsel." *Political Science and Politics* 32, no. 3 (September 1999): 546–49.

Fleegler, Robert L. *Brutal Campaign: How the 1988 Election Set the Stage for Twenty-First-Century American Politics.* Chapel Hill: University of North Carolina Press, 2023.

Fried, Amy. *Muffled Echoes: Oliver North and the Politics of Public Opinion.* New York: Columbia University Press, 1997.

Friedman, Andrew. *Covert Capital: Landscapes of Denial and the Making of U.S. Empire in the Suburbs of Northern Virginia.* Berkeley: University of California Press, 2013.

Galeotti, Anna Elisabetta. "Liars or Self-Deceived? Reflections on Political Deception." *Political Studies* 63, no. 4 (2015): 887–902.

George, Larry N. "Tocqueville's Caveat: Centralized Executive Foreign Policy and American Democracy." *Polity* 22, no. 3 (Spring 1990): 419–41.

Gesell, Gerhard A. "United States v. Oliver North." *Federal Sentencing Reporter* 2, no. 2 (July–August 1989): 59–64.

Ghio, R. S. "The Iran-Contra Prosecutions and the Failure of Use Immunity." *Stanford Law Review* 45, no. 1 (November 1992): 229–61.

Glabe, Scott. "The Original Privatization of Intelligence: Iran-Contra Revisited." *American Intelligence Journal* 28, no. 1 (2010): 113–20.

Gleijeses, Piero. *Conflicting Missions: Havana, Washington, and Africa, 1959–1976.* Chapel Hill: University of North Carolina Press, 2002.

Gleijeses, Piero. *Visions of Freedom: Havana, Washington, Pretoria, and the Struggle for Southern Africa 1976–1991.* Chapel Hill: University of North Carolina Press, 2013.

Goodman, Allan E. "Reforming U.S. Intelligence." *Foreign Policy* 67 (Summer 1987): 121–36.

Grandin, Greg. *Empire's Workshop: Latin America, the United States, and the Rise of the New Imperialism.* New York: Metropolitan Books, 2006.

Green, Stuart P. "Uncovering the Cover-Up Crimes." *American Criminal Law Review* 42, no. 1 (Winter 2005): 9–44.

Hacker, Jacob S., and Paul Pierson. *Off Center: The Republican Revolution and the Erosion of American Democracy.* New Haven, CT: Yale University Press, 2005.

Hameleers, Michael. "My Reality Is More Truthful Than Yours: Radical Right-Wing Politicians' and Citizens' Construction of 'Fake' and 'Truthfulness' on Social Media—Evidence from the United States and The Netherlands." *International Journal of Communication* 14 (2020): 1135–52.

Hamilton, Alexander, James Madison, and John Jay, *The Federalist Papers*, ed. Lawrence Goldman. Oxford: Oxford University Press, 2008.

Haque, Akhlaque. *Surveillance, Transparency, and Democracy: Public Administration in the Information Age, Public Administration: Criticism and Creativity.* Tuscaloosa: University Alabama Press, 2015.

Harmer, Tanya. *Allede's Chile and the Inter-American Cold War.* Chapel Hill: University of North Carolina Press, 2011.

Hayek, F. A. *The Constitution of Liberty.* Vol. 17 of *The Collected Works of F. A. Hayek*, ed. Ronald Hamowy. London: Routledge, 1960; 2011.

Hayward, Steven F. *The Age of Reagan: The Conservative Counterrevolution, 1980–1989.* New York: Crown Forum, 2009.

Hemmer, Nicole. *Partisans: The Conservative Revolutionaries Who Remade American Politics in the 1990s.* New York: Basic, 2022.

Heyboer, Kelly. "A Furor over the CIA and Drugs." *American Journalism Review* 18, no. 9 (November 1996).

Hinson, Christopher L. "Negative Information Action: Danger for Democracy." *American Behavioral Scientist* 53, no. 6 (2010): 826–47.

Hollyer, James R., B. Peter Rosendorff, and James Raymond Vreeland, "Democracy and Transparency." *Journal of Politics* 73, no. 4 (2011). https://doi.org/10.1017/s0022381611000880.

Hyde, Henry J. "'Leaks' and Congressional Oversight." *American Intelligence Journal* 9, no. 1 (Summer 1988): 24–27.

Hyde, Henry, and George Mitchell. "Pardoning Ollie North: Was Reagan Wrong Not to Grant a Pretrial Pardon?" *ABA Journal* 75, no. 2 (February 1989): 42–43.

Inboden, William. *The Peacemaker: Ronald Reagan, the Cold War, and the World on the Brink.* New York: Dutton, 2022.

Jay, Martin. *The Virtues of Mendacity: On Lying in Politics*. Charlottesville: University of Virginia Press, 2010.

Johns, Andrew, ed. *A Companion to Ronald Reagan*. Malden, MA: Wiley, 2015.

Johnson, Loch K. "The Contemporary Presidency: Presidents, Lawmakers, and Spies: Intelligence Accountability in the United States." *Presidential Studies Quarterly* 34, no. 4 (December 2004): 828–37.

Johnson, Scott P. "President Donald J. Trump and the Potential Abuse of the Pardon Power." *Faulkner Law Review* 9, no. 2 (Spring 2018): 289–328.

Jordan, Sandra. "Classified Information and Conflicts in Independent Counsel Prosecutions: Balancing the Scales of Justice after Iran-Contra." *Columbia Law Review* 91, no. 7 (November 1991): 1651–98.

Kabaservice, Geoffrey. *Rule and Ruin: The Downfall of Moderation and the Destruction of the Republican Party, from Eisenhower to the Tea Party*. New York: Oxford Press, 2012.

Kalt, Brian C. "Pardon Me? The Constitutional Case against Presidential Self-Pardons." *Yale Law Journal* 106, no. 3 (December 1996): 779–809.

Keeley, Theresa. *Reagan's Gun-Toting Nuns: The Catholic Conflict over Cold War Human Rights Policy in Central America*. Ithaca, NY: Cornell University Press, 2020.

Kenworthy, Eldon. "Where Pennsylvania Avenue Meets Madison Avenue: The Selling of Foreign Policy." *World Policy Journal* 5, no. 1 (Winter 1987/1988): 107–27.

Kiehl, William P. "Seduced and Abandoned: Strategic Information and the National Security Council Process." in *Affairs of State: The Interagency and National Security*, ed. Gabriel Marcella. Strategic Studies Institute, US Army War College, 2008.

Koh, Harold Hongju. *The National Security Constitution: Sharing Power after the Iran-Contra Affair*. New Haven, CT: Yale University Press, 1990.

Kornbluh, Peter. "Crack, Contras, and the CIA: The Storm over 'Dark Alliance' (Anatomy of a Story)." *Columbia Journalism Review* 35, no. 5 (January-February 1997).

Landon-Murray, Michael, and Edin Mujkic. "Disinformation in Contemporary U.S. Foreign Policy." *Public Integrity* (2019): 512–22.

Ledeen, Michael A. "Secrets." *The National Interest* 10 (Winter 1987/1988): 48–55.

LeoGrande, William. *Our Own Backyard: The United States in Central America, 1977–1992*. Chapel Hill: University of North Carolina Press, 1998.

Levy, Deborah M. "Advice for Sale." *Foreign Policy* 67 (Summer 1987): 64–86.

Lobel, Jules. "Emergency Power and the Decline of Liberalism." *Yale Law Journal* 98, no. 7 (May 1989): 1385–433.

Locke, John. *Second Treatise of Government*. South Bend, IN: Infomotions, 2000.

Love, Margaret Colgate. "Reinventing the President's Pardon Power." *Federal Sentencing Reporter* 20, no. 1 (October 2007): 5–15.

Lynch, Michael, and David Bogen. *The Spectacle of History: Speech, Text, and Memory at the Iran-Contra Hearings*. Durham, NC: Duke University Press, 1996.

Maddow, Rachel, and Michael Yarvitz. *Bag Man: The Wild Crimes, Audacious Cover-up and Spectacular Downfall of a Brazen Crook in the White House*. New York: Crown, 2020.

Mann, Thomas E., and Norman J. Ornstein. *It's Even Worse Than It Looks*. New York: Basic Books, 2012.

Maravall, José María, and Adam Przeworski, *Democracy and the Rule of Law*. Cambridge: Cambridge University Press, 2003.

Marshall, Jonathan, Peter Dale Scott, and Jane Hunter. *The Iran Contra Connection: Secret Teams and Covert Operations in the Reagan Era*. Boston, MA: South End, 1987.

Mayer, Jane, and Doyle McManus. *Landslide: The Unmaking of the President, 1984–1988*. Boston, MA: Houghton Mifflin, 1988.

McCormick, James M., and Steven S. Smith. "The Iran Arms Sale and the Intelligence Oversight Act of 1980." *Political Science and Politics* 20, no. 1 (Winter 1987): 29–37.

McCoy, Alfred W. "Covert Netherworld: An Invisible Interstice in the Modern World System." *Comparative Studies in Society and History* 58, no. 4 (2016): 847–79.

McGranahan, Carole. "An Anthropology of Lying: Trump and the Political Sociality of Moral Outrage." *American Ethnologist* 44, no. 2 (May 2017): 243–48.

Mearsheimer, John J. *Why Leaders Lie: The Truth about Lying in International Politics*. New York: Oxford University Press, 2013.

Meiers, Franz-Josef. "The Return of the Imperial Presidency? The President, Congress, and U.S. Foreign Policy after 11 September 2001." *Amerikastudien [American Studies]* 55, no. 2 (2010): 249–86.

Meitl, P. J. "The Perjury Paradox: The Amazing Under-Enforcement of the Laws regarding Lying to Congress." *Quinnipiac Law Review* 25, no. 3 (2007): 547–72.

Mervin, David. "Deception in Government." *Society* 37, no. 6 (September/October 2000): 25–27.

Miller, Herbert J., Jr., and John P. Elwood. "The Independent Counsel Statute: An Idea Whose Time Has Passed." *Law and Contemporary Problems* 62, no. 1 (Winter 1999): 111–29.

Montesquieu. *The Spirit of Laws*. Vol. 1, trans. Thomas Nugent. Cincinnati, OH: Robert Clarke, 1873.

Montgomery, Bruce P. "Source Material: Nixon's Ghost Haunts the Presidential Records Act: The Reagan and George W. Bush Administrations." *Presidential Studies Quarterly* 32, no. 4 (December 2002): 789–809.

Myres, Jason David. "Post-Truth as Symptom: The Emergence of a Masculine Hysteria." *Philosophy and Rhetoric* 51, no. 4 (2018): 392–415.

Newland, Chester A. "Faithful Execution of the Law and Empowering Public Confidence." *Presidential Studies Quarterly* 21, no. 4 (Fall 1991): 673–86.

Nichols, Ray. "Of Arms and the Man: The Iran-Contra Affair as 'Representative Anecdote.'" *Australasian Journal of American Studies* 11, no. 2 (December 1992): 19–36.

Nicolescu-Waggonner, Cristina. *No Rule of Law, No Democracy: Conflicts of Interest, Corruption, and Elections as Democratic Deficits*. Albany: SUNY Press, 2016.

Nincic, Miroslav. "Getting What You Want: Positive Inducements in International Relations." *International Security* 35, no. 1 (Summer 2010): 138–83.

Olmsted, Kathryn S. "The Truth Is Out There: Citizen Sleuths from the Kennedy Assassination to the 9/11 Truth Movement." *Diplomatic History* 35, no. 4 (September 2011): 671–93.

Olmsted, Kathryn S. "Fringe Paranoia Goes Mainstream." *Modern American History* 1 (2018): 243–46.

Parry, Robert, and Peter Kornbluh. "Iran-Contra's Untold Story." *Foreign Policy* 72 (Autumn 1988): 3–30.

Patterson, James. *Restless Giant: The United States from Watergate to Bush v. Gore*. New York: Oxford University Press, 2005.

Perlstein, Rick. *Nixonland: The Rise of a President and the Fracturing of America*. New York: Scribner, 2008.
Perlstein, Rick. *Reaganland: America's Right Turn 1976–1980*. New York: Simon and Schuster, 2020.
Persico, Joseph E. *Casey: The Lives and Secrets of William J. Casey: From the OSS to the CIA*. New York: Viking, 1990.
Pfiffner, James P. " 'The Contemporary Presidency': Presidential Lies." *Presidential Studies Quarterly* 29, no. 4 (December 1999): 903–17.
Pfiffner, James P. "Donald Trump and the Norms of the Presidency." *Presidential Studies Quarterly* 51, no. 1 (March 2021): 96–124.
Pyle, Christopher H. "The Law: Barack Obama and Civil Liberties." *Presidential Studies Quarterly* 42, no. 4 (December 2012): 867–80.
Raz, Joseph. *The Authority of Law: Essays on Law and Morality*. Oxford: Oxford University Press, 1979.
Reske, Henry J. "Walsh Winds Up Probe." *ABA Journal* 79, no. 1 (January 1993): 14–6.
Richardson, Heather Cox. *To Make Men Free: A History of the Republican Party*. Boulder, CO: Basic Books, 2014.
Robinson, Michael J., and Andrew Kohut. "Believability and the Press." *Public Opinion Quarterly* 52, no. 2 (Summer 1988): 174–89.
Rozell, Mark J. "Executive Privilege in the Reagan Administration: Diluting a Constitutional Doctrine." *Presidential Studies Quarterly* 27, no. 4 (Fall 1997): 760–72.
Scheffer, David J. "U.S. Law and the Iran-Contra Affair." *American Journal of International Law* 81, no. 3 (July 1987): 696–723.
Schimdli, William Michael. *Freedom on the Offensive: Human Rights, Democracy Promotion, and US Interventionism in the Late Cold War*. Ithaca, NY: Cornell University Press, 2022.
Schmitter, Philippe C., and Terry Lynn Karl. "What Democracy Is . . . and Is Not." *Journal of Democracy* 2, no. 3 (1991). https://doi.org/10.1353/jod.1991.0033.
Seib, Gerald F. *We Should Have Seen It Coming: From Reagan to Trump—A Front-Row Seat to a Political Revolution*. New York: Random House, 2020.
Shapiro, Saul B. "Citizen Trust and Government Cover-Up: Refining the Doctrine of Fraudulent Concealment." *Yale Law Journal* 95, no. 7 (June 1986): 1477–99.
Sharpe, Kenneth E. "The Post-Vietnam Formula under Siege: The Imperial Presidency and Central America." *Political Science Quarterly* 102, no. 4 (Winter 1987–1988): 549–69.
Shendow, William. "An Analysis of Foreign Affairs Powers: A Perspective for the Public Administrator on the Iran-Contra Affair." *Public Administration Quarterly* 15, no. 2 (Summer 1991): 171–87.
Silverberg, Marshall. "Separation of Powers and Control of the CIA's Covert Operations." *Texas Law Review* 68, no. 3 (February 1990): 575–622.
Singer, P. W. *Corporate Warriors: The Rise of the Privatized Military Industry, Updated Edition*. Ithaca, NY: Cornell University Press, 2008.
Solomon, Norman. *War Made Easy: How Presidents and Pundits Keep Spinning Us to Death*. Hoboken, NJ: Wiley, 2005.
"The Summer of 1987." *Foreign Affairs* 66, no. 1 (Fall 1987): 1–6.

Tamanaha, Brian Z. *On the Rule of Law: History, Politics, Theory*. Cambridge: Cambridge University Press, 2004.

Thelen, David. *Becoming Citizens in the Age of Television: How Americans Challenged the Media and Seized Political Initiative during the Iran-Contra Debate*. Chicago: University of Chicago Press, 1996.

Thompson, Dennis. "Democratic Secrecy." *Political Science Quarterly* 114, no. 2 (Summer 1999): 181–93.

Timbers, Edwin. "Legal and Institutional Aspects of the Iran-Contra Affair." *Presidential Studies Quarterly* 20, no. 1 (Winter 1990): 31–41.

Tucker, Robert W. "Fouling Up." *National Interest* 7 (Spring 1987): 93–6.

Turner, Robert F. "The Constitution and the Iran-Contra Affair: Was Congress the Real Lawbreaker?" *Houston Journal of International Law* 11 (1988): 83–127.

Vile, M. J. C. *Constitutionalism and the Separation of Powers*. 2nd ed. Indianapolis: Liberty Fund, 1998.

Voß, Klaas. "Plausibly Deniable: Mercenaries in U.S. Covert Interventions during the Cold War, 1964–1987." *Cold War History* 16, no. 1 (2016): 37–60.

Waldron, Jeremy. "Is the Rule of Law an Essentially Contested Concept (in Florida)?" *Law and Philosophy* 21, no. 2 (March 2002): 137–64.

Weaver, William G., and Robert M. Pallitto. "State Secrets and Executive Power." *Political Science Quarterly* 120, no. 1 (Spring 2005): 85–112.

Weinberger, Caspar W. "In Defense of the Presidency." *Presidential Studies Quarterly* 18, no. 1 (Winter 1988): 17–21.

Weinberg, Steve. "October Surprise: Enter the Press." *Columbia Journalism Review* 31, no. 6 (March 1992): 33–41.

Whiting, Alex. "Controlling Tin Cup Diplomacy." *Yale Law Journal* 99, no. 8 (June 1990): 2043–62.

Williams, Robert. "The Last Word on the Iran-Contra Affair?" *Crime, Law and Social Change* 23 (1995): 367–85.

Wiltz, John. *In Search of Peace: The Senate Munitions Inquiry, 1934–36*. Baton Rouge: Louisiana State University Press, 1963.

Wood, Gordon S. *The Creation of the American Republic: 1776–1787*. New York: W. W. Norton, 1993.

Woodward, Bob. *VEIL: the Secret Wars of the CIA 1981–1987*. New York: Simon and Schuster, 1987.

Wroe, Ann. *Lives, Lies and the Iran-Contra Affair*. London: I. B. Tauris, 1992.

Zakaria, Fareed. "The Rise of Illiberal Democracy Essay." *Foreign Affairs* 76, no. 6 (1997): 22–43.

DIGITAL SOURCES

"Biden's Approval Rating Surges." Quinnipiac University/Poll, August 31, 2022. https://poll.qu.edu/poll-release?releaseid=3854. Accessed July 12, 2024.

Dabis, Cherien, dir. *Only Murders in the Building*. Season 2, episode 5, "The Tell." Aired July 19, 2022, on Hulu. www.hulu.com/watch/349dea4a-63a9–4e06–86f7-ea45adcf5392.

"Democracy." United Nations. www.un.org/en/global-issues/democracy. Accessed February 24, 2023.

Diamond, Larry. "What Is Democracy?" Hilla University for Humanistic Studies, January 21, 2004. https://diamond-democracy.stanford.edu/events/lecture/what-democracy. Accessed July 12, 2024.

Digital National Security Archive Collection: Iran-Contra Affair. https://nsarchive.gwu.edu/special-exhibits/iran-contra-affair.

"Evans and Novak." Transcript. *Cable News Network*, October 11, 1986.

"Executive Order 12575." American Presidency Project. www.presidency.ucsb.edu/documents/executive-order-12575-presidents-special-review-board. Accessed July 12, 2024.

"Guidance Note of the Secretary-General on Democracy." United Nations, 2008. www.un.org/democracyfund/sites/www.un.org.democracyfund/files/un_sg_guidance_note_on_democracy.pdf. Accessed July 12, 2024.

Hamilton, Alexander. *Federalist No. 74*. Library of Congress. https://guides.loc.gov/federalist-papers/text-71–80#s-lg-box-wrapper-25493466. Accessed July 12, 2024.

"Judicial Independence." Annenberg Classroom. www.annenbergclassroom.org/glossary_term/judicial-independence/. Accessed July 12, 2024.

National Security Decision Directive 276. Federation of American Scientists, Intelligence Resource Program. https://irp.fas.org/offdocs/nsdd/nsdd-276.htm. Accessed July 12, 2024.

"Public Trust in Government, 1958–2024." Pew Research Center. June 24, 2024. www. https://www.pewresearch.org/politics/2024/06/24/public-trust-in-government-1958-2024/. Accessed July 12, 2024.

"Remarks by President Biden on the Continued Battle for the Soul of the Nation." White House, September 1, 2022. www.whitehouse.gov/briefing-room/speeches-remarks/2022/09/01/remarks-by-president-bidenon-the-continued-battle-for-the-soul-of-the-nation/. Accessed July 12, 2024.

"Tempered Expectations and Hardened Divisions a Year into the Biden Presidency." Bright Line Watch. http://brightlinewatch.org/tempered-expectations-and-hardened-divisions-a-year-into-the-biden-presidency. Accessed July 12, 2024.

"Threats to American Democracy Ahead of an Unprecedented Presidential Election." Public Religion Research Institute, October 25, 2023. www.prri.org/research/threats-to-american-democracy-ahead-of-an-unprecedented-presidential-election/. Accessed July 12, 2024.

V-Dem Institute. *Democracy Report 2022: Autocratization Changing Nature?* University of Gothenburg, March 2022. https://v-dem.net/media/publications/dr_2022.pdf. Accessed July 12, 2024.

Wallenfelt, Jeff. "Did George Washington Really Say, 'I Can't Tell a Lie'?" *Brittanica*. www.britannica.com/story/did-george-washington-really-say-i-cant-tell-a-lie. Accessed July 12, 2024.

INDEX

Page numbers in italics refer to illustrations.